Praise for *Financial Data Engineering*

This book transforms complex technical concepts into practical tools, empowering professionals to unlock new dimensions of innovation in finance. A rare blend of depth, clarity, and forward-thinking insight.

—Shivani Gole, Data Engineer, McKinsey & Company

Financial Data Engineering is a helpful and thorough guide on using data engineering in the financial sector. Tamer does a great job of mixing theory with practical examples, making it useful for both professionals and academics. This book is well-organized, with real-world examples that make complex ideas easy to understand. It is very relevant in today's data-driven financial world.

—Pankaj Gupta, Manager, Data Engineering,
Discover Financial Services

This book navigates through both the complex regulatory landscape and the deep technical workings of financial data engineering. Tamer's approach simplifies challenging concepts, serving as both an accessible introduction to the topic and a valuable reference for professionals in the field.

—Aakash Atul Alurkar, Senior Product Manager,
Financial Services, Zoom

In *Financial Data Engineering*, Tamer Khraisha provides a comprehensive overview of the many different aspects of financial data as well as the engineering capabilities required. Through helpful frameworks and many real-world examples, this book is a great resource for experienced practitioners as well as people new to the industry.

—Martijn Groot, Financial Data Management Executive

An essential read for those exploring financial data. This book offers clear guidance on building scalable, efficient, and compliant data solutions in finance.

—*Ganesh Harke, Tech Lead at Citibank N.A.*

Financial Data Engineering by Tamer Khraisha is an indispensable resource that masterfully bridges the worlds of finance and data engineering. This book offers a uniquely comprehensive approach with its careful balance between foundational finance concepts and cutting-edge data engineering applications. Its insightful blend of theory, practical examples, and contemporary case studies makes it a must-read for anyone involved in the dynamically changing world of financial data. Whether you are a finance professional seeking to deepen your data engineering knowledge or a data engineer exploring and developing financial applications, this book provides the clarity and depth needed to navigate today's complex financial data landscape and master tomorrow's financial data engineering challenges.

—*Brian Buzzelli, Head of Data Practice, Meradia*

Data from various sources demands diverse skills to prepare it for modeling. Tamer has done an outstanding job in illustrating these tools and processes, making financial data engineering much more accessible and understandable.

—*Abdullah Karasan, Founder of Leveragai*
and Adjunct Faculty at UMBC

Financial Data Engineering is a necessary read for those data engineers planning to work in the financial sector—or within financial organizations of any corporation or government agency. Key takeaways from the book include a focus on the financial data ecosystem (regulatory responsibilities from a public institution and government perspective), financial data governance, and the significance of data engineers committing to developing knowledge of the financial domain.

—*Johnnie Jones, Director of Data Engineering,*
Boeing Employee Credit Union (BECU)

This book balances finance concepts and modern data practices, making it a clear guide for professionals in the finance and data fields. Whether you're new to finance and data or experienced in the field, you'll find valuable insights here.

—*William Jamir Silva, Senior Software Engineer*

This book masterfully bridges the gap between data engineering and financial data, offering a well-balanced exploration of both fields with practical insights and timeless principles. The author's ability to distill complex concepts into an accessible and comprehensive guide makes it an invaluable resource for professionals navigating the intersection of financial data and data engineering.

—*Vipul Bharat Marlecha, Senior Data Engineer, Netflix*

Financial Data Engineering

Design and Build Data-Driven
Financial Products

Tamer Khraisha
Foreword by Martijn Groot
Afterword by Brian Buzzelli

Beijing · Boston · Farnham · Sebastopol · Tokyo

Financial Data Engineering

by Tamer Khraisha

Published by O'Reilly Media, Inc., 1005 Gravenstein Highway North, Sebastopol, CA 95472.

O'Reilly books may be purchased for educational, business, or sales promotional use. Online editions are also available for most titles (*https://oreilly.com*). For more information, contact our corporate/institutional sales department: 800-998-9938 or *corporate@oreilly.com*.

Acquisitions Editor: Michelle Smith	**Indexer:** nSight, Inc.
Development Editor: Jill Leonard	**Interior Designer:** David Futato
Production Editor: Gregory Hyman	**Cover Designer:** Karen Montgomery
Copyeditor: Liz Wheeler	**Illustrator:** Kate Dullea
Proofreader: Sonia Saruba	

October 2024:   First Edition

Revision History for the First Edition

2024-10-09:   First Release

See *http://oreilly.com/catalog/errata.csp?isbn=9781098159993* for release details.

978-1-098-15999-3

[LSI]

To my wife Marti, my constant cheerleader and greatest inspiration, and to our wonderful baby Mark, whose laughter is the melody that accompanies my writing. This book is a small reflection of the love and joy you bring into my world.

Table of Contents

Part I.   Foundations of Financial Data Engineering

Part II. The Financial Data Engineering Lifecycle

Foreword

The common metaphor for data in financial services is that of oil, lifeblood, or more generally life-giving fuel. However, equally important is how firms use this fuel to the benefit of their business. Data is often raw material that needs to be processed, refined and blended before it can be used. How this material is then used in decision-making workflows is a critical differentiator. From strategy formulation, product development down to process implementation, operations and reporting to investors, customers and regulators, how firms manage information can be the difference between thriving, surviving or indeed declining.

The rapid changes in how data is captured, aggregated, distilled, consumed and distributed have led to faster cycle times, new insights and a much more close-knit integration of computer science into business operations. The wide variety of traditional as well as new data sets that often don't fit the mold of traditional computer science, brings opportunities for business differentiation and provides the burgeoning field of financial data engineering with the raw materials it needs.

This variety has fostered rapid development of data governance and a better appreciation of the various aspects of data quality. Data pipelines do not exist in isolation but are shaped by the context of business goals, external reporting considerations as well as legal and commercial constraints. Cloud transition and the range of data sets, tools and data engineering techniques available can make us feel spoiled for choice. Invariably, trade-offs take place, quality can be in the eye of the beholder and the right combination of data and engineering methods bridges business and technology. However, getting this combination right is no mean feat and there are many challenges that can easily derail any financial data engineering project.

Perhaps a more apt metaphor for data in financial services is that of food with data as the ingredients and financial data engineering being similar to the process of cooking. The number of both basic ingredients and spices has grown and so has the number of culinary techniques and recipes, leading to a proliferation of options on the menu. How the kitchen is staffed is a key differentiator.

What Tamer Khraisha has done in his book, *Financial Data Engineering,* is to provide us with a comprehensive guide that helps to better understand the vast and varied landscape of financial information and how best to apply financial data engineering concepts to make the most of it. It provides 'data chefs' a structured overview of financial data engineering and the raw materials to work with: from the different types of data sets and their identification to a structured treatment of the different aspects of data quality and data integrity. Subsequently, we get to work on these raw materials step by step, treating the entire financial data engineering lifecycle and taking the business context and trade-offs into account. Whether cloud adoption, database and data warehouse developments, tokenization, machine learning or gen AI, Tamer puts it into business context.

I especially liked that Tamer interlaced his overview and guidelines with many real-world case studies and ends the book with several in-depth data engineering projects. This will help practitioners build and finesse their own judgement as to what tools and data sets are fit for purpose and what controls or guardrails make sense.

With his training in financial economics, background in network science and as a fintech practitioner, Tamer bridges business and technology and brings a unique perspective to the field of financial data engineering. This book connects different topics that are often treated in a dispersed way, not least in financial services organizations themselves.

This book will be a source to technologists looking to get a better appreciation of the business context of financial data engineering, as well as to those in financial services trying to get a better sense of the art of the possible in financial data engineering. It will be helpful to people fresh in the job market but will also serve as a reference to experienced practitioners.

Financial data engineering bridges the old divide between computer science and business and this book will be a great help to successfully navigate that road.

— Martijn Groot
Financial Data Management expert
Author of Managing Financial Information in the
Trade Lifecycle *(Elsevier, 2008) and* A Primer in
Financial Data Management *(Elsevier, 2017)*
St. Paul's Bay, Malta, September 2024

Preface

With this book, you will learn fundamental concepts, common challenges, best practices, innovative frameworks, and cutting-edge technologies essential for successfully designing and building data-driven financial products and services. This book is intended to establish foundational knowledge that is accessible to individuals from diverse backgrounds, be they finance, computer science, software engineering, or academic research. It covers a wide range of carefully selected topics chosen for their market, technological, and scientific relevance. Each concept in the book is presented in straightforward language, accompanied by case studies and finance-specific examples for deeper insights. Moreover, to facilitate practical application, the final chapter presents four hands-on projects addressing various data-driven challenges related to financial markets.

To fully appreciate the story, read the chapters in order, though each chapter can also be read on its own if you prefer.

Who Should Read This Book?

This book serves a wide audience. This includes individuals working at institutions such as banks, investment firms, financial data providers, asset management companies, security exchanges, regulatory bodies, financial software vendors, and many more. It is designed for data engineers, software developers, quantitative developers, financial analysts, and machine learning practitioners who are managing and/or working with financial data and financial data-driven products. Furthermore, the book appeals to scholars and researchers working on data-driven financial analysis, reflecting the growing interest in big data research in the financial sector. Whether you're a practitioner seeking insights into data-driven financial services, a scholar investigating finance-related problems, or a newcomer eager to venture into the financial field with a technology-oriented role, this book is designed to meet your needs.

Prerequisites

To get the most out of the hands-on exercises in Chapter 12, I recommend having some basic knowledge of the following:

- Python programming
- SQL and PostgreSQL
- Using tools like Python JupyterLab, Python Notebooks, and Pandas
- Running Docker containers locally
- Basic Git commands

However, if you're unfamiliar with all of these, don't worry! You can still dive into the projects and learn as you go along.

What to Expect from This Book

This book aims to combine two domains—data engineering and finance—each encompassing numerous concepts, practices, theories, problems, and applications. The sheer number of topics within each of these two domains exceeds the scope of a single book. Consequently, I've aimed to achieve a balance among various considerations to provide a comprehensive yet scoped exploration.

The key consideration is determining how to allocate emphasis between finance and data engineering throughout the discussion. The initial five chapters (Part I) predominantly lean toward finance, which may cover familiar ground for people with experience in the field. Reading these initial chapters is highly recommended for those without a finance background and those who are seeking to refresh their knowledge of financial data and its associated challenges. Similarly, the last seven chapters (Part II) focus primarily on data engineering, offering a comprehensive treatment of data storage concepts, data modeling, databases, workflows, data ingestion mechanisms, data transformations, and more. Even if you're well-versed in data engineering, these chapters will prove invaluable for understanding their specific applications and challenges within the financial domain.

Another consideration is finding the right balance between covering a wide range of topics and providing in-depth explanations. The choice of topics in this book was driven by the author's experience, a literature review, market analysis, expert insights, regulatory requirements, and industry standards. At its core, this book is about financial data and the associated methodological and technological challenges. However, it's important to note this is not meant to be a book on financial analysis, financial machine learning, or statistics. Nonetheless, given that a substantial portion of AI and machine learning projects revolve around data preparation and preprocessing—approximately 50–80% of the time[1]—this book can significantly aid in streamlining these crucial tasks. In addition, some topics receive more extensive coverage due to their significance, while others are briefly addressed as their detailed explanation exceeds the book's scope and length.

Lastly, a major and intricate consideration is finding the right balance between emphasizing timeless (immutable) principles and illustrating contemporary issues. While a book emphasizing immutable concepts remains valuable over time, it's equally beneficial for readers to gain insight into current challenges and receive practical guidance through case studies and technologies. This book aims to strike a delicate balance between foundational concepts and practical applications, offering readers a comprehensive understanding of both immutable principles and current trends in the field. For example, Chapter 8 covers the most popular topic in data engineering: databases. Due to the rapid evolution of database technologies, this chapter takes an abstract approach, focusing on data storage models rather than specific technologies. Each model is examined in terms of its primary use cases, data modeling principles, technological implementations, and applications within the financial domain. This approach ensures relevance and longevity in light of emerging database innovations.

Book Resources and References

In this book, I use more than one thousand references spanning various sources: scientific journals, books, blog posts, online articles, opinion pieces, and white papers. Many of these references are cited throughout the chapters to support the content and offer a solid foundation for the information delivered. For those who want to dig deeper, an extensive list of additional references is available on the GitHub page (*https://oreil.ly/jpMIc*) for this book. I will periodically update this list to include new and relevant references.

---

1 Gil Press, "Cleaning Big Data: Most Time-Consuming, Least Enjoyable Data Science Task, Survey Says" (*https://oreil.ly/af6Vm*), *Forbes*, March 23, 2016.

Conventions Used in This Book

The following typographical conventions are used in this book:

Italic
> Indicates new terms, URLs, email addresses, filenames, and file extensions.

`Constant width`
> Used for program listings, as well as within paragraphs to refer to program elements such as variable or function names, databases, data types, environment variables, statements, and keywords.

This element signifies a tip or suggestion.

This element signifies a general note.

This element indicates a warning or caution.

Using Code Examples

Supplemental material (code examples, exercises, etc.) is available for download at *https://oreil.ly/FinDataEngCode*.

Should you encounter any challenges while setting up or executing any step in the projects outlined in Chapter 12, please don't hesitate to create an issue on the project's GitHub repository (*https://oreil.ly/XCV4f*). I will make sure to reply to you in a very short time.

If you have a technical question or a problem using the code examples, you may also send an email to *support@oreilly.com*.

This book is here to help you get your job done. In general, if example code is offered with this book, you may use it in your programs and documentation. You do not need to contact us for permission unless you're reproducing a significant portion of the code. For example, writing a program that uses several chunks of code from this book does not require permission. Selling or distributing examples from O'Reilly books does require permission. Answering a question by citing this book and quoting example code does not require permission. Incorporating a significant amount of example code from this book into your product's documentation does require permission.

We appreciate, but generally do not require, attribution. An attribution usually includes the title, author, publisher, and ISBN. For example: "*Financial Data Engineering* by Tamer Khraisha (O'Reilly). Copyright 2025 Tamer Khraisha, 978-1-098-15999-3."

If you feel your use of code examples falls outside fair use or the permission given above, feel free to contact us at *permissions@oreilly.com*.

O'Reilly Online Learning

 For more than 40 years, *O'Reilly Media* has provided technology and business training, knowledge, and insight to help companies succeed.

Our unique network of experts and innovators share their knowledge and expertise through books, articles, and our online learning platform. O'Reilly's online learning platform gives you on-demand access to live training courses, in-depth learning paths, interactive coding environments, and a vast collection of text and video from O'Reilly and 200+ other publishers. For more information, visit *https://oreilly.com*.

How to Contact Us

Please address comments and questions concerning this book to the publisher:

> O'Reilly Media, Inc.
> 1005 Gravenstein Highway North
> Sebastopol, CA 95472
> 800-889-8969 (in the United States or Canada)
> 707-827-7019 (international or local)
> 707-829-0104 (fax)
> *support@oreilly.com*
> *https://oreilly.com/about/contact.html*

We have a web page for this book, where we list errata, examples, and any additional information. You can access this page at *https://oreil.ly/FinancialDataEngineering*.

For news and information about our books and courses, visit *https://oreilly.com*.

Find us on LinkedIn: *https://linkedin.com/company/oreilly-media*.

Watch us on YouTube: *https://youtube.com/oreillymedia*.

Acknowledgments

Writing this book has been an incredible journey, and it would not have been possible without the support, guidance, and encouragement of many individuals.

First and foremost, special thanks to Michelle Smith, the content acquisition editor, for giving me the opportunity to write this book and believing in my vision from the beginning.

I am very thankful to Jill Leonard, the book editor, for her careful attention to detail and for guiding me through the editing process with patience and expertise. Her hard work and dedication ensured that every aspect of this book was thoroughly checked and refined.

I want to express my thanks to Greg Hyman, the production editor, for his essential role in overseeing the production process and ensuring that the final version of the book met the highest standards.

I would like to express my deepest gratitude to the technical reviewers who provided invaluable input and keen insights that greatly enhanced the quality of this work. My sincere thanks go to Aakash Atul Alurkar, Rahul Arulkumaran, Brian Buzzelli, Shivani Gole, Martijn Groot, Pankaj Gupta, Ganesh Harke, Abdullah Karasan, Vipul Bharat Marlecha, Mukund Sarma, Chandra Shukla, William Jamir Silva, and Kushan Vora.

Special thanks to Prof. Rosario Nunzio Mantegna, Yousef Ibrahim, and Máté Sándor for their valuable comments, input, and support.

Lastly, I would like to extend my sincere gratitude to the authors of the numerous references, books, articles, and blog posts that have greatly contributed to this book. With around one thousand sources consulted, your work has been invaluable in shaping the content and providing the insights needed for this project.

## PART I

Foundations of Financial Data Engineering

The first part of this book consists of five chapters, focusing on the core concepts and fundamental elements of financial data, along with the challenges associated with its management. These chapters discuss the various systems and practices employed across financial markets to manage financial data effectively.

Chapter 1 provides an introduction to the fundamentals of finance, highlighting its unique data challenges and the foundational ideas of financial data engineering. Chapter 2 dives into the complexities of the financial data ecosystem, examining its structure and key characteristics. Chapters 3 and 4 discuss financial identification and entity systems, emphasizing their significance as critical data engineering challenges within financial markets. Lastly, Chapter 5 presents a detailed framework for establishing robust data governance practices within financial institutions.

Together, these chapters establish the basic principles and concepts required to understand and practice financial data engineering.

## CHAPTER 1

Financial Data Engineering Clarified

Given all the payments, transfers, trades, and numerous financial activities that take place on a daily basis, can you imagine how much data the global financial sector generates? According to a 2011 report by *McKinsey Global Institute* (*https://oreil.ly/UCWHq*), the banking and investment sector in the US alone stores and manages more than one exabyte of data. To put that in perspective, an exabyte is the equivalent of one billion gigabytes, and it translates into trillions of digital records. The same report shows that on average, financial services firms generate and store more data than firms in other sectors. Some statistics are even more astonishing; for instance, JPMorgan Chase, the largest bank in the United States by market capitalization, manages more than 450 petabytes of data (*https://oreil.ly/b3IWP*). Bank of New York Mellon, a global financial services company specializing in investment management and investment services, manages over 110 million gigabytes of global financial data (*https://oreil.ly/svSHz*).

Naturally, we might extrapolate these estimates and figures to tens or even hundreds of exabytes if we take into account the global context and the constantly expanding financial landscape. As a result, data sits at the heart of the financial system, serving as both the input for different financial operations and the output generated from them. Importantly, to guarantee a healthy and well-functioning system, a reliable and secure data infrastructure is needed for generating, exchanging, storing, and consuming all kinds of financial data. In addition, this infrastructure must adhere to the financial sector's specific requirements, constraints, practices, and regulations. This is where financial data engineering comes into the scene. To get started, this chapter will introduce you to finance, financial data engineering, and the role and skills of the financial data engineer.

Defining Financial Data Engineering

Data engineering has always been a vibrant and innovative field from both industry and research standpoints. If you are a data engineer, you are likely aware of how many data-related technologies are released and popularized every year. Several factors drive these developments:

- The growing importance of data as a key input in the creation of digital products and services

- Large digital companies, such as LinkedIn, Netflix, Google, Meta, and Airbnb, transitioning the data frameworks they developed internally to handle massive volumes of data and traffic to open source projects

- The impressive success of open source alternatives, which has fueled interest from individuals and businesses in developing and evaluating new tools and ideas

As an industry practice, data engineering has undergone several conceptual and technological evolution episodes. Without offering a detailed historical account, I would simply say that the birth of data engineering started with the introduction of Structured Query Language (SQL) and data warehousing in the 1970s/1980s. Companies like IBM and Oracle were early pioneers in the field, playing a key role in developing and popularizing many of the fundamental principles of data engineering.

Until the early 2000s, data engineering responsibilities were primarily handled by information technology (IT) teams. Roles such as database administrator, database developer, and system administrator were prevalent in the data job market.

With the global rise and adoption of the internet and social media, the so-called *big data* revolution marked a major step toward contemporary data engineering. Using the release date of Apache Hadoop as a reference, I would say that the big data era started around 2005. Pioneers like Google, Airbnb, Meta, Microsoft, Amazon, and Netflix have popularized a more specialized and advanced version of data engineering. This includes big data frameworks, open source tools, cloud computing, alternative data, and streaming technologies.

The financial sector has actively participated in this dynamic environment as both an observer and an adopter of data technologies. This active involvement stems from the financial industry's continuous evolution in response to market demands and regulatory changes, which often necessitates the adoption of new technologies. Importantly, data engineering practices in finance are heavily domain driven, given the distinct requirements of the financial sector in terms of security, governance, and regulation, as well as the complex nature of the financial data landscape and financial data management challenges.

Considering these factors, this book will present financial data engineering as a domain-driven field within data engineering, specifically tailored to the financial sector, thereby setting it apart from traditional data engineering. To further justify the need for financial data engineering, the upcoming sections will provide a brief introduction to the finance domain, outline the data-related challenges encountered in financial markets, offer definitions of data engineering and financial data engineering, and provide an overview of the role and responsibilities of a financial data engineer.

First of All, What Is Finance?

Despite the extensive use of the term *finance*, there could be a lot of confusion about what it really means. This is because finance is a multifaceted concept that can be approached from different angles (see Figure 1-1). To prepare you with a basic domain knowledge, the next sections present a short conceptual illustration of finance from four main perspectives: economics, market, science, and technology.

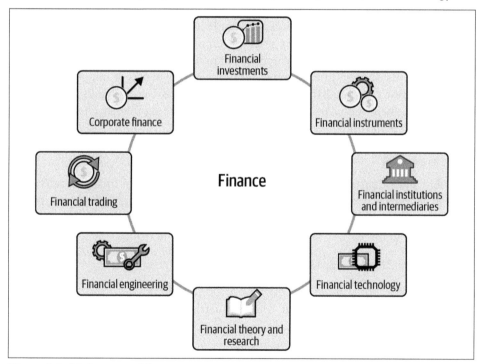

Figure 1-1. Main areas of finance

Finance as an economic function

In economic theory, finance is an institution that mediates between agents who are in *deficit* (who need more money than they have) and those in *surplus* (who have more money than they spend). To secure funds, agents in deficit offer to borrow money from agents with a surplus in exchange for an interest payment.

This perspective highlights the vital role of finance in the economy: it offers individuals a means to invest their savings, allows families to purchase a house through a mortgage, provides businesses with capital to get started, empowers universities to invest their assets and expand their campus, and enables governments to finance public projects to fulfill societal needs.

For economists, finance is one of the primary drivers of *economic growth*. This is why good economies tend to have large, efficient, and inclusive financial markets. To ensure financial markets' stability and fairness, several regulatory agencies and regulations were established.

A major subject that financial economists often investigate is *market equilibrium*, which describes a state where demand and supply intersect, resulting in a stable market price. In financial markets, this price is commonly represented by the interest rate, with supply and demand reflecting the quantity of money in circulation. When demand exceeds supply, interest rates typically rise, whereas if supply surpasses demand, interest rates tend to decrease. Entities such as central banks were established to implement monetary policies aimed at maintaining market interest rates as closely aligned with equilibrium as possible.

Finance as a market

To enable individuals and companies to engage efficiently in financial activities, *financial markets* have emerged, hosting a vast array of financial institutions, products, and services. Nowadays, if we take a well-developed financial sector, we can find a large variety of market players. These may include the following:

- Commercial banks (e.g., HSBC, Bank of America)
- Investment banks (e.g., Morgan Stanley, Goldman Sachs)
- Asset managers (e.g., BlackRock, The Vanguard Group)
- Security exchanges (e.g., New York Stock Exchange [NYSE], London Stock Exchange, Chicago Mercantile Exchange)
- Hedge funds (e.g., Citadel, Renaissance Technologies)
- Mutual funds (e.g., Vanguard Mid-Cap Value Index Fund)
- Insurance companies (e.g., Allianz, AIG)
- Central banks (e.g., Federal Reserve, European Central Bank)

- Government-sponsored enterprises (e.g., Fannie Mae, Freddie Mac)
- Regulators (e.g., Securities and Exchange Commission)
- Industry trade groups (e.g., Securities Industry and Financial Markets Association)
- Credit rating agencies (e.g., S&P Global Ratings, Moody's)
- Data vendors (e.g., Bloomberg, London Stock Exchange Group [LSEG])
- FinTech companies (e.g., Revolut, Wise, Betterment)
- Big tech companies (e.g., Amazon Cash, Amazon Pay, Apple Pay, Google Pay)

 The terms "financial institution," "financial firm," "financial company," and "financial organization" might often be used interchangeably. However, from an economic theory standpoint, "financial institution" may be the most appropriate term to use, as it represents an abstract concept encompassing any company, agency, firm, or organization that serves a specific purpose or function within financial markets. For this reason, I will be mostly using the term "financial institution" throughout this book.

The primary unit of exchange in financial markets is commonly referred to as a financial *asset, instrument, or security.* There is a large number of financial assets that can be bought and sold in financial markets. Here are a few:[1]

- Shares of companies (e.g., common stocks)
- Fixed income instruments (e.g., corporate bonds, treasury bills)
- Derivatives (e.g., options, futures, swaps, forwards)
- Fund shares (e.g., mutual funds, exchange-traded funds)

Given the large and diverse number of financial instruments and transactions, financial markets are further classified into categories, such as the following:

- Money markets (for liquid short-term exchanges)
- Capital markets (long-term exchanges)
- Primary markets (for new issues of instruments)
- Secondary markets (for already issued instruments)

---

1 If you want to learn more in depth about financial instruments, I encourage you to read *Investments* by Zvi Bodie, Alex Kane, and Alan Marcus (McGraw Hill, 2023).

- Foreign exchange markets (for trading currencies)
- Commodity markets (for trading raw materials such as gold and oil)
- Equity markets (for trading stocks)
- Fixed-income markets (for trading bonds)
- Derivatives markets (for trading derivatives)

Investopedia: The Online Resource for Financial Education

If you want a quick introduction to a specific financial term, Investopedia (*https:// oreil.ly/oO9gS*) is the place to go. Investopedia is the world's leading source of online financial and investment content. This includes information on financial terminology, definitions, news, investments, and financial education. Investopedia is a valuable resource for anyone interested in learning more about finance, whether they are a novice learner or an investor looking to gain more in-depth financial knowledge. Investopedia's articles are written, reviewed, and fact-checked by financial experts, which adds to the credibility and quality of the published content.

Interestingly, financial markets are highly reliant on and driven by research and methodologies developed by finance departments at prominent universities and specialized finance institutes. The next section will briefly explore the nature and key areas of financial research.

Finance as a research field

Finance is a well-known and extensive field of academic and empirical research. One major area of investigation is *asset pricing theory*, which aims to understand and calculate the price of claims to risky (uncertain) assets (e.g., stocks, bonds, derivatives, etc.). Within this theory, low prices often translate into a high rate of return, so we can think of financial asset pricing theory as a way to explain why certain financial assets pay (or should pay) higher average returns than others.

Another major field of financial research is *risk management*, which focuses on measuring and managing the uncertainty around the future value of a financial asset or a portfolio of assets. Other areas of investigation include portfolio management, corporate finance, financial accounting, credit scoring, financial engineering, stock prediction, and performance evaluation.

To publish financial research findings, a variety of peer-reviewed journals have been established. Some of these journals offer broad coverage, while others are more specialized. Here are some examples:

The Journal of Finance
Covers theoretical and empirical research on all major areas of finance

The Review of Financial Studies
Covers theoretical and empirical topics in financial economics

The Journal of Banking and Finance
Covers theoretical and empirical topics in finance and banking, with a focus on financial institutions and money and capital markets

Quantitative Finance
Covers theoretical and empirical interdisciplinary research on quantitative methods of finance

The Journal of Portfolio Management
Covers topics related to finance and investing, such as risk management, portfolio optimization, and performance measurement.

The Journal of Financial Data Science
Covers data-driven research in finance using machine learning, artificial intelligence, and big data analytics

The Journal of Securities Operations & Custody
Covers topics and issues related to securities trading, clearing, settlement, financial standards, and more

In addition to academic journals, a large number of conferences, events, and summits are regularly held to share and discuss the latest developments in financial research. Examples include the Western Finance Association meetings, the American Finance Association meetings, and the Society for Financial Studies Cavalcades. Furthermore, globally renowned certifications like the Chartered Financial Analyst (CFA) are available to aspirant financial specialists who wish to acquire strong ethical and technical foundations in investment research and portfolio management.

Finance as a technology

Finally, finance can refer to the set of technologies and tools enabling all kinds of financial transactions and activities. Examples include the following:

- Payment systems (mobile, contactless, real-time, digital wallets, gateways, etc.)
- Blockchain and distributed ledger technology (DLT)
- Financial market infrastructures (e.g., Euroclear, Clearstream, Fedwire, T2, CHAPS)
- Trading platforms
- Stock exchanges (e.g., NYSE, NASDAQ, Tokyo Stock Exchange)

- Stock market data systems
- Automated teller machine (ATM)
- Order management systems (OMSs)
- Risk management systems
- Algorithmic trading and high-frequency trading (HFT) systems
- Smart order routing (SOR) systems

This diverse array of technologies in the financial sector is crucial for maintaining the efficiency and reliability of global financial markets.

Defining Data Engineering

Now that we have a foundational understanding of finance, let's explore what financial data engineering is. To do this, I'll first explain traditional data engineering, as it is a widely recognized term in the industry.

If we Google the words "what is data engineering," we get more than two billion search results. That's quite a lot, but to be more pragmatic, we can do a more advanced inquiry by searching Google Scholar for all papers and books where the term "data engineering" occurs in the title. Such a query returns a relatively large number of results (around 2,290 scientific publications), as shown in Figure 1-2.

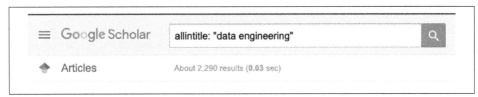

Figure 1-2. Google Scholar search for publications with data engineering in the title

I highly recommend you read some of the publications that Google Scholar returns for data engineering. Interestingly, you will quickly notice that there is quite a high variety of definitions for data engineering. This is expected, as the field of data engineering sits at the intersection between multiple fields, including software engineering, infrastructure engineering, data analysis, networking, software and data architecture, data governance, and other data management-related areas.[2]

---

2 Data management is a broader term than data engineering. It refers to all plans and policies put in place to make sure that data is strategically managed and optimized for business value creation. To read about data management, I highly recommend *Data Management at Scale* by Piethein Strengholt (O'Reilly, 2023).

For illustrative purposes, let's consider the following selected definitions:

> Data engineering is the development, implementation, and maintenance of systems and processes that take in raw data and produce high-quality, consistent information that supports downstream use cases, such as analysis and machine learning. Data engineering is the intersection of security, data management, DataOps, data architecture, orchestration, and software engineering.
>
> —Joe Reis and Matt Housley, *Fundamentals of Data Engineering* (O'Reilly, 2022)

> Data engineering is all about the movement, manipulation, and management of data.
>
> —Lewis Gavin, *What Is Data Engineering?* (O'Reilly 2019)

> Data engineering is the process of designing and building systems that let people collect and analyze raw data from multiple sources and formats. These systems empower people to find practical applications of the data, which businesses can use to thrive.
>
> —Dremio (*https://oreil.ly/GW18h*)

As you can see, all three definitions are quite different, but if we make an effort to extract the main defining elements, we can infer that data engineering revolves around the *design* and *implementation* of an *infrastructure* that enables an organization to *retrieve* data from one or more sources, *transform* it, *store* it in a target destination, and make it *consumable* by end users. Naturally, in practice, the complexity of such a process would depend on the technical and business requirements and constraints, which vary on a case-by-case basis. Given this context, I will use the following definition of data engineering throughout this book:

> Data engineering is a field of practice and research that focuses on designing and implementing data infrastructure intended to reliably and securely perform tasks such as data ingestion, transformation, storage, and delivery. This infrastructure is tailored to meet varying business requirements, industry practices, and external factors such as regulatory compliance and privacy considerations.

Throughout this book, we'll focus on the concept of *financial data infrastructure* as the cornerstone of financial data engineering. Along the way, we will examine the *components* of a financial data infrastructure, which include physical (hardware) and virtual (software) resources and systems for storing, processing, managing, and transmitting financial data. Furthermore, we will discuss the essential *capabilities* and *features* of a financial data infrastructure, such as security, traceability, scalability, observability, and reliability.

With this definition in mind, let's now proceed to clarify the meaning of financial data engineering.

Defining Financial Data Engineering

Financial data engineering shares most of the traditional data engineering tools, patterns, practices, and technologies. However, when designing and building a financial data infrastructure, relying only on traditional data engineering is not sufficient. You are very likely going to deal with domain-specific issues such as the complex financial data landscape (e.g., a large number of data sources, types, vendors, structures, etc.), the regulatory requirements for reporting and governance, the challenges related to entity and identification systems, the special requirements in terms of speed and volume, and a variety of constraints on delivery, ingestion, storage, and processing.[3]

Given such domain-driven particularities, financial data engineering deserves to be treated as a specialized field that sits at the intersection between traditional data engineering, financial domain knowledge, and financial data (as illustrated in Figure 1-3). More formally, this book defines financial data engineering as follows:

> Financial data engineering is the domain-driven practice of designing, implementing, and maintaining data infrastructure to enable the collection, transformation, storage, consumption, monitoring, and management of financial data coming from mixed sources, with different frequencies, structures, delivery mechanisms, formats, identifiers, and entities, while following secure, compliant, and reliable standards.

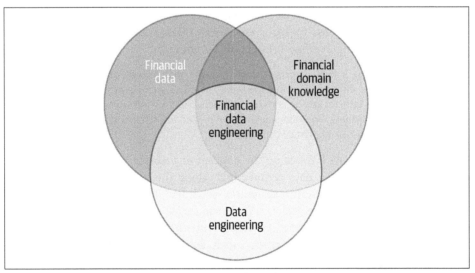

Figure 1-3. Financial data engineering and related fields

---

3 For a good reference on these challenges, see Antoni Munar, Esteban Chiner, and Ignacio Sales, "A Big Data Financial Information Management Architecture for Global Banking" (*https://oreil.ly/v2P2Z*), presented at the 2014 International Conference on Future Internet of Things and Cloud (IEEE, August 2014): 385–388.

Don't confuse financial data engineering with financial engineering. Financial engineering is an interdisciplinary applied field that uses mathematics, statistics, econometrics, financial theory, and computer science to develop financial investment strategies, financial products, and financial processes.[4]

Domain-Driven Design

Designing software systems following domain-specific knowledge and requirements is a common practice. The most prominent approach in this context is *Domain-Driven Design* (DDD). DDD emphasizes modeling and designing the business domain to ensure that the software aligns with business requirements in terms of quality and features. This approach necessitates close collaboration between engineers and domain experts to establish a common understanding and a unified language, known as the "ubiquitous language," which is consistently used throughout the project.

DDD divides a given business problem into domains. A domain is the problem space that the software application is being developed to solve. For example, in a banking application, domains could be accounts, payments, transactions, customers, cash management, and liquidity management. Domains can further be decomposed into subdomains; for example, cash management may have subdomains such as collections management and cash flow forecasting, which are bounded by a given context.

Now that you know what financial data engineering is, you may be wondering why it matters to financial institutions and markets and why we should write a book about it. The next section addresses these questions in detail.

Why Financial Data Engineering?

One of the main goals of this book is to illustrate how financial data engineering is unique in terms of the domain-driven elements that characterize it. To understand why the market demands financial data engineering, it is crucial to examine the main factors shaping and driving data-driven needs and trends in the financial sector. The next few sections will provide a detailed account of these factors.

---

4 To know more about this topic, check this excellent reference: Tanya S. Beder and Cara M. Marshall's *Financial Engineering: The Evolution of a Profession* (Wiley, 2011).

Volume, Variety, and Velocity of Financial Data

One of the primary factors that have been transforming the financial sector is *big data*. In this book, big data is simply defined as a combination of three attributes: large size (*volume*), high dimensionality and complexity (*variety*), and speed of generation (*velocity*). Let's explore each of these Vs in detail.

Volume

When referencing big data, it is hard to deny that it is primarily about size. Data can be large, either in *absolute* or *relative* terms. Data is said to be large in absolute terms if it gets generated in a remarkably enormous and nonlinear quantity. An absolute increase in data size is often the result of socio-technological changes that induce a structural alteration to the data generation process. For example, in the past, card payments were primarily reserved for major purchases and were relatively limited, whereas today, the widespread adoption of card and mobile payment methods has transformed everyday transactions, with people now using cards and phones to pay for almost everything, from groceries to electronics. This, in turn, has led to a (remarkable) absolute increase in the amount of payment data being generated and collected.

In addition, the rapid development and adoption of digital automated technologies, in particular electronic exchange mechanisms, have resulted in an absolute increase in the sheer volume of financial data generated. The emergence of high-frequency trading is a good example. For instance, a single day's worth of data from the New York Stock Exchange's high-frequency dataset (*https://oreil.ly/4a0B1*), Trade and Quotes (TAQ), comprises approximately 2.3 billion records. With the implementation of high-frequency trading technologies, financial data began to be recorded at incredibly fine intervals, including the millisecond (one-thousandth of a second), microsecond (one-millionth of a second), and even nanosecond (one-billionth of a second) levels.

On the other hand, data is considered relatively large if its size is big compared to other existing datasets. Improved data collection is perhaps the main driver behind the relative increase in financial data volumes. This has been facilitated by technological advancements enabling more efficient data collection, regulatory requirements imposing stricter data collection and reporting requirements, the increasing complexity of financial instruments necessitating the collection of data for risk management, and the growing demand for data-driven insights within the financial sector. As an example, the Options Price Reporting Authority (OPRA), which collects and consolidates all the trades and quotes from member option exchanges in the United States, reported an astonishing peak rate of 45.9 million messages per second in February 2024.[5]

With large volumes of financial data comes a new space of opportunities:

- Overcoming sample selection bias that might exist in small datasets
- Enabling investors and traders to access high-frequency market data
- Capturing patterns and financial activities not represented in small datasets
- Monitoring and detecting frauds, market anomalies, and irregularities
- Enabling the use of advanced machine learning and data mining techniques that can capture complex and nonlinear signals
- Alleviating the problem of high dimensionality in machine learning, where the number of features is significantly high compared to the number of observations
- Facilitating the development of financial data products that are derived from data, improve with data, and produce additional data

However, such opportunities come with technical challenges, mostly related to data engineering:

- Collecting and storing large volumes of financial data from various sources efficiently
- Designing querying systems that enable users to retrieve extensive datasets quickly
- Building a data infrastructure capable of handling any data size seamlessly
- Establishing rules and procedures to ensure data quality and integrity
- Aggregating large volumes of data from multiple sources
- Linking records across multiple high-frequency datasets

The frequency at which data is generated and collected greatly impacts financial data volumes. A process that produces one million records per second generates significantly larger data volumes compared to a process that produces one thousand records per second. This rate of data generation is known as data *velocity* and will be discussed in the following section.

---

5 See the Operating Metrics file in the official OPRA document library page (*https://oreil.ly/apOY2*).

Velocity

Data velocity refers to the speed at which data is generated and ingested. Recent years have seen an increase in the velocity of data generation in financial markets. High-frequency trading, financial transactions, financial news feeds, and finance-related social media posts all produce data at high speeds.

With increased financial data velocity, new opportunities emerge:

- Quicker reaction times as data arrives shortly after generation
- Deeper and more immediate insights into intraday dynamics, such as price fluctuations and patterns emerging within an hour, minute, or second
- Enhanced market monitoring
- Development of new trading strategies, including algorithmic trading and high-frequency trading

Crucially, high data velocity introduces critical challenges for data infrastructures:

Volume
> How to build event-driven systems that can handle the arrival of large amounts of data in real time

Speed
> How to build a data infrastructure that can reliably cope with the speed of information transmission in financial markets

Reaction time
> How to build pipelines that can react as quickly as possible to new data arrival yet guarantee quality checks and reliability

Variety/multistream
> How to handle the arrival of many types of data from multiple sources in real time

The exponential increase in financial data volumes and the velocity of data generation doesn't occur uniformly. Alongside this growth, new data types, formats, and structures have emerged to fulfill various business and technical requirements. The following section will explore this diversity of data in depth.

Variety

The third feature that defines big data is variety, which refers to the presence of many data types, formats, or structures. To better describe this concept, let's illustrate the three types of structures that data can have:

Structured data
> This data has a clear format and data model, is easy to organize and store, and is ready to analyze. The most common example is tabular data organized as rows and columns.

Semi-structured data
> This type of data lacks a straightforward tabular format but has some structural properties that make it manageable. Often, semi-structured data is parsed and stored in a tabular format for ease of use. Examples include XML and JSON, which store data in a hierarchical tree-like format.

Unstructured data
> This data lacks any predefined structure or formatting and requires parsing and preprocessing using specialized techniques before analysis. The majority of data worldwide is unstructured, including formats like PDF, HTML, text, video, and audio.

The variety of financial data has significantly increased in recent years. For example, the US Securities and Exchange Commission's Electronic Data Gathering, Analysis, and Retrieval system (EDGAR) receives and handles about two million filings a year (*https://oreil.ly/v0BjW*). Such filings can be complex documents, many of which contain multiple attachments, scores of pages, and several thousands of pieces of information or details. Another example is alternative data sources such as news, weather, satellite images, social media posts, and web search activities, which have been shown to be highly valuable for financial analysis and product development.[6]

Increased variety in financial data opens up new opportunities:

- Incorporating new variables into financial analysis for enhanced predictions
- Capturing new economic and financial activities that can't be analyzed using structured data alone
- Facilitating the development and integration of innovative financial products like news analytics, fraud detection, and financial networks
- Enhancing regulatory capabilities to capture complex market structures for more effective oversight

---

6 Alternative datasets and their use cases in finance are discussed in detail in Chapter 2.

However, data variety also presents several data engineering challenges:

- Building a data infrastructure capable of efficiently storing and managing diverse types of financial data, including structured, semi-structured, and unstructured formats

- Implementing data aggregation systems to consolidate different data types into a single access point

- Developing methodologies for cleaning and transforming new structures of financial data

- Establishing specialized pipelines to process varied types of financial data, such as natural language processing for text and deep learning for images

- Implementing identification and entity management systems to link entities across a wide range of data sources

---

Be Wary of the Curse of Dimensionality in Financial Data

Although the volume of financial data has experienced significant growth in recent decades, special consideration should be given to the ratio of data observations to the number of variables. For example, assume we have an initial sample of 10 firms and 5 features about their performance (e.g., revenues, net profit, and so on). If data increases in size both in terms of observations (more firms) and variables (more features), then we can conduct reliable analysis using the new, larger sample. However, if the increase in data size concerns mainly the features and not the observations (i.e., no more firms added to the dataset), then we might encounter the issue known as the *curse of dimensionality* (*https://oreil.ly/TnxXI*). It states that for a statistical or machine model to produce valid predictions, the number of observations needs to grow exponentially with the number of features. Some researchers have argued (*https://oreil.ly/jE62C*) that this has been the case in some financial applications, such as asset management. A number of techniques can be used to counteract the curse of dimensionality: *data augmentation* (collecting or generating more data) and *dimensionality reduction* (reducing the number of features in the data).

Finance-Specific Data Requirements and Problems

The financial industry has always witnessed constant transformation: new players joining and disrupting the competitive landscape, new technologies emerging and revolutionizing the way financial markets function, new data sources expanding the space of opportunities, and new standards and regulations getting released, promoted, and enforced.

Given these dynamics, the financial industry sets itself apart in terms of the issues and challenges that its participants face. A few key ones are listed here:

- There is a lack of a standardization in some key areas:
  - Identification system for financial data
  - Classification system for financial assets and sectors
  - Financial information exchange
- Lack of established data standards for financial transaction processing
- Dispersed and diverse sources of financial data
- Adoption of multiple data formats by companies, data vendors, providers, and regulators
- Complexity in matching and identifying entities within financial datasets
- Lack of reliable methods to define, store, and manage financial reference data (discussed in Chapter 2)
- Lack of relevant data for understanding and managing various financial problems due to poor data collection processes (e.g., granular data on financial market dependencies and exposures necessary for systemic risk analysis)
- The constant need to adapt data and tech infrastructure to meet new market and regulatory demands (e.g., the EU's *Instant Payments Regulation* requires all payment service providers to offer 24/7 euro payments within seconds, necessitating upgrades to legacy systems)
- The constant need to record, store, and share financial data for various regulatory and market purposes (e.g., the EU's *Central Electronic System of Payment Information* mandates payment system providers to track cross-border payment data and share it with the tax authorities of EU member states).
- Absence of standardized practices for cleaning and ensuring the quality of financial data
- Difficulty in aggregating data across various silos and divisions within financial institutions

- Creating consolidated tapes, which integrate market data from multiple sources including trade and quote information across various venues, continues to pose technological and market challenges

- Balancing innovation and competitiveness with regulatory compliance

- Persisting concerns regarding security, privacy, and performance in cloud migration strategies

- Continued reliance on legacy technological systems due to organizational inertia and risk aversion

Over the years, a number of industry and regulatory initiatives were proposed to tackle these issues. For example, to facilitate a standardized delivery of financial services and products, the United States established the *Accredited Standards Committee X9* (ASC X9) (*https://oreil.ly/_xsi6*) to create, maintain, and promote voluntary consensus standards for the financial industry. In addition to setting national standards in the United States, ASC X9 can submit standards to the International Organization for Standardization (ISO) in Geneva, Switzerland, to be considered an international ISO standard. ASC X9 develops standards for many different areas and technologies, including electronic legal orders for financial institutions, electronic benefits and mobile payments, financial identifiers, fast payment systems, cryptography, payment messages, and more.

Additionally, international agencies such as the Association of National Numbering Agencies (ANNA) were established to coordinate and foster the adoption of ISO-based financial identifiers (covered in Chapter 3). Frameworks such as *eXtensible Business Reporting Language* (XBRL) (discussed in Chapter 7) were developed to standardize the communication and reporting of business information. Following the financial crisis of 2007–2008, the financial industry realized the need for a standardized identifier for legal entities involved in market transactions, which led to the development (*https://oreil.ly/-GmxD*) of the celebrated Legal Entity Identifier (LEI), discussed in Chapter 3.

Furthermore, financial market players have also been actively contributing and providing solutions to the above-mentioned problems. To give a few examples, Bloomberg is currently promoting its *Financial Instrument Global Identifier* (FIGI) as an open standard for identifying financial instruments; LSEG released its *Permanent Identifier* (PermID) to complement existing market identifiers; and financial institutions such as JPMorgan have been pioneers in promoting market practices such as Value at Risk (VAR) (*https://oreil.ly/_KbIQ*) in the 90s, and more recently the use of financial APIs (*https://oreil.ly/iuFY_*) to support fast, real-time data transactions.

Financial Machine Learning

Machine learning (ML) stands out as one of the most promising investments for shaping the future of the financial industry. To understand what machine learning is, it's better first to understand what artificial intelligence (AI) is. Although there is no well-accepted definition of artificial intelligence, in its simplest form, AI aims to understand the nature of intelligence to build systems that can reliably perform tasks that usually would require human intelligence, such as speech recognition, visual perception, decision-making, and language understanding. Figure 1-4 illustrates the various fields of inquiry in artificial intelligence.

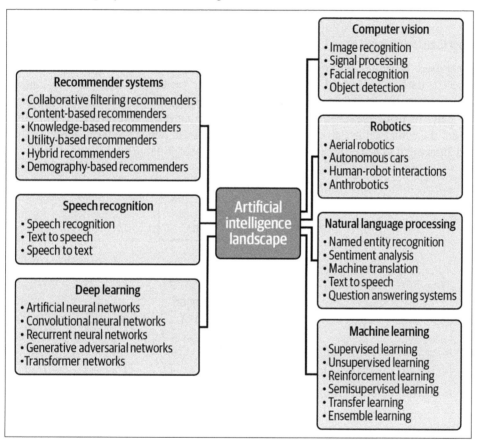

Figure 1-4. An outline of artificial intelligence fields

Machine learning stands out as a highly popular and significant subfield within AI. It focuses on building systems that can discover patterns from data, learn from their mistakes, and make predictions. The key word in machine learning is *learning*, which the computer scientist Tom Mitchell eloquently illustrates as follows:[7]

> A computer program is said to learn from experience E with respect to some class of tasks T and performance measure P, if its performance at tasks in T, as measured by P, improves with experience E.

Machine learning scientists and practitioners often develop models based on three types of learning: supervised, unsupervised, and reinforcement learning. Let's explore each in detail.

Supervised learning

Supervised learning describes a learning approach that relies on an annotated (labeled) dataset comprised of a set of explanatory variables (called *features*) and a response variable (called a *label*). In a supervised setting, the model is trained to identify patterns using explanatory variables. The training process involves showing the model the actual value (label) it should have predicted, hence the term "supervised," and allowing it to learn from its mistakes (as illustrated in Figure 1-5).

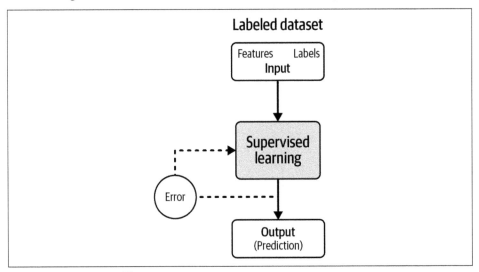

Figure 1-5. Supervised learning process

---

7 Tom Mitchell, *Machine Learning* (McGraw-Hill, 1997), p. 2.

When building a supervised system, modelers start by fitting one or more models on training data, where features and labels are known, via a selected optimization process such as *gradient descent*. Successively, the fit model(s) is tested on a second chunk of the data, called the validation dataset. The goal of the validation dataset is to allow the machine learning expert to fine-tune the so-called model *hyperparameters* via a process called *regularization*. Regularization is a technique used to achieve a balance between *bias* (how well a model learns the training data) and *variance* (how good the model is at generalizing to new instances unseen during training). Finally, a test dataset is used to evaluate the performance of the model that did best on the validation dataset. Performance metrics include accuracy, precision, root mean square error (RMSE), and mean square error (MSE), to name a few.[8]

Supervised learning can be divided into two categories: *classification*, which predicts a class label for a categorical variable, and *regression*, which predicts a quantity for a numerical variable. Linear regression, autoregressive models, generalized additive models, neural networks, and tree-based models are well-known regression methods. For classification tasks, methods such as logistic regression, support vector machines, linear discriminant analysis, tree models, and artificial neural networks are commonly used.

In finance, supervised learning is extensively employed for both classification and regression tasks. Examples of financial regression problems include stock price forecasting, volatility estimation and prediction, asset pricing, and risk assessment. Classification problems are also plenty in finance, for example, credit scoring, default prediction, corporate action prediction, fraud detection, and credit risk rating.

---

8 For a good reference on performance metrics, I recommend Aurélien Géron's book, *Hands-On Machine Learning with Scikit-Learn, Keras, and TensorFlow* (O'Reilly, 2022).

Unsupervised learning

Unsupervised learning is used to extract patterns and relationships within data without relying on known target response values (labels). Unlike supervised learning, it does not have a teacher (supervisor) correcting the model based on knowledge of the correct answer (as illustrated in Figure 1-6).

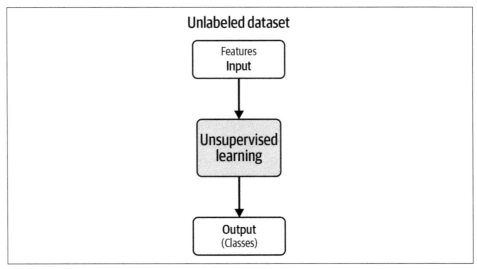

Figure 1-6. Unsupervised learning process

There are two main types of unsupervised learning: *clustering*, where a model is trained to learn and find groups (clusters) in the data, and *density estimation*, which tries to summarize the distribution of the data. Examples of clustering techniques include k-means, k-nearest neighbor, principal component analysis, and hierarchical clustering, while the kernel density estimator is perhaps the most common example of density estimation techniques.[9]

Unsupervised learning applications in finance are still in their early stages, but the future trend is promising. For example, clustering can be used to group similar financial time series, cluster stocks into groups based on sector or risk profile, analyze customer and market segmentation, and find similar firms or customers to assign similar scores or ratings.

---

9 For an overview of clustering techniques, I recommend the official documentation of scikit-learn (*https://oreil.ly/KUWiS*).

Reinforcement learning

In reinforcement learning, an artificial agent is placed in an environment where it can perform a sequence of actions over a state space and learn to make better decisions via a feedback mechanism. The key difference between this technique and supervised learning is that the feedback from the teacher is not about providing the right answer (true label); instead, the agent is given a reward (positive or negative) in order to encourage certain behaviors (actions) and punish others (see Figure 1-7).

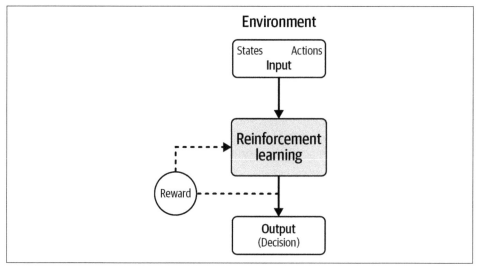

Figure 1-7. Reinforcement learning process

As many financial activities entail decision-making by agents, there has been a considerable interest among financial practitioners and researchers in reinforcement learning, which centers on optimal decision-making. Financial applications of reinforcement learning include portfolio selection and optimization, optimal trade execution, and market-making.[10]

---

10 An excellent reference on reinforcement learning in finance is the book by Ashwin Rao and Tikhon Jelvis, *Foundations of Reinforcement Learning with Applications in Finance* (CRC Press, 2022).

Generative AI and Large Language Models in Finance

Recently, an emerging field of AI, known as generative AI, has received remarkable attention following the introduction by OpenAI of the large language model (LLM) ChatGPT. In generative AI, a system is trained to generate one or more outcomes, such as text, image, and video, in response to prompts. In the case of ChatGPT, the user interacts with a chatting machine in a conversational way, where the machine can answer a wide variety of questions, solve problems, generate code, make and challenge statements, admit its mistakes, and at the same time reject inappropriate prompts.

Language modeling is quite popular in finance. For example, it's used in sentiment analysis, news classification, named entity recognition, fraud detection, and question answering. However, as of the time of writing of this book, no LLM has been tuned and adapted for the financial domain. As a first step in this direction, Bloomberg developed BloombergGPT (*https://oreil.ly/8FnP-*), a 50-billion parameter LLM developed with a mixed approach that focuses on financial domain-specific capabilities, while also maintaining a competitive performance on general-purpose tasks.

BloombergGPT was trained on a massive dataset consisting of English financial documents such as filings, news, press releases, web-scraped documents, and social media pulled from the Bloomberg archives. This data was augmented with public datasets such as The Pile, the Colossal Clean Crawled Corpus (C4), and Wikipedia. In total, this has led to a comprehensive dataset of almost 700 billion tokens, half domain-specific and half general-purpose. The resulting model has outperformed existing open source models on financial-specific tasks while guaranteeing on par and sometimes better performance on general language tasks.

As an alternative to BloombergGPT, a group of researchers, in collaboration with the AI4Finance Foundation, developed and released FinGPT (*https://oreil.ly/tkWun*), an open source framework that allows the development of LLMs for the financial domain. The data sources used to develop FinGPT include financial news, social media, filings, trends, and academic datasets.

GenAI applications are rapidly expanding within the finance industry. For instance, FactSet, a leading data and analytics provider, has launched Portfolio Commentary (*https://oreil.ly/69jEt*). This tool uses AI to generate explanations of portfolio performance attribution analysis—the practice of explaining portfolio performance relative to a benchmark—within FactSet's renowned Portfolio Analytics application.

Applied machine learning systems rely on data and computational resources; thus, having access to more data and computing power leads to better and faster predictions. In finance, where computational resources and datasets have grown, financial machine learning has emerged as a promising yet challenging area of research and practice.

According to Marcos López de Prado (*https://oreil.ly/255DX*), a leading hedge fund manager and quantitative analyst, financial machine learning has proven to be very successful and is likely to be a major factor in shaping the future of financial markets, but it shouldn't be ignored that it presents major challenges that need to be taken into consideration. Perhaps the most relevant challenge that's worth mentioning is the problem of false discoveries. This refers to the practice of finding what seems like a valid pattern in the data, yet in reality is a spurious relationship.[11] Other challenges include the interpretability/explainability of the models, performance, costs, and ethics.

For financial institutions to effectively invest in and leverage financial machine learning, they must ensure they are machine learning ready. This involves having the right team with expertise in both finance and machine learning, a sufficient quality and quantity of financial data for ML algorithms, a robust data infrastructure, dedicated ML-oriented data pipelines, DevOps (or MLOps) practices for seamless deployment and integration, and monitoring tools. With this foundation, financial data engineering becomes crucial. Financial data engineers collaborate closely with financial ML scientists and ML engineers to define data requirements, automate data transformations, perform quality checks, and structure ML workflows for fast and high-performance computations.

The Disruptive FinTech Landscape

Following the 2007–2008 financial crisis, traditional financial institutions have faced a significant increase in regulatory requirements. Consequently, the focus of market participants has shifted substantially toward compliance. At the same time, as customers became more accustomed to using services online, demand for simple and user-friendly online financial products has increased. These factors paved the way for a new wave of technological innovation in the financial sector, commonly known as *FinTech*.

The term FinTech has emerged as a market portmanteau to describe both innovative technologies developed for the financial sector and the startup firms that develop these technologies. FinTech firms have attracted particular attention in the media and the market due to their innovative, flexible, and experimental approach. Not being constrained by regulatory debt, FinTechs have been employing modern and nonconventional approaches to solving and improving a wide range of financial problems, such as payments, lending, investment, fraud detection, and cryptocurrency. Traditional financial institutions would lack this flexibility due to factors such as

---

11 The problem of false discoveries is well-known in finance. For an introduction to this topic, please refer to the article by Campbell R. Harvey, Yan Liu, and Heqing Zhu, "… and the Cross-Section of Expected Returns" (*https://oreil.ly/7vaqK*), *Review of Financial Studies* 29, no. 1 (January 2016): 5–68.

organizational inertia, regulatory constraints, security concerns, and a lack of innovative culture.

The main distinguishing features of FinTech services are *specialization* and *personalization*. As small firms, FinTechs tend to focus on penetrating only specific and niche areas of the financial system. Figure 1-8 illustrates the different areas of specialization of FinTech firms. As the figure illustrates, the FinTech landscape spans all segments of the financial sector, from fundamental functions such as payments and investment to more specialized areas such as regulatory compliance (often called *regtech*) and analytics.

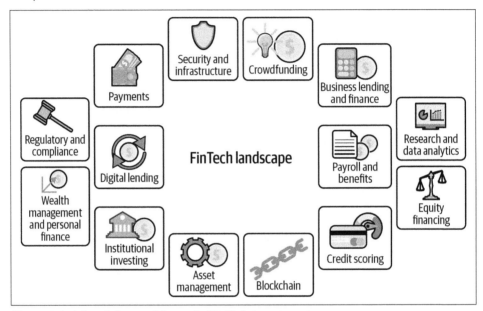

Figure 1-8. A breakdown of the main FinTech investment areas

Moreover, the FinTech business model has demonstrated competitiveness through its customizable and personalized offerings. For example, digital wealth management platforms like Betterment and Wealthfront provide clients with detailed surveys to assess their financial goals and risk preferences, enabling them to offer investment plans tailored to each investor's unique objectives and expectations.

Overall, the FinTech market has seen rapid growth since its inception. According to a report published by Boston Consulting Group (*https://oreil.ly/rzLUV*), as of 2023, there were roughly 32,000 FinTech firms globally, securing more than $500 billion in funding. The same report predicts that by 2030, the annual revenue of the FinTech sector is expected to reach $1.5 trillion, with banking FinTech representing 25% of the overall banking evaluations.

Payments: The Dynamic Heart of Innovation in Financial Technology

In the rapidly evolving landscape of financial technology, payments represent the most active and vibrant area of innovation. As the central mechanism for the exchange of value, payments have undergone a dramatic transformation, driven by technological advancements, changing consumer expectations, and regulations. Today, the payments sector is not merely about transferring money; it is about creating the seamless, secure, and instantaneous financial experiences that are integral to our daily lives.

With the proliferation of smartphones, the rise of ecommerce, and the demand for real-time transactions, the payments industry is at the forefront of FinTech innovation. This sector is pioneering the use of cutting-edge technologies such as cloud computing, real-time systems, blockchain, open banking APIs, biometric authentication, and artificial intelligence to enhance security, efficiency, and user experience. As a result, payments are reshaping the financial ecosystem, promoting financial inclusion, and driving economic growth.

There are many types of entities involved in the payment ecosystem. Examples include the following:

Issuers
> Financial institutions that provide consumers with payment cards (credit, debit, or prepaid), such as JPMorgan Chase, Bank of America, and Citibank.

Acquirers
> Financial institutions that manage and process payment transactions for merchants, like Wells Fargo Merchant Services, First Data, and Elavon.

Payment processors
> Companies that handle the technical aspects of processing transactions between issuers and acquirers, including PayPal, Square, and Stripe.

Payment networks
> Networks that connect issuers and acquirers to facilitate card transactions, such as Visa, Mastercard, and American Express.

Payment gateways
> Services that act as an intermediary in electronic financial transactions. Examples include Authorize.net, Braintree, and Cybersource.

Digital wallet providers
> Companies offering electronic devices or software for storing payment information and making transactions, such as Apple Pay, Google Wallet, and Samsung Pay.

FinTech startups
   Innovative companies creating new payment solutions using advanced technology, including Revolut, Stripe, and Square.

Settlement institutions
   Entities that facilitate the final transfer of funds between financial institutions to complete payment transactions, such as Fedwire and the Clearing House Interbank Payments System (CHIPS).

Payment infrastructures
   Systems and networks that facilitate the processing, authorization, and settlement of financial transactions between parties. Examples include the Society for Worldwide Interbank Financial Telecommunication (SWIFT) for financial messaging and interbank communication and Australia's New Payments Platform (NPP) for fast payments.

Additionally, there are several payment-related regulatory frameworks currently being developed and adopted. For instance, the European Union is moving forward with the following regulations:

Instant Payments Regulation
   Requires all payment service providers (PSPs) to offer the capability to send and receive euro payments within seconds, 24/7, across the EU.

Central Electronic System of Payment Information (CESOP)
   Mandates payment system providers to track cross-border payment data and share it with the tax authorities of EU member states.

Markets in Crypto-Assets (MiCA) regulation
   Aims to harmonize EU market rules for crypto-assets.

Eurosystem Collateral Management System (ECMS)
   A unified system for managing assets used as collateral in Eurosystem credit operations.

Third Payment Services Directive (PSD3) and Payment Services Regulation (PSR)
   Seek to further harmonize the payment market and reduce national variations.

E-Money Directive
   Provides the legal framework for issuing and managing electronic money within the European Union.

For financial data engineering aspirants, diving into payments promises not just a career path but a gateway to shaping the future of digital transactions and financial services on a global scale.

To thrive in this technology-intensive, high-performance, and data-driven landscape, aspiring FinTech companies must prioritize their software and data engineering strategies. To compete with and/or collaborate with incumbent financial institutions, FinTechs must ensure the highest standards of quality, reliability, and security. In this context, financial data engineers play a crucial role by designing efficient and reliable data ingestion, processing, and analysis pipelines that can scale and seamlessly integrate with other solutions.

Regulatory Requirements and Compliance

Financial institutions, and banks in particular, have a special status in the economic system. This is justified by the fact that the financial sector forms a complex network of asset cross-holdings, ownerships, investments, and transactions among financial institutions. As a consequence, a market shock that leads to the failure of one or more financial institutions can trigger a cascade of failures that might destabilize the entire financial system and cause an economic meltdown.[12] The global financial crisis of 2007–2008 is the best example of such a scenario.

To avoid costly financial crises, the financial sector has been subjected to a large number of regulations, both national and international. Crucially, a significant part of financial regulatory requirements concerns the way banks should collect, store, aggregate, and report data. For example, following the financial crisis of 2007–2008, the Basel Committee on Banking Supervision noted that banks, and in particular *Global Systemically Important Banks* (G-SIBs), lacked a data infrastructure that could allow for quick aggregation of risk exposures to identify hidden risks and risk concentrations. To overcome this problem, the Basel Committee issued a list of 13 principles on data governance and infrastructure (*https://oreil.ly/dSCF7*) that banks need to implement to strengthen their risk data aggregation and reporting capabilities.

Beyond banks, other financial institutions are also considered systemically important. These include *Financial Market Infrastructures* (FMIs), which facilitate the processing, clearing, settlement, and custody of payments, securities, and transactions. Examples of FMIs are stock exchanges, multilateral trading facilities, central counterparties, central securities depositories, trade repositories, payment systems, clearing houses, securities settlement systems, and custodians. FMIs are critical to the functioning of financial markets and the broader economy, making them subject to extensive regulation.[13]

---

12 To read more about the topic of systemic risk, I recommend Jaime Caruana's article, "Systemic Risk: How to Deal With It?" (*https://oreil.ly/69XKq*), Bank for International Settlements (February 2010).

13 To read more about FMI regulation, see "Principles for Financial Market Infrastructures" (*https://oreil.ly/BGLoR*), the Bank for International Settlements (April 2012), and "Core Principles for Systemically Important Payment Systems" (*https://oreil.ly/EWSlw*), the Bank for International Settlements (January 2001).

Occasionally, regulators may require financial institutions to collect new types of data. For example, the European directive known as the Markets in Financial Instruments Directive (*https://oreil.ly/U-AMN*), or MiFID, requires firms providing investment services to collect information regarding their clients' financial knowledge to assess whether their level of financial literacy matches the complexity of the desired investments.

To comply with regulations, financial institutions need dedicated financial data engineering and management teams to design and implement a robust data infrastructure. This infrastructure must capture, process, and aggregate all relevant data and metadata from multiple sources while ensuring high standards of security and operational and financial resilience. It should enable risk and compliance officers to quickly and accurately access the data needed to demonstrate regulatory compliance. Financial data engineers will also be tasked with creating and enforcing a financial data governance framework that guarantees data quality and security, thereby increasing trust among management, stakeholders, and regulators. In Chapter 5, Financial Data Governance, we will explore these topics in detail.

The Financial Data Engineer Role

The financial data engineer is at the core of everything we've discussed so far. Working in the financial industry can be a very rewarding and exciting career. A decade ago, the most in-demand roles in finance were analytical, such as financial engineers, quantitative analysts (or quants), and analysts. But with the digital revolution that took place with big data, the cloud, and FinTech, titles such as data engineer, data architect, data manager, and cloud architect have established themselves as primary roles within the financial industry. In this section, I will provide an overview of a financial data engineer's role, responsibilities, and skills.

Description of the Role

The role of a financial data engineer is in high demand, though the title, required skills, and responsibilities can vary significantly between positions. For example, the title of a financial data engineer could be any of the following:

- Financial data engineer
- Data engineer, finance
- Data engineer, fintech
- Data engineer, finance products
- Data engineer, data analytics, and financial services
- Financial applications data engineer
- Platform data engineer, financial services

- Software engineer, financial data platform
- Software engineer, financial ETL pipelines
- Data management developer, FinTech
- Data architect, finance platform

In many cases, other titles that don't include the term "data engineering" involve, to a large extent, practices and skills related to financial data engineering. For example, the role of a machine learning engineer could involve many responsibilities concerning the creation, deployment, and maintenance of reliable analytical data pipelines for machine learning. The role of quantitative developer, common among financial institutions, often involves tasks relating to developing data pipelines, data extraction, and data transformations.

It is important to know that the role of a financial data engineer is neither a closed circle nor a professional lock-in. Even though financial domain knowledge is a major plus for financial data engineering roles, many financial institutions would accept people with data engineering experience who come from different backgrounds. Similarly, working as a financial data engineer would easily allow you to fit into other domains, given the rich variety of technical problems and challenges you might encounter in the financial industry.

Where Do Financial Data Engineers Work?

The demand for financial data engineers primarily arises from financial institutions that generate and store data and are willing or required to invest in data-related technologies. Let's consider a few examples.

FinTech

FinTech firms are technology oriented and data driven; therefore, they are one of the best places to work as a financial data engineer. One of the main advantages of working for a FinTech is that you get to witness the entire lifecycle of product development. This provides engineers a solid overview of how data, business, and technology are combined to make a successful product. Another advantage is that you get to contribute original ideas and solutions to major infrastructural and software problems (e.g., choosing a database or finding a financial data vendor).

Commercial banks

Commercial banks are financial institutions that accept deposits from individuals and institutions while providing loans to consumers and investors, process a significant volume of daily transactions, and adhere to numerous regulatory requirements. To effectively manage their internal operations and ensure timely reporting, commercial banks typically employ teams of software and data engineers. These are responsible for developing and maintaining database systems, data aggregation and reporting mechanisms, customer analytics infrastructure, and transactional systems for various banking activities such as accounts, transfers, withdrawals, and deposits. Working as a data engineer at a commercial bank offers the opportunity to gain valuable insights into industry standards and best practices related to security, reliability, and compliance.

Interestingly, commercial banks frequently form collaboration agreements (*https:// oreil.ly/0-aKi*) with FinTech firms to extend their services to the public. These partnerships necessitate a robust data infrastructure that facilitates secure and efficient server communication, often through financial APIs. Consequently, banks and FinTech firms need to hire financial data engineers to design and implement backends for data collection, transmission, aggregation, and integration.

Investment banks

An investment bank is a financial institution that provides corporate finance and investment services, such as mergers and acquisitions, leveraged buyouts, and initial public offerings (IPOs). Unlike commercial banks, investment banks do not accept deposits or give loans. Sometimes, they invest their own money via proprietary trading.

Investment banks engage in various activities that involve the generation, extraction, transformation, and analysis of financial data. These include building and backtesting investment strategies, asset pricing, company valuation, and market forecasting. This requires frequent and easy access to different types of financial data. Additionally, investment banks must regularly report compliance-related data to regulatory authorities. To facilitate quick and straightforward access to this data, investment banks need a team of financial data engineers to design and maintain systems for data collection, transformation, aggregation, and storage.

Asset management firms

Asset management firms are financial institutions that provide investment and asset management services to customers looking to invest their money. These can be independent entities or divisions within a large financial institution. Typically, asset managers operate on an institutional level, with clients such as mutual funds, pension funds, insurance companies, universities, and sovereign wealth funds.

To provide investment services, asset managers require access to a wide array of financial data to build investment strategies, construct portfolios, analyze financial markets, manage risks, and report on behalf of their clients. To manage such data, asset management firms employ in-house financial data engineers to design and maintain effective data strategies, governance, and infrastructure. Even when using third-party data management solutions, in-house engineers are crucial for overseeing and enhancing the data infrastructure.

Hedge funds

Hedge funds are financial institutions that actively invest a large pool of money in various market positions (buy and sell) and asset classes (equity, fixed income, derivatives, alternative investments) to generate above-market returns. To meet their financial return objectives, hedge funds build and test (backtest) a large number of complex investment strategies and portfolio combinations.

To achieve their goals, hedge funds rely on a large number of heterogeneous financial data sources from various providers. Financial engineers and quantitative developers working at hedge funds need high-quality and timely access to financial data. Moreover, hedge funds may invest in algorithmic and high-frequency strategies, which require robust and efficient data infrastructure for easy data read and write operations. This environment makes hedge funds an ideal workplace for financial data engineers.

Regulatory institutions

A variety of national and international regulatory bodies have been established to oversee financial markets. Examples include national entities like central banks and local market regulators, as well as international bodies such as the Bank for International Settlements, its Committee on Payments and Market Infrastructures, and the Financial Stability Board.

These institutions perform a wide variety of activities that require significant investments in financial data engineering and management. For example, if a regulatory agency establishes mandatory reporting and filing requirements, it requires a scalable data infrastructure capable of processing and storing all the reported data. Additionally, regulatory agencies might provide their members with principles and best practices on financial data infrastructure and governance system design. This requires internal teams of data engineers, data managers, and industry experts who can develop and formulate market recommendations.

Financial data vendors

Data vendors are key players in financial markets, providing subscription-based access to financial data collected from numerous sources. Notable examples include Bloomberg, LSEG, and FactSet. Due to their business model, these companies face various challenges related to data collection, curation, formatting, ingestion, storage, and delivery. Consequently, they offer some of the best opportunities for developing a career in financial data engineering.

Security exchanges

Security exchanges are centralized venues where buyers and sellers of financial securities conduct their transactions. Prominent examples include the New York Stock Exchange, NASDAQ, and the London Stock Exchange.

Exchanges need to record all activities and transactions that they facilitate on a daily basis. Some exchanges offer paid subscriptions to their transaction and quotation data. Additionally, they manage tasks like symbology, i.e., assigning identifiers and tickers to listed securities. All this makes exchanges an ideal place to develop a career as a financial data engineer, especially if you want to be at the heart of the financial center.

Big tech firms

Big tech companies such as Google, Amazon, Meta, and Apple have developed into major platforms for user interactions, transactions, and various online activities (*https://oreil.ly/SXoWH*). Tech companies rely on two mechanisms to expand their activities: user data and network effect. The more activities happen on an online platform, the more data can be collected. Data is then used to study customer behavior to offer new products and services. This, in turn, encourages others to join the platform, which generates yet more data, and so on.

Relying on these self-reinforcing mechanisms, tech giants like Amazon, Apple, Google, and Alibaba have expanded into financial services, offering products like payments, insurance, loans, and money management. This move capitalizes on their extensive customer data, wide-reaching networks, and advanced technology, leading to the creation of user-friendly services such as mobile device payments. Consequently, dedicated teams of data engineers, finance specialists, and machine learning experts are required to support these operations.

Responsibilities and Activities of a Financial Data Engineer

The financial data engineer's set of tasks and responsibilities will depend on the nature of the job and business problems, the hiring institution, and, most importantly, the firm's data maturity.

Data maturity is an important concept that relates to *data strategy*. A data strategy is a long-term plan that describes the roadmap of objectives, people, processes, rules, tools, and technologies required to manage an organization's data assets. To measure data strategy progress, data maturity approaches are often used. With a data maturity framework, an organization can illustrate the stages of development toward data usability, analytical capabilities, and integration. To further illustrate the concept, I borrow and build on the framework proposed by Joe Reis and Matt Housley in their book, *Fundamentals of Data Engineering*, which organizes data maturity into three steps: starting with data, scaling with data, and leading with data.

Starting with data

A financial institution that is starting with data is at the very early stage of its data maturity. Note that this doesn't necessarily mean that the institution is new; old institutions (e.g., traditional banks) might decide to initiate digital transformation plans to automate and modernize their operations (e.g., cloud migration).

When starting with data, the financial data engineer's responsibilities are likely to be broad and span multiple areas such as data engineering, software engineering, data analytics, infrastructure engineering, and web development. This early phase prioritizes speed and feature expansion over quality and best practices.

Scaling with data

During this stage, the financial institution needs to assess its processes, identify bottlenecks, and determine current and future scaling requirements. With these insights in hand, the institution can proceed to enhance the scalability, reliability, quality, and security of its financial data infrastructure. The primary objective here is to eliminate/handle any technological constraints that may be an obstacle to the company's growth.

During this stage, financial data engineers will be able to focus on adopting best practices for building reliable and secure systems, e.g., codebase quality, DevOps, governance, security, standards, microservices, system design, API and database scalability, deployability, and a well-established financial data engineering lifecycle.

Leading with data

Once a financial institution reaches the stage at which it is able to lead the market with data, it is considered data driven. In this stage, all processes are automated, requiring minimal manual intervention; the product can scale to any number of users; internal processes and governance rules are well established and formalized; and feature requests go through a well-defined development process.

During this stage, financial data engineers can specialize in and focus on specific aspects of the financial data infrastructure. There will always be space for further optimizations via roles and departments like site reliability engineering, platform engineering, data operations, MLOps, FinOps, data contracts, and new integrations.

Skills of a Financial Data Engineer

Financial data engineers bring together three types of skills: financial domain knowledge, technical data engineering skills, and soft and business skills. We'll briefly illustrate these skillsets in the upcoming sections.

Financial domain knowledge

Having a good understanding of finance, financial markets, and financial data is an essential and competitive asset in any finance-related job, including financial data engineering. Examples of financial domain skills include the following:

- Understanding the different types of financial instruments (stocks, bonds, derivatives, etc.)
- Understanding the different players in financial markets (banks, funds, exchanges, regulators, etc.)
- Understanding the data generation mechanisms in finance (trading, lending, payments, reporting, etc.)
- Understanding company reports (balance sheet, income statement, prospectus, etc.)
- Understanding the market for financial data (vendors, providers, distributors, subscriptions, delivery mechanisms, coverage, etc.)
- Understanding financial variables and measures (price, quote, volume, yield, interest rate, inflation, revenue, assets, liability, capitalization, etc.)
- Understanding financial theory terms (risk, uncertainty, return, arbitrage, volatility, etc.)
- Understanding of compliance and privacy concepts (personally identifiable information (PII), anonymization, etc.)
- Knowledge of financial regulation and data protection laws is a plus (Basel rules, MiFID, Solvency II, GDPR, the EU's General Data Protection Regulation, etc.)

Technical data engineering skills

Financial data engineering requires strong technical skills, which can vary across financial institutions, depending on their business needs, products, technological stack, and data maturity. Crucially, it's important to keep in mind that the data engineering landscape is quite dynamic, with new technologies emerging and diffusing every year. For this reason, this book will focus more on immutable and technology-agnostic principles and concepts rather than on tools and technologies. But to give you an illustrative and nonexhaustive overview of the current landscape (as of 2024), expect as a financial data engineer to be asked about your knowledge of the following areas:

Database query and design

- Experience with relational database management systems (RDBMSs) and related concepts, in particular Oracle, MySQL, Microsoft SQL Server, and PostgreSQL
- Solid knowledge of database internals and properties such as transactions, transaction control, ACID (atomicity, consistency, isolation, durability), BASE (basically available, soft state, evenutally consistent), locks, concurrency management, WAL (write-ahead logging), and query planning
- Experience with data modeling and database design
- Experience with the SQL language, including advanced concepts such as user-defined functions, window functions, indexing, clustering, partitioning, and replication
- Experience with data warehouses and related concepts and design patterns

Cloud skills

- Experience with cloud providers (Amazon Web Services, Azure, Google Cloud Platform, Databricks, etc.)
- Experience with cloud data warehousing (Redshift, Snowflake, BigQuery, Cosmos, etc.)
- Experience with serverless computing (lambda functions, AWS Glue, Google Workflows, etc.)
- Experience with different cloud runtimes (Amazon EC2, AWS Fargate, cloud functions, etc.)
- Experience with infrastructure as code (IaC) tools such as Terraform

Data workflow and frameworks

- Experience with ETL (extract, transform, load) workflow solutions (AWS Glue, Informatica, Talend, Alooma, SAP Data Services, etc.)
- Experience with general workflow tools such as Apache Airflow, Prefect, Luigi, AWS Glue, and Mage
- Experience with messaging and queuing systems such as Apache Kafka and Google Pub/Sub
- Experience in designing and building highly scalable and reliable data pipelines (dbt, Hadoop, Spark, Hive, Cassandra, etc.)

Infrastructure

- Experience with containers and container orchestration such as Docker, Kubernetes, AWS Fargate, and Amazon Elastic Kubernetes Service (EKS)
- Experience with version control using Git, GitHub, GitLab, feature branches, and automated testing

- Experience with system design and software architecture (distributed systems, batch, streaming, lambda architecture, etc.)
- Understanding of the Domain Name System (DNS), TCP, firewalls, proxy servers, load balancing, virtual private networks (VPNs), and virtual private clouds (VPCs)
- Experience building integrations with and reporting datasets for payments, finance, and business systems like Stripe, NetSuite, Adaptive, Anaplan, and Salesforce
- Experience working in a Linux environment
- Experience with software architecture diagramming and design tools such as draw.io, Lucidchart, CloudSkew, and Gliffy

Programming languages and frameworks
- Experience with Object-Oriented Programming (OOP)
- Experience optimizing data infrastructure, codebase, tests, and data quality
- Experience with generating data for reporting purposes
- Experience working with Pandas, PySpark, Polars, and NumPy
- Experience working with financial vendor APIs and feeds like the Bloomberg Server API, LSEG's Eikon, FactSet APIs, the OpenFIGI API, and LSEG's PermID
- Experience with web development frameworks such as Flask, FastAPI, and Django
- Understanding of software engineers' best practices, Agile methodologies, and DevOps

Analytical skills
- Knowledge of data matching and record linkage techniques
- Knowledge of financial text analysis such as extracting entities from text, fraud detection, and know your customer (KYC)
- Knowledge of financial data cleaning techniques and quality metrics
- Experience performing financial data analysis and visualization using various tools such as Microsoft Power BI, Apache Superset, D3.js, Tableau, and Amazon QuickSight
- Basic experience in machine learning algorithms and generative AI

Business and soft skills

For most financial institutions, data represents a valuable asset. Therefore, financial data engineers need to ensure that their work aligns with the data strategy and vision of their institution. To do so, they can complement their technical skills with business and soft skills such as the following:

- Ability to comprehend technical aspects of the product and technology to communicate effectively with engineers, and to explain these concepts in simpler terms to finance and business stakeholders
- Understanding the value generated by financial data and its associated infrastructure for the institution
- Collaborating closely with finance and business teams to identify their data requirements
- Staying informed about the evolving financial and data technology landscape
- Establishing policies for company members to access and request new financial data
- Interest in data analysis and machine learning, leveraging financial data
- Proactively gathering and analyzing high-value financial data needs from business and analyst teams, and clearly communicating deliverables, timelines, and tradeoffs
- Providing guidance and education on financial data engineering, expectations from a financial data engineer, and how to search, find, and access financial data
- Participating in the assessment of new financial data sources, technologies, products, or applications suitable for the company's business

Certainly, not every job demands proficiency in all these skills. Instead, a tailored combination is often sought based on the specific business needs. Throughout this book, you'll learn about several of the aforementioned skills, diving deeply into some while experiencing an overview of others, all with demonstrations of their importance and practical application within the financial domain.

Summary

This chapter provided an overview of financial data engineering, summarized as follows:

- Defining financial data engineering and outlining its unique challenges
- Justifying the need for financial data engineering and illustrating its applications
- Describing the role and responsibilities of the financial data engineer

Now that you have an idea about financial data engineering, it's time to learn about the most important asset in this field: financial data. In Chapter 2, you will gain a thorough understanding of financial data, including its sources, types, structures, and distinguishing features. You will also learn about key benchmark financial datasets that are widely used in the financial industry.

Financial Data Ecosystem

As discussed throughout this book, data will be placed at the heart of financial market operations. As digital transformation and cloud migration efforts make their way through the financial arena, more and more financial activities will leave a digital trace. Consequently, the amount, variety, and speed of financial data generation is constantly increasing. This, in turn, has given rise to a vast and complex financial data landscape, encompassing numerous sources, types, structures, providers, delivery methods, and datasets essential for market participants to conduct their financial and business activities.

This chapter breaks down the key components of the financial data ecosystem and illustrates their features and issues.

These include the following key areas:

- The different sources of financial data
- The data structures used in finance, along with their technical details
- The variety of data types that the financial industry generates and consumes

Then, I'll give an overview of some of the most important financial datasets used by practitioners and researchers.

Sources of Financial Data

Financial data can originate from a variety of sources, so let's establish a few baselines. In this book, the term data source will be used to indicate the location, entity, or mechanism behind the generation of financial data. These sources may differ in a number of ways:

Accessibility
    Whether the data is open access, commercially licensed, or proprietary

Usability
    Whether the data source is easy to use and extract data from, and whether the data is provided in a raw format or in a clean structure that is ready to use

Coverage
    Whether the data source offers complete and wide coverage of financial data

Reliability
    Whether a source is trusted, secure, timely, and durable

Quality
    Whether the data provided by the sources is of high quality (i.e., absence of errors, biases, duplicates, etc.)

Documentation
    Whether additional information is available on the data structures, fields, and content of the data source

There are many different data sources in the financial data ecosystem. In this book, I categorize them into six main types: publicly available data, data generated by security exchanges, commercial data provided by vendors and distributors, survey data, alternative data, and confidential data. Let's explore the main features of each data source in detail.

Public Financial Data

Public data is information that is freely accessible by anyone, without a license or fees, primarily through the internet. Public financial data exists for a number of reasons, such as regulatory disclosure and reporting requirements, publicly released data by governmental and nongovernmental organizations, public research data, and free stock market APIs. Let's explore each of these sources in detail.

Regulatory disclosure requirements

Many financial institutions are subject to data disclosure and reporting obligations established by national and international regulations. Such requirements aim to increase market transparency, efficiency, investor protection, and liquidity, as well as reduce the cost of capital for firms. For example, in the United States, companies are required to submit different reports about their operations to the Securities and Exchange Commission (SEC) as established by the Securities Act of 1933, the Securities Exchange Act of 1934, the Trust Indenture Act of 1939, and the Investment Company Act of 1940.

A variety of SEC public forms are available (*https://oreil.ly/UP-8L*) for companies to file periodic financial statements and various other disclosures. The most common form is the *10-K*, which is filed annually and provides a comprehensive overview of the company's financial performance. The *10-Q*, a comparable but less detailed document, is submitted following each of the three quarters for which a 10-K filing is not required. A special form, called *8-K*, is used to notify investors or the SEC about special and relevant events that might occur between 10-K and 10-Q filings. Another well-known type of disclosure is the *prospectus*, which is a document providing details about a stock, bond, or mutual fund investment offering to the public.

The main advantage of regulatory disclosures is that they constitute a reliable, unbiased, and regular source of data, covering a wide range of regulated entities. The main challenge, however, is that reporting data is often provided in raw and unstructured or semi-structured formats (e.g., HTML, TXT, or XML). Another issue is the potential for incomplete data due to the tradeoff between market efficiency and disclosure precision, which arises from regulators' demands that businesses reveal just enough data to ensure market efficiency without jeopardizing competition.[1]

Electronic Data Gathering, Analysis, and Retrieval (EDGAR)

EDGAR (*https://oreil.ly/rF5QE*) is the primary data management system used by the SEC, designed to provide a seamless experience for businesses and individuals required to file reports with the agency. The EDGAR Business Office (EBO) is the official owner of EDGAR and is responsible for its administration and maintenance, strategic planning and development, and SEC staff customer support. The EDGAR database is public and free, providing access to millions of company and individual filings. The system handles roughly 3,000 filings per day, serves about 3,000 terabytes of data annually, and accommodates an average of 40,000 new filers per year.

---

1 If interested in this topic, I recommend Itay Goldstein and Liyan Yang's article, "Information Disclosure in Financial Markets" (*https://oreil.ly/_Qo5F*), *Annual Review of Financial Economics* 9 (November 2017): 101–125, and Anat R. Admati and Paul Pfleiderer's "Forcing Firms to Talk: Financial Disclosure Regulation and Externalities" (*https://oreil.ly/QlzH1*), *The Review of Financial Studies* 13, no. 3 (July 2000): 479–519.

Public institutional and governmental data

A number of national and international financial institutions regularly collect, curate, and freely publish financial and economic data. Such institutions are often regulatory or multinational agencies. Examples include the following:

World Bank Open Data (https://oreil.ly/QFqDs)
Published and maintained by the World Bank, this resource provides a large collection of financial and macroeconomic indicator datasets.

Data.europa.eu
Published by the European Union, this site provides a central point of access to open data published by European institutions and national data portals. It provides access to 1,536,561 datasets, grouped into 179 catalogs and originating from 36 countries.

The ECB Statistical Data Warehouse (https://oreil.ly/d2y0f)
Published by the European Central Bank (ECB), this resource provides data on all Eurozone economic, financial, and monetary statistics released by the ECB and Eurostat in relation to monetary policy.

Federal Reserve Economic Data (FRED) (https://oreil.ly/ogvMO)
Published by the Federal Reserve Bank of St. Louis, this database provides a central point of of access to hundreds of thousands of economic data time series collected from national, international, public, and private sources.

Public research data

Researchers in financial markets may create and make publicly available research-oriented datasets that can be freely accessed and used for further empirical investigation. For example, Professor Kenneth French has created an online library, the Ken French Data Library (*https://oreil.ly/dfpqo*), that provides public and freely accessible financial data on US monthly Fama/French 3 factors and 5 factors, as well as other economic and financial variables. Another example is datasets made public on Kaggle, where researchers and machine learning practitioners publish their models alongside the datasets that they used for training.

Free stock market APIs

A number of commercial companies, both financial and nonfinancial, offer free online financial data services such as news, prices, quotes, press releases, financial reports, and more. Examples include Yahoo Finance, Google Finance, and Alpha Vantage. Such services frequently have APIs that enable programmatic access to financial data (e.g., Yahoo's API (*https://oreil.ly/X7zL6*)).

While free APIs provide convenient and cost-free access to financial data, I recommend using them with caution. For classroom-level financial analysis or experimental purposes, it's perfectly fine to use such data. However, for real financial applications and academic research, the data might lack the necessary quality guarantees. Potential quality issues may include errors, lack of adjustment for corporate actions, biases, incompleteness, and lack of proper identifiers. Companies like Yahoo and Google do not prioritize financial data services as a key element of their competitive strategy, so they may not be motivated to offer the highest quality financial data for free.

Security Exchanges

Market exchanges like the London Stock Exchange, New York Stock Exchange, and Chicago Mercantile Exchange gather and manage diverse datasets on the transactions they handle. Being the hub of transaction activities, these exchanges provide detailed and up-to-date data crucial for trading and investment purposes. Additionally, they maintain historical archives and reference data, offering valuable insights for analysis.

It's important to note that not all market trading takes place on official exchange venues. Some financial products, like bonds and various derivatives, are traded over the counter (OTC). This term refers to trading conducted off-exchange through broker-dealer networks. Consequently, statistics on OTC transactions are often unavailable or challenging to gather and access.

Commercial Data Vendors, Providers, and Distributors

One of the most valuable and reputable sources of financial data are commercial companies specializing in financial data and software. These providers collect and curate data from a large number of sources, including regulatory filings, news agencies, surveys, company websites, brokers, banks, rating agencies, company reports, bilateral agreements with companies, exchange venues, and many more.

Case Study: Morningstar Data Acquisition Process

Morningstar, Inc. (*https://oreil.ly/z8IVA*), is a well-known financial data vendor that collects, analyzes, and provides financial market data, in particular stock and fund data. In one of their 8-K filings (*https://oreil.ly/Jc-P2*), Morningstar experts provided a detailed overview of their data collection and acquisition process. Here's an excerpt from the original filing:

> We [Morningstar] collect most of our data from original source documents that are publicly available, such as regulatory filings and fund company documents. This is the main source of operations data for securities in our open-end, closed-end,

exchange-traded fund, and variable annuity databases, as well as for financial statement data in our equity database. This information is available at no cost.

For performance-related information (including total returns, net asset values, dividends, and capital gains), we receive daily electronic updates from individual fund companies, transfer agents, and custodians. We don't need to pay any fees to obtain this performance data. In some markets we supplement this information with a standard market feed such as Nasdaq for daily net asset values, which we use for quality assurance and filling in any gaps in fund-specific performance data. We also receive most of the details on underlying portfolio holdings for mutual funds, closed-end funds, exchange-traded funds, and variable annuities electronically from fund companies, custodians, and transfer agents.

...Our separate account and hedge fund databases require more specialized information, which we obtain by sending surveys to the management companies. We also survey for some specialized portfolio and operations data in our other databases to enhance our proprietary portfolio statistics. We supplement information gathered electronically or through surveys by licensing a few third-party data feeds for market indices and individual securities.

As you can see, financial data vendors rely on a variety of data sources in their data collection process. This is done to supplement and enhance their data offers. Clearly, financial data vendors are continually expanding their offerings and services by including new and larger datasets derived from new sources.

Compared to other data sources, commercial datasets offer the following advantages:

- Providing structured and standardized data that is highly suited for analysis, thus reducing the need for extensive data cleaning and preprocessing

- Enriching financial datasets with additional fields and identifiers for better analysis

- Providing comprehensive documentation on data usage and field metadata

- Providing a wide range of data delivery options and formats that can suit various business applications

- Providing customized solutions and packages that fit different business needs

- Providing customer support

There is a large variety of financial data vendors, some of which create their own content (often called data providers); others specialize in aggregating or distributing data, while others act as both distributors and creators of financial data. Generally speaking, financial data companies compete along the following axes:

Data coverage
    The universe of financial instruments, entities, sectors, and variables is quite massive. Some vendors focus on a subset of financial data (e.g., asset classes,

geographical areas, and sectors), while others tend to act as global aggregators or serve as a one-stop shop, offering a breadth of financial data coverage (such as prices, quotes, news, press releases, macroeconomic data, ratings, and volatility indicators).

Delivery mechanisms

Different providers offer their data via one or more delivery mechanisms. These may include SFTP (Simple File Transfer Protocol), cloud, data feed, API, desktop, web access, and others.

Delivery formats

Providers can differ in the file formats they use for data delivery. Examples include CSV (comma-separated values), XML, HTML, JSON, SQL query, and Zip Archive.

Data history

Some providers, especially older ones, could have longer historical coverage than others. Additionally, some providers might provide point-in-time snapshots of their data, while others provide only the latest data releases.

Delivery frequency

Data can be provided continuously (real time) or with fixed frequency such as second, minute, day, market closing time, week, or month.

Data standardizations and adjustments

Some providers might apply data transformations or standardization, while others would deliver the data in its original format. Here are a few examples:

Adjusted stock prices

A vendor might deliver adjusted stock prices that take into account corporate events such as stock splits and dividends, while another provider would leave the data unadjusted.

Data aggregation

Some vendors provide data at the exchange level, while others aggregate the data across exchanges. If you are interested in trading on a specific exchange, you might want to check if a data provider sells data for that exchange.

Standardization of accounting figures across countries

This might impact analysis if a company uses a specific accounting method that gets lost during standardization.

Data reliability and quality

Accuracy, quality, and timely access to financial data are crucial to financial institutions. Providers who guarantee high data quality, low error and bias rates, and high availability are likely to be more trusted.

Value-added services

Providers who enrich the data with extra fields, identifiers, documentation, and customer support are likely to have a competitive advantage.

Pricing

Many subscription plans are available, and they vary by vendor. Some offer large packages that can be more expensive, while others offer various package sizes that can fit multiple usage patterns and needs.

Technical limitations

Vendors might impose certain limits and quotas on their servers, such as the maximum daily requests, the maximum number of instruments that can be queried, or the request timeout.

The market for financial data is competitive and innovative, and it is continuously evolving to accommodate new products, markets, technologies, data types, and delivery mechanisms. One of the winning strategies that financial data vendors seem to invest in is the *one-stop shop* model, where a financial data vendor provides an integrated platform with access to a wide range of financial data as well as complementary services such as analytics and insights, export options, artificial intelligence tools, visualizations, messaging and chatting, trading, and search capabilities. Another competitive strategy is the *network effect*, where the value of a data vendor's solution increases as more people use it. The more users and traders engage with a specific data vendor platform, the more appealing it becomes for new customers to join.

A significant share of the financial data market is dominated by a few players. This includes Bloomberg, LSEG, FactSet, S&P Global Market Intelligence, Morningstar, SIX Financial Information, Nasdaq Data Link, NYSE, Exchange Data International (EDI), Intrinio, and WRDS. There are also smaller players that tend to offer innovative products focused on a specific market niche. For example, firms such as Pitch-Book and DealRoom provide private market data on startups, private equity, and venture capital.

Next, I'll present an introductory overview of some of the most important providers in the market.

Bloomberg

Bloomberg is the whale in the financial data market, comprising almost one-third of the total market share. Bloomberg's flagship product is the Bloomberg Terminal (*https://oreil.ly/3xxgA*), a computer system well-known for its black interface that provides users with access to real-time market data, news, quotes, insights, and a number of valuable complementary services. Bloomberg is best suited for buy-side and asset management professionals such as traders and portfolio managers.

A valuable feature of Bloomberg is Instant Bloomberg (IB), a messaging service that allows users to chat with a large pool of financial professionals who are using the Bloomberg Terminal. Additionally, users of the Bloomberg Terminal can place trading orders via an end-to-end secure trading service (Tradebook). Recently, Bloomberg introduced BloombergGPT, an AI-powered language model that helps financial professionals with challenging language tasks such as sentiment analysis, news classification, question answering, and more. Additionally, Bloomberg provides API services (*https://oreil.ly/YbjkC*) that allow developers to access Bloomberg data programmatically using various programming languages.

LSEG Eikon

LSEG Eikon (*https://oreil.ly/VELTQ*) is Bloomberg's main competitor, and it holds a significant market share. Similar to Bloomberg, Eikon has a rich collection of financial datasets, a feature-rich user interface, developer APIs, an instant messaging service (LSEG Messenger), and trade execution capabilities. Compared to Bloomberg, Eikon has much cheaper options for more limited offerings.

FactSet

FactSet (*https://oreil.ly/DHaNW*) offers an affordable solution to access real-time financial data, combining proprietary, third-party, and user data. Some of FactSet's advantages include the user-friendly UI, PowerPoint integrations for PitchBooks, personalization options, a large variety of alternative datasets, and portfolio analysis tools.

S&P Global Market Intelligence

S&P Global Market Intelligence (*https://oreil.ly/DZSU7*) is a leading financial data and market intelligence service provider. It provides financial and industry data, analytics, news, and research. Among the most well-known solutions of S&P GMI is Capital IQ, a web-based platform that provides a rich set of data points on company financials, transactions, estimates, private company data, ownership data, and more.

Wharton Research Data Services

Wharton Research Data Services (WRDS) (*https://oreil.ly/15CjL*) is the leading platform in financial and business research and analysis and is among the most popular data distributors in finance. WRDS offers a globally accessed, user-friendly web interface with more than 600 datasets from more than 50 data vendors across multiple domains, with a particular focus on finance. Through WRDS, users can access multiple data sources, documentation, analytics, and query-building tools simultaneously. WRDS establishes distribution and resale agreements with data vendors and allows their clients to access vendor data directly through their platform. For some datasets, WRDS requires their clients to buy and maintain a separate license for the data.

How Do I Choose a Financial Data Vendor?

Most financial institutions use services from at least one financial data vendor. However, finding and choosing the right vendor can be quite challenging. My advice is to start by formalizing your company's or project's financial data needs. Then, using the vendor differentiating criteria mentioned previously, you can ask yourself some key questions:

What type of data am I looking for?
> For example, if you are looking for data on Chinese stock prices, you might want to find a local data provider specializing in the Chinese market.

Which fields are mandatory, and which are optional?
> For example, if you want adjusted stock prices, you need to choose a data provider that provides already adjusted data or the necessary fields to perform the adjustment.

What is the universe of assets that I want?
> For example, if you want data on European and American stocks, as well as fixed-income data, you might need a global data provider with international coverage (e.g., Bloomberg).

Do I need data quality guarantees?
> Some providers ensure their data is free from errors, biases, and other quality issues, while others offer less assurance, necessitating data cleaning.

What is the planned budget?
> For example, if your company has a limited budget, you might need to look for a data provider that offers small packages or on-demand pricing.

What purpose do I need the data for?
> For example, buy-side professionals (e.g., traders) often need a wide variety of data, such as prices, news, macroeconomic variables, and market volatility, while sell-side professionals (e.g., investment bankers) need more specific data, such as asset prices and corporate events.

What data update frequency do I want?
> For example, if you have a machine learning model that you train weekly, then there is no need for very frequent updates. However, if you are working at an algorithmic trading company, then data would be needed at a very high frequency.

Do I need specific delivery mechanisms?
> For example, if you are developing a web application, you will very likely need to fetch data via an API. However, if you have data extraction running in the background, receiving files via SFTP or direct website download should work fine.

Do I need predictable delivery performance?

Some providers may offer guarantees on latency, throughput, and uptime, which are crucial for time-sensitive applications.

Can I tolerate vendor limitations?

For example, if your workload is predictable, you can adapt your application and consumption patterns to the limitations established by the data vendor. However, if your data needs are unpredictable or growing, you might want to find a data vendor that does not impose strict limitations or negotiate custom quotas.

Do I need a simple solution?

For example, if you want a simple user interface with Microsoft Excel or CSV export capabilities, you may not want to choose a very sophisticated financial data solution.

Survey Data

A survey is a set of questions designed to collect information from a specific group of people on a particular topic. Survey data can enhance existing datasets and provide deeper insights. For instance, banks might ask clients to complete a survey to assess their financial knowledge and risk appetite level. This information can help assess and tailor investment plans to fit each customer's profile. Similarly, financial data vendors may rely on surveys as a mechanism to gather data from companies by sending them questions related to their operations, performance, and structure.

Survey data could serve as the main ingredient in creating other types of data. For example, the Institute for Supply Management (ISM) publishes the *Purchasing Managers' Index* (PMI) (*https://oreil.ly/lTAND*), a monthly figure used by market agents as an indicator of the direction of the economy. To calculate the PMI, the ISM sends a survey to a list of companies that make up a representative sample of the entire economy. Once respondents return the filled-in surveys, the index is computed by aggregating and weighing the individual responses.

The main advantage of survey data is its flexibility, enabling the questioner to design the questions to guarantee valuable answers and organize the information optimally. However, a few challenges might arise. For example, if the survey is voluntary, some respondents might have no incentive to provide answers, which can bias the final outcome. In other cases, some candidates may choose not to complete the survey. This could be due to a reluctance to report poor financial performance, organizational inertia, concerns about reputational risk, competition, or issues related to security and confidentiality. Additionally, the questioner might (intentionally or unintentionally) induce *framing bias* in the survey by choosing questions intended to force the respondent to give a desired answer. For this reason, a strong emphasis on ethical practices and bias checks is highly recommended when conducting surveys.

Alternative Data

In recent years, the term "alternative data" has emerged in the financial world to describe data sources not traditionally used in financial analysis and investment. These nonconventional data sources are not inherently embedded within the financial system, unlike trading venues, payment systems, and commercial banking. The sources of alternative data are quite heterogeneous. A few are mentioned here:

- Satellites (e.g., collecting shipping images)
- Social media (e.g., tweets)
- Articles
- Blog posts (e.g., Medium, Substack)
- News channels (e.g., Thomson Reuters, Bloomberg)
- Weather observers
- Online clicking patterns and browsing history
- Shipping and pipeline trackers
- Emails and chats
- Product and service reviews
- Security, social, and environmental scores and ratings

Confidential and Proprietary Data

Financial institutions generate and store large amounts of data when conducting their internal operations. The most essential and valuable type of internal data involves contextual, nontransactional information about the various business entities. This includes, for example, data about clients, employees, suppliers, products, subscriptions, offerings, discounts, pricing, financial structures (e.g., cost centers), and locational information (e.g., branches).

A second type of internal business data is *transactions*. In performing their daily activities, financial institution clients generate a large amount of transaction data, such as payments, deposits, trading, purchases, credit card transactions, and money transfers.

Finally, financial institutions might collect *internal analytical data* from research teams and analysts conducting market and financial analysis. This includes, for example, sales analysis and forecasting, customer segmentation, credit scoring, default probabilities, investment strategies, stock predictions, macroeconomic analysis, and customer churn probabilities.

In specific situations, financial institutions must report various types of confidential data to regulatory bodies. This includes trade details, large transaction information, suspicious activity reports, data gathered during anti-money laundering (AML) and know your customer (KYC) processes, as well as information related to tax, compliance, liquidity, risk management, and capital adequacy.

Now that you have an idea about the different sources of financial data, the next section will discuss the various structures in which financial data can be represented.

Structures of Financial Data

Financial data can be stored and represented using various structures. These may range from simple data structures such as tabular times series, cross-section, or panel data to more complex structures such as matrices, graphs, and text. Throughout this section, we will explore these structures in detail.

Time Series Data

A time series is a collection of records for one or more variables associated with a single entity, observed at specific intervals over time. Time series are indexed in time order and can be represented mathematically as follows:

$$\mathbf{X} = \{X_1, X_2, \ldots, X_N\}$$

where N is the length of the time series and X is the observed variable, or:

$$\mathbf{X} = \{X_t, t \in T\}$$

where T is a time index set and X is the observed variable.

In tabular format, a time series with S variables observed over N periods can be represented as shown in Table 2-1. The first column stores the temporal dimension (T_N), while the other columns (X_S) store the time series values for each variable. A single cell (X_{SN}) records the time series values observed at a specific time for a given variable.

Table 2-1. Tabular representation of time series

Time/variable	X_1	X_2	X_3	...	X_S
T_1	X_{11}	X_{21}	X_{31}	...	X_{S1}
T_2	X_{12}	X_{22}	X_{32}	...	X_{S2}
...	...	...	...	...	...
T_N	X_{1N}	X_{2N}	X_{3N}	...	X_{SN}

The time series is the most common data structure in financial markets, mainly due to the dynamic and transactional nature of financial activities that happen over time. Examples of financial activities that generate time-series data include trading, pricing, payment, investment, estimation, valuation, risk measures, volatility figures, corporate events, performance and accounting, and many more.

Extensive literature on financial time series has been produced where a large number of temporal phenomena have been investigated. For an excellent treatment of financial time series analysis, I recommend the seminal book *Analysis of Financial Time Series* by Ruey Tsay (Wiley, 2010).

Cross-Sectional Data

A cross-section is a collection of records for one or more variables observed across multiple entities at a single point in time. In cross-sectional data, the time series dimension is irrelevant, and the emphasis is on the variables themselves. Entities in a cross-section often share common characteristics, such as firms within the same sector, investments in a specific strategy, fund managers, and more.

A cross-section dataset can be represented mathematically as follows:

$$\left\{ X_{t=z, i, j}, i = 1, \ldots, N, j = 1, \ldots, S \right\}$$

where t is the time index (fixed), i is the entity index, and j is the variable index.

In tabular format, we can draw a cross-section of N entities and S variables as shown in Table 2-2. The first column stores the names of the entities (E_N), while the other columns store the cross-section value of the S variables (V_S). A table cell ($X_{i,j}$) stores the cross-section value of a given entity for a given variable.

Table 2-2. Tabular representation of cross-section data

Entity/variable	V_1	V_2	V_3	...	V_S
E_1	X_{11}	X_{21}	X_{31}	...	X_{S1}
E_2	X_{12}	X_{22}	X_{32}	...	X_{S2}
...	...	...	...	...	...
E_N	X_{1N}	X_{2N}	X_{3N}	...	X_{SN}

Financial cross-section data is generated from the presence of many participants in financial markets, including financial institutions, brokers, investors, consumers, traders, and managers, as well as a variety of other entities such as financial assets, investment strategies, and consumer and firm choices and behaviors, among others.

Financial cross-sectional data can be used to understand and explain significant point-in-time differences between financial entities, such as why different stocks have different returns, why firms behave differently, or why performance across fund managers varies. Furthermore, cross-sectional analysis is a key tool for identifying correlations, causations, or anomalies across different entities, which can be critical for investment decisions, policy formulation, and understanding market dynamics.

Panel Data

Panel data combines both time series and cross-sectional structures, representing data for a set of variables across multiple entities at different points in time. Mathematically, a panel has the following form:

$$\{X_{i,j,t}, i = 1, \ldots, N, j = 1, \ldots\ldots, S, t = 1, \ldots\ldots, T\}$$

where i is the entity index, j is the variable index, and t is the time index.

In tabular format, we can draw a panel of two entities, two time periods, and three variables as shown in Table 2-3. The first column stores the names of the entities, the second column stores the time, and the last three columns store the observed panel values for all three variables. This panel representation is called *wide format*, as it expands horizontally when new variables are added to the panel. Another option is the long format, where the variable name and value are stored in separate columns, expanding the table vertically with new entries. An example is shown in Table 2-4.

Table 2-3. Wide tabular representation of panel data

Entity	Time	V_1	V_2	V_3
E_1	t=1	X_{111}	X_{112}	X_{113}
E_1	t=2	X_{121}	X_{122}	X_{123}
E_2	t=1	X_{211}	X_{212}	X_{213}
E_2	t=2	X_{221}	X_{222}	X_{223}

Table 2-4. Long tabular representation of panel data

Entity	Time	Variable name	Variable value
E_1	t=1	V_1	X_{111}
E_1	t=2	V_2	X_{122}
E_2	t=1	V_1	X_{211}
E_2	t=2	V_2	X_{222}

Financial panel data arises from numerous market entities engaging in various activities over time. For instance, stocks are continuously traded and priced, companies regularly submit quarterly and annual reports, and individuals conduct daily payments and transactions. Hence, most financial datasets are essentially panel datasets.

Panel data may vary in terms of their cross-section and time series components. For example, annual balance sheets tend to have a large cross-section component (many firms) and a small history. On the other hand, some stock price panel datasets tend to have a long history (e.g., high-frequency trading prices) and a smaller cross-section component (asset universe).

An important characteristic of panel datasets is their degree of balance (*https://oreil.ly/lwqFA*). Assume a panel has N entities, T time periods, and S variables. The panel is said to be *balanced* if all N × T × S observations are available; otherwise, the panel is called *unbalanced*. Table 2-5 shows a balanced panel where data are available for all entities, time periods, and variables. Table 2-6 instead illustrates an unbalanced panel as it has six cells with null values, resulting in half of the observations being missing.

Table 2-5. Balanced panel

Entity	Time	V_1	V_2	V_3
E_1	t=1	X_{111}	X_{112}	X_{113}
E_1	t=2	X_{121}	X_{122}	X_{123}
E_2	t=1	X_{211}	X_{212}	X_{213}
E_2	t=2	X_{221}	X_{222}	X_{223}

Table 2-6. Unbalanced panel

Entity	Time	V_1	V_2	V_3
E_1	t=1	Null	X_{112}	Null
E_1	t=2	X_{121}	X_{122}	X_{123}
E_2	t=1	X_{211}	Null	X_{213}
E_2	t=2	Null	Null	Null

Similar to time-series data, a large literature, both theoretical and empirical, has been produced for panel data analysis. For an excellent introduction, I highly recommend Badi H. Baltagi's seminal book *Econometric Analysis of Panel Data* (Springer, 2021).

Matrix Data

A matrix is a two-dimensional array of elements arranged as rows and columns. Here is an example:

$$\begin{pmatrix} 2 & 5 & 7 \\ 3 & 4 & 6 \\ 7 & 7 & 3 \end{pmatrix}$$

This is a matrix with three rows and three columns, often referred to as a 3×3 matrix.

The use of matrix structures is quite common in finance. The best example is perhaps portfolio optimization theory, in particular Markowitz's mean-variance optimization (MVO). According to MVO, when constructing a financial investment portfolio, three elements should be taken into consideration:

- The expected return on the assets in the portfolio
- The variance (risk) of the asset returns
- The covariances between the asset returns

For example, let's imagine a portfolio with three assets: A, B, and C. Let's denote the expected return of any asset i with $E(R_i)$, the variance with $var(R_i)$, and the covariance between two assets i and j with $cov(R_i, R_j)$. Using MVO, two matrix representations would be constructed as follows:

- 3×1 portfolio return matrix

$$\begin{pmatrix} E(R_A) \\ E(R_B) \\ E(R_C) \end{pmatrix}$$

- 3×3 covariance matrix

$$\begin{pmatrix} var(R_A) & cov(R_A, R_B) & cov(R_A, R_C) \\ cov(R_B, R_A) & var(R_B) & cov(R_B, R_C) \\ cov(R_C, R_A) & cov(R_C, R_B) & var(R_C) \end{pmatrix}$$

Using these matrix representations, MVO relies on matrix algebra to optimize the portfolio's expected return for a given level of risk appetite. Portfolio optimization means choosing the best asset allocation strategy (how much to invest in each asset) to achieve a desired investment goal.[2]

Graph Data

Financial markets are an outstanding example of a complex system of myriad relationships, transactions, dependencies, and flows. Understanding such complex interactions can provide valuable information and insights into market structures, systematic risks, contagion mechanisms, dominant market positions, fraudulent behavior, and market inefficiencies.

The kind of analysis that focuses on studying the complex interactions in a system is called *network analysis* or *network science*.[3] To employ network science in finance, traditional time-series or cross-section data would lack the depth and granularity required to build and analyze financial networks. To this end, graph data is required. This type of data is also frequently referred to as connections, networks, or nodes and links. A graph dataset consists of two sets of data: a set of nodes (aka vertices) together with node attributes (e.g., name, country, type, and so on), and a set of links (aka edges) with link attributes (e.g., type, value, sign, and so on).

When working with graph data, an important challenge concerns the decision about how to structure the data for quick access and analysis. Structuring nodes' data and their attributes is straightforward, and a tabular structure will do the job. However, things get more complicated when it comes to structuring link data. To this end, special graph structures are often used. Generally speaking, a graph dataset can be represented in four main ways:

Network visualization
> A 2-D drawing of the nodes (often as circles) and links (using straight lines). This method is useful for illustrative purposes and works best with small networks.

Adjacency matrix
> An N × N matrix (N being the number of nodes). If there is a link between nodes i and j, it stores 1 at positions (i, j) and (j, i).

---

2 If interested in learning more about portfolio theory, I recommend the excellent book by Jack Clark Francis and Dongcheol Kim, *Modern Portfolio Theory: Foundations, Analysis, and New Developments* (Wiley, 2013).

3 For a good introduction to network science, I highly recommend Mark Newman's book *Networks*, 2nd ed. (Oxford University Press, 2018).

Adjacency list

An array of length N (N being the number of nodes) where each item in the array contains the index of the node and a list of its neighbors represented via a linked list.

Edge list

A simple array that stores all edges of a graph. An item of an edge list is a tuple where the first element is the source node and the second is the target, with optional elements that may represent link attributes such as weight, sign, and time.

Figure 2-1 visually illustrates these four types of graph data representations.

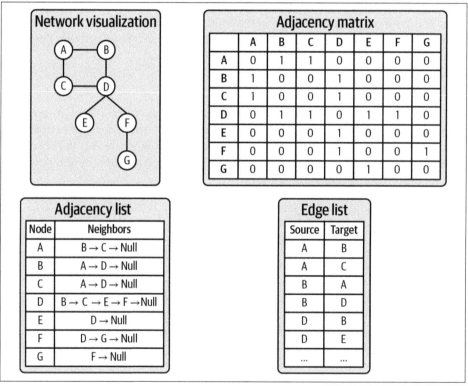

Figure 2-1. Different representations of graph data

Financial markets rely on a range of graph data types and representations. In the upcoming sections, I will discuss six pertinent graph structures: simple, directed, weighted, temporal, multipartite, and multiplex.

Simple graphs

A simple graph consists of a set of homogeneous nodes (nodes of the same type, e.g., companies) and a set of homogeneous, unweighted, and undirected links. Figure 2-2 illustrates an example with two nodes (A, B).

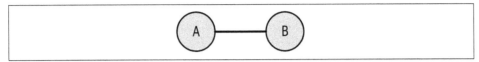

Figure 2-2. A simple graph with two nodes

The adjacency matrix, adjacency list, and edge list representations of simple graphs are similar to those shown in Figure 2-1. In financial markets, simple graphs can represent the *presence* of relationships between entities, such as payment agreements between banks, partnership agreements, and statistical correlations between financial assets.

Directed graphs

In a directed graph, links have a direction indicating an *orientation* between the nodes. Directed graphs are used to represent relationships where nodes at each end of the link play different roles. For example, A borrows from B, where A is the borrower and B is the lender. Figure 2-3 illustrates an example with two nodes, A and B, where node A points to node B but not vice versa.

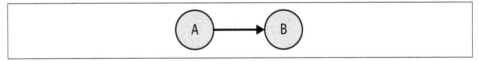

Figure 2-3. A simple directed graph with two nodes

The adjacency matrix of a directed network will have a value of 1 at position (i, j) if there is a link pointing from node i to j, but will have a value of 0 in position (j, i) if j doesn't have a link pointing toward i. Similarly, a directed graph's adjacency and edge list will only store records for nodes that point toward other nodes. Figure 2-4 illustrates the four representations for a directed graph.

Network visualization	Adjacency matrix				Adjacency list		Edge list	
		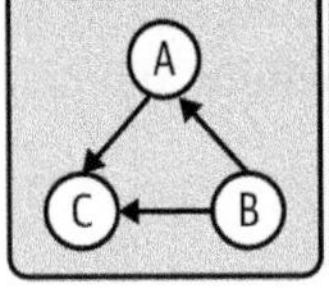 A	B	C	Node	Neighbors	Source	Target
	A	0	0	1	A	C → Null	A	C
	B	1	0	1	B	A → C → Null	B	A
	C	0	0	0	C		B	C

Figure 2-4. Directed graph representations

Directed graphs can represent a variety of financial activities, such as cross-holding among banks, transfers, transactions, and interbank lending.

Weighted graphs

In weighted graphs, links are assigned a numerical value to indicate the relationship's magnitude or strength. When representing a weighted graph, the weight needs to be added to the adjacency matrix, adjacency list, and edge list as illustrated in Figure 2-5.

Network visualization	Adjacency matrix				Adjacency list		Edge list		
		A	B	C	Node	Neighbors	Source	Target	Weight
	A	0	0	3	A	C|3 → Null	A	C	3
	B	5	0	12	B	A|5 → C|12 → Null	B	A	5
	C	0	0	0	C		B	C	12

Figure 2-5. Weighted graph representations

Most types of graphs can be weighted (including simple and directed graphs). In finance, weights can represent the value of the assets one bank holds at another in a cross-holding network, the amount of money transferred in a transaction, or the number of securities sold in a market trade.

Multipartite graphs

A graph representation is called *multipartite* when it includes more than one type of node and only allows links between different types of nodes. Graphs with two types of nodes are referred to as *bipartite*, those with three types of nodes as *tripartite*, and the generalized case with k types is called *k-partite*. A *k-partite projection*, often applied to bipartite graphs, is a common operation that builds a graph that contains one type of the k available node types, and edges exist based on whether two nodes share a common link to another type of node in the original network. Figure 2-6 presents a bipartite graph along with its projected graph and adjacency matrix.

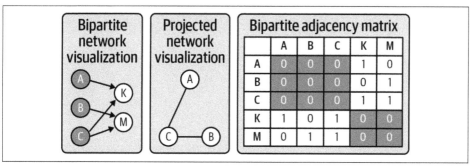

Figure 2-6. Bipartite graph representations

The leftmost graph in Figure 2-6 has two types of nodes, shaded and white, and links exist only between a shaded and a white node. The middle graph illustrates a bipartite projection on one type of node (the shaded nodes in the leftmost graph). The projected graph shows that nodes A and C have a link because in the bipartite graph on the left, both A and C share a connection to K. The same goes for C and B, which share a connection to M. The adjacency matrix in Figure 2-6 has a block structure, where links between the same type of nodes will be absent and represented with zeros (shaded blocks) whereas links between different types of nodes exist in the white blocks.

Examples of bipartite relationships in finance include the following:

Interlocking directorate
Nodes of type "person" (node type 1) act as a member of the board of directors (link) of one or more firms (node type 2).

Syndicated lending
Multiple lenders (node type 1) jointly provide a loan (link) to one or more borrowing entities (node type 2).

Corporate control hierarchies
Parent firms (node type 1) have ownership rights (link) over child firms (node type 2).

Correspondence banking
A correspondent banking relationship is an arrangement between two banks, typically in different countries, where one bank (the correspondent bank) provides services on behalf of another bank (the respondent bank).

Working with multipartite graphs is much easier when nodes are labeled by category, often referred to as a colored graph in mathematics. For instance, a bipartite graph can be colored with two colors, where each node category has the same color. Without such labels, identifying a k-partite graph can be challenging, especially when k is greater than two.[4]

---

4 For more on this topic, see Celina M.H. de Figueiredo's article "The P versus NP—Complete Dichotomy of Some Challenging Problems in Graph Theory" (*https://oreil.ly/x5dU1*), *Discrete Applied Mathematics* 160, no. 18 (December 2012): 2681–2693.

Temporal graphs

In a temporal graph, links have a temporal dimension indicating the time at which they were active. The network representation of temporal graphs is snapshot based or time based. As illustrated in Figure 2-7, both the network and adjacency representations are temporal snapshots storing the state of links at each time period. For example, nodes A and B established a link at times t1, t3, and t4, but they didn't interact at time t2. The adjacency matrix is represented as a multidimensional matrix storing a snapshot for each time period. The edge list stores all links and the time at which they were active.

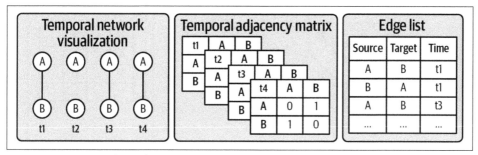

Figure 2-7. Temporal graph representations

Many financial relationships are temporal in nature, such as interbank lending, trading, payments, transactions, and many more.

Multilayer graphs

A multilayer graph is a complex structure used to represent relationships between different types of nodes and links. The most common type is the *multiplex* graph, where nodes are of the same type but have different types of links depending on the interaction context. For instance, a financial institution may operate in various markets such as commercial banking, wealth management, and financial consulting.

Multilayer network representations are very useful in finance. They can reveal potential cascading mechanisms that might amplify a local shock, help understand power structures spanning multiple areas, and enhance fraud detection (e.g., when the same individual operates in different systems using the same connection patterns). An illustration of multiplex graph representation is provided in Figure 2-8.

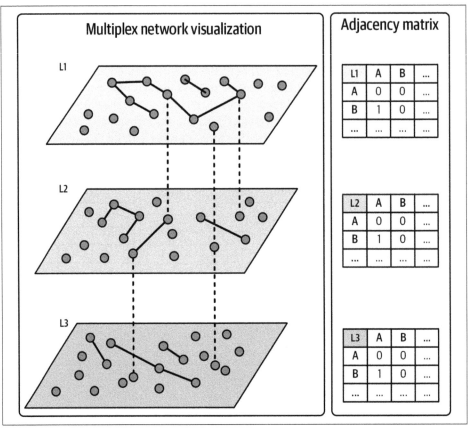

Figure 2-8. Multiplex graph representation

What Are the Sources of Financial Graph Data?

An important feature of financial graph data is that it is often derived from other types of data sources. For example, to build a graph of the interbank loan market (*https://oreil.ly/lK30D*), you would need a historical panel of interbank transactions containing information on borrowers, lenders, and the transaction amount and time. Similarly, say you want to build a bipartite network of interlocking directorates (*https://oreil.ly/dXg-J*) to see which directors sit on multiple boards, then you would need a dataset (e.g., the LSEG Officers and Directors dataset) that contains information on executive individuals and the companies they are associated with. In some cases, more work is required. For example, if you want to build a network of similarities between stocks (*https://oreil.ly/cFN3H*), you would first need a historical panel of price data (e.g., CRSP), and then you need to compute the pair-wise similarity (correlation) between the stocks in order to get the links needed to build the graph.

It is possible in some cases to find connection datasets curated by financial data vendors. For example, S&P Global provides a number of datasets about business and company relationships (*https://oreil.ly/sydqG*), such as ownership, supply chain, investment, and many more types of relationships.

Text Data

Text data refers to information available in any unstructured or semi-structured format. Its extensive use and versatility make it arguably the most available type of data in financial markets (*https://oreil.ly/5ZUgg*). With the advent of generative AI and large language models (LLMs), the importance of text data has significantly increased. Generative models such as GPT-4 and BloombergGPT are trained on massive amounts of text data. For specialized financial tasks such as fraud detection, sentiment analysis, know your customer (KYC), and anti-money laundering (AML), finance domain-specific text data is essential for customizing and fine-tuning an LLM.

It can be any text-based medium, including news, analyst reports, company filings, prospectus documents, emails, social media posts, system logs, patent documents, legal and technical documents, research papers, web pages, blog posts, and much more.[5]

Text data can take various forms, including plain text consisting of words and sentences, semi-structured documents with keys and values, tabular formats, or complex specialized data structures like word embeddings (*https://oreil.ly/5Ajf5*).

Financial text data exhibits certain characteristics that set it apart from other forms of textual data. Terms such as "liability," "risk," "default," and "exposure" may carry negative connotations in certain contexts, yet they are commonly used and frequent terminology in financial markets. Additionally, financial documents can contain both explicit content (such as a firm merging with another) and implicit content (factual information implying a positive or negative emotion).[6]

Now that you're familiar with financial data's main sources and structures, the following section will explore the various types of financial data employed for analytical and operational purposes.

---

5 For a good introduction to the different sources of financial text data, I recommend Mirjana Pejić Bach, Živko Krstić, Sanja Seljan, and Lejla Turulja's article, "Text Mining for Big Data Analysis in Financial Sector: A Literature Review" (*https://oreil.ly/HsYET*), *Sustainability* 11, no. 5 (January 2019): 1277.

6 More on this topic in Marjan Van de Kauter, Diane Breesch, and Véronique Hoste's "Fine-Grained Analysis of Explicit and Implicit Sentiment in Financial News Articles" (*https://oreil.ly/vts8V*), *Expert Systems with Applications* 42, no. 11 (July 2015): 4999–5010.

Types of Financial Data

The financial data structures we discussed in the previous section can represent a variety of financial variables, content, and phenomena. This section will categorize these financial phenomena by discussing the most crucial types of financial data in detail, illustrating their features and challenges.

Fundamental Data

Financial fundamental data, also called financial statements data, balance sheet data, or corporate finance data, conveys information about firms' structures, operations, and performance. Firms themselves generate and produce fundamental data, partly because it's a regulatory requirement and partly because it helps the management understand the financial and operational situation of the firm. Many companies have accounting departments liable for generating and maintaining financial statements, but it is also possible to do so via accounting service providers such as consulting and audit firms. In general, there are three main financial statements:

Balance sheet
> Provides figures on what a firm owns (assets), what it owes (liabilities), and what its shareholders own (*shareholders' equity*)

Income statement
> Provides figures on a firm's financial performance over a specific period, such as the annual revenues and net profit

Cash flow statement
> Provides information on a firm's cash movements (in and out), which can help determine whether the firm is generating enough cash to carry out its operations

Each financial statement contains a large number of items representing different quantities. A special type of financial statement item is *ratios,* which represent relationships between two or more items. For example, a popular ratio is *Return on Equity* (ROE), which is calculated by dividing the company's net income by the value of its shareholders' equity. A high ROE is an indicator that the company is efficient at generating net income using shareholders' equity.

Financial fundamental data statements have a number of characteristics that need to be taken into account. First, due to the time it takes to prepare them, fundamental data statements are released with *low frequency,* such as quarterly, each semester, or yearly. Second, fundamental data reports are often published with a *time lapse,* meaning that data for a specific period is released at a future date. Data can be reported in the form of *reinstatements*, which happens when a figure gets revised and corrected after it has been released. Data *backfilling* can also take place, which happens when a firm and its entire fundamental data history get added to a dataset that has never had information on that firm before.

If not handled properly, these characteristics could lead to *non-point-in-time* (PIT) fundamental data (*https://oreil.ly/BH6U0*). PIT data is data that is recorded with a timestamp reflecting the filing or release data. With PIT data, one can ask the questions "When was the data released?" and "What data was known at that time?" On the other hand, non-PIT data is stamped with the fiscal year-end date or the latest update date. Non-PIT data reflects the latest data release, and it gets overwritten when an update or reinstatement happens. Table 2-7 illustrates the difference. With three versions of the data available, a PIT dataset would keep track of all historical snapshots (101, 110, 120), while a non-PIT dataset would show only the latest version (120).

Table 2-7. PIT versus non-PIT data

Data type	Preliminary result	Fiscal year-end release	Correction
Version	101	110	120
PIT	101	110	120
Non-PIT	120	120	120

Non-PIT data poses several challenges. First is the problem of *look-ahead bias*, which happens when conducting historical studies and assuming that data was known at a specific historical moment, which, due to a release time lapse, may not be the case. Second is *reproducibility*, which becomes challenging if non-PIT data used for past research is updated and may not yield the same results. The third challenge is *transparency*, which may be an issue if, for example, a company updates an accounting record to hide past fraudulent behavior.

Reading Financial Highlights from a Bank Annual Report

Being able to understand the main items in an annual report is a good skill, even for financial data engineers. The table below illustrates the annual financial highlights of an imaginary bank, ADK. If you check the annual report of any real bank, you will find a similar table. Examining the figures for 2020, we can see that the bank realized more *total net revenues* compared to 2021 ($bln 102 versus 99) but with a lower *net income* ($bln 23 versus 25). This translates into lower returns for shareholders, which we can see from the *return on common equity* figure of 11% compared to 16% in 2019. ADK is quite a large bank, which we can see from the *total assets* figure that equals $2,987,245 million (almost $3 trillion) and the *headcount* of 150,432. Moreover, ADK seems to be financially stable, which we can infer from the *Tier 1 capital ratio* of 15%, a measure introduced by the Basel III accord, which tells how stable a financial institution is by comparing its core equity against its risk-weighted assets. Basel III established that the Tier 1 capital ratio must be at least 6%. ADK probably has a large market share, which we can see from its considerable market capitalization of $240,876 million (roughly $240 billion). A dividend was distributed every year to shareholders, which we know from the *cash dividends per share* figure.

Item	2020	2019	2018
Total net revenue ($ mln)	102,000	99,340	96,345
Total noninterest expense ($ mln)	55,000	49,000	45,865
Net income ($ mln)	23,100	25,987	19,628
Cash dividends per share ($)	3.5	2	1.7
Return on common equity	11%	16%	8%
Tier 1 capital ratio	15.0%	14.1%	14%
Total capital ratio	18.9%	17%	17%
Loans ($ mln)	986,865	956,586	916,865
Deposits ($ mln)	1,298,456	1,187,456	1,062,456
Total assets ($ mln)	2,987,245	2,445,853	2,200,119
Total stockholders' equity ($ mln)	72,876	71,664	70,345
Market capitalization ($ mln)	250,876	300,897	280,986
Headcount	150,432	144,983	139,709

Market Data

Market data includes price and related information for financial instruments traded on market venues such as the New York Stock Exchange (NYSE) or in off-exchange OTC markets. It is extensively available for many types of instruments, such as stocks, derivatives, indexes, currencies, bonds, and funds. Moreover, market data is released frequently, often becoming available just seconds after its generation.

A financial instrument's market data may include fields such as the following:

- Identifiers such as tickers, e.g., IBM
- Trading venue code such as the exchange code, e.g., NYSE
- Last day (adjusted) closing price, e.g., $40.30
- Current day open price, e.g., $40.15
- Current day highest price, e.g., $42.30
- Current day lowest price, e.g., $39.42
- Current day price range, e.g., $39–42.30
- Current day volume, e.g., 50,000

- Latest bid/ask prices and quantities, e.g., bid of $40.02 × 2200 and ask of $40.03 × 3000
- Last trade/quote date, e.g., today at 14:12:10 p.m.

 In financial markets, the term *bid* is used to indicate the price at which buyers are willing to buy a financial asset, while the *ask* is the price at which sellers are willing to sell an asset.

Some stock exchanges and media platforms enrich market data with fundamentals such as market capitalization, revenues, and net profit, as well as various financial ratios and corporate event dates, such as the latest dividend date.[7]

At the core of market data generation lies the *order book*, an electronic ledger of buy and sell orders for a specific security at a given trading venue. Order books have two representations: *Market by Order* (MBO) and *Market by Price* (MBP). MBO shows each individual order separately, detailing the price, quantity, and time of entry for each buy and sell order. In contrast, MBP aggregates orders by price level, consolidating them into price buckets to display the total quantity of orders at each price level instead of showing each order individually.

Orders in an order book can be matched through an *Order Matching System* (OMS), which uses algorithms to ensure the best execution. The two most common match algorithms are price/time priority (also known as First In, First Out, or FIFO) and pro rata.[8] Price/time priority matches orders based on price first, and then by the time of entry at the same price level; for example, if two buy orders are placed at the same price, the earlier one gets matched first. Pro rata matching, on the other hand, matches orders at the same price level proportionally based on their sizes; for instance, if there are two buy orders at the same price, one for 100 shares and another for 200 shares, and a sell order for 150 shares arrives, the matching will be split proportionally, giving 50 shares to the first order and 100 shares to the second.[9]

An example of an order book is illustrated in Table 2-8. The example shows that the highest bid price level is $55.11, while the lowest ask price level is $55.13. The highest bid and lowest ask are called the *top of the book*, while the difference between them is

---

7 To see a real example, check out the information provided by Yahoo Finance for Google stock (*https://oreil.ly/sq3Fr*).

8 For a more comprehensive list, check CME Group's list of match algorithms (*https://oreil.ly/-Llzc*).

9 For a deeper explanation of the order book mechanism, I recommend Jean-Philippe Bouchaud, Julius Bonart, Jonathan Donier, and Martin Gould's book, *Trades, Quotes and Prices: Financial Markets Under the Microscope* (Cambridge University Press, 2018).

called the *bid/ask spread* (=$0.02). The *order book depth* is a measure of the number of distinct price levels available in an order book. Another term, the *market depth*, is often used as an indicator of liquidity and is defined as the size of market orders that can be executed without causing a large impact on the price level.

Table 2-8. Example of an order book

Buy-side		Sell-side	
Bid volume	Bid price	Ask price	Ask volume
220	$ 55.11	$ 55.13	1000
1000	$ 55.11	$ 55.14	500
50	$ 55.9	$ 55.66	200
20	$ 55.55	$ 55.66	10
560	$ 55.1	$ 66.68	50
...	...	...	...

Different types of orders can be submitted to an order book. For example, a *market order* is used to buy or sell at the best bid/ask price available. A *limit order* is an order to sell at a specified minimum ask price or buy at a maximum bid price. A *stop-loss order* is triggered and submitted to buy or sell if the price level reaches a predefined maximum or minimum value. A *trailing stop order* is triggered if the market price moves up or down by a specific percentage or dollar amount.

Market data exhibits several features that are worth considering. First, market data, such as prices, are computed quantities. When an investment firm submits an order to buy or sell a financial asset, the order price is often calculated using a specific valuation method. For example, company stock prices can be calculated using methods such as the net present value, earning multiples, the dividend discount model, or the discounted cash flow model.[10]

Importantly, when different market participants submit orders with varying prices across different markets, determining the final market price for investors becomes crucial. Ideally, the bid price is the highest among all bid prices, and the ask price is the lowest among ask prices. To enforce this rule, regulators such as the SEC passed the Regulation National Market System (NMS) regulation (*https://oreil.ly/VE01I*), which introduced the *National Best Bid and Offer* (NBBO). With the NBBO in action, brokers are required to ensure that their client orders are executed against the best bid and ask prices, which need to be at least equal to the NBBO.[11]

---

10 For an excellent reference on this topic, I recommend Aswath Damodaran's *Investment Valuation: Tools and Techniques for Determining the Value of Any Asset*, 3rd ed. (Wiley, 2012).

11 To calculate the NBBO, stock exchanges report their best bid/ask prices to a system called the Securities Information Processor (SIP), which aggregates all the quotes in a single NBBO and releases it to the market.

Nevertheless, not all financial markets ensure an NBBO. This is particularly true in OTC markets like foreign exchange (Forex) markets where currencies are traded. There is no enforced exchange rate for a currency pair in the Forex market. The exchange rate you will get is specific to the Forex quote provider, which can be your bank or, most commonly, a *Forex broker*. This means that the quote you see on Google for EUR/USD is not the market price, and you should not expect it to match the one you get offered when you convert money from one currency to another.

Price discreteness is another important attribute of market data. It means that the price of a listed stock cannot change by less than a specific amount known as *tick size*. For example, according to SEC Rule 612 on the minimum pricing increment (*https://oreil.ly/U_vBG*):

> The Rule prohibits market participants from displaying, ranking, or accepting quotations, orders, or indications of interest in any NMS stock priced in an increment smaller than $0.01 if the quotation, order, or indication of interest is priced equal to or greater than $1.00 per share. If the quotation, order, or indication of interest is priced less than $1.00 per share, the minimum pricing increment is $0.0001.

Finally, a quite important feature of market data, and in particular price data, is its *nonsynchronous history*. This means that given two securities, A and B, security A could trade at least once every minute, while security B trades only once every five hours. Such discrepancies in market behavior are often due to market liquidity varying from one security to another.

Transaction Data

A financial transaction is a legal agreement between two or more parties to exchange financial securities, services, goods, risks, or commodities in return for money. Financial markets generate massive volumes of transaction data triggered by activities such as investments, payments, trading, hedging, speculation, and lending.

Most financial transactions are conducted either fully or partially electronically. Generally speaking, a financial transaction can be characterized by at least five elements: transaction specifications, transaction parties, initiation date, settlement date, and settlement method.[12] Next, we discuss each of these five elements in detail.

Transaction specifications

Before initiating a transaction, parties agree on its details and specifications. In securities exchange, this phase is often called pre-trade. To provide examples, a stock purchase transaction would specify the name and identifiers of the shares being

---

12 Readers interested in a comprehensive coverage of the financial transaction lifecycle can read the excellent book by Robert P. Baker, *The Trade Lifecycle: Behind the Scenes of the Trading Process* (Wiley, 2015).

exchanged, the quantity of each share, the price, and the currency. For financial instruments such as options on stocks, additional details would be needed, such as option type (call versus put), expiry date, and exercise price. For cross-border payments, parties may need to agree on the amount, currency pair, Forex conversion rate, and any spread margin.

Initiation date

The initiation date of a transaction is the date at which parties enter into an agreement to execute a transaction.

Settlement date

The settlement date is when a transaction is finalized, and the exchange of money and transfer of ownership takes place. In securities exchange, this phase is called post-trade. Importantly, in many financial transactions, the settlement date falls on a future date, following the initiation date. Such a delay can be due to various reasons such as the transaction verification process, technological constraints, errors due to missing information, bureaucratic steps such as the issuance of a certificate of ownership (e.g., stock certificate), lengthy payment process, and any manual intervention steps that may be necessary (e.g., review).

Financial market participants have been investing in technologies to shorten the transaction settlement time. The term *straight-through processing* (STP) is often used to designate the ideal transaction processing system that does not involve manual intervention, leading to decreased processing time, reduced operational risks, and lowered costs. Additionally, financial markets have adopted common conventions for settlement periods. For example, the current convention in securities transactions is *T +2 (trade date plus two days)*, which indicates that a security transaction should be settled two business days after the transaction initiation date. Recently, the term *same-day affirmation* (SDA) or *T0* has received attention from markets and regulators as it promotes the idea of completing the transaction verification process on the same day the transaction took place. Reducing the time of financial transaction lifecycles via STP and SDA can be quite challenging, as it requires significant investments by multiple market participants in a data infrastructure that provides real-time transaction data, while at the same time meeting the requirements of security and reliability (luckily, this is the topic of this book!).

Settlement method

Financial market transactions can be settled differently based on the transaction type. In securities markets, the most common settlement method is *Delivery versus Payment* (DVP), which guarantees that the cash payment for securities is made either before or at the same time as the delivery of the securities. In a *Delivery versus Free*

(DVF) mechanism, the delivery of securities occurs for free, for example, when delivering the collateral to a securities loan.

In payments, multiple settlement mechanisms exist. A common example is *Payment versus Payment* (PvP), widely used in Forex transactions. In a PvP system, the payment of one currency occurs only if the payment of the corresponding currency takes place. Another prominent mechanism is *Real-Time Gross Settlement* (RTGS), where funds are transferred in real time on a gross basis, meaning transactions are processed continuously throughout the day and settled individually. Conversely, in a *Deferred Net Settlement* (DNS) mechanism, transactions are accumulated over a period (e.g., end of the day) and then settled in batches at specific intervals. In DNS, only the net difference between debits and credits is settled. For example, if Citibank is to pay JPMorgan Chase $1.5 million, and JPMorgan Chase is to pay Citibank $1 million, a DNS system would aggregate this to a single payment of $500,000 from Citibank to JPMorgan Chase. Conversely, an RTGS system would require two separate payments for the full amounts ($1.5 million to JPMorgan Chase and $1 million to Citibank).

Transaction parties

Financial market transactions are often conducted by two parties, the buyer and the seller. However, transactions are not risk free. The term *settlement risk* refers to the risk that one side of a transaction does not honor their contractual obligation, e.g., failure to pay the amount due, failure to pay on time, or failure to transfer the asset ownership. To mitigate such risk, a third party is often involved in financial transactions to act as a guarantor. Examples include the following:

Clearing house
    Clearing houses act as intermediaries between sellers and buyers. They facilitate and guarantee a successful settlement of transactions by acting as buyers for the seller and sellers for the buyer. Examples of clearing houses include exchange clearing house divisions such as Nasdaq Clearing and CME Clearing, as well as credit card clearing houses such as Visa and Mastercard.

Central Securities Depository (CSD)
    A CSD is a specialized financial institution that holds financial securities such as shares and derivatives on behalf of other institutions. Similar to a clearing house, CSDs act as a third party to financial transactions to guarantee successful settlement and transfer of security ownership against the payment of money. A prominent example of a CSD is Clearstream.

Custodian
    A custodian or custodian bank is a financial institution that offers securities and post-trade services to institutional investors, asset managers, banks, and other financial institutions. Custodians provide a range of services, such as holding and

safekeeping their client's securities, conducting transactions on their client's behalf, and providing clearing and settlement services.

Payment systems

Payment systems facilitate the secure transfer of funds between financial institutions while effectively managing settlement risks. The most prominent example is RTGS systems such as the Federal Reserve's Fedwire in the United States, the Bank of England's CHAPS in the UK, and the European Central Bank's T2 (part of TARGET2 services). RTGSs are typically preferred for fast transactions and reduced settlement risk. Other services allow for deferred and netted payments, such as the US Clearing House Interbank Payments System (CHIPS). These systems are typically used for less-time-critical payments, which makes them less expensive than RTGSs.

Analytics Data

A valuable type of financial data is analytics data, which is often derived from other types of data such as fundamental, market, and transaction data. This data is typically computed using simple formulas, statistical models, machine learning techniques, and financial theories. Examples include news and market sentiment analytics (novelty, score, relevance, impact), financial risk measures (e.g., Value at Risk, option Greeks, bond duration, implied volatility), market indexes (e.g., MSCI Global Indexes), ESG (environmental, social, and governance) scores, stock analysis, company valuation, estimates (e.g., Institutional Brokers' Estimate System estimates), and competition analysis.

The main advantage of analytics data is that it offers pre-calculated patterns and signals, ready for immediate use in decision-making. Nevertheless, the calculation methodology used by the analytics data provider might be proprietary, which makes it a mystery box. Furthermore, as the same data becomes accessible to all market participants, maintaining a sustainable competitive advantage becomes increasingly difficult (sooner or later, someone will get the same data and replicate your strategy).

Alternative Data

Alternative data refers to a variety of nonconventional data that can be used for financial analysis, investment, or forecasting. It is regarded as nonconventional since it does not primarily originate within the traditional context of financial markets, such as trading, prices, transactions, and corporate finance operations. Examples include news, social media posts, satellite images, patents, Google trends, consumer behavior, technology analysis, political analysis, environmental and reliability scores, and many more. A large number of alternative datasets are available through data vendors, but it is also possible to extract similar data from the internet and other public repositories.

The main advantage of alternative data lies in its novelty and diversity. A financial institution equipped with the expertise and resources to extract and clean alternative data sources stands to gain a competitive informational advantage, which can significantly improve portfolio analysis and returns. For example, one study (*https://oreil.ly/FH1iQ*) used satellite image data to show that the number of cars in the parking lots of a sample of public US companies may be used as a predictor of financial performance.

A variety of challenges might be encountered when working with alternative data. The main issue is that these datasets are often available in an unstructured and raw format, necessitating substantial investment to structure the data and extract valuable insights. Another challenge is the lack of standardized entity identifiers and references, unlike conventional financial datasets. Moreover, alternative data can be imbalanced or incomplete because its observations and events are not consistently captured, unlike the systematic data collection for traditional datasets such as publicly traded stocks. Finally, alternative datasets can easily be biased yet provide no additional information to detect such biases.[13]

Reference Data

Financial reference data is a type of metadata used to identify, classify, and describe financial instruments, products, and entities. It is crucial for various financial operations, including transactions, trading, clearing and settlement, regulatory reporting and compliance, data consolidation, and investment.

To understand what reference data is, it's helpful first to review the concept of a financial instrument. Simply put, a financial instrument is a contract between two parties that has monetary value and can be traded on financial markets. Examples include debt instruments such as bonds and loans, equity instruments such as stocks, derivative instruments such as options and futures, and foreign exchange instruments such as currency pairs and currency futures. Importantly, each financial instrument comes with its own set of terms and conditions that define its contractual specifications. In this context, reference data is typically used as a metadata resource to describe these terms and conditions. Table 2-9 presents a few examples of reference data for several financial assets.

---

13 For more on this topic, see Ashby Monk, Marcel Prins, and Dane Rook's article, "Rethinking Alternative Data in Institutional Investment" (*https://oreil.ly/Q_Oil*), *Journal of Financial Data Science* 1, no. 1 (Winter 2019): 14–31.

Table 2-9. Reference data for different asset classes

Asset category	Reference data fields
Fixed income (bonds)	• *Issuer information:* name, country, sector • *Security identifiers:* ISIN; CUSIP, etc. • *Instrument information:* issue date, maturity date, coupon rate and frequency, currency, current price, yield to maturity, accrued interest • *Bond features:* callable, putable, convertible, payment schedule, settlement terms • *Credit information:* credit rating, credit spread
Stocks	• *Basic information:* identifiers such as ticker or ISIN, company name, exchange, sector, industry • *Price and volume information:* current, open, close, high, low prices, volume, average volume • *Dividend information:* dividend yield, dividend per share, dividend payment date, ex-dividend date • *Corporate actions:* stock splits, dividend distribution, buybacks, and mergers and acquisitions • *Fundamental information:* earnings per share, price-to-earnings ratio, book value per share
Funds	• *Fund structure:* umbrella fund, subfunds, share classes • *Identification information:* fund/subfund/share class name, type, identifiers such as ISIN, inception date, currency, domiciliation • *Fund management:* fund manager, management company, custodian, distributor, investment strategy, and fees such as management and advisory fees • *Performance:* net asset value (NAV), NAV calculation frequency, historical returns, benchmark index • *Holdings and allocation:* top holdings, sector, geographical, and asset allocation • *Risk profile:* volatility, Sharpe ratio, beta, alpha, hedging policy • *Investment, distribution, and dividends:* distribution frequency, distribution restrictions, dividend yield, subscription and redemption terms, cutoff times, minimum investment
Derivatives	• *Basic information:* instrument type, underlying asset, identifiers, classification • *Contract specifications:* contract size, expiration date, settlement date, exercise style, strike price • *Pricing information:* premium, mark-to-market price, bid/ask price • *Underlying asset information:* underlying asset price, volatility, dividend yield • *Risk metrics:* delta, gamma, theta, implied volatility, etc. • *Trading information:* open interest, volume • *Counterparty information:* name, credit rating, collateral requirements • *Corporate action adjustments:* stock splits on the underlying asset

Managing reference data is one of the most outstanding challenges in financial markets. In some cases, reference data is simple. For example, a stock is a standard financial instrument widely understood to represent an ownership stake in a firm. Stock reference data includes identifiers such as its ticker, the dividend rate if it pays dividends, and the legal issuing entity. Nevertheless, exotic and more complex financial instruments have been introduced with the evolution of financial markets. This is particularly the case with financial derivative instruments. For example, identifying an option contract requires information about the underlying asset, strike price, expiration date, option type (e.g., call or put), style (American versus European), and possibly other factors such as dividend yields or implied volatility. Furthermore, derivative instruments come in great variety, each with unique characteristics and terms. Such characteristics might even change with time, either through contractual adjustments or market events, or be customized to meet clients' specific needs.[14]

Many financial transactions and settlements fail due to operational errors, often linked to poor reference data. These errors can stem from inaccuracies in settlement instructions, trade-specific details, client and counterparty information, instrument data, or corporate actions data. For example, incorrect client details, mismatched account information, or erroneous security identifiers can lead to misrouted payments and failed trades. Consequently, maintaining accurate and up-to-date reference data is crucial for smooth transaction processing and minimizing operational risks.[15]

This has led to the development of proprietary or firm-specific reference data descriptions. As a result, market participants and regulators have struggled to agree on standard terms, definitions, and formats for financial instruments, which is the primary challenge in reference data management.

Another significant challenge with reference data is the absence of a unified identification system for financial instruments. Various financial identifiers have been created, each serving different purposes and possessing unique features. Market participants' use of different identifiers makes it increasingly difficult to match financial instruments across different identification systems. This issue is explored in greater detail in Chapter 3.

Several initiatives have been launched to address the challenges of reference data in financial markets. The International Organization for Standardization established a dedicated committee (*https://oreil.ly/Gwb_E*), ISO/TC 68/SC 8, whose scope is "standardization in the field of reference data for financial services." In the United States, the Dodd-Frank Wall Street Reform and Consumer Protection Act of 2010 mandated that the *Office of Financial Research* (OFR) prepare and publish a financial instrument reference database (*https://oreil.ly/nRGOx*). In the European Union, the *Financial Instruments Reference Data System* (FIRDS) was established to collect and publish reference data on financial instruments (*https://oreil.ly/VbSMb*). This system operates under Article 27 of Regulation (EU) No 600/2014 (MiFIR) and Article 4 of Regulation (EU) No 596/2014 (MAR). Managed by the European Securities and Markets Authority (ESMA), FIRDS ensures the availability and transparency of financial instrument data, aiding in regulatory compliance and market supervision.

---

14 For example, consider a stock option with a strike price of $100 and 100 shares underlying it. If a two-for-one stock split event takes place, managing reference data involves adjusting the option specifications to reflect 200 shares with a new strike price of $50, ensuring all related systems and records are updated accurately.

15 A more detailed discussion of this problem can be found in Allan D. Grody, Fotios Harmantzis, and Gregory J. Kaple's article, "Operational Risk and Reference Data: Exploring Costs, Capital Requirements and Risk Mitigation" (*https://oreil.ly/1TUB7*), *Journal of Operational Risk* 1, no. 3 (2006).

In the financial data market, several commercial reference data solutions stand out. Notable examples include Bloomberg's reference data (*https://oreil.ly/OC0r7*) and LSEG's reference data (*https://oreil.ly/IDpuM*) offerings. Reference data could be offered in a form that matches the requirements set by specific regulatory regimes, such as MiFID II, Europe's Securities Financing Transactions Regulation (SFTR), and the Basel Committee's Fundamental Review of the Trading Book (FRTB). Additionally, some reference data services focus on financial entities, such as SwiftRef (*https://oreil.ly/NEwa1*), which provides comprehensive international payment reference data. SwiftRef offers detailed information on BICs (Business Indentifier Codes), IBAN (International Bank Account Number) validation, and various other identifiers crucial for identifying entities involved in global payments.

In Chapter 3, we will explore the most essential types of reference data, focusing specifically on financial security identifiers.

Entity Data

Entity data includes information about corporate entities and their characteristics. It is frequently used alongside reference data to offer more detailed insights into a specific entity. Examples of entity data elements include the company name, identifiers, year of establishment, legal corporate form, ownership structure, sector classification, associated individuals, credit rating, ESG score, risk exposures, major corporate events, and more.

A number of commercial entity datasets are available, such as LSEG's legal entity data and services (*https://oreil.ly/OwcOq*), Moody's Orbis database (*https://oreil.ly/2-G-_*), and SwiftRef's entity data (*https://oreil.ly/WRxWt*). These datasets are used for many useful purposes such as corporate finance analysis, risk management (e.g., supplier or credit risk), and compliance and financial crime prevention through anti-money laundering (AML), know your customer (KYC), and client due diligence (CDD).

Benchmark Financial Datasets

As you have seen from our discussion thus far, financial data is abundantly available from multiple sources and in a variety of types and structures. To extract analytical and economic value from this data, commercial vendors, financial institutions, and researchers create *financial datasets*. I define a financial dataset as a bundled collection of variables and data points that provide information on a specific financial entity or topic, such as loans, stock prices, index prices, bond markets, and derivative markets. A financial dataset can include a mix of data types, such as fundamentals, market data, transactions, analytics, reference data, and entity data.

A considerable number of financial datasets already exist in the market, and new datasets are continuously being created and published. Next, I'll provide an overview of some of the world's most trusted and used financial datasets.

Center for Research in Security Prices

Financial datasets provided by the Center for Research in Security Prices (CRSP) are among the most prominent and trusted sources of market data. In particular, the CRSP US Stock dataset (*https://oreil.ly/syxTE*) provides comprehensive daily and monthly stock market data on over 32,000 securities listed on US stock exchanges such as the NYSE and NASDAQ and on a broad range of market indexes. The CRSP US Stock dataset contains information on price and quote data as well as external identifiers, shares outstanding, market capitalization, delisting information, and corporate action details.

Compustat Financials

Compustat Financials (*https://oreil.ly/2vVPz*), also called Compustat Fundamentals or Compustat Global, is the world benchmark dataset for company fundamentals. It provides standardized information on more than 80,000 international public companies. Compustat provides point-in-time snapshots of fundamental data, allowing researchers to conduct reliable historical and backtesting analyses. The dataset is quite comprehensive, with over 3,000 fields conveying information on financial statements, ratios, corporate actions, industry specifications, identifiers, and more.

Trade and Quote Database

The daily Trade and Quote (TAQ) dataset (*https://oreil.ly/dak4D*) provides daily high-frequency data on all trades and quotes that take place on the NYSE, NASDAQ, and other regional exchanges. TAQ data is available starting from 2003. The distinguishing feature of TAQ is the time precision it offers: seconds (HHMMSS) since 1993, milliseconds (HHMMSSxxx) since 2003, microseconds (HHMMSSxxxxxx) since 2015, and nanoseconds (HHMMSSxxxxxxxxx) since 2016.

Institutional Brokers' Estimate System

The Institutional Brokers' Estimate System (I/B/E/S) (*https://oreil.ly/DnDlJ*) is a database maintained by LSEG, serving as the market benchmark for stock analysts' earnings estimates for publicly traded companies. Over 950 firms and more than 19,000 analysts from 90+ countries regularly contribute to the I/B/E/S. The database provides extensive coverage of over 60,000 companies, with data available from 1976 for North America and from 1987 for international markets.

IvyDB OptionMetrics

IvyDB (*https://oreil.ly/11soK*) is the market benchmark dataset for historical equity and index options data. The most popular version of IvyDB is the US database, but since 2008, IvyDB Europe has been available as well. IvyDB provides a rich set of options data fields, such as daily quotes, identifiers, volume, computed implied volatility, option Greeks, open interest, interest rates, maturity, exercise, and exercise price. Information on the underlying instruments is also available, including closing prices, dividends, and corporate action information.

Trade Reporting and Compliance Engine

Trade Reporting and Compliance Engine (TRACE) (*https://oreil.ly/4_NLG*) is a financial dataset on bond and fixed-income transactions. TRACE represents an indispensable data source as most bond transactions happen OTC, making it a less transparent market than centrally exchanged instruments such as stocks.

TRACE itself is a program created by the Financial Industry Regulatory Authority (FINRA) to enable market participants who are FINRA members to report their fixed-income OTC transactions. FINRA members are required to report their transactions within 15 minutes of execution, which is then made available in real time to TRACE subscribers. Data available via TRACE includes fields such as execution time, price, volume, and bond yield.

Orbis Global Database

Orbis (*https://oreil.ly/FI-K0*) is the industry's primary resource for global entity data. Published by Moody's Analytics, it contains information on more than 450 million private and listed companies worldwide, offering detailed financial information for many of them.

In addition to its global coverage, Orbis provides comparable information on company ownership structure and financial strength metrics. Orbis collects data from more than 170 data providers and hundreds of its own data sources. The data is further enriched and standardized to enable easy querying, analysis, and comparison.

SDC Platinum

SDC Platinum (*https://oreil.ly/Cn-I2*), offered by the London Stock Exchange Group (LSEG), is a premier source of comprehensive global corporate finance and market deal event data. It provides detailed information on various financial transactions, including mergers and acquisitions, alliances, private equity, venture capital, new issues, leveraged buyouts, and syndicated loans, among many others.

Standard & Poor's Dow Jones Indices

Standard & Poor's Dow Jones Indices (SPDJI) (*https://oreil.ly/C_qDU*) is a leading global index provider and a primary source of historical index data, offering a wide range of indexes across various markets, including equities, derivatives, fixed income, and commodities. Examples include the S&P 500, S&P MidCap 400, and S&P Small-Cap 600, which are widely recognized as leading indicators of US equity market performance. S&P DJI provides detailed data features such as index names, constituents and their weights, closing prices, market capitalization, constituent company information, and index-related events.

Alternative Datasets

The datasets illustrated so far are general in scope and generated through the traditional mechanisms of financial markets. Interestingly, alternative, more specialized datasets have been gaining popularity among market participants. Let's look at a few examples.

BitSight Security Ratings

BitSight Security (*https://oreil.ly/L_6K8*) is a world leader in cybersecurity rating and related analytics. BitSight ratings convey comparable insights and visibility into a company's cybersecurity risk. It provides adaptive ratings correlated with the changing ransomware risk landscape. BitSight ratings are calculated using objective and observable factors such as server software, open ports, TLS/SSL (Transport Layer Security/Secure Sockets Layer) certificates and configuration, web application headers, and system security.

Global New Vehicle Registrations

The Global New Vehicle Registrations dataset (*https://oreil.ly/MeRvC*), offered by S&P Global Mobility, provides daily information and analysis on vehicle registrations from more than 150 countries, 350 brands, multiple fuel types (diesel, petrol, etc.), and body types (e.g., car, van, SUV). The dataset provides valuable information that can be used to analyze trends in the automotive market, such as the transition to electric vehicles.

Weather Source

The Weather Source dataset (*https://oreil.ly/8WBKh*) provides hourly and daily weather-related data for a large number of locations worldwide. Weather Source collects and standardizes weather data from many input sources and provides weather insights relevant to different businesses.

Patent data

Patent data is unstructured data that conveys information on patent details such as the inventor and assignee name, related patent citations, patent abstract, patent summary, detailed description, and claims. This data is often used to understand technological innovation problems. In recent years, the use of patent data has gained increasing importance in financial analysis. One of the primary sources of patent data is the United States Patent and Trademark Office (USPTO) (*https://oreil.ly/GEOi5*), which provides public access to detailed patent and trademark information. Another useful source is Google Patents, which aggregates patent data from a variety of sources, including the USPTO, and makes it easily searchable via its search engine.

In conclusion, it's important to keep in mind that the number of datasets created and used by financial markets is immense, and we have only scratched the surface in this section. As a financial data engineer, one of the most valuable skills that you can develop is the ability to search and navigate the financial data landscape and identify the right dataset for a particular business problem.

Summary

This chapter provided an overview of the financial data landscape, which we can summarize as follows:

- Classifying and explaining the sources of financial data
- Distinguishing between the different structures used to represent financial data
- Illustrating the main types of financial data generated by the various market activities
- Providing a short list of benchmark datasets widely recognized among market participants and researchers

Now that you have an understanding of what financial data engineering entails and the intricacies of the financial data ecosystem, we'll shift gears with the next few chapters, where you will learn about specific financial data engineering topics. The following three chapters will address in depth the following problems, which have been selected based on their prominent importance for financial markets:

- Financial identification systems and their main features and challenges (Chapter 3)
- The process and methods for financial entity recognition and resolution (Chapter 4)
- Financial data governance through data quality, integrity, privacy, and security (Chapter 5)

Let's keep going!

Financial Identification Systems

A key aspect of financial data, such as prices and transactions, is that it can provide informational value only if we can reliably assign each record to its corresponding entity. Being able to filter a dataset to get data for a specific entity unlocks the ability to analyze the data in meaningful ways.

To this end, financial market participants have developed and employed different types of financial identifiers. Nevertheless, data identification remains notably challenging and is widely regarded as one of the most critical problems in financial data management. The outstanding issue of reference data management, presented in the previous chapter, fundamentally revolves around financial identification and the matching of various identifiers that reference the same financial market entity.

This chapter will discuss the problem of financial data identification, illustrate the desired properties of financial identification systems, and examine the key features and limitations of current systems.

If you are going to become a financial data engineer, dealing with financial identifiers and knowing how to manage their shortcomings will be one of the main challenges you will regularly face. So, let's dive into this issue.

Financial Identifiers

The predominantly digital nature of financial market operations and transactions necessitates recording and querying them through information and database systems. At its heart, a reliable financial information system is an identification system: a way of telling who interacts with whom, a way of distinguishing one financial entity from another, and a way of finding all records that belong to the same entity. Consequently, well-identified financial data will deliver valuable insights and a significant competitive edge. To learn more, let's further detail what financial identifiers and identification systems are, why they are essential for financial markets, and who creates and maintains financial data identification systems.

Financial Identifier and Identification System Defined

From our discussion so far, you've seen how financial data is produced in large volumes and various formats, which are subsequently organized into more coherent collections known as financial datasets. Typically, each financial dataset must have an *observation unit* (or *statistical unit*) that represents the object for which information (*data points*) is available. For example, a company fundamentals dataset would have the company as the unit of observation. To distinguish data points for one unit from the others, such as company A's data from company B's, a data identifier (company identifier in our example) should be attached to each data point. Without an identifier, financial datasets would be of no practical use. Figure 3-1 illustrates the concept. The tables shown in the figure convey information about the annual revenues of different companies observed at multiple periods. The data in the left table is not very useful as it is hard to determine which firm the statistics are referencing. When the company_id identifier is added in the right table, it becomes possible to distinguish between several companies that the data references.

Unidentified data		Identified data		
Date	Annual revenues	company_id	Date	Annual revenues
31-12-2020	$2,100,000	company_a	31-12-2020	$2,100,000
31-12-2021	$1,880,790	company_a	31-12-2021	$1,880,790
31-12-2022	$2,250,000	company_a	31-12-2022	$2,250,000
31-12-2023	$2,405,000	company_a	31-12-2023	$2,405,000
31-12-2022	$1,600,00	company_b	31-12-2022	$1,600,00
31-12-2020	$500,000	company_b	31-12-2020	$500,000
31-12-2019	$20,000,000	company_c	31-12-2019	$20,000,000

Figure 3-1. Unidentified dataset (left) versus identified dataset (right)

In this book, I define a financial identifier and financial identification system as follows:

> A financial identifier is a character sequence associated with a particular financial entity (e.g., company, individual, transaction, asset, document, sector group, event, etc.), enabling accurate identification of said entity across one or more financial datasets or information systems. A financial identifier can be any combination of numeric digits (0-9), alphabet letters (a-z, A-Z), and symbols. A financial identification system creates principles and procedures for generating, interpreting, storing, assigning, and maintaining financial identifiers.

There are a few more key terms that are important to establish. First, calling an identifier a code, ID, or symbol is common. Second, financial identification systems can generate identifiers following an *encoding* system or as *arbitrary IDs*. An encoding system converts words, letters, numbers, and symbols into a short, standardized format for identification, communication, and storage. The reverse process is decoding, which converts the code sequence back to its original form to make it easier to understand. Identifiers that do not adhere to an encoding system are often described as arbitrary; they are randomly created and assigned and have no particular meaning. Third, the field that deals with building financial identification systems is frequently referred to as *symbology*, a term you will often hear when learning and working with financial identifiers.

The Need for Financial Identifiers

Financial data identifiers serve various purposes, one of the most common being the identification of financial instruments and entities involved in market transactions. This type of identification data is often referred to as reference data, as we discussed in Chapter 2.

In any financial transaction, it is crucial to include the identifiers of the exchanged instruments and the entities participating in the agreement. Additionally, the transaction itself may be assigned an identifier for tracking purposes. As a result, identifiers are integral throughout the entire lifecycle of a financial transaction, from pre-trade to trade to post-trade settlement. They facilitate swift and efficient market transactions, enhance communication among market participants, increase transparency, and reduce operational costs and errors.[1]

Another important use of financial identifiers is for reporting purposes. Regulatory authorities can demand various information from financial institutions, such as market exposure, capital, risk concentration, liquidity, assets and liabilities, and trades. Financial institutions need to aggregate data from multiple sources and divisions to prepare the required report. Financial identifiers are crucial in this situation since they enable data collection and consolidation, ensuring accurate and timely reporting. In addition, by adding identifiers to the reported data, regulators would find it simple to examine the information and judge the reporting institution's compliance. Several regulatory frameworks, such as MiFID II, mandate that reporting institutions use certain financial identities when reporting data. This, in turn, imposes an extra

---

1 If you are interested in this topic, I highly recommend Martijn Groot's book, *Managing Financial Information in the Trade Lifecycle: A Concise Atlas of Financial Instruments and Processes* (Elsevier, 2008).

obligation on reporting institutions to establish a reliable financial identification system.[2]

Financial identifiers are essential for exchange listing and trading purposes. To list and trade a financial security on a trading venue, it must be assigned an identifier. This enables investors, traders, and market makers to easily locate, track, buy, sell, and analyze financial instruments.

Last but not least, financial identifiers are required as an essential data field when performing financial data analysis. A substantial portion of financial analysis is cross-sectional, where the focus is on studying the behavior and differences among different financial entities (e.g., assets, companies, etc.). Using financial identities would enable the analyst to pick the right data sample, run quality checks and filters, eliminate duplicates, and match the same entity across numerous datasets.

Who Creates Financial Identification Systems?

Various organizations, spanning both public and private sectors, may generate and assign a financial identifier. Some organizations develop recommendations for financial identification systems but do not issue the identifier for those who require it; others issue identifiers based on existing standards or recommendations; and still others develop and issue the identifier. Let's explore this variety of roles and functions with some examples.

International Organization for Standardization (ISO)

The *International Organization for Standardization* (ISO) is an independent organization that creates and promotes voluntary and consensus-based international standards for various technical and nontechnical fields. It is composed of representatives from the national standards organizations of 169 countries.

Throughout the years, the ISO has demonstrated considerable interest and involvement in developing international financial identifiers. For example, the ISO standard known as the International Securities Identification Number (ISIN) has emerged as the leading identifier in international security trading, clearing, and settlement. Later in this chapter, I will cover the ISIN identifier as well as other ISO-based identifiers in detail.

Crucially, the ISO does not issue and assign identifiers for market participants; instead, this job is delegated to so-called National Numbering Agencies, which we will examine in the following section.

---

2 For an interesting read, see Richard Young's article, "The Identifier Challenge: Attributes of MiFID II That Cannot Be Ignored" (*https://oreil.ly/mBYIs*), *Journal of Securities Operations & Custody* 9, no. 4 (Autumn 2017): 313–320.

How Does the ISO Develop a Standard?

Familiarity with industry standards is essential for a financial data engineer to excel. However, how do organizations such as the ISO create a standard? As reported by the official website (*https://oreil.ly/blG7M*), the ISO does not unilaterally decide when to create a standard; instead, it responds to a market need raised by stakeholders such as companies, consumer associations, academia, NGOs, and government and consumer groups. A typical scenario involves an industry group reporting the need for a standard to its national member, who subsequently approaches the ISO.

Once a market need for a standard emerges, the ISO appoints a committee composed of independent technical experts nominated by ISO members. A committee may have subcommittees and working groups. For example, ISO/TC 68 is the ISO committee tasked with overseeing financial services standards globally, and it has three main subcommittees:

ISO/TC 68/SC 2
> Covers information security in financial services

ISO/TC 68/SC 8
> Covers reference data for financial services

ISO/TC 68/SC 9
> Covers information exchange for financial services

The nominated committee starts the process by discussing the nature, scope, and key elements of the standard and submitting a draft proposal that meets the market need. The draft is then shared for further review and recommendations. Reaching a final agreement is consensus based and relies on a voting mechanism. If a consensus is not reached, then the draft will be modified and voted on again. Developing an ISO standard typically takes three years from initial proposal to final publication.

National Numbering Agencies

A *National Numbering Agency* (NNA) is a national organization that issues and promotes ISO-based financial identifiers. Each country is free to assign the role of NNA to a local market player, which can be a stock exchange, central bank, regulator, clearing house, financial data provider, or custodian. For example, the UK NNA is the London Stock Exchange, and Luxembourg's is Clearstream Banking (a central securities depositary). Some countries don't have an NNA; in such cases, a Substitute Numbering Agency (SNA) is appointed. Examples of SNAs include CUSIP Global Services in the US and WM Datenservice in Germany.

The Association of National Numbering Agencies (ANNA) was established to coordinate between the different national NNAs. ANNA collects and aggregates identifier data from all its members into a global centralized dataset called the ANNA Service Bureau (ASB) to ensure data quality and guarantee global interoperability.

Financial data vendors

Most financial data vendors create their own identification systems to support the development of their products and services. For instance, when aggregating data from many sources, the data vendor might face the issue of identifier heterogeneity, which can be hard to resolve. It may also be the case that the data has no identifier, for example, when working with unstructured data such as news and text. Additionally, external identifiers might lack some of the properties the vendor needs (e.g., uniqueness). In such cases, creating a new vendor-based identification system is a common practice. Vendors such as S&P Global Market Intelligence, LSEG, Bloomberg, and FactSet all have their own in-house identifiers.

In certain instances, financial data vendors develop their identifiers because they create, rather than aggregate, their content. For example, news analytics providers such as RavenPack create and provide structured news and event data from unstructured content for a large number of entities. Since RavenPack independently extracts entities from text, it has developed its proprietary unique entity identifier system, known as the RavenPack Unique Entity Identifier.

Finally, given the increasing value of financial identifier data (e.g., for reference data management), financial data vendors may find it a profitable opportunity to create and license their financial identifiers.

Financial institutions

Financial institutions create identifiers to facilitate internal processes, such as transactions, account management, client identification, and payment card number generation. Additionally, they might collect financial data from various sources, both internal and external, which may come with different identifiers. In these cases, a financial institution may opt to create its internal identification system to allow for a flexible design that matches business requirements and enables easy data retrieval and aggregation.

In conclusion, financial identifiers are critical to the efficiency, interoperability, and transparency of financial markets. All market participants deal with identifiers, either as users or as participants in their development. At this point, you may be wondering why it is so difficult to design a financial identification system that works in all circumstances and meets all market demands. To answer this question, we must first examine the desirable attributes of financial identification systems and understand the various constraints and challenges involved. This is what I'll talk about next.

Desired Properties of a Financial Identifier

Designing and maintaining a good financial identification system is one of the most persistent challenges in the financial industry. The difficulty stems from the need to balance various desirable properties, each of which may conflict with others. In this section, I build upon the framework proposed in the seminal work of Jules J. Berman, *Principles and Practice of Big Data* (Academic Press), to derive a minimal set of desired properties for a financial identification system. These properties include uniqueness, globality, scalability, completeness, accessibility, authenticity, granularity, permanence, immutability, and security. Let's explore each property in detail.

Uniqueness

Uniqueness refers to the quality of being one of a kind. For instance, fingerprints are unique to each human; no two humans on earth can have the same fingerprint. In the same way, a financial identification system must uniquely identify financial entities and never assign the same identifier to distinct entities. Figure 3-2 illustrates the concept of uniqueness. The identification system on the left is not unique since it assigns the identifier 56H128 to two separate entities: WTK Inc. and XYZ Inc. However, the system on the right is unique as it assigns a distinct identifier to all three financial entities.

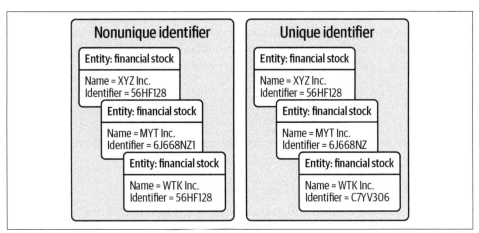

Figure 3-2. Unique (right) versus nonunique (left) identification systems

Crucially, the concept of a unique identifier can become ambiguous when applied to financial markets. To illustrate how, let's consider the following scenarios:

- A company is listed on two stock exchanges, A and B. Should the listed stock have two identifiers, one for each market, or a single identifier for both?

- A financial instrument is trading in two countries; do we need separate identifiers for each country?

- A financial instrument can have multiple issues. Should we treat each issue as a unique instrument or use a single identifier for all?

- Following a company merger or acquisition, does the resulting entity represent a new, unique company or maintain the identity of the original?

- A financial transaction contains multiple instructions that relate to various instruments. Should each instruction have its own identifier or simply use the parent transaction identifier?

Quite challenging, no? Now, I imagine that you might have a solution for the above scenarios. But this is exactly where the issue lies; different market participants make different assumptions about what a unique financial identifier should be, and this has led to the development and adoption of numerous identifiers that differ in the way they define uniqueness. This can explain the common practice of using multiple identifiers within a dataset, for example, to identify the security with one identifier and the market where it is traded with another. If you are designing a financial identification system, my advice for you is to carefully think about the concept of uniqueness and discuss it with your business team to avoid serious shortcomings that might arise later.

Globality

Financial markets are complex and dynamic systems that are in continuous evolution and expansion. To illustrate how, let's consider the following facts:

- New companies are established and listed on the market.

- New financial instruments are created, listed, and traded in different markets and jurisdictions.

- Trading activities take place in various venues, such as centralized exchanges, trading platforms, and OTC markets.

- Consumer demand and preferences for financial products and services are constantly evolving, creating opportunities for the introduction of new offerings.

- Financial transactions span multiple countries, markets, and jurisdictions.

- New markets are established for exchanging new financial products.

- New financial entities are recognized and extracted from financial data.
- New exchange platforms and mechanisms gain popularity (e.g., cryptocurrencies).
- New types of data on financial activities are recorded and consumed.
- New financial regulatory requirements are published and enforced.
- New market standards are released, promoted, and adopted.
- New financial technologies emerge and diffuse among market participants.

These dynamics, among others, have contributed to a significant increase in the number and variety of financial entities that require identification. To meet this demand, a financial identification system must be able to accommodate the expanding ecosystem of financial activities and entities. I call such property *globality*. For example, a global identification system can do the following things:

- Expand from assigning identifiers at a national level to an international scale
- Expand its scope from assigning identifiers solely within centralized markets to OTC and other types of markets
- Expand its coverage to include various financial instruments such as indices, derivatives, digital assets, and loans

Figure 3-3 illustrates a straightforward example showcasing the concept of globality. The system on the top is global, as it expands its coverage to new areas that emerge from market expansion. The system on the bottom is nonglobal, as it covers only three areas and can't expand further.

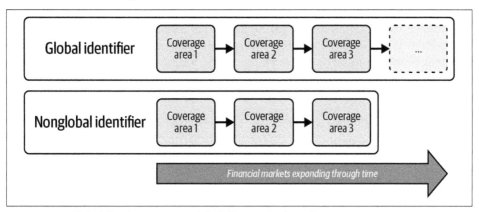

Figure 3-3. Global (top) versus nonglobal (bottom) identification systems

Several identifiers, in particular vendor-specific identifiers, are limited to certain markets (e.g., stocks, bonds), exchanges (e.g., NYSE trades and quotes), or jurisdictions (e.g., US stocks, UK stocks). However, some identifiers have been developed to cover a broader range of market entities. The best example is perhaps Bloomberg's Financial Instrument Global Identifier (FIGI), which we will discuss in more detail later in this chapter.

Scalability

A scalable financial identification system does not exhaust its pool of assignable identifiers. Several reasons could lead to a shortage in the available supply of identifiers in a financial identification system:

Rapid market growth

If the number of financial entities requiring identifiers increases rapidly, the identification system may struggle to keep up with the demand. One example is the issuance of a high volume of short-term financial instruments, such as commercial papers, repurchase agreements, and certificates of deposit. These instruments typically have short maturities and are frequently rolled over, creating a constant demand for new identifiers. If each instrument requires a unique identifier, it can quickly reduce the available pool of new identifiers.

Limited character length

If the identifier format is limited in character length, exclusively employs numeric characters, or imposes format constraints, there may be a finite number of possible combinations, causing the identification system to exhaust its identifiers soon. For example, the Issuer Identification Number (IIN), presented later in this chapter, was expanded from a six-digit to an eight-digit format due to a shortage in the supply of assignable identifiers (*https://oreil.ly/FsiM_*). Another example is the SEDOL identifier, discussed later in this chapter, which was changed from a numeric to an alphanumeric format following plans to expand its market coverage.

Poor allocation strategy

If the identification system does not allocate the identifiers optimally, it might lead to early exhaustion. Examples of poor allocation strategies include the following:

Category-based allocation

Allocating identifiers based on specific categories (e.g., different types or classes of stocks, bonds, derivatives) can lead to the exhaustion of available identifiers for a particular category if it grows more quickly than others. For instance, if bond instruments are allocated identifiers from 00000-29999 and stock instruments from 30000-49999, the bond category might run out of identifiers much earlier if there is a surge in bond issuance.

Reserved ranges

Reserving large ranges of identifiers for future use or specific purposes, such as special market events, regulatory reporting, or new financial instruments, can significantly reduce the pool of identifiers available for general use.

Addressing these issues entails proactive planning, market growth projection, periodic evaluations, and adaptability of the identification system to the ever-changing financial market ecosystem.

Completeness

Completeness requires that an identifier be assigned to each uniquely identifiable entity covered by the identification system. In other words, if an identification system is created to identify a set of financial entities, then each entity in the set must have an identifier. Table 3-1 illustrates the concept by comparing complete and incomplete identifiers. Identification system A is incomplete because it lacks identifiers for entities 3, 4, and 6. In contrast, Identification system B is complete, as it assigns identifiers to all six entities.

Table 3-1. Comparing complete and incomplete identifiers

Entity	Identifier A (incomplete)	Identifier B (complete)
Entity 1	19982243	A5J234HS
Entity 2	87987924	B5J874GS
Entity 3	NULL	T3H7Z589
Entity 4	NULL	GQ16B437
Entity 5	23987912	N9M3F16S
Entity 6	NULL	K485GV1Z

A financial identification system may suffer from incompleteness for various reasons. For instance, a newly established company identification system might not backfill the history of its covered universe because some companies have failed, gone bankrupt, delisted, merged with other companies, or changed their names. Another common scenario arises when merging different datasets with different identifiers. For example, if you join data using a US-based identifier with data using a global identifier, many entities might lack the US identifier.

Accessibility

Financial identifier data should be accessible, meaning it should not be restricted by license fees or usage limits, or monopolized by market players. Limited access to financial identifiers can result in market inefficiencies and a lack of transparency when conducting transactions and reporting.[3] Logically, there are situations where financial identifiers, like credit card numbers or bank account IDs, must be secured.

In some cases, financial identifiers are freely available (e.g., on online trading platforms or stock exchange websites). However, collecting and aggregating this data in a structured format for a large number of entities can be overwhelming. Financial data vendors provide such products, often sold as reference data, but these are often subscription based.

Some market players launched initiatives to promote open-access financial identifiers. For example, LSEG openly released its Permanent Identifier (PermID) system (*https://oreil.ly/Zvx15*), which provides comprehensive coverage across a wide variety of entity types, including companies, financial instruments, issuers, funds, and people. Another example is OpenFIGI, an open-access system that allows anyone to request Bloomberg's Financial Instrument Global Identifier (FIGI), which I discuss later in this chapter.

Timeliness

The timeliness of a financial identification system refers to its ability to process and generate identifiers quickly and efficiently. When a new financial entity enters the market or is created within a system (e.g., a new issue of a financial instrument), a timely financial identification system should do the following:

- Enable market participants to request an identifier quickly, ideally in real or near-real time
- Process requests quickly, allowing the issuing entity to allocate identifiers promptly
- Make accessible the newly allocated identifiers to other market participants without delay

Efficient and timely generation and dissemination of financial identifiers are essential for enhancing the efficiency of financial market operations and transactions.

---

3 In 2011, the European Commission concluded (*https://oreil.ly/n1hi0*) that Standard and Poor's (S&P) was abusing its dominant position and violating antitrust rules as the unique issuing agency of US security ISINs by charging European financial institutions high access fees. The Commission made it legally binding for S&P to abolish licensing fees paid by banks for using US ISINs.

Authenticity

An authentic financial identification system can confirm whether a specific identifier was generated by it. To draw an analogy, this is the same as telling whether a watch displaying the label *Rolex* is indeed an authentic Rolex.

Financial identifiers are often designed following a specific symbology specification, which can be a formula or standardized format. This, in turn, enables the development of programs that can verify the identifier's adherence to these specifications. A common practice involves the addition of a *check digit* to the identifier string. When a check digit is included, typically at the end of the identifier, an algorithm can be used to authenticate the identifier based on this digit. Later in this chapter, I will illustrate various examples of identifier check digits and their calculation logic.

Granularity

In financial markets, it is quite common to observe hierarchical arrangements and structures within and between entities:

- Asset origination chain (e.g., issuing company → securities → stocks → common stocks → issues).
- Trading context (e.g., international → continental → national → market).
- Pyramid organizational structures (e.g., CEO → president → vice-president → middle management → team leaders → employees) .
- Company ownership structures (e.g., parent company A owns B (child), B owns D, and D owns F, G, K).
- Asset classifications, where assets are organized in groups, categories, and subcategories (e.g., derivatives → options → stock options → call stock option).
- Sector classifications, which structure economic sectors using an industry taxonomy (e.g., sectors → industry groups → industries → sub-industries).
- Packaged transactions such as syndicated loans (package →facilities).
- Complex financial instruments such as multi-leg options or interest rate swaps, where the same instrument has multiple child instruments.
- In the fund industry, an umbrella fund structure allows for the creation of multiple subfunds, each with distinct investment strategies, further divided into various share classes tailored to different investor needs.[4]

---

4 For more details, see Angeliki Skoura,, Julian Presber, and Jang Schiltz's article, "Luxembourg Fund Data Repository" (*https://oreil.ly/AyR5B*), *Data* 5, no. 3 (July 2020): 62.

A financial identification system is *granular* if it can scale to provide different levels of details that reflect market hierarchies. Figure 3-4 illustrates this concept. In this example, the entity requiring identification should be recognizable at international, national, and market levels. The identification system on the left is nongranular because it uses the same identifier for the entity across all levels. In contrast, the system on the right is granular because it assigns a unique identifier to the entity at each level.

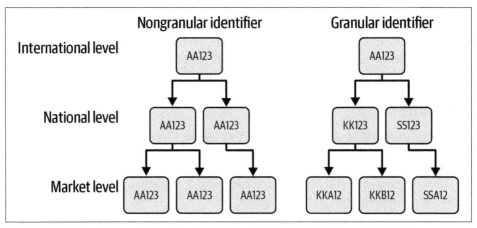

Figure 3-4. Granular versus nongranular financial identification systems

Permanence

A reliable financial identification system must ensure that identifiers and their associated data are permanent and durable. This is essential for guaranteeing market trust and confidence and allowing the tracking and referencing of financial instruments and transactions over time. For example, a bank client should be able to go to the bank at any time and ask for a statement about their past transactions. If the customer closes their accounts with the bank, their identification data should not disappear from the system.

In some cases, a financial identifier can be interrupted; for example, a commercial data vendor might stop maintaining an identifier as they develop a new identification system or switch to using an industry-wide system. Additionally, an identification system might be replaced with a new one if it fails to meet certain desired properties, such as uniqueness, globality, and granularity. The concept of permanent versus nonpermanent identifiers is shown in Figure 3-5. The identification system on the left is permanent as it could return the associated data at time t and time t+n. In contrast, the system on the right is nonpermanent as it returns data at time t but returns none at time t+n.

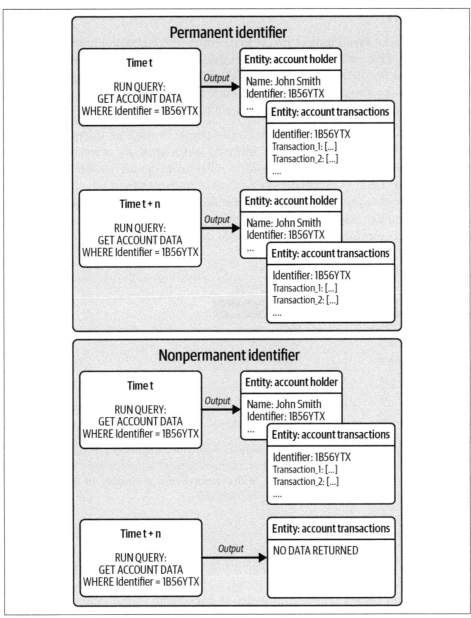

Figure 3-5. Permanent versus nonpermanent identification systems

Immutability

A robust financial identification system must ensure the immutability of its identifiers over time. This means that an identifier associated with a specific entity should neither change nor be reassigned to another entity. If the identified entity ceases to exist, its identifier should never be reused. Such a property is essential for maintaining transparency, traceability, and effective monitoring.

Besides temporal immutability, identifiers must persist through all stages of financial activities. For example, a transaction's lifecycle, which typically comprises multiple steps from initiation, through execution, to settlement, should consistently use the same identifier. Table 3-2 illustrates the concept of mutable versus immutable identifiers. Identifier A is immutable, as all three entities have the same identifier in 2005 and 2022. Identifier B is not mutable, as entities 1 and 3 changed their identifier in 2022. Moreover, the identifier of entity 1 used in 2005 was reassigned to entity 3 in 2022.

Table 3-2. Mutable versus immutable identifiers

Entity	Year	Identifier A (immutable)	Identifier B (mutable)
Entity 1	2005	XZY743	XZY743
Entity 2	2005	ABC376	ABC376
Entity 3	2005	MNT098	MNT098
Entity 1	2022	XZY743	KKH654
Entity 2	2022	ABC376	ABC376
Entity 3	2022	MNT098	XZY743

Corporate events such as mergers, acquisitions, spin-offs, corporate restructurings, and rebranding might change a company's structure, potentially resulting in the creation of a new entity. In these cases, a new identifier may be assigned.

Security

Security must be prioritized when designing a financial identification system, as these systems are vulnerable to malicious attacks. Consider the damage that an attacker could inflict, for instance, if they succeeded in hacking an identification system and irreversibly changing its identifiers. Even worse is the scenario in which sensitive identifying data is compromised and utilized to commit financial crimes against the entities identified in the data.

To summarize, developing an optimal financial identification system is challenging since it involves multiple complex properties that may be difficult to achieve in a single system. For this reason, financial markets have developed a plethora of financial identification systems, each serving a particular purpose and offering unique characteristics. Some of these systems are widely adopted, while others are gaining attention in response to evolving market needs. The next section will provide you with an overview of current financial identification systems.

Financial Identification Systems Landscape

The current landscape of financial identification systems is extensive, comprising open source and proprietary systems designed with different properties and for various purposes. Several standardization efforts have been initiated, yet a universally accepted standard has not been established. To give you an idea of the current scale, a Wikipedia search for "security identifier" (*https://oreil.ly/a5vsU*) yields results for 16 different identifiers. The ISO conducted an inventory of the current national and international financial identification standards (*https://oreil.ly/qE18s*) and identified a total of 19 different systems. These identifiers and several others are illustrated in Figure 3-6.

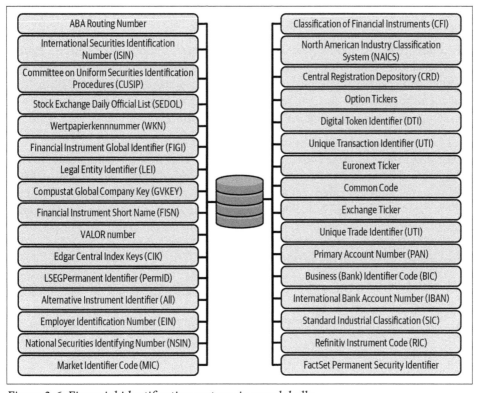

Figure 3-6. Financial identification systems in use globally

In the following sections, I will discuss some of the most important financial identification systems used by markets, along with their key characteristics and challenges.

International Securities Identification Number

The *International Securities Identification Number* (ISIN) is a 12-character alphanumeric code, defined in ISO 6166 (*https://oreil.ly/Lov0_*), that uniquely identifies a wide range of financial securities such as stocks, bonds, derivatives, fund share classes, and indexes.

In principle, an ISIN should represent a set of fungible financial instruments. For instance, the common stocks of a given company are fungible with each other, regardless of the issuance date, as they all share the same specifications. In this scenario, the same ISIN is typically used to represent the company's common stock. However, if the company issues different classes of stocks, such as preferred stocks, each class would receive a different ISIN. Similarly, multiple bond issues from the same company would have distinct ISINs, since each issue has unique specifications such as the start date, end date, and interest rate. The same principle applies to more complex financial products, such as derivatives.

ISIN codes are issued and maintained by each country's National Numbering Agency or the Substitute Numbering Agency. The ISIN system has gained widespread market adoption and is increasingly recognized as the global standard for financial instrument identification. Due to their reliability, ISIN identifiers are predominantly used for trading, settlement, clearing, and regulatory reporting.

The 12 characters of an ISIN can be divided into three parts: the first two characters are the ISO 3166-1 alpha-2 code (*https://oreil.ly/K-_mq*) of the issuing country. The middle nine alphanumeric characters represent the security identifier. This nine-digit alphanumeric code is often called the National Securities Identifying Number (NSIN). Examples of NSINs include CUSIP in the USA, SEDOL in the UK, and WKN ("Wertpapierkennnummer") in Germany.[5] The last character is a check digit computed using the modulus 10 double-add-double or Luhn algorithm. Figure 3-7 offers a visual breakdown of the ISIN.

Figure 3-7. Structural breakdown of the ISIN code

---

[5] CUSIP and SEDOL are discussed in the next few sections. For details on WKN, refer to the definition offered by Börse Frankfurt (*https://oreil.ly/uic6Y*).

One potential drawback of the ISIN is its international scope, which means it does not specify the trading location or currency. If a given stock trades on multiple different exchanges, the associated ISIN will be the same. For instance, IBM's common stock is listed on almost 25 trading platforms and exchanges around the world. In this case, some identifiers for IBM stock would vary depending on where it is traded (e.g., the ticker). However, IBM stock will have only one ISIN for each security.[6] To overcome this limitation, the *Market Identifier Code* (MIC), defined in ISO 10383 (*https://oreil.ly/oLO28*), is commonly used alongside the ISIN to specify exchanges, trading venues, and both regulated and nonregulated markets.

Another limitation is that the ISIN does not provide detailed information about the contract terms or variations within a particular type of security. In other words, an ISIN cannot describe a contract uniquely.

An ISIN might become inactive or be replaced with a new one following corporate actions such as mergers and acquisitions, company name changes, stock splits, and the redemption/conversion of debt instruments.

Another limitation of the ISIN is that it does not cover all instruments, especially over-the-counter instruments. In this case, alternative instrument identifiers are often used.[7]

Luhn Algorithm: The Industry Standard for Financial Identifier Validation

The Luhn algorithm or Luhn formula, also known as the modulus 10 or mod 10 algorithm, named after its creator, IBM scientist Hans Peter Luhn, and specified in ISO/IEC 7812-1 (*https://oreil.ly/M-JO_*), is a widely used checksum formula for financial identifier validation. The algorithm is not meant to be a security measure against malicious attacks but rather a mechanism to protect against errors and distinguish valid identifiers from incorrect ones.

To validate an identifier such as ISIN using the Luhn formula, six steps are required:

1. If the identifier already contains the check digit, remove it. In most cases, the check digit is located at the end of the string. The remaining string constitutes the *payload*.

2. Starting from the rightmost digit in the payload, double the value of every second digit.

---

6 Example taken from the ISIN organization web page (*https://oreil.ly/z26Fb*).

7 Keep in mind that many financial identification systems are always expanding, so just because an identifier doesn't cover a certain market segment now doesn't imply it won't tomorrow.

3. If doubling the digit results in a number that is greater than 9 (e.g., 18), then sum the digits of the doubled number to get a single digit (e.g., 12 becomes $1 + 2 = 3$).

4. Sum all the digits.

5. Compute the sum's modulus 10 as $(10 - (\text{sum mod } 10)) \text{ mod } 10$. The result of this operation can be interpreted as the smallest number that needs to be added to the sum (possibly 0) to make it a multiple of 10.

6. If the modulus 10 obtained in step 5 is equal to the check digit, then the number is valid. Otherwise, it's not.

For an example, let's validate the ISIN of Microsoft, US5949181045:

1. To get a numerical string, we convert the country letters to digits by taking the ASCII code (American Standard Code for Information Interchange) of the capital letter and subtracting 55. The ASCII code for U is 85, while for S, it's 83; therefore, the new digit is [85-55][83-55]5949181045 = 30285949181045.

2. Remove the check digit (=5) to get the payload → 3028594918104.

3. Starting from the right, we double the value of each second digit, and we get [6] 0 [4] 8 [10] 9 [8] 9 [2] 8 [2] 0 [8].

4. Take the sum of the multidigit numbers (>9). We have one, which is [10], and by summing $1 + 0$, we get 1; therefore, the new sequence is [6] 0 [4] 8 [1] 9 [8] 9 [2] 8 [2] 0 [8].

5. Add up all the digits: $6 + 0 + 4 + 8 + 1 + 9 + 8 + 9 + 2 + 8 + 2 + 0 + 8 = 65$.

6. Calculate the check digit using the formula: $10 - (65 \text{ mod } 10) \text{ mod } 10 = 5$.

7. As the final result (5) is equal to the check digit, we can tell that the identifier is a valid ISIN.

A Python implementation for this ISIN check digit validation is available in the GitHub repo for this book (*https://oreil.ly/8Ym6G*).

Classification of Financial Instruments

The *Classification of Financial Instruments* (CFI) is a six-letter code defined in ISO 10962 (*https://oreil.ly/oldKF*) that describes and classifies financial instruments. It was developed to address a major problem in financial markets, namely the need for a uniform and consistent approach to categorizing and grouping financial instruments. The ISO has appointed SIX Group, the national numbering agency of Switzerland, as the maintenance agency for the CFI code. SIX publishes a list of all CFI codes and modifications on its website (*https://oreil.ly/ZMrOf*).

Since July 1, 2017, CFI codes are globally assigned alongside the ISIN when a new financial instrument is issued. In most cases, an instrument's CFI remains unmodified during its lifespan. However, corporate-related events such as changes to voting rights or ownership restrictions could cause a CFI to change.

In a CFI code, the first letter indicates the instrument category, the second denotes the subcategory, and the remaining letters indicate various attributes of the instrument. Both the second and remaining letters are optional. For example, the CFI code ESVXXX is for equity (E), common/ordinary share (S) with voting right (V), while code FXXXXX indicates a future (F), and OCXXXX is an option (O) of type call (C). Figure 3-8 offers a visual illustration of the CFI code.

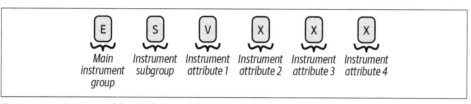

Figure 3-8. Structural breakdown of the CFI code

Financial Instrument Short Name

The *Financial Instrument Short Name* (FISN), defined in ISO 18774 (*https://oreil.ly/ OGcgl*), is a human-readable code used to provide a consistent, uniform, and global description of financial instruments. Since July 1, 2017, the FISN has been globally assigned alongside the ISIN and CFI at the time of issuance of a new financial instrument.

Unlike ISINs, which are primarily used for clearing and settlement, FISNs are utilized by market participants to enhance the readability, efficiency, reliability, data consistency, and transparency of financial services transactions and reference data.

The FISN code has a maximum length of 35 alphanumeric characters. Of these, 15 are reserved for the issuer name, and 19 for the description of the instrument, with the character "/" as the separator between the issuer name and description. Figure 3-9 illustrates the structure of the FISN code.

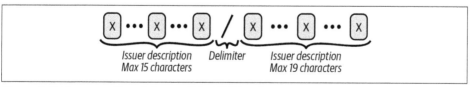

Figure 3-9. Structural breakdown of the FISN code

Committee on Uniform Security Identification Procedures

The *Committee on Uniform Security Identification Procedures* (CUSIP) is a nine-character alphanumeric code used to identify financial securities in the United States and Canada. CUSIP codes are mainly used for trading, settlement, and clearing. They are issued and managed by CUSIP Global Services (CGS) (*https://oreil.ly/poJ_k*), which acts as the US national numbering agency and is operated by FactSet Research Systems, Inc., as of the time this book was written.

The first six characters of a CUSIP uniquely identify an issuer (company, municipality, agency). The seventh and eighth characters identify the instrument type and issue using a hierarchical alphanumeric convention. The last character is a check digit.

For US securities, the CUSIP number makes up the middle nine characters of a US ISIN. For example, Amazon's ISIN is US0231351067, and Amazon's CUSIP is 023135106. Figure 3-10 offers a visual representation of the CUSIP code.

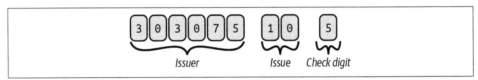

Figure 3-10. Structural breakdown of the CUSIP code

To check the validity of a CUSIP code, the following steps are required:

1. Convert non-numeric characters to digits according to their ordinal position in the alphabet plus 9 (e.g., A = (1 + 9) = 10).

2. Convert the characters * to 36, @ to 37, and # to 38.

3. Multiply every even digit by 2. If the result is a two-digit number, add the digits together (e.g., 13 → 1 + 3 = 4).

4. Get the sum of all values.

5. Get the floored value of the sum: (10 − (sum modulo 10)) modulo 10.

A Python implementation for ISIN check digit validation is available in the GitHub repo for this book (*https://oreil.ly/ACvCK*).

Recently, a new identifier, called *CUSIP Entity Identifier* (CEI), was introduced by CGS (*https://oreil.ly/7oU7C*) to identify legal parties involved in the syndicated lending market.[8] The CEI was developed in collaboration with the Loan Syndications and Trading Association (LSTA) and syndicated loan solution providers.

---

8 The syndicated lending market is where a group of financial institutions (the syndicate) jointly extend a loan (often large loans) to a single borrower.

Legal Entity Identifier

The *Legal Entity Identifier* (LEI), defined in ISO 17442 (*https://oreil.ly/UKFb9*), is a 20-character alphanumeric code used to identify legal entities engaged in financial transactions. Each LEI contains information about an entity's ownership structure and thus answers the questions of "who is who" and "who owns whom." This concept aligns closely with know your customer (KYC) practices in financial markets, which aim to verify the identity of clients within financial institutions. The LEI identifier is a global, unique, and freely accessible identifier. Its official maintainer is the Global Legal Entity Identifier Foundation (GLEIF).

As illustrated in Figure 3-11, the first four characters of the LEI form a prefix that identifies the Local Operating Unit (LOU) that issued the LEI. Characters 5 to 18 constitute the entity identifier assigned by the LOU. Finally, characters 19 and 20 are two check digits.

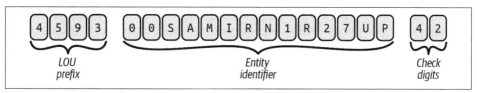

Figure 3-11. Structural breakdown of the LEI identifier

ISO 17442 classifies (*https://oreil.ly/VSXaQ*) the following as legal entities:

- All financial intermediaries
- Banks and finance companies
- International branches
- All entities that issue equity, debt, or other securities for other capital structures
- All entities listed on an exchange
- All entities that trade financial instruments or are otherwise parties to financial transactions, including business entities, pension funds, and investment vehicles such as collective investment funds (at umbrella and subfund levels) and other special purpose vehicles that have a legal form
- All entities under the purview of a financial regulator and their affiliates, subsidiaries, and holding companies
- Sole traders (as an example of individuals acting in a business capacity)

On April 4th, 2019, ANNA and GLEIF launched a collaborative initiative to associate ISIN identifiers with the LEI identifiers of their issuers. This initiative aims to enhance market transparency by establishing a direct link between the issuer and the issuance of securities.

Lehman Brothers and the Establishment of the Legal Entity Identifier

The introduction of the LEI has been celebrated as a major milestone in financial markets, generating numerous discussions and publications about its beneficial impact on improving market efficiency and stability. The question is, why all this attention?

The issue started shortly after the collapse of Lehman Brothers in 2008. As explained by a McKinsey report (*https://oreil.ly/vsiLd*), "After Lehman's demise, participants in the global financial system could not assess their exposure to Lehman, its subsidiaries, and each other because there was no standard system for identifying counterparties in the maze of subsidiaries and affiliates from which banks, insurers, asset managers, and other market participants transact."

To give an illustrative example, when Lehman Brothers collapsed in 2008, it had an estimated 8,000 subsidiaries working in various jurisdictions (*https://oreil.ly/mirmV*), while Morgan Stanley had roughly 3,500 subsidiaries. Consider the potential number of bilateral agreements and transactions between any of Lehman's 8,000 subsidiaries and Morgan Stanley's 3,500 and assume that such agreements are specified using different identification systems. Now, assume that you want to calculate the total exposure of Morgan Stanley to Lehman Brothers. This would require aggregating millions of positions, each identified using the subsidiary's convention.

Unsurprisingly, it took quite a lot of time for Lehman Brothers's counterparties to calculate their total exposure to the consolidated entity. To mitigate this issue and ensure that financial institutions can quickly aggregate their exposures and risk information, the ISO led an initiative to develop an international legal entity identification standard, resulting in the LEI.

In addition to the LEI, the ISO created the *Entity Legal Forms* (ELF), described in ISO 20275 (*https://oreil.ly/3Aal3*), to uniquely identify entity forms/types globally using a standardized four-character code. GLEIF maintains ELF codes that can be accessed and downloaded from its web page (*https://oreil.ly/dUb8y*).

Transaction Identifiers

Identifiers are the backbone of the lifecycle of financial transactions. During its processing, a single transaction often traverses various systems and parties. Consequently, the same transaction might be recorded with different IDs as it moves from one system to the next. This makes it difficult to unambiguously identify transactions and all related messages across disparate systems and databases. To overcome this issue, unique transaction identifiers have been developed.

One example is the *Unique Swap Identifier* (USI),[9] specific to the United States and mandated (*https://oreil.ly/DSry9*) by the Commodity Futures Trading Commission (CFTC) and the Securities and Exchange Commission (SEC) as part of the Dodd-Frank Act. The USI is a fixed-length identifier assigned to all swap transactions, identifying the transaction uniquely throughout its lifecycle. To expand the scope of the USI identifier for global reporting of financial transactions, the *Unique Trade Identifier* (UTI) was introduced (*https://oreil.ly/9N5Eb*).

To ensure consistency across different jurisdictions and reporting platforms, the ISO introduced the ISO 23897 (*https://oreil.ly/3E2U8*)—the *Unique Transaction Identifier* (UTI) standard. It provides specifications aimed at standardizing transaction identifiers globally, ensuring unique identification throughout a financial transaction's lifecycle. This is essential for facilitating transaction reporting, improving traceability, and reducing operational errors, especially as cross-border trading expands.[10]

The format of these transaction identifiers is generally similar. ISO 23897 specifies a max length of 52 characters for UTI code, but a variable length is possible. There is a consensus that a unique transaction identifier should include a prefix identifying the issuing entity, followed by a string that uniquely identifies the transaction. A market preference has emerged in favor of using international standards such as LEI identifiers for the prefix part.[11] For example, in 2013, the ISDA working group proposed a best practice recommendation for the UTI (*https://oreil.ly/kMRUi*), where the prefix consists of characters 7–16 of the LEI, followed by a 32-character string, as illustrated in Figure 3-12.

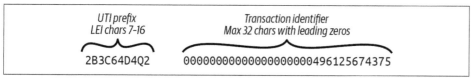

Figure 3-12. ISDA-based Unique Trade Identifier (UTI) structure

---

9 In finance, a swap is a type of derivative instrument in which two parties agree to exchange financial instruments, cash flows, or payments over a specified period of time.

10 To explore the utility of UTIs in financial markets, I recommend reading Swift's article on "The Unique Transaction Identifier and Its Value in Securities Settlement" (*https://oreil.ly/00Rob*).

11 Refer to BIS (editors): Committee on Payments and Market Infrastructures Board of the International Organization of Securities Commissions Technical Guidance, "Harmonisation of the Unique Transaction Identifier" (*https://oreil.ly/QlZK8*), February 2017.

Stock Exchange Daily Official List

The *Stock Exchange Daily Official List* (SEDOL) is a seven-character alphanumeric code mainly used to identify securities traded on the London Stock Exchange (LSE) and other smaller exchanges in the UK. The LSE (the National Numbering Agency of the UK) assigns SEDOL codes upon request from the security issuer.[12]

Over the years, the SEDOL system has expanded, and SEDOL codes can now be issued at the country level to represent securities listed in multiple jurisdictions. SEDOLs are issued globally across all jurisdictions and multiple asset classes. If a security is traded on a different exchange in a different country, it will be assigned a separate SEDOL code. This makes SEDOLs unique across countries, which is ideal for international trading and security identification.

For UK securities, SEDOLs are embedded within the UK ISIN codes by adding the country code at the beginning, followed by two padding zeros, then the SEDOL, and finally, the ISIN check code. For example, the UK banking group HSBC has a SEDOL code of 0540528 and an ISIN code of GB0005405286.[13]

SEDOL codes issued prior to March 2004 were exclusively numeric. Afterward, the SEDOL system moved to an alphanumeric format that starts with an alphabetic character, followed by five alphanumeric characters and a trailing numeric check digit. Figure 3-13 illustrates the structure of SEDOL.

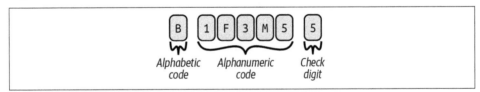

Figure 3-13. The structural breakdown of the SEDOL identifier

To check if a SEDOL is valid, the check digit is chosen to make the weighted sum of all SEDOL characters a multiple of 10. The steps to validate a SEDOL are as follows:

1. Convert non-numeric characters to digits according to their ordinal position in the alphabet plus 9 (A = (1 + 9) = 10).

2. Multiply each of the first six numbers by their corresponding weight: 1 for first position, 3 for second, 1 for third, 7 for fourth, 3 for fifth, 9 for sixth.

---

12 Sedol technical documentation is available on the LSE website (*https://oreil.ly/PHL4m*).

13 Information taken from the official company page of HSBC on the LSE website (*https://oreil.ly/t2xTa*).

3. Get the sum of all values.

4. Get the floored value of sum: (10 − (sum modulo 10)) modulo 10.

A Python implementation for SEDOL check digit validation is available in the Git-Hub repo for this book (*https://oreil.ly/iTLnc*).

Ticker Symbols

A ticker symbol is a short and unique series of letters assigned to financial securities (mostly stocks) for listing and trading purposes. There is no standard for tickers, and they can be generated and assigned by various organizations, including exchanges and trading venues, financial data providers, and financial institutions.

The allocation process and formatting conventions of tickers are specific to each issuing organization. Among US exchanges, tickers are typically one to four characters long, and they resemble the company name when possible. For example, the ticker for Apple, Inc. on the NYSE is AAPL, while Ford Motor has the ticker F. Some exchanges, such as NASDAQ, add a fifth symbol to their tickers (*https://oreil.ly/G9hMy*) to convey information about the trading status and special features of the stock. For example, in BRK.A, the first three represent the stock symbol for Berkshire Hathaway, Inc. (BRK), and the last letter (.A) indicates that the shares are of class A type, which traditionally holds more voting rights.

In addition to exchanges, financial data providers assign proprietary ticker symbols to financial instruments. For example, Bloomberg created its own Bloomberg ticker to identify a financial entity uniquely within the Bloomberg ecosystem. A Bloomberg ticker can include the exchange-specific ticker, the market sector, the exchange code, instrument-specific information (e.g., bond maturity, option expiry, option type, etc.), and the Bloomberg database (e.g., EQUITY for stocks).

Another well-known proprietary ticker symbol is the *Refinitiv Instrument Code* (RIC), which is issued and maintained by LSEG. RIC tickers are mainly used to look up information on specific financial instruments on LSEG platforms. The main component of the RIC is the security's ticker symbol with an optional character that identifies the exchange. For example, the RIC symbol IBM.N refers to IBM stock (IBM) traded on the New York Stock Exchange (.N).

Stock tickers can vary by exchange and country, which implies that they may not be unique across different exchanges and countries. As a result, to reliably identify a stock, both the ticker and the exchange or country of listing are often required.

Tickers are not immutable and might change to reflect corporate actions such as mergers and acquisitions. For example, prior to the 1999 merger with Mobil Oil, Exxon used the phonetic spelling of the company (XON) as its ticker symbol. After the merger, the symbol changed to XOM.

Importantly, tickers are not guaranteed to remain unique, as they can be reassigned over time. For example, until 2017, the ticker SNOW was assigned by NYSE to Intrawest Resorts Holdings, Inc. In May 2017, Henry Crown and Company and KSL Capital Partners acquired Intrawest and transformed it into a privately owned company. After delisting Intrawest, the ticker SNOW was reassigned to Snowflake. A Wikipedia search of both company names would confirm this, as illustrated in Figure 3-14.

Figure 3-14. NYSE tickers for Intrawest and Snowflake

Derivative Identifiers

Derivatives are among the most exchanged financial securities in financial markets. As a quick reminder, a derivative is a contract that derives its value from an underlying financial asset or variable such as stocks, commodities, foreign exchange, interest rates, indexes, and many more.

Crucially, identifying derivative instruments is more challenging than identifying other types of financial instruments. First, several constituent elements must be considered to identify a derivative instrument. Second, due to their flexible and customizable nature, derivatives can easily turn into very complex products. Third, a substantial deal of derivatives is traded OTC, complicating their tracking and identification. Nonetheless, as I will demonstrate next, market participants have developed various initiatives to identify both exchange-traded and OTC derivative instruments.

Option symbol

Option symbols are derived symbols used to identify an option and its characteristics on a given exchange.[14] The current market standard for option symbols is based on the *Options Clearing Corporation*'s (OCC) *Options Symbology Initiative* (OSI). The OSI format consists of a 21-character alphanumeric code that can be split into four parts:

---

14 An option is financial derivative instrument that gives its holder the right, but not the obligation, to buy or sell a specific quantity of an underlying asset at a given strike price on or before a specified future date, depending on the option style.

- A root (ticker) symbol of the underlying stock or ETF (exchange-traded fund).
- An expiration date, which is six digits in the format YYMMDD.
- An option type, either C for a call or P for put.
- The strike price. This is represented by the price times 1,000, with the front padded with 0s to 8 digits. The decimal point falls three places from the right in the options symbol: 00000.000.

The structure of the OSI option symbol is illustrated in detail in Figure 3-15.

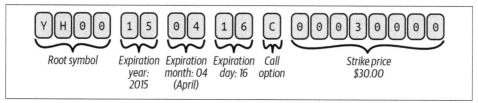

Figure 3-15. The structural breakdown of the OSI option symbol

CFI, UPI, and OTC ISIN

To identify OTC derivatives, a combined identification scheme has been put in place that relies on three identifiers:

OTC ISIN
> This is allocated by the *Derivatives Service Bureau* (DSB), with the initial two characters starting with the custom "EZ" code.

Unique Product Identifier (UPI)
> This is defined in ISO 4914 (*https://oreil.ly/V-dgy*) for the identification of OTC derivative products.

Classification of financial instruments (CFI)
> This is generated by the DSB as part of the OTC ISIN generation process.

The three identifiers are combined to provide different levels of detail. Malavika Solanki, of the management team at the DSB, illustrated the combined use of the three identifiers with the following example (*https://oreil.ly/_qMRN*): at the highest level, the CFI can tell that a derivative instrument is a "single currency, fix-float, interest rate swap with a constant notional schedule and cash delivery." The UPI would tell a bit more about the product, for example, that it has a "three-month reference rate term, a USD reference rate, and that the name of the reference rate was USD-LIBOR-BBAR." Finally, the OTC ISIN can provide more granular details about the specific instrument that has been transacted, such as "the standardized ISO reference rate name, the price multiplier associated with the instrument, the full name and short names of the instrument, the expiry date."

Alternative Instrument Identifier

The *Alternative Instrument Identifier* (AII) has been adopted within the European Union for reporting purposes to identify derivatives traded on regulated markets without an ISIN assigned to them. Rather than being a code, the AII is a concatenation of descriptive fields that identify the instrument. The fields include the exchange code, exchange product code, derivative type, put/call identifier, expiry/delivery/prompt date, and strike price, as illustrated in Figure 3-16.

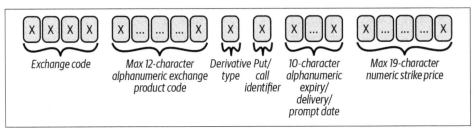

Figure 3-16. The structural breakdown of the AII identifier

Financial Instrument Global Identifier

The *Financial Instrument Global Identifier* (FIGI) is a 12-character alphanumeric ID covering hundreds of millions of active and inactive instruments around the world.

The history of FIGI started in 2009 when Bloomberg decided to release its Open Symbology (BSYM) system for identifying financial securities across asset classes. The BSYM provides a library of identifiers for hundreds of millions of securities, known as Bloomberg Global Identifiers (BBGIDs). In 2014, the BSYM symbology system was adopted by the Object Management Group (OMG), a nonprofit standards consortium, in order to promote it as an open industry standard. Subsequently, the BBGID was renamed to FIGI. Since its introduction, FIGI has received a lot of market attention. For example, the Accredited Standards Committee X9 adopted FIGI as an official US data identification standard (*https://oreil.ly/f6-_a*).

FIGI codes are unique across all markets and countries and remain unchanged once issued. For example, if IBM stock is traded on 12 stock exchanges, there will be 12 different FIGIs.

Furthermore, FIGI was designed as a global system capable of identifying any type of financial instrument, including stocks, bonds, derivatives, loans, indexes, funds, and digital assets. FIGIs are also free to access. An open source tool called OpenFIGI (*https://oreil.ly/VPX6F*) was released to identify, map, and request a free FIGI via an API.

The FIGI identification system has a hierarchical structure composed of three levels:

Global FIGI

This is the most granular level, identifying a financial asset at the trading-venue level. It is unique to a specific instrument at a particular trading venue.

Composite global FIGI

This level aggregates multiple venue-level FIGI identifiers within the same country, providing a broader identification that encompasses all trading venues for a specific instrument within that country.

Share class global FIGI

This level further aggregates FIGI identifiers to cover financial instruments across multiple countries. It provides a global view of a single instrument regardless of the country and venue.

For example, Amazon trades on multiple stock exchanges in the US. When Amazon common stock trades on the New York Stock Exchange, it has the FIGI code BBG000BVPXP1. When the same stock trades on the NASDAQ Global Select exchange, it has a FIGI of BBG000BVQ4Z3. But if you don't care about which US exchange Amazon trades on, you can use the Amazon composite FIGI (BBG000BVPV84) to generically reference Amazon stock traded in the US. If you want to globally identify Amazon common stock regardless of trading venue and country, the share class code (BBG001S5PQL7) can be used.[15] Figure 3-17 illustrates the hierarchical structure of FIGI.

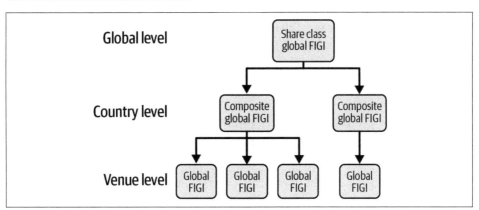

Figure 3-17. Hierarchical representations of FIGI

---

15 To explore for yourself, please use this link (*https://oreil.ly/p1La-*).

All three levels of FIGI identifiers have the same structure and limitations. The identifier may contain only letters in [B, C, D, F, G, H, J, K, L, M, N, P, Q, R, S, T, V, W, X, Y, Z], and zero to nine digits.

The structure of FIGI codes is as follows:

- The first two characters identify the certified issuer that created the FIGI code. Currently, Bloomberg generates the majority of FIGI codes, hence the presence of the prefix BB in most identifiers.
- The third character is the letter G, used to indicate that it's a global identifier.
- Characters 4–11 are alphanumeric characters that constitute the reference ID.
- A trailing check digit.

Figure 3-18 illustrates this structure visually.

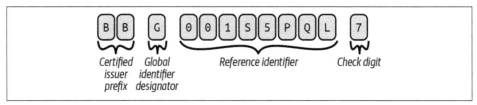

Figure 3-18. The structural breakdown of FIGI

The check digit procedure is based on the Luhn algorithm, following five steps:

1. Get the identifier, e.g., BBG000BLNQ16, and remove the check digit, BBG000BLNQ1.
2. Convert non-numeric characters to digits according to their ordinal position in the alphabet plus 9 (A = (1 + 9) = 10). In our example, we get [11][11][16][0][0] [0][11][21][23][26][1].
3. Double every second digit: [11][22][16][0][0][0][11][42][23][52][1].
4. Compute the sum of the resulting values: $1 + 1 + 2 + 2 + 1 + 6 + 0 + 0 + 0 + 1 + 1 + 4 + 2 + 2 + 3 + 5 + 2 + 1 = 34$.
5. Get the floored value of the sum: (10 − (34 modulo 10)) modulo 10 = 6, which is the check digit attached to the identifier.

A Python implementation for FIGI check digit validation is available in this book's GitHub repo (*https://oreil.ly/-BwrQ*).

FactSet Permanent Identifier

The *FactSet permanent identifier (https://oreil.ly/LNMqf)* is a proprietary identification system developed by FactSet to offer a stable and unified identifier. It includes three levels:

Security
Identifying the security globally

Regional
Identifying the security at the regional level per currency (e.g., US/USD)

Listing
Identifying the security at the market level (e.g., US/NYSE/USD)

FactSet provides the FactSet Symbology API (*https://oreil.ly/QHQAn*), a symbol/identifier resolution service that allows users to map a wide variety of identifiers to FactSet's native symbology or third-party identifiers such as CUSIPs, SEDOLS, ISINs, Bloomberg FIGI, and many more. In addition, FactSet offers the FactSet Concordance API (*https://oreil.ly/UbD3r*), which enables users to programmatically match the FactSet identifier for a specific entity based on attributes, such as name, URL, and location.

LSEG Permanent Identifier

The *Permanent Identifier* (PermID) (*https://permid.org*) is a unique identifier used within the London Stock Exchange Group (LSEG) information model to identify and reference various objects, including organizations, instruments, funds, issuers, and people. It ensures that these objects are accurately and unambiguously referenced and linked together, even as their relationships change over time.

What makes PermID especially valuable is that it's linked to a unique web address or Uniform Resource Identifier (URI), offering a permanent, direct link to the identified entity. LSEG has made PermID open source, enabling access via web pages or through API-based entity search and matching services.

For example, the following PermID URLs can be used to retrieve information about the technology company Apple:

https://permid.org/1-4295905573
Provides organizational details identifying Apple, Inc.

https://permid.org/1-8590932301
Contains instrument details identifying Apple's ordinary shares.

https://permid.org/1-25727408109
Includes quote information identifying Apple's ordinary shares on the New York Stock Exchange.

Digital Asset Identifiers

Following the emergence and diffusion of blockchain and distributed ledger technologies, *digital assets* have been established as a new type of financial market entity. According to the ISO 22739 vocabulary for blockchain (*https://oreil.ly/--xjQ*), a digital asset is an "asset that exists only in digital form or which is the digital representation of another asset." In many cases, digital assets are referred to as *digital tokens*. A digital token can be *fungible* if it's identical and interchangeable with similar assets (e.g., one dollar in New York is the same as one dollar in Australia), or *nonfungible* if they are unique and nondivisible (e.g., a painting or a boat). The most common place for exchanging digital assets is a *blockchain*, which, according to ISO 22739 vocabulary, refers to a "distributed ledger with confirmed blocks organized in an append-only, sequential chain using cryptographic links."[16] The process of converting something to a digital asset and adding it to a blockchain system is called *tokenization*.

Over the past years, a wide variety of fungible digital assets have been developed, for example the following:

Crypto assets
Assets developed using cryptographic techniques. The most notable examples are cryptocurrencies such as Bitcoin and Ethereum. Crypto assets can serve as a means of payment or investment.

Security token
A financial security or instrument converted into a digital token and exchanged on a distributed ledger like blockchain (e.g., Microsoft Stock Token). Similar to traditional security certificates, security tokens represent an ownership right in a company or asset.

Nonfungible tokens
These represent ownership rights over a unique digital asset such as images, videos, and games.

Utility token
A token used to access a specific service or feature within a blockchain-based ecosystem.

---

16 More on blockchain internals will be discussed in Chapter 8.

As digital assets have grown in popularity, the requirement to identify the issued, stored, and transacted digital tokens and crypto assets has become more urgent. A first initiative was established with the introduction of the *Digital Token Identifier* (DTI), defined in ISO 24165-1 (*https://oreil.ly/Y1yar*), to identify fungible tokens and digital ledgers. In defining the DTI, the ISO realized the need for a new methodology for assigning the identifier. This is because digital assets are often not associated with a particular issuing entity, such as central banks, unlike traditional assets.

The standard helps in reducing confusion and increasing trust in the crypto assets market by providing a universal method of identification.

Industry and Sector Identifiers

Industry and sector identifiers are classification frameworks used to categorize and group businesses into various categories and subcategories. Financial firms use industry identifiers to analyze market exposure, classify stocks, measure concentration risks, and understand cross-industry differences. Two main industry classification frameworks are widely used: the *Standard Industrial Classification* (SIC) and the *North American Industry Classification System* (NAICS).

The SIC identifier is a four-character numerical code used to classify industries based on their primary activities. The SIC system was created in 1937 by the US government to facilitate economic analysis across industries and agencies and to promote standardization and uniformity in the collection and recording of industrial data.

As illustrated in Figure 3-19, the official SIC classification code consists of three parts. The first two digits, which are mandatory, identify the major sector group. The third digit further categorizes the business into an industry group. The fourth digit provides the most granular classification, specifying the particular sector of the business. For example, SIC code 6021 (National Commercial Banks) (*https://oreil.ly/aqQWh*) belongs to industry group 602 (Commercial Banks), which is part of major group 60 (Depository Institutions), which belongs to the division of (Finance, Insurance, and Real Estate).

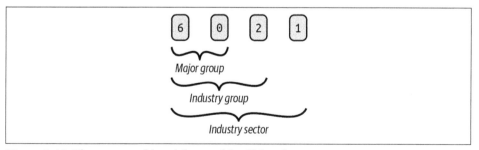

Figure 3-19. The structural breakdown of the SIC code

The SIC system had several shortcomings. First, it produced ambiguous, mismatched, and overlapping classifications generated by SIC. Second, the four-digit system restricted the addition of new, emerging business sectors and industries. To overcome these issues, the SIC system was replaced in 1997 by the North American Industrial Classification System (NAICS), which introduced a more flexible six-character numeric code.

As shown in Figure 3-20, the first two digits of an NAICS code indicate the major sector of the business. The third digit indicates the subsector, and the fourth digit designates the industry group. The fifth digit indicates the specific industry of operation, while the sixth code specifies the national industry. For example, NAICS code 522110 (*https://oreil.ly/0V87L*) is used to identify commercial banks. The first two digits, 52, define the sector (Finance and Insurance), the first three digits (522) identify the subsector (Credit Intermediation and Related Activities), the first four digits (5221) define the industry group (Depository Credit Intermediation), and the last two digits identify the industry (Commercial Banking).

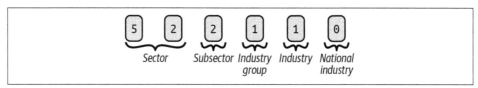

Figure 3-20. The structural breakdown of the NAICS code

Other industrial classification frameworks are in use worldwide. These include the Statistical Classification of Economic Activities in the European Community, known as NACE and predominantly used in the European Union, the UK Standard Industrial Classification of Economic Activities (UK SIC), and the Australian and New Zealand Standard Industrial Classification (ANZSIC).

Bank Identifiers

Banks are the cornerstones of financial markets. They provide a secure and reliable place for individuals and organizations to deposit, transfer, and invest money, obtain loans, and make credit and debit card payments. Additionally, they support various online applications and offer a platform for FinTech firms to offer their services. Therefore, bank identifiers are essential for identifying banks, customers, and payment cards.

The most prominent example is the *Business Identifier Code* (BIC), also called SWIFT or Bank Identifier Code. This alphanumeric code, defined in ISO 9362 (*https://oreil.ly/vnegN*), is used to identify banks, financial institutions, and nonfinancial institutions worldwide when conducting international money transfers and routing exchanging messages. SWIFT issues BIC codes.

A SWIFT/BIC consists of either 8 or 11 alphanumeric characters that identify the country, city, bank, and optionally the branch:

Bank code
Four-character alphabetic characters identifying the bank. It usually looks like a shortened version of that bank's name.

Country code
A two-character ISO 3166-1 alpha-2 code indicating the country where the bank is located.

Location code
Two-character alphanumeric code that designates where the bank's main office is.

Branch code
An optional three-character alphanumeric code representing a specific branch. XXX is used to indicate the bank's head office.

Figure 3-21 illustrates the structure of the BIC. The example shown refers to the Italian bank UniCredit Banca. The displayed code can be read as follows: UNCR identifies UniCredit Banca, IT is the country code for Italy, MM is the office location code for Milan, and XXX indicates the head office.

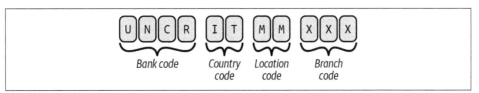

Figure 3-21. The structural breakdown of the BIC code

The use of the BIC code to identify financial institutions is quite common, especially when identifying financial institutions in international transactions. Nevertheless, certain countries employ their own local bank or branch identification codes. For instance, Australia uses the *Bank State Branch* (BSB), a six-digit code, to identify branches of Australian financial institutions. Similarly, in the United States, financial institutions involved in various payment operations are identified using the *ABA Routing Number*, consisting of nine digits.

Another well-known bank identifier is the *International Bank Account Number* (IBAN). It is defined in ISO 13616 (*https://oreil.ly/PXeiy*) and serves as an international system of unique codes used to identify bank accounts when conducting money transfers. The IBAN system was originally developed for use within the EU, but it was later adopted by regions such as the Caribbean and Middle East.

The length of the IBAN varies by country, but it cannot exceed 34 characters. For instance, Belgian IBANs have 16 alphanumeric characters, Luxembourg's are 20, and Germany's are 22.

An IBAN code is composed of three main parts (see Figure 3-22 for an illustration):

- Country code following the ISO 3166-1 alpha-2 convention.

- Two check digits.

- *Basic Bank Account Number* (BBAN)—up to 30 alphanumeric characters that include the bank code, branch identifier, and account number. The length of BBAN may vary across countries.

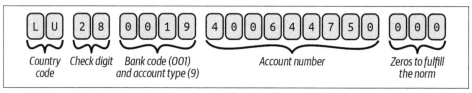

Figure 3-22. The structural breakdown of the IBAN number for Luxembourg

An IBAN code is validated through a mod-97 algorithm (as described by ISO 7064 (*https://oreil.ly/OESpA*)) that works as follows:

1. Make sure the IBAN has a valid length. For example, let's take a random Luxembourgish IBAN: LU280019400644750000. The length is 20, which matches the country's specified length.

2. Move the first four characters to the end of the string → 0019400644750000LU28.

3. Convert non-numeric characters to digits according to their ordinal position in the alphabet plus 9 (A = (1 + 9) = 10). In our example, we get 0019400644750000213028.

4. Treat the result as an integer and check if the modulo 97 of the number is equal to 1, 19400644750000213028 mod 97 = 1.

A Python implementation for IBAN validation is available in the GitHub repo for this book (*https://oreil.ly/7JbCy*).

Last but not least, an important bank identifier is the payment card number or *Primary Account Number* (PAN), defined in ISO/IEC 7812 (*https://oreil.ly/M-JO_*). This is used to define payment cards and identify their issuer and cardholder. Most payment cards, such as credit, debt, and gift cards, have their PAN laser-printed on the front (yes, it's your credit card number!).

The PAN is a numeric code with variable length ranging from 8 to 19 digits. The first six to eight digits represent the *Issuer Identification Number* (IIN), which identifies the card issuer. The first digit in the IIN is the *Major Industry Identifier* (MII), which identifies the industry/sector of the card issuer (for example, 4 and 5 are commonly used to identify financial institutions). The remaining characters are the individual account numbers used to identify the cardholder's account. The last digit is a check digit, which can be validated using the Luhn algorithm.[17] Figure 3-23 illustrates the structure of the PAN.

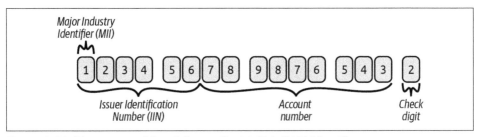

Figure 3-23. The structural breakdown of a 16-digit PAN Identifier

Summary

This chapter offered an in-depth treatment of financial identifiers and identification systems, which can be summarized as follows:

- Defining financial identifiers and identification systems and highlighting their critical role in financial market operations.
- Providing an overview of the entities involved in the creation, issuance, and maintenance of financial identifiers and identification systems.
- Outlining the desired properties of an optimal financial identification system.
- Discussing existing financial identification systems in detail, highlighting their main features and shortcomings.

The key takeaway from this chapter is that financial identification presents significant challenges for financial markets. In addition, as new products and market requirements emerge, the complexity of the issue continues to evolve. I highly recommend you stay informed about emerging trends in the development, standardization, and adoption of financial identification systems, as well as the evolving characteristics of existing systems.

---

17 Here is an exercise: take the Luhn algorithm that we defined previously in the International Securities Identification Number and use it to validate a credit or debt card number (BE CAREFUL: don't use your own card number; a list of test credit card numbers is available online (*https://oreil.ly/8Smmy*)).

Now that you have a solid understanding of financial identification systems, let's move on to explore another related and crucial problem in financial markets: financial entity systems. You build a financial entity system when you want to extract, recognize, identify, and match financial entities within and across various sources of financial data.

The next chapter is all about financial entity systems—let's keep moving!

CHAPTER 4
Financial Entity Systems

In the last chapter, you learned about financial identifiers and identification systems and their critical role in financial markets. Importantly, before a financial entity can be identified, it must first be extracted and ready for identification. However, in finance, it's quite common for data to exist in an unstructured format, where entities are not immediately identifiable. In fact, analysts estimate (*https://oreil.ly/5ZUgg*) that the vast majority of data in the world exists in unstructured formats, such as text, video, audio, and images. Moreover, it is quite frequent that different identifiers are used to reference the same financial entity across both structured and unstructured data. These factors collectively pose significant challenges when trying to extract value and insights from the data.

To this end, many financial institutions develop systems to extract, recognize, identify, and match financial entities within financial datasets. These systems, which I will call *financial entity systems* (FESs), constitute the main topic of this chapter. As a financial data engineer, understanding FESs and the challenges they entail is essential in navigating today's complex financial data landscape.

In the first part of this chapter, I will clarify the notion of financial entities and provide an overview of their various types. Next, I will illustrate the problem of financial entity extraction and recognition using a popular FES called *named entity recognition*. After that, I'll cover the issue of financial data matching and record linkage using another FES known as *entity resolution*.

Financial Entity Defined

Generally speaking, the term *entity* refers to any real-world object that can be recognized and identified. By narrowing the scope to financial markets, we can use the term *financial entity* to denote any real-world entity operating within financial markets. In this book, I define financial entity and financial entity systems as follows:

> A financial entity is a real-world object that may be recognized, identified, referenced, or mentioned as an essential part of financial market operations, activities, reports, events, or news. A financial entity may be human or not. It can be tangible (e.g., an ATM machine), intangible (e.g., common stock), fungible (e.g., one-dollar bills), or infungible (e.g., loans). A financial entity system is an organized set of technologies, procedures, and methods for extracting, identifying, linking, storing, and retrieving financial entities and related information from different sources of financial data and content.

As financial markets evolve and expand, so do the diversity and types of financial entities. A frequently used benchmark classification system (*https://oreil.ly/kinx6*) categorizes entities into four main groups: individuals (PER), corporations (ORG), places (LOC), and miscellaneous entities (MISC).

Naturally, based on your institution's needs, it might be necessary to categorize entities into a broader or more granular range. For example, let's say that your financial institution decides to collect data on the digital asset market. In this case, you might want to create a new entity type (digital asset) to represent objects such as cryptocurrencies, digital currency, utility tokens, security tokens, stablecoins, bitcoin, and many more. Other examples include the following:

- *Persons*, e.g., bankers, traders, directors, account holders, investors, market makers, regulators, brokers, financial advisors
- *Locations*, e.g., New York, Japan, Africa, Benelux (Belgium, the Netherlands, and Luxembourg)
- *Nationalities,* e.g., Italian, Australian, Chinese
- *Companies*, e.g., Bloomberg L.P., JPMorgan Chase & Co., Aramco, Ferrero
- *Organizations*, e.g., Securities and Exchange Commission, European Central Bank, London Stock Exchange, International Monetary Fund
- *Sectors*, e.g., financial services, food industry, agriculture, construction, microchips
- *Currency*, e.g., dollar ($), pound (£), euro (€)

- *Commodity*, e.g., gold, copper, silver, wheat, coffee, oil, steel
- *Financial security*, e.g., stocks, bonds, derivatives
- *Corporate events*, e.g., mergers, acquisitions, leveraged buyouts, syndicated loans, alliances, partnerships
- *Financial variables*, e.g., interest rate, inflation, volatility, index value, rating, profits, revenues
- *Investment strategies*, e.g., passive investment, active investment, value investing, growth investing, indexing
- *Corporate and market hierarchies*, e.g., parent company, holding company, subsidiary, branch
- *Products*, e.g., iPhone, Alexa, Siri, Dropbox, Gmail

Now that you know what financial entities are and how to categorize them, let's move on to understand how to identify and extract these entities from financial data. As previously mentioned, the systems designed for this purpose are referred to as *named entity recognition* (NER) systems.

Financial Named Entity Recognition

As a financial data engineer, if you ever get assigned to a project that involves recognizing and identifying financial entities from unstructured or semi-structured text, you will likely design and build an NER system. In this section, I will first define NER and give a few illustrative examples. Then, I will describe how NER works and the steps involved in designing an NER system. Third, I will give an overview of the available methods and techniques for conducting NER. Lastly, I will discuss a few examples of open source and commercial software libraries and tools that you can use to do NER.

Named Entity Recognition Described

NER, also known as entity extraction, entity identification, or entity chunking, is the task of detecting and recognizing named entities in text, such as persons, companies, locations, events, symbols, time, and more. NER is a key problem in finance, given the large volumes of finance-related text generated on a daily basis (e.g., filings, news, reports, logs, communications, messages) combined with the growing demand (*https://oreil.ly/413sX*) for advanced strategies for working with unstructured and text data.

The outcome of NER analysis is used in a variety of financial applications, such as enriching financial datasets with entity data, information extraction (e.g., extracting relevant financial information from financial reports and filings), text summarization (e.g., ensuring adherence to legal requirements), fraud detection (identifying suspicious entities and transactions), adverse media screening (i.e., screening an entity against a negative source of information), sentiment analysis (assessing market sentiment from news and social media), risk management (e.g., recognizing potential financial risks and exposures), and extracting actionable insights from financial news, market events, players, competition, trends, and products.

RavenPack Analytics: The Market Leader in Financial Named Entity Recognition

The market for products and services that depend on named entity recognition methods is rapidly expanding. Prominent names in this field include RavenPack, Info-Ngen, OptiRisk Systems, and LSEG's Machine Readable News.

RavenPack News Analytics (RNA) (*https://oreil.ly/paVLa*) is the world-leading news insights and analytics resource. RavenPack collects and analyzes unstructured content from more than 40,000 sources such as Dow Jones Newswires, the *Wall Street Journal*, *Barron's*, MT Newswires, PR Newswire, Alliance News, MarketWatch, The Fly, and providers of regulatory news, press releases, and articles.

RavenPack News Analytics computes 20+ years of point-in-time data and provides event and sentiment data on more than 350,000 entities in over 130 countries, including the following:

- 110,000+ global, public, and private companies across all sectors
- 165,000+ macro entities such as places, currencies, persons, and organizations
- 7,000+ key business and geopolitical and macroeconomic events detected and enriched with sentiment and relevance scores

For each record in RavenPack News Analytics, information is available on:

- The entity (e.g., name, domicile, RavenPack's unique entity identifiers, and other identifiers)
- Event Category
- Event Sentiment Score (how negative or positive an event is [range $-1 \rightarrow 1$])
- Event Similarity Days (how novel is the event, measured as the number of days passed [range $0 \rightarrow 365$] since a similar event occurred)
- Event Relevance Score (how relevant is an event [range $0 \rightarrow 100$] based on where it occurs—e.g., a headline has a high ERS)

To identify and extract these relevant aspects from news data, RavenPack built a proprietary named entity recognition system. RavenPack maintains a database of predefined entities with more than 50 distinct entity types to provide timely and high-quality data. Moreover, RavenPack expands and extends its database as new and relevant types of entities or events appear in the market.

In building its NER system, RavenPack faced a special requirement for the financial sector: entity names may change over time, and the same name may refer to different entities at different times. This might lead to problems such as survivorship bias, where only the latest assignee or an identifier or surviving entities are considered, skewing the data and the analysis. To solve this issue, RavenPack constructed a point-in-time-aware NER system.

The main idea behind NER is to take an annotated text such as...

> Google has invested more than $1 Billion in Renewable Energy projects in the United States over the past 5 years

... and produce a new block of text that highlights the position and type of entities, as illustrated in Figure 4-1. In this example, six types of entities are recognized: company, currency, amount, sector, time, and location.

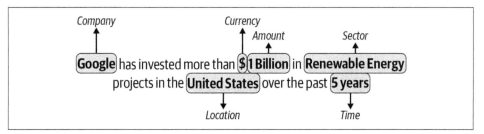

Figure 4-1. An illustration of the outcome of NER

For the sake of illustration, let's walk through a practical example. A well-known financial dataset is LSEG Loan Pricing Corporation DealScan (*https://oreil.ly/vyDek*), which offers comprehensive coverage of the syndicated loans market. A syndicated loan (also known as a syndicated facility) is a special type of loan where a group of lenders (the syndicate) jointly provide a large loan to a company or an organization. Within the syndicate, different agents assume various roles (e.g., participating bank, lead arranger, documentation agent, security agent, etc.). LSEG and similar data providers collect information about syndicated loans from multiple sources, with SEC filings such as 8-Ks as the primary source.

Let's consider a scenario where your team is tasked with creating a dataset on syndicated loans using a collection of SEC filings. Your first step involves extracting data from the text, identifying various elements that characterize a syndicated facility, and then organizing this information into a structured format. Let's take the following example of an SEC filing for a syndicated facility agreement given to an Australian company (the text below is quoted and highlighted from the SEC filing (*https://oreil.ly/Bq5ER*)):

> *Exhibit 10.1*
>
> *SYNDICATED FACILITY AGREEMENT*
>
> *dated as of **September 18, 2012***
>
> *among*
>
> ***THE MAC SERVICES GROUP PTY LIMITED** ,*
>
> *as Borrower,*
>
> *THE LENDERS NAMED HEREIN,*
>
> *J .P. MORGAN AUSTRALIA LIMITED ,*
>
> *as **Australian Agent** and **Security Trustee** ,*
>
> ***JPMORGAN CHASE BANK, N.A.** ,*
>
> *as **US Agent** ,*
>
> *JPMORGAN CHASE BANK, N.A.,*
>
> *as **Issuing Bank***
>
> *and*
>
> *JPMORGAN CHASE BANK, N.A.,*
>
> *as **Swing Line Lender***
>
> *J.P. MORGAN SECURITIES LLC ,*
>
> *as **Lead Arranger** and **Sole Bookrunner***
>
> *…*
>
> *The Borrower has requested the Lenders to extend credit, in the form of **Loans or Credits** (as hereinafter defined), to the Borrower in an aggregate principal amount at any time outstanding not in excess of **AUD$300,000,000** .*

As you can see, the text includes details regarding the borrower, lenders, and their respective roles, as well as information about the facility type, amount, and currency. Leveraging NER, we can extract this information and construct a structured dataset. For simplicity, let's design a dataset with three tables: one to store facility data, another for borrower details, and a third for lender information. Figure 4-2 shows what the *Entity Relationship Model* of our dataset looks like. In the facility table, the facility_id is an arbitrarily assigned unique identifier. In the borrower and lender tables, the facility_id is present as a foreign key, meaning that records will exist in these tables only for facilities that exist in the facility table.

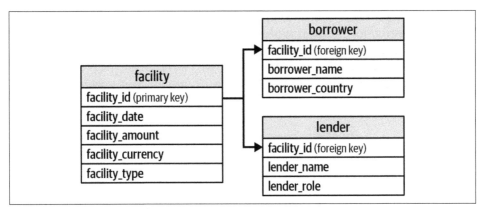

Figure 4-2. Entity Relationship Model (ERM) of the syndicated loan database

The result of a successful NER-based entity extraction would look like the data present in Tables 4-1, 4-2, and 4-3.

Table 4-1. Facility table

facility_id	facility_date	facility_amount	facility_currency	facility_type
89763	2012-09-18	300,000,000	AUD	Loans or Credits

Table 4-2. Borrower table

facility_id	borrower_name	borrower_country
89763	The Mac Services Group PTY Limited	Australia

Table 4-3. Lender table

facility_id	lender	lender_role
89763	J.P. Morgan Australia Limited	Australian Agent and Security Trustee
89763	JPMorgan Chase Bank, N.A.	US Agent
89763	JPMorgan Chase Bank, N.A.	Issuing Bank
89763	JPMorgan Chase Bank, N.A.	Swing Line Lender
89763	J.P. Morgan Securities LLC	Lead Arranger
89763	J.P. Morgan Securities LLC	Bookrunner

Crucially, although an NER system can identify the occurrence of a specific entity in the text, it typically does not link it to the corresponding real-world object. For example, if you refer back to Figure 4-1, Google was labeled as COMPANY, but at this point, we still don't know which real-world company this is. To accomplish this task, an additional technique, called *named entity disambiguation* (NED) or entity linking, is often used.

Many books treat NED as a separate problem from NER and dedicate a separate section to it. However, for financial applications, linking the identified entities to their real-world matches is essential. For this reason, I consider NED an additional step in the NER process. Figure 4-3 demonstrates how NED works in conjunction with NER to link the recognized entity (COMPANY) to its specific real-world counterpart (Google).

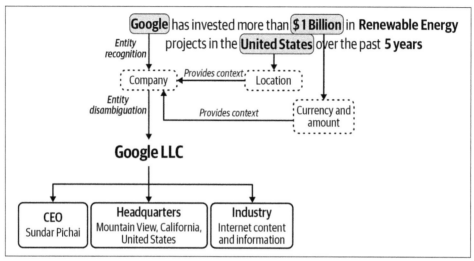

Figure 4-3. Named entity recognition and disambiguation

In NED, entities identified in the text are mapped to their unique real-world counterparts using a *knowledge base*. A knowledge base is a central repository that contains information about a vast array of subjects. These can be general-purpose or specialized and may be public or private. For example, Wikipedia is a well-known public, general-purpose knowledge base, while Investopedia serves a similar role but focuses specifically on finance. Other notable examples include GeoNames, Wikidata, DBpedia, and YAGO. Financial institutions and data vendors may also create proprietary knowledge bases tailored to their specific needs using their own data.

How Does Named Entity Recognition Work?

In this section, we will explore the various steps involved in building an NER system. As illustrated in Figure 4-4, the first step is data preprocessing, which ensures the data is structured, cleaned, harmonized, and ready for analysis. The second step, entity extraction, involves identifying the locations of all candidate entities. In the third step, these candidate entities are categorized into their respective entity types. Subsequently, the quality and completeness of the extracted data and the performance of the model are assessed in the evaluation step. Finally, the recognized entities can optionally be linked to their unique real-world counterparts through the disambigua-tion process.

Note that NER is an iterative process. Once the model is evaluated, the modeler can determine if improvements in data preprocessing, model selection, or training tech-niques are necessary to enhance the NER system's performance.

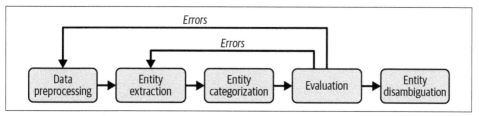

Figure 4-4. Named entity extraction and disambiguation process

Data preprocessing

Methodologically speaking, NER is a subtask of the field of *natural language process-ing* (NLP) (*https://oreil.ly/NbKiz*). As with most NLP tasks, NER achieves good results if applied to clean and high-quality data. A variety of NLP-specific data preparation techniques can be used with NER. These include the following:

Tokenization
> Tokenization is the process of breaking down the text into smaller units called *tokens*. Word tokenization breaks down the text into single words; for example, "Google invests in Renewable Energy" becomes ["Google", "invests", "in", "Renew-able", "Energy"]. Sentence tokenization breaks down text into smaller individual sentences; for example, "Google invests in Renewable Energy" gets converted into ["Google", "invests in", "Renewable Energy"].

Stop word removal
> Stop words are common and frequent words that have very little or no value for modeling or performance. For example, the English words "is," "the," and "and" are often classified as stop words. In most NLP tasks, including NER, stop words are filtered out.

Canonicalization
> In NLP, the form and conjugation of the word are often of no value. For example, the words "invest, investing, invests, invested" convey the same type of action; therefore, they can all be mapped to their base form, i.e., "invest." The process of mapping words in a text to their root/base forms is known as *canonicalization*.
>
> Two types of canonicalization techniques are often used: *stemming* and *lemmati-zation*. Stemming is a heuristic technique that involves removing affixes from a word to produce its stem. This method is quick and efficient but can produce

imprecise results, as it often leads to over-stemming (reducing words too much) or under-stemming (not reducing them enough). To address the limitations of stemming, lemmatization techniques are often used. Using vocabulary and morphological analysis, a lemmatizer tries to infer the dictionary form (lemma) of words based on their intended meaning. There are several common lemmitization techniques:

Lowercase conversion
This consists of converting all words to lowercase.

Synonym replacement
This technique involves replacing words with one of their synonyms.

Contractions removal
Contractions are words written as a combination of a shortened word with another word. Contraction removal consists of transforming the words in a contraction into their full-length form, e.g., "she'd invest in stocks" becomes "she would invest in stocks."

Standardization (normalization) of date and time formats
For example, dates are converted to YYYYMMDD format, and timestamps to YYYMMDDHH24MMSS.

 NER is highly sensitive to data preprocessing, where even minor changes can significantly impact the results. It's essential to carefully assess the consequences of each preprocessing step. For example, converting all words to uppercase could disrupt rules dictating entity characteristics, such as the expectation that country names begin with uppercase letters.

Entity extraction

During entity extraction, an algorithm is applied to a corpus of clean text to detect and locate candidate entities. In this step, the NER system designer should know which type of entities they are looking for in the text. The extraction process is a *segmentation* problem, where the goal is to find all meaningful segments of text that represent an entity. In this case, the name "Bank of England" needs to be identified as a single entity, even if the word "England" could also be a meaningful entity.

Since the goal of this step is to locate references to an entity, it might produce correct yet imperfect results. For example, unnecessary tokens might be included, as in "Banking giant JP Morgan Chase". In other cases, some tokens might be omitted, such as missing "Inc." in "JP Morgan Chase Inc." or "Michael" in "Michael Bloomberg."

Entity categorization

Once all candidate entities in the text have been extracted, the next step is to accurately map each valid entity to its corresponding entity type. For example, "Bank of America" should be classified as a company (COMP), "United States" as a country (LOC), "Bill Gates" as a person (PER), and any other token should be labeled as "O" to indicate that it is not a relevant entity.

The main challenge in this step is language ambiguity. For example, the words *bear* and *bull* are frequently used to indicate two species of animals. However, in financial markets, the word bull is often used to indicate an upward trend in the market, while bear describes a receding market.

Another example involves similar names that could refer to different entities. For instance, "JP Morgan" might describe the well-known financial institution JPMorgan Chase, but it could also refer to John Pierpont Morgan, the American financier who founded J.P. Morgan Bank.

To illustrate the NER process up to this step, we should be able to take a text such as...

> Gold prices rose more than 1% on Wednesday after the U.S. Federal Reserve flagged an end to its interest rate hike cycle and indicated possible rate cuts next year.[1]

...and produce a structured categorization, as illustrated in Table 4-4. In this example, five types of entities were extracted: commodity (CMDTY), variable (VAR), nationality (NAL), organization (ORG), and miscellaneous (O).

Table 4-4. Outcome of entity extraction and categorization of a news title

entity_type	text
CMDTY	Gold
VAR	Prices
NAL	U.S.
ORG	Federal Reserve
O	rose more than 1% on Wednesday after the
O	flagged an end to its interest rate hike cycle and indicated possible rate cuts next year.

---

1 Ashitha Shivaprasad and Sherin Elizabeth Varghese, "Gold Climbs Over 1% After Fed Signals End of Rate Hikes" (*https://oreil.ly/isQBl*), Reuters (December 2023).

Entity disambiguation

If you aim to extend beyond merely extracting entities, which is crucial in numerous financial applications, you must proceed to disambiguate the identified and validated entities. This involves establishing a link between each correctly recognized entity in the data and its unique real-world counterpart.

The entity disambiguation step can present some challenges. One major issue is name variations. For example, a company can be mentioned in multiple ways, such as Bank of America, Bank of America Corporation, BoA, or BofA. Entity ambiguity is another challenge. For example, Bloomberg can refer to the company Bloomberg L.P. or its CEO, Michael Bloomberg. Finally, the knowledge bases used to disambiguate the entities might not always contain up-to-date information on all specific or novel entities that emerge in the market.

If we take our example, illustrated in Table 4-4, adding entity disambiguation would result in real-world references, as illustrated in Table 4-5. This example is illustrative, and more precise references could be used. For instance, the spot and future prices could be linked to a specific commodity exchange such as CME.

Table 4-5. Outcome of an entity extraction, categorization, and disambiguation of a news title

entity_type	text	reference
CMDTY	Gold	Chemical element with symbol AU
VAR	Prices	Spot price and future price on commodity exchanges
NAL	U.S.	Country in North America
ORG	Federal Reserve	Central Bank of the United States of America
O	rose more than 1% on Wednesday after the	
O	flagged an end to its interest rate hike cycle and indicated possible rate cuts next year.	

Evaluation

Evaluating the performance of NER systems in terms of their accuracy and efficiency is the last step in NER. An accurate NER system should detect and recognize all valid entities, correctly assign them to the appropriate entity types, and optionally link them to their real-world counterparts. Besides analytical performance, NER systems must also be assessed based on their computational efficiency, which includes runtime, memory consumption, storage requirements, CPU usage, and scalability to handle large-scale financial applications with millions of records.

To compute performance metrics for an NER system, four kinds of results are needed:

False positive (FP)
    An instance incorrectly identified as an entity by the NER system

False negative (FN)
    An instance that the NER system fails to classify as an entity, even though it is an actual entity in the ground truth

True positive (TP)
    An instance correctly identified as an entity by the NER system

True negative (TN)
    An instance correctly identified as a nonentity, consistent with the ground truth

These four values are often represented in a special tabular format known as a *confusion matrix*, as illustrated in Figure 4-5.

		Actual values	
		Actually is an entity	Is not an actual entity
Predicted values	Recognized as entity	True positive (TP)	False postive (FP)
	Not recognized as entity	False negative (FN)	True negative (TN)

Figure 4-5. Confusion matrix of NER

To compute the confusion matrix of a given NER model, you need to have a ground truth dataset with the actual values. The ground truth is mainly used for model training, where predicted values are compared against their true counterparts. This is usually a major challenge in NER, especially if you have big datasets. You, as a financial data engineer, will play a primary role in building and maintaining a labeled database to be used as the ground truth for NER systems.

Using the confusion matrix, the following performance evaluation metrics can be computed:

Accuracy
    Accuracy measures the overall performance of the NER model and answers the question, "Out of all the classifications that were made, how many were correct?" In NER, this can be used as a measure of the ability of the model to distinguish

between what is an entity from what is not. Accuracy works well as an evaluation metric if the cost of false positives and false negatives is more or less similar. This can be represented as a formula as follows:

$$Accuracy = \frac{TP + TN}{TP + TN + FP + FN}$$

Precision

Precision measures the proportion of true positives to the number of all positives that the model predicted. It answers the question, "Of all instances that were classified as true positives, how many are correct?" In NER, this could be interpreted as the percentage of tokens (words or sentences) that were correctly recognized as entities out of all the tokens that are actually entities. A low precision value would indicate that the model is not good at avoiding false positives. Precision is a good measure when the cost of false positives is quite high. This can be represented as a formula as follows:

$$Precision = \frac{TP}{FP + TP}$$

Recall

Recall measures the true positive rate of the model by answering the question, "Out of all instances that should be classified as true positives, how many were correctly classified as such?" Low recall indicates that the model is not good at avoiding false negatives. The recall is a good measure to use when the cost of a false negative is high. This can be represented as a formula as follows:

$$Recall = \frac{TP}{TP + FN}$$

F1 score

The F1 score is a harmonic mean of precision and recall. It is widely used when the class representation in the data is imbalanced or when the cost of both false positives and false negatives is high. In financial NER, this is likely to be the case, as the vast majority of data tokens are not entities and the cost of mistakes is high. This can be represented as a formula as follows:

$$F1score = \frac{2 * (Recall * Precision)}{Recall + Precision}$$

Additional evaluation metrics can be derived from the confusion matrix.[2] In many research papers on NER, the F1 score is used as the default metric. However, I highly recommend that you compute all four metrics to have an overview of your NER performance from different angles. For example, a low precision might tell you that you have a rule in your model that easily classifies a token as an entity. Similarly, a low recall might tell you that your model hardly classifies an entity as such; maybe your rules are too strict.

Now that you understand the necessary steps for developing an NER system, let's explore the main modeling approaches that can be employed to build and operationalize an NER system.

Approaches to Named Entity Recognition

Numerous NER methods and techniques have been proposed in academic literature and by market participants. Frequently, these solutions are tailored or fine-tuned to suit particular domains. In this book, I will offer a taxonomy of seven modeling approaches: lexicon-based, rule-based, feature-engineering-based machine learning, deep learning, large language models, wikification, and knowledge graphs.

One thing to keep in mind is that these approaches aren't necessarily mutually exclusive. In many cases, especially when building complex NER systems, developers employ a combination of techniques. In the upcoming sections, I will discuss each of the seven approaches with some level of detail.

Lexicon/dictionary-based approach

This approach works by first constructing a lexicon or dictionary of vocabulary using external sources and then matching text tokens with entity names in the dictionary. A financial dataset, like reference or entity datasets, can function as a lexicon. Lexicons are flexible and can be tailored to any domain. For this reason, this approach could be a good choice for domain-specific tasks where the universe of entities is small or constant, or evolves slowly. Examples include sector names, financial instrument classes, and company names. Other examples might include accounting or legal texts, which rely on standard principles and formal language that doesn't change much over time.

Lexicons serve a dual purpose in NER. They can function as the primary extraction method or complement other techniques, as I'll illustrate later. Furthermore, a lexicon can be used for entity disambiguation. For example, a lexicon mapping company names to their identities can handle both recognition and disambiguation tasks.

---

2 Have a look at the confusion matrix Wikipedia page (*https://oreil.ly/IUCXZ*) for more details.

The main advantages of lexicons are processing speed and simplicity. If you have a lexicon, then the extraction process can be viewed as a simple dictionary lookup. Keep in mind, however, that lexicons cannot recognize new entities that are not in the dictionary (e.g., new types of financial instruments). Additionally, lexicons are highly sensitive to the quality of data preprocessing and the presence of errors. As they cannot deal with exceptions or erratic data types, lexicons tend to guarantee better performance on high-quality data. Finally, lexicons might produce false positives if the context is not taken into account. For example, a stock ticker lexicon might contain the symbol AAPL for Apple, Inc. However, the abbreviation AAPL may also refer to "American Association of Professional Landmen" or "American Academy of Psychiatry and the Law."

Rule-based approach

The rule-based approach employs a set of rules, created either manually or automatically, to recognize the presence of an entity in text. For example:

- *Rule N.1*: the number after currency symbols is a monetary value, e.g., $200.
- *Rule N.2*: the word after Mrs. or Mr. is a person's name.
- *Rule N.3*: the word before a company suffix is a company name, e.g., Inc., Ltd., Inc., Incorporated, Corporation, etc.
- *Rule N.4*: alphanumeric strings could be security identifiers if they match the length of the identifier and can be validated with a check-digit method.

Similar to the lexicon approach, rule-based methods tend to be domain-specific, making their transferability to other domains challenging. They are also particularly sensitive to data preprocessing issues, exceptions, and textual ambiguity, which can result in an large set of rules. Complex rule-based approaches are difficult to maintain, hard to understand, and can be slow to run. Therefore, they are recommended in cases where the language is either simple or subject to formal standards, such as accounting, annual reports, or SEC filings.

Feature-engineering machine learning approach

Lexicon- and rule-based methods commonly face challenges when complex data patterns need to be identified for accurate NER. In such cases, modeling presents a compelling alternative. One prominent method involves feature-engineering machine learning, wherein a multiclass classification model is trained to predict and categorize words in a text. Being supervised, this approach requires the existence of labeled data for training.

To apply supervised machine learning, the modeler must select, and in most cases engineer, a set of features for each token.[3] To give a few examples, features can be something like the following:

- Part-of-speech tagging (noun, verb, auxiliary, etc.)
- The word type (all-capitalized, all-digits, alphanumeric, etc.)
- Whether it's a courtesy title (Mr., Ms., Miss, etc.)
- The word match from a lexicon or gazetteer (e.g., San Francisco: City in California)
- Whether the previous word is a courtesy title
- Whether the word is a currency symbol (¥, $, etc.)
- Whether the previous word is a currency symbol
- Whether the word is at the beginning or end of the paragraph
- Context aggregation features that capture the surrounding context of a word (e.g., the previous and subsequent n words)[4]
- Prediction of another ML classifier[5]

Once all relevant features have been carefully engineered, a variety of algorithms can be used. Among the most popular choices are logistic regression, Random Forests, Conditional Random Fields, Hidden Markov Models, support vector machines, and Maximum Entropy Models.

Feature-based models offer several advantages, such as speed of training and feature interpretability. However, several challenges might arise, such as the need for financial domain expertise, the complexity of feature engineering, difficulty modeling nonlinear patterns, and the inability to capture complex contexts for longer sentences. This is where more advanced machine learning techniques, such as deep learning, come into play, which I will introduce next.

---

3 For a detailed discussion on how to design features for NER, see Lev Ratinov and Dan Roth's article, "Design Challenges and Misconceptions in Named Entity Recognition" (*https://oreil.ly/FBOOo*), in *Proceedings of the Thirteenth Conference on Computational Natural Language Learning (CoNLL-2009)*: 147–155, and Rahul Sharnagat's "Named Entity Recognition: A Literature Survey" (*https://oreil.ly/gXgGK*), *Center For Indian Language Technology* (June 2014): 1–27.

4 To learn more about context aggregation, see the method proposed in Hai Leong Chieu and Hwee Tou Ng's "Named Entity Recognition with a Maximum Entropy Approach" (*https://oreil.ly/rqs0C*), in *Proceedings of the Seventh Conference on Natural Language Learning at HLT-NAACL 2003*: 160–163.

5 To learn more about this advanced technique, see Radu Florian, Abe Ittycheriah, Hongyan Jing, and Tong Zhang's "Named Entity Recognition Through Classifier Combination" (*https://oreil.ly/BWMFm*), in *Proceedings of the Seventh Conference on Natural Language Learning at HLT-NAACL 2003*: 168–171.

Deep learning approach

In recent years, deep learning (DL) has established itself as the state-of-the-art approach for NER.[6] DL is a prominent subfield of machine learning that works by learning a hierarchical representation of data via a neural network composed of multiple layers and a set of activation functions. A neural network can be thought of as a computational graph where each layer of nodes performs nonlinear function compositions of simpler functions produced at the previous layer. Interestingly, this process of repeated composition of functions has significant modeling power, which has contributed to the success of deep learning in solving complex problems.

There are several advantages to applying DL to NER. First, the modeler doesn't need to worry about the complexities involved in feature engineering, as deep neural networks are capable of learning and extracting features automatically. Second, DL can model a large number of complex and nonlinear patterns in the data. Third, neural networks can capture long-range correlations and context dependencies in the text. Fourth, DL offers high flexibility through network specifications (depth, width, layers, hyperparameters, etc.), which allows the modeling of a large number of domain-specific problems on large datasets.

A wide variety of network structures exist within the DL field. The ones that have shown remarkable success in NER-related tasks are Recurrent Neural Networks and their variants, such as Long Short-Term Memory, Bidirectional Long Short-Term Memory, and, most recently, attention mechanism-based models, such as Transformers.[7]

Deep learning is a powerful and advanced technique. However, I advise against using it by default for your NER task. DL models are hard to interpret and may require special hardware (e.g., a graphics processing unit, or GPU) and time to train. Try a simple approach first. If it doesn't work, then use more complex techniques.

Given the remarkable performance of complex models like DL in text-related tasks, development has extended to even more sophisticated models, such as large language models (LLMs), which I'll explore next.

---

6 For a good survey of the use of deep learning in NER, see Jing Li, Aixin Sun, Jianglei Han, and Chenliang Li's "A Survey on Deep Learning for Named Entity Recognition" (*https://oreil.ly/vCBtQ*), *IEEE Transactions on Knowledge and Data Engineering* 34, no. 1 (January 2020): 50–70.

7 A good read on the use of Transformers for NER is offered by Cedric Lothritz, Kevin Allix, Lisa Veiber, Jacques Klein, and Tegawendé François D. Assise Bissyande in "Evaluating Pretrained Transformer-Based Models on the Task of Fine-Grained Named Entity Recognition" (*https://oreil.ly/MHueQ*), in *Proceedings of the 28th International Conference on Computational Linguistics* (2020): 3750–3760.

Large language models

A large language model (LLM) is an advanced type of generative artificial intelligence model designed to learn and generate human-like text. Most LLMs leverage a deep learning architecture known as a Transformer, proposed in the seminal paper "Attention Is All You Need" (*https://oreil.ly/58cuk*). Techniques such as Reinforcement Learning from Human Feedback (RLHF) are often used to align LLMs to human preferences. LLMs may also utilize other techniques such as transfer learning, active learning, ensemble learning, embeddings, and others.

LLMs are quite massive, often trained on vast amounts of text data and comprising millions or even billions of parameters. General-purpose LLMs are commonly known as *foundational models*, highlighting their versatility and wide-ranging applicability across numerous tasks. Prominent examples include OpenAI's Generative Pre-trained Transformer (GPT) series, such as GPT-3 and GPT-4, Google's BERT (Bidirectional Encoder Representations from Transformers), Meta's Llama, Mistral, and Claude. LLMs are capable of performing a wide range of general-purpose natural language processing tasks, including text generation, summarization, entity recognition, translation, question answering, and more.

LLMs can also be fine-tuned to specific domains. Fine-tuning is the process of retraining a pre-trained LLM on a domain-specific dataset, allowing it to adapt its knowledge and language understanding to suit better the terminology, vocabulary, syntax, and context of the target domain. For example, the FinBERT (*https://oreil.ly/J5vhT*) is a domain-specific adaptation of the BERT model, fine-tuned specifically for the financial domain. It is trained on a vast amount of financial texts, such as news articles, earnings reports, and financial statements, to understand and process financial language and terminology effectively. FinBERT can be used for various tasks in the financial domain, including sentiment analysis, named entity recognition, text classification, and more.

LLMs can be a powerful technique for financial NER. This is because they are able to understand and process complex and domain-specific language, recognizing entities such as financial instruments, accounting, and regulatory terms, as well as company and person names within the context of financial markets. For example, an LLM may be able to distinguish "Apple Inc." as a tech company listed on NASDAQ from the word "apple" as a fruit, using contextual clues from surrounding text. They can also identify financial terms such as "S&P 100," "NASDAQ Composite," and "Dow Jones Industrial Average" as indexes rather than just random phrases. Similarly, LLMs may be able to distinguish between terms like "call option" and "put option," understanding that they refer to specific types of financial derivatives, despite their similar structure.

Crucially, while LLMs may show outstanding performance in many financial language processing tasks, they can still encounter challenges with specialized and evolving financial terminology. For example, financial terms such as "interest rate swap" (CDS), "collateralized debt obligation" (CDO), and "mortgage-backed securities" (MBS) necessitate a deep understanding of financial instruments and their contexts. Similarly, terms such as "bonds" and "equity" have completely different meanings in finance than in the general sense. Furthermore, terms like "bitcoin," "blockchain," "cryptocurrency," and "DeFi" (decentralized finance) have emerged relatively recently and require continuous model updates to stay current.

Retrieval-Augmented Generation

Retrieval-augmented generation (RAG) is an advanced technique employed to enhance the factual grounding, contextual relevance, and response accuracy of language models, especially in specialized domains like finance. RAG operates by retrieving relevant information from external sources, such as databases or documents, and incorporating this data into a language model's input prompt, thereby providing additional context to produce more accurate and contextually relevant responses.

In finance-specific tasks like financial NER, RAG enhances accuracy by disambiguating entities, staying up-to-date with rapidly changing information, and integrating domain-specific knowledge from financial documents and databases. This capability makes RAG particularly effective for identifying financial entities and handling complex jargon. Crucially, the success of RAG largely depends on the availability of reliable external data sources, highlighting its foundation in data engineering.

Another major challenge with LLMs is *hallucination*, which happens when an LLM generates irrelevant, factually wrong, or inconsistent content. Interpretability and transparency represent additional challenges, particularly in finance, where regulatory compliance and trust in decision-making are crucial.

Wikification

Wikification is an entity disambiguation technique that links recognized named entities to their corresponding real-world Wikipedia page. Figure 4-6 illustrates this technique through an example. In the first step (entity recognition), two entities (Seattle and Amazon) are identified. In the next step, the identified entities are linked to their unique matching Wikipedia page.

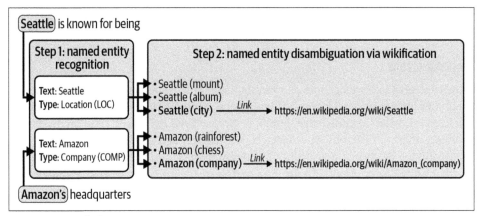

Figure 4-6. Wikification process

Several wikification techniques have been proposed, the majority of which utilize similarity metrics to determine which Wikipedia page is most similar to the recognized entity. One prominent implementation was first presented in Silviu Cucerzan's groundbreaking work (*https://oreil.ly/BIhsI*). Cucerzan proposed a knowledge base that incorporates the following elements:

Article entity/concept
    Most Wikipedia articles have an entity/concept associated with them.

Entity class
    Person, location, organization, and miscellaneous.

Entity surface forms
    The terms used to reference the entity in text.

Contexts
    Terms that co-occur or describe the entity.

Tags
    Subjects the entity belongs to.

For example, the term *Berkeley* (*https://oreil.ly/vT5eq*) can refer to a large number of real-world entities, including places, people, schools, and hotels. Assume we are interested in identifying the University of California, Berkeley. In this case, the entity type is school or university; the context could be California, a public university, or a research university; tags might include education, research, science, and others; and the entity surface form might be simply Berkeley.

An entity is disambiguated by first identifying its surface form. Subsequently, two vector representations that encode contexts and tags are constructed: one for the Wikipedia context that occurs in the document and another for the Wikipedia entity.

Finally, the assignment to a Wikipedia page is made via a process that maximizes the similarity between the document and entity vectors.

Knowledge graphs

Knowledge graphs have become an essential technique in internet-based information search and have been widely applied in entity disambiguation. There isn't yet a clear definition of what a knowledge graph is (*https://oreil.ly/xHyFe*). Still, it basically involves gathering different types of facts, knowledge, and content from many sources, organizing them into a network of nodes and links, and using it to provide more information to users upon submitting a search query. In other words, a knowledge graph can be thought of as a network of real-world entities—i.e., persons, locations, materials, events, and organizations—related together via labeled directed edges. Figure 4-7 presents a simple illustrative example of a knowledge graph around the company Dell Technologies. The graph illustrates Dell Technologies and several related entities, such as its CEO, Michael Dell, and its supplier, Intel Corporation.

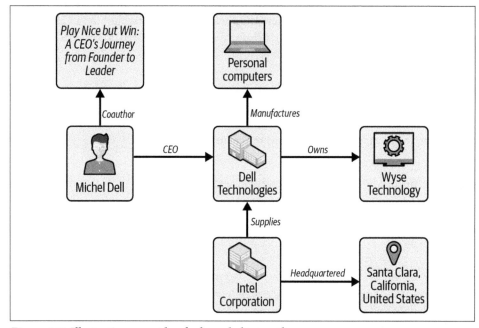

Figure 4-7. Illustrative example of a knowledge graph

The power of knowledge graphs stems from their extreme flexibility, which allows them to encompass a wide range of elements and interactions. This, in turn, can improve search results and reveal hidden data links that might otherwise go undetected using more traditional approaches.

Knowledge graphs have been proposed as an advanced approach to entity disambiguation within NER systems. A well-known implementation is the Accurate Online Disambiguation of Named Entities (*https://oreil.ly/Kzd_0*), or AIDA. It constructs a "mention-entity" graph, where nodes represent mentions of entities found in the text, as well as the potential entities these mentions could refer to. These nodes are connected with weighted links based on the similarity between the context of the mention and the context of each entity. This helps the system figure out which entity the mention is most likely referring to. Additionally, AIDA connects the entities themselves with each other using weighted links. This allows AIDA to capture coherence among entities within the graph, aiding in the disambiguation process.

AIDA utilizes the *densest subgraph algorithm* to search the mention-entity graph. The densest subgraph algorithm helps identify the most densely connected subgraph within the larger graph. In the context of AIDA, this subgraph represents the set of mentions and entities that are most closely related to each other based on their connections and similarities. By identifying this densest subgraph, AIDA can determine the most coherent and relevant set of mentions and entities for a given context.

Two challenges may arise when finding such dense subgraphs. First, you need a reliable definition of the notion of a dense subgraph that ensures coherence and context similarity. Second, dense-subgraph problems are computationally expensive and almost NP-hard problems. This means that a heuristic or efficient algorithm is needed to guarantee a fast graph search to find the optimal dense subgraph.

Named Entity Recognition Software Libraries

Practitioners in industry and academia have created several software tools for NER. Several open source tools are available, including spaCy, NLTK, OpenNLP, CoreNLP, NeuroNER, polyglot, and GATE.

In addition to open source solutions, financial institutions and data providers build proprietary NER solutions. The most famous example is RavenPack analytics, which we discussed earlier in this chapter. Another prominent example is NERD (Named Entity Recognition and Disambiguation) (*https://oreil.ly/9lpaZ*), developed by S&P Global's AI accelerator, Kensho. NERD is one of the few entity recognition and disambiguation tools tailored specifically for financial entities. NERD takes a text document as input and identifies mentions of named entities such as companies, organizations, and people. It also links the extracted entities to their real-world entries in the S&P Global comprehensive Capital IQ database.

FactSet provides a Natural Language Processing API (*https://oreil.ly/7l-f7*) that can be used to recognize and locate a wide range of entities in structured and semi-structured texts. This includes companies, people, locations, health conditions, drug names, numbers, monetary values, and dates. In addition to NER, the API allows entity disambiguation by finding the best matching FactSet identifiers for companies and people found in the text.

Another tool that might be used for NER is *Automated Machine Learning* (AutoML). These solutions offer simple and user-friendly interfaces to automatically choose, train, and tune the best ML model/algorithm for a particular problem. One of the main advantages of AutoML is that it allows nonexperts to use sophisticated ML models. Examples of AutoML tools include open source libraries such as Auto-sklearn, AutoGluon, AutoKeras, and H20 AutoML, as well as cloud-based managed solutions such as Google AutoML and Amazon Sagemaker.[8]

AWS offers a specialized NLP AutoML service called Amazon Comprehend. Comprehend already has trained NER capabilities that you can immediately interact with, and it also offers the option to customize an NER system to your specific task (e.g., detecting financial entities). In addition, AWS introduced Bedrock, a managed service that allows users to build and fine-tune generative AI applications with foundation models.

Financial Entity Resolution

Once entities have been recognized and identified, a system should be available whereby the data associated with a unique entity in one dataset can be matched with data held in another dataset for the same unique entity. This process is very common in finance and is known as entity resolution (ER). In this section, you will learn what ER is and why it is important in finance. Then, you will learn how ER systems work and the different approaches to ER. Finally, I will present a list of software libraries and tools available for performing ER.

---

8 One thing to keep in mind is that AutoML may be too generic to deal with the peculiarities of NER. For more on this issue, see Matteo Paganelli, Francesco Del Buono, Marco Pevarello, Francesco Guerra, and Maurizio Vincini's "Automated Machine Learning for Entity Matching Tasks" (*https://oreil.ly/Slvk4*), in the *Proceedings of the 24th International Conference on Extending Database Technology (EDBT 2021)*, Nicosia, Cyprus, March 23–26, 2021: 325–330.

Entity Resolution Described

Entity resolution, also known as record linkage or data matching, refers to the process of identifying and matching records that refer to the same unique entity within a single data source or across multiple sources, particularly when a unique identifier is unavailable. When ER is applied to a single dataset, it is often done to identify and remove duplicate records (*record deduplication*). When it is applied to multiple datasets, the goal is to match and aggregate all relevant information about an entity (*record linkage*).

Mathematically, let's represent two data sources as A and B and denote records in A as a and records in B as b. The set of records that represent identical entities in A and B can be written as:

$$M = \{(a, b); a = b; a \in A; b \in B\}$$

And the set of records that represent distinct entities as:

$$U = \{(a, b); a \neq b; a \in A; b \in B\}$$

As we will see later in this chapter, the main objective of an ER system is to distinguish the set of matches M from the set of non-matches U.

The Importance of Entity Resolution in Finance

Entity resolution is a common practice and represents a main challenge in the finance domain. As a financial data engineer, you will likely encounter the need to develop an ER system. Various industry initiatives have been established to address the financial ER problem. For instance, the Financial Entity Identification and Information Integration (FEIII) Challenge (*https://oreil.ly/dTFQB*) was initiated to create methodologies for aligning the various financial entity identification schemes and identifiers. Despite these efforts, the problem remains unresolved for several reasons, which I will outline next.

Multiple identifiers

As you learned in Chapter 3, financial markets rely on a large number of data identification systems, each developed with a specific goal, structure, and scope. As such, it is typical that different financial datasets come with different identifiers. One financial identifier is typically sufficient to identify and distinguish unique entities when working with a single dataset. However, in many cases, people need to work with multiple datasets at once. For example, financial analysts or machine learning experts might require a sample of data and features that span multiple data sources. To this end, different datasets might need to be merged via an ER system to create a comprehensive dataset for the analysis.

Figure 4-8 illustrates a basic ER example where two datasets with different identifiers are matched. The table on the left contains six records identified by identifier B, while the table on the right holds data for the same records but uses identifier A. ER is performed by matching identifiers A and B, as depicted by the arrows. The resulting identifier mapping is as follows: 111 maps to BBB, 333 maps to AAA, and 222 maps to CCC.

Dataset with identifier B				Dataset with identifier A		
Feature 4	Feature 3	Identifier B		Identifier A	Feature 1	Feature 2
record_value	record_value	BBB		111	record_value	record_value
record_value	record_value	BBB		111	record_value	record_value
record_value	record_value	AAA	Entity resolution	333	record_value	record_value
record_value	record_value	AAA		333	record_value	record_value
record_value	record_value	CCC		222	record_value	record_value

Figure 4-8. Entity resolution in the presence of two different identifiers

Keep in mind that if the datasets you want to merge use the same data identifier, then the task becomes a simple database join operation, and there would be no need to develop an ER system.

Missing identifiers

In some cases, a financial dataset may lack a proper identifier or may have an arbitrary identifier that does not match the specific one you need. For instance, data generated from nonregulated or decentralized markets, such as OTC, may not include appropriate data identifiers. A stock prices dataset might use the stock ticker as an identifier, while you may require the ISIN. Another common scenario involves agents engaged in financial activities who may intentionally obscure their identities to commit fraud. In such cases, an ER system is essential to identify entities based on the available data attributes. Figure 4-9 illustrates the process of ER where identifiers are assigned to an unidentified dataset. The table on the right displays multiple features without entity identifiers. Using ER, records are mapped to their corresponding identifiers, as indicated by the arrows.

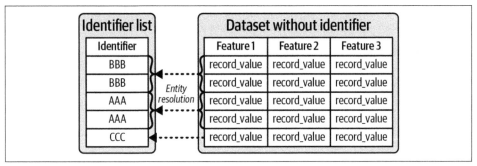

Figure 4-9. Entity resolution with unidentified data

Entity Resolution for Fraud Detection and Identify Verification

One of the most important applications of ER in finance is fraud detection and identity verification. ER can help identify financial records that can be linked to the same real-life person or company using features such as name, email, bank account, country code, address, phone number, etc. Additionally, ER can identify anomalous activities when criminals attempt to conceal their identity and unlawful intentions by omitting crucial information or presenting it in an inaccurate manner.

One of the most common types of financial crimes is *money laundering*, an activity that makes illegally generated money look as if it comes from a legitimate source. A variety of money laundering schemes exist, and they continue to emerge over time. A typical example involves the same individual appearing as the owner of numerous companies, some of which provide no actual service but only shift money between different ends.

In banking, it is a common practice to verify the identity of an applicant when opening a bank account or conducting a financial transaction to ensure they are who they claim to be. This process is known as *know your customer* (KYC) and is aimed at preventing a pervasive form of fraud known as *identity fraud*. ER can be used for KYC to identify potential fraudsters who use different identities, email addresses, phone numbers, and other patterns to open new bank accounts and conduct financial transactions.

Data aggregation and integration

Information regarding various operations and activities within financial institutions is typically decentralized and scattered across multiple divisions. Data integration refers to the process of combining these multiple data sources to provide a comprehensive view of the organization. This process is highly relevant for financial institutions for purposes such as regulatory reporting and risk monitoring. In Chapter 5, you will learn more about the importance of data aggregation in the financial sector.

To facilitate data integration, an ER system would be needed to match data across the different units and divisions within a financial institution. Figure 4-10 provides a simple example illustrating this process. In this scenario, data originates from two divisions, 1 and 2. The data from each division is initially mapped to a common identifier before being merged into a single unified dataset.

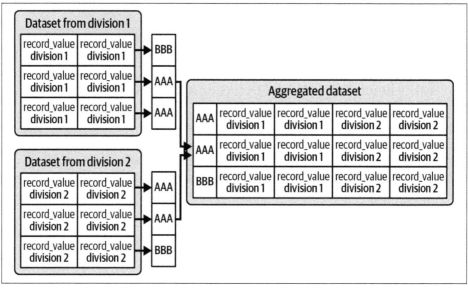

Figure 4-10. Entity resolution for data aggregation

Data deduplication

A frequent problem with financial data is the presence of duplicates, i.e., multiple records that convey the same information about an entity. Duplicate records are often encountered when using nonstandard identifiers such as person or company names, which can be recorded with multiple variations. Chapter 5 will have a dedicated section detailing the problem of financial data duplicates.

The process of identifying and removing data duplicates is called data deduplication. Since deduplication requires matching similar entities in the same dataset, it can be treated as an ER problem. Figure 4-11 shows an example illustrating this process. The table on the left contains two duplicate instances, (1,2) and (7,8). Using ER, it is possible to identify these duplicates and perform data deduplication, as shown in the table on the right.

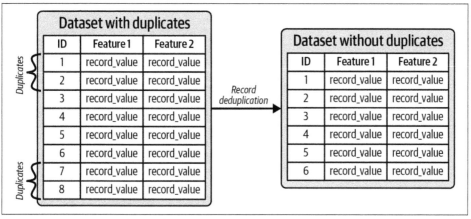

Figure 4-11. Entity resolution for data deduplication

How Does Entity Resolution Work?

A typical ER process involves five iterative steps, which I illustrate in Figure 4-12. In the first step, *preprocessing* is applied to the input datasets to ensure their high quality for the task. The second step, *blocking,* is often required to reduce computational complexity when matching large datasets. In the third step, candidate pair records are *generated* and *compared* using a selected methodology. Successively, comparisons are *classified* into matches, non-matches, or possible matches. Finally, in the fifth step, the goodness of the matching process is *evaluated.* In the next few sections, we will explore each of these five steps in detail.

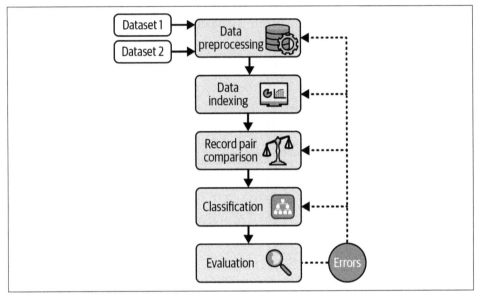

Figure 4-12. Entity resolution process

Data preprocessing

ER is highly sensitive to the quality of the input datasets. Therefore, before starting the matching process, it is crucial that the necessary rules are established and applied for quality assessment and data standardization. Such rules are particularly important for the data fields that will be used in the matching process, especially identifier fields. Table 4-6 illustrates an example where three datasets store data about the same financial entity using different formatting styles.

Table 4-6. Nonstandardized data representations

	Entity name	Headquarter	Market capitalization	Ex-dividend date
Dataset 1	JP Morgan Chase	New York City	$424.173B	Jul 05, 2023
Dataset 2	JPMorgan Chase & Co.	New York City, NY	$424,173,000,000	2023-07-05
Dataset 3	J.P. Morgan Chase & Co.	New York	$424,000.173M	5/7/23

As the table shows, the three records are the same but look different as they use different formats. Keep in mind that formatting heterogeneity may occur within the same dataset.[9]

To guarantee optimal data-matching results, data should be standardized using a consistent formatting method. The most common approach involves rule-based techniques, which employ a set of data transformation rules such as the following:

- Remove dots from entity names (e.g., J.P. Morgan Chase & Co. → JP Morgan Chase & Co).

- Remove stop words (e.g., The Bank of America → Bank of America).

- Expand abbreviations (e.g., Corp. → Corporation).

- Remove postfixes (e.g., FinTech firm → FinTech).

- Names should appear as "Given name, Surname".

- Convert dates to the format "YYYY/MM/DD".

- Parse fields into smaller segments (e.g., divide a field that contains full addresses like "270 Park Avenue, New York, NY" into multiple fields for the city, state, and street).

- Infer missing fields (e.g., zip code can be inferred from the street address).

- Remove duplicate records.

When performing data preprocessing, make sure you don't modify the original tables. Instead, make a new copy of the data and apply the transformations to it.

---

9 For a good read on this topic, please see Erhard Rahm and Hong Hai Do's article, "Data Cleaning: Problems and Current Approaches" (*https://oreil.ly/F8Ilg*), *IEEE Data Eng. Bull.* 23, no. 4 (December 2000): 3–13.

Indexing

Once the input datasets are cleaned and standardized, they should be ready for matching. In a typical scenario, the matching process will involve a comparison between each element in the first dataset with all elements in the second one. If the datasets at hand are small, then such a comparison can be done in a reasonable amount of time. However, with large datasets, the computational complexity may increase significantly. Consider a scenario where you want to match two datasets with 500k records each. If all pair-wise comparisons were to be performed, there would be a total of 500,000 × 500,000 or 250 billion candidate comparisons. Even at a processing speed of one million comparisons per second, it would still take 69 hours to match the two datasets. If both datasets have one million records each, then it will take around 11 days!

Crucially, in most ER problems, the majority of pair-wise comparisons will result in non-matches. This is because records in the first dataset often match a small subset of records in the second dataset. For this reason, it is common to observe that the number of pair-wise comparisons increases quadratically with the number of data records (i.e., $O(x^2)$, where x approximates the number of records in the datasets to match), while the number of true matches increases linearly.[10]

To overcome this issue, a number of data optimization techniques have been developed. Such techniques are often referred to as *indexing*, which aims to reduce the number of pair-wise comparisons needed by generating pair records that are likely to match and filter out the rest. The most common indexing technique is called *blocking*. It works by splitting the datasets to match into a smaller number of blocks and performing pair-wise comparisons among the records within each block only. To perform the splitting, a *blocking key* needs to be defined using one or more features from the datasets. For example, a blocking key might place records in the same block if they have the same zip code or country.

Blocking presents a few challenges. First, it is highly sensitive to data quality. Small variations in the data (*https://oreil.ly/uucpQ*) might lead a blocking key to place a record in the wrong block. Second, blocking might entail a tradeoff between computational complexity and block granularity (*https://oreil.ly/aYJjs*). By defining a very specific blocking key, you will end up with many blocks, which is good for performance. But this comes at the risk of excluding true matches. On the other hand, using a more generic blocking key could result in a small number of blocks, which will lead to a large number of pair-wise comparisons that increase computational complexity.

---

10 For more on this topic, refer to Mikhail Bilenko, Beena Kamath, and Raymond J. Mooney's "Adaptive Blocking: Learning to Scale Up Record Linkage" (*https://oreil.ly/SagB_*), in the *Sixth International Conference on Data Mining (ICDM'06)* (IEEE, 2006): 87–96.

Figure 4-13 illustrates a simple blocking process. In this example, we have two datasets, A and B, that contain company information such as the market capitalization, the headquarters' country, and the exchange market on which the company is listed. If we were to perform all pair-wise comparisons, we would need to do 6 × 6 = 36 comparisons. However, using blocking criteria that group records in blocks based on the headquarters' country and exchange market, we reduce the number of pair comparisons to five.

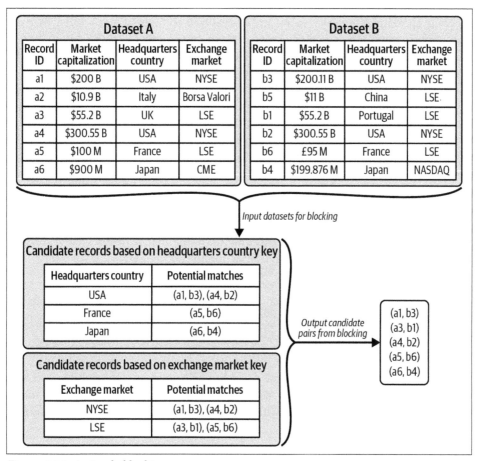

Figure 4-13. A simple blocking process

In addition to blocking, a number of other indexing techniques have been developed (*https://oreil.ly/iV2wo*). Examples include Sorted Neighborhood Indexing, Q-Gram-Based Indexing, Suffix Array-Based Indexing, Canopy Clustering, and String-Map-Based Indexing.

Comparison

Once the candidate pairs have been generated, the next step involves the actual comparison between the records. The traditional approach to record comparison is based on pair similarity. This is often performed by aggregating all features into a single string and then comparing the string similarity between the pairs. Alternatively, comparing pair features individually by computing their similarities and combining them into a single similarity score is also possible.

Generally speaking, similarity scores are normalized to be between 0 and 1. A pair has a perfect match if its similarity score is 1, whereas a non-match is indicated by a score of 0. The comparison is called *exact matching* if it only allows for either a match or a non-match. Crucially, it is normal for similarity ratings to fall within the 0–1 range, in which case the matching is *approximate* or *fuzzy*. Approximate matching may occur due to differences in the datasets, such as the number of features (one dataset has a feature that the other does not), different formats (e.g., values reported in different currencies), information granularity (i.e., one dataset has a more granular identifier than the other), and information precision (one dataset rounds values to two decimals while the other uses three).

During the comparison phase, there are three types of matching scenarios:

One-to-one
  Each record in the first dataset can only have one match in the second dataset (e.g., matching the same financial transaction in two datasets).

One-to-many
  One record in the first dataset may have numerous matches in the second dataset (e.g., matching all transactions in one dataset associated with a specific credit card in another dataset).

Many-to-many
  Numerous records from the first dataset can be matched to multiple records from the second dataset (e.g., matching multiple transactions within a trade recorded in a broker's database with transactions recorded by the clearing house or stock exchange).

As an illustrative example, Table 4-7 shows the similarity scores for the five candidate pairs from Figure 4-11. Records are first standardized (numbers expressed without decimals or multiples; all letters are uppercase), and then concatenated in a single string. Successively, the similarity is calculated between the concatenated strings using the *Longest Common Substring* (LCS) algorithm.[11]

---

11 The LCS implementation used to compute the similarities is the Python SequenceMatcher class in the difflib package (*https://oreil.ly/bEfgs*).

Table 4-7. Illustration of record comparison

Record pair	Pair string	Similarity score
(a1, b3)	a1: "$200000000000USANYSE" b3: "$200110000000USANYSE"	0.9
(a3, b1)	a4: "$55200000000UKLSE" b1: "$552000000000PORTUGALLSE"	0.75
(a4, b2)	a4: "$300550000000USANYSE" b2: "$300550000000USANYSE"	1
(a5, b6)	a5: "$100000000FRANCELSE" b6: "£95000000FRANCELSE"	0.81
(a6, b4)	a6: "$900000000JAPANCME" b6: "$199876000JAPANNASDAQ"	0.51

In addition to the LCS algorithm, there are several other methods available for computing pair similarities. These include Jaro–Winkler approximate string comparison, Levenshtein distance, edit distance, Jaccard similarity, Q-gram distance, and more.

Classification

Once all similarities have been computed, the next step is the classification of the candidate pairs into matching categories. In its most basic form, classification is binary: match or non-match. However, a less restrictive approach allows for three classes: match, non-match, and potential match. In either case, a match indicates a pair that refers to the same real-world entity in both datasets, while a non-match means that records in the pair refer to two different entities. A potential match is a pair of records that are likely to be a match but require a final clerical review for confirmation.

A variety of pair classification methods have been proposed, including the threshold-based approach, rule-based approach, probabilistic approach, and machine learning approach. Later in this chapter, we will discuss these models in more detail. To make a simple example, let's use a basic threshold-based approach to classify the results of the previous step (comparison) that were reported in Table 4-7. Let's assume that a match has a similarity score greater than or equal to 0.9, a potential match has a score of 0.8 and above, and anything below 0.8 is a non-match. Using this approach, the outcome of the classification is illustrated in Table 4-8.

Table 4-8. Illustration of a threshold-based pair classification

Record pair	Similarity score	Classification
(a1, b3)	0.9	MATCH
(a3, b1)	0.75	NON-MATCH
(a4, b2)	1	MATCH

Record pair	Similarity score	Classification
(a5, b6)	0.81	POTENTIAL MATCH
(a6, b4)	0.51	NON-MATCH

Evaluation

The final step in an ER process is performance evaluation. A highly performant ER system is able to find and correctly classify all valid matches in the input datasets. Additionally, it needs to ensure computational efficiency in terms of runtime, memory consumption, storage needs, and CPU usage.

In most cases, ER systems are implemented for real-world financial applications; therefore, they need to scale to large applications with millions of records. Measuring computational complexity (e.g., in terms of O() notation) is fundamentally important, even if optimization techniques such as indexing are applied. This is especially important when developing a streaming-based real-time record linkage system. In this case, complexity metrics and disk and memory usage figures can orient the implementation in terms of hardware, data infrastructure, and algorithmic optimizations. Additionally, as proposed by Elfeky et al. in their research paper (*https://oreil.ly/qz5Ld*), performance can be measured in terms of the effectiveness of indexing techniques in reducing the number of record pairs to be matched (*reduction ratio*) while at the same time capturing all valid matches (*pair completeness*).

To evaluate the quality of the matching results of an ER system, a common practice is to use the binary classification quality metrics employed in machine learning and data mining, which we used for evaluating NER systems. In building such metrics, four numbers need to be calculated. *True positives* are the number of pairs correctly classified as matches, while *true negatives* are pairs correctly classified as non-matches. Similarly, *false positives* are non-matches that were mistakenly classified as matches, while *false negatives* are pairs that were classified as non-matches, but in reality, they refer to actual matches. Figure 4-14 shows the confusion matrix representation of these figures.

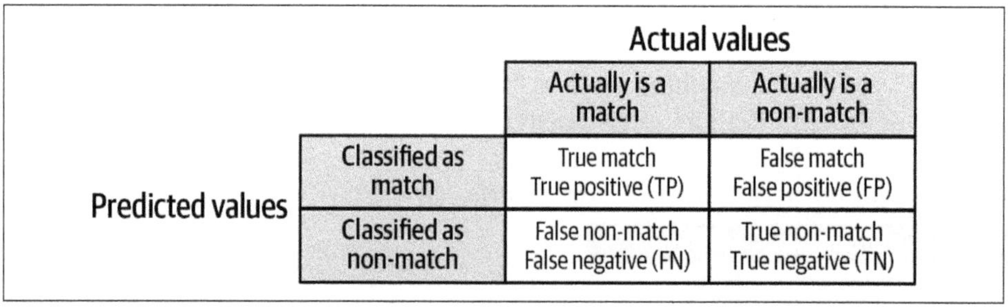

		Actual values	
		Actually is a match	Actually is a non-match
Predicted values	Classified as match	True match True positive (TP)	False match False positive (FP)
	Classified as non-match	False non-match False negative (FN)	True non-match True negative (TN)

Figure 4-14. Confusion matrix of ER

Based on these four metrics, a variety of quality measures can be calculated (*https:// oreil.ly/CxnpK*). For example, accuracy detects the ability of the system to make a correct classification (match vs. non-match). Precision measures the ability of the system to correctly classify true matches (i.e., how good the system is at avoiding false positives). Recall is another metric that measures the ability of the system to detect all true matches (i.e., how good the system is at avoiding false negatives). The F1 score is a harmonic mean of precision and recall and is used to find a balance between recall and precision.

Let's use our Table 4-8 example to compute these four metrics. As illustrated in Table 4-9, the final predictions are available in the column called "Predicted class after human review," while the ground truth values are available in the column "Ground truth class."

Table 4-9. Final ER classifications and their ground truth value

Record pair	Predicted class	Predicted class after human review	Ground truth class
(a1, b3)	MATCH	MATCH	MATCH
(a3, b1)	NON-MATCH	NON-MATCH	NON-MATCH
(a4, b2)	MATCH	MATCH	MATCH
(a5, b6)	POTENTIAL-MATCH	MATCH	MATCH
(a6, b4)	NON-MATCH	NON-MATCH	MATCH

From the data in Table 4-7, we can compute the confusion matrix values as follows:

- TP: 3
- TN: 1
- FP: 0
- FN: 1

Then, we can compute the four quality metrics, as illustrated in Table 4-10.

Table 4-10. Computed quality metrics

Quality measure	Value
Accuracy	0.8
Precision	1
Recall	0.75
F1 score	0.85

As a general performance metric, an accuracy of 0.8 is not bad, but it wouldn't be ideal in a critical application. The precision value of 1 tells us that the model doesn't produce false positives; if a pair is classified as a match, then it will be a match with 100% certainty. Recall tells us that the model couldn't find all true matches and made a few false negative classifications. The F1 score of 0.85 shows an OK model performance, but one that is still not ideal for a good ER system.

Approaches to Entity Resolution

Numerous ER techniques have been proposed in the literature and by market participants. Such techniques are often named and classified differently; therefore, I summarize them into three categories: deterministic linkage, probabilistic linkage, and machine learning. These aren't necessarily mutually exclusive, and they can be combined to build an ER system. For example, a simple rule-based approach can be used to match high-quality records, while a probabilistic or machine learning approach is used for records with poor data quality. In the following sections, I will illustrate each approach in some detail.

Deterministic linkage

The simplest ER technique, known as deterministic linkage, performs data matching via a set of deterministic rules based on the available data fields. Various deterministic linkage methods have been proposed, including link tables, exact matching, and rule-based matching, which I'll cover next.

Link tables.   A link table contains a mapping between two or more data identifiers. If two datasets use different identifiers mapped in a link table, then the datasets can be matched via an SQL join operation between them and the link table. Figure 4-15 illustrates this approach.

For financial applications, link tables need to be built with a *point-in-time* feature to keep track of the possibility that identifiers might change, get reassigned, or become inactive. To this end, a good financial link table would include additional information such as the start and end date of the link, the link status, and any additional comments. For example, Table 4-11 illustrates a link table that contains three links, where only one link (a1, b55) is active and has no end date, while link (a4, a20) ended in 31-12-2007 as the stock got delisted, and link (199, b44) ended in 20-01-1995 because the company merged with another one.

Figure 4-15 Tables

Dataset with identifier A

Record ID	Attribute A	Attribute B
a1	200.44	2954
a2	33.654	54244
a3	20.65437	43286
a4	534	765
a5	12.555	346
a6	55	754

Link between identifiers A and B

a1	b6
a2	b4
a3	b1
a4	b2
a5	b3
a6	b5

Dataset with identifier B

Record ID	Attribute C	Attribute D
b3	0.11	A
b5	0.23	B
b1	0.5	A
b2	0.32	C
b6	0.8	A
b4	0.55	B

Matched dataset

Identifier A	Identifier B	Attribute A	Attribute B	Attribute C	Attribute D
a1	b6	200.44	2954	0.8	A
a2	b4	33.654	54244	0.55	B
a3	b1	20.65437	43286	0.5	A
a4	b2	534	765	0.32	C
a5	b3	12.555	346	0.11	A
a6	b5	55	754	0.23	B

Figure 4-15. An ER process using a link table

Table 4-11. Example of a link table

Identifier A	Identifier B	Link start date	Link end date	Status	Comment
a1	b55	01-02-1990	-	Active	
a4	b20	20-01-2005	31-12-2007	Inactive	Stock delisted
a99	b44	20-01-1995	20-01-1995	Inactive	Merged with another company

The main advantages of link tables are simplicity, performance, and readability. However, they might be laborious to construct and require extensive maintenance and updating.

Financial institutions might create their own link tables internally. This is where you, as a financial data engineer, will play a major role. Additionally, a variety of financial link tables are available as commercial products. This includes, for example, reference datasets that match different financial identifiers and other instrument characteristics. Another example is the famous data distributor Wharton Research Data Services (WRDS), which has created its own linking suite (*https://oreil.ly/8QLGK*) to enable users to link tables between the most popular databases on the WRDS platform.

Another notable example involves the series of initiatives established (*https://oreil.ly/Nseut*) by the Global Legal Entity Identifier Foundation (GLEIF) in partnership with market participants to link the LEI with other financial identifiers. The result includes a list of open source link tables, such as the BIC-to-LEI, ISIN-to-LEI, and MIC-to-LEI mappings.

Case Study: CRSP/Compustat Merged (CCM) Link Table

One of the most common use cases of entity resolution in finance is merging stock price data with company fundamentals data. If you have ever checked a financial news website, you will notice that data about stock close/open prices, bid/ask prices, and volume are available, together with fundamental data such as market capitalization and dividend distributions. This is done by matching data across price and fundamental datasets for the same entity.

A good example of a price/fundamentals ER system is the CRSP/Compustat Merged Database (CCM) (*https://oreil.ly/zXBdq*). The CCM database is a link table that matches historical events and market data from the CRSP database with company fundamentals data from S&P's Compustat database (both discussed in Chapter 2). As described by the vendor documentation (*https://oreil.ly/SpJtG*), the identifiers used in creating the link table are the following:

GVKEY
    Compustat's company identifier.

ID
    Compustat's issue identifier. One GVKEY may be associated with multiple GVKEYs.

PRIMISS
    Compustat's primary security identifier.

PERMCO
    CRSP's company identifier.

PERMNO
    CRSP's issue identifier. One PERMCO may be associated with multiple PERMNOs.

The resulting link table matches all security identifiers with information on the link start date, link end date, CRSP identifiers, and Compustat identifiers.

Exact matching. In exact matching, records in two datasets are linked via a common unique identifier or via a linkage key (*https://oreil.ly/RcS2R*) that combines a set of data attributes into a single matching key. If a common unique identifier is available in both datasets, then the matching process becomes a simple SQL join operation on the unique key. The issue here is that financial datasets often use different identifiers. Additionally, an identifier may exist only from a certain point in time, and old records might lack identification. The same procedure can be followed with a linkage key, but instead of a unique identifier, a linkage key is constructed to merge the datasets. For linkage keys to provide good results, data must be of high quality (complete, standardized, deduplicated, and without errors).

Rule-based matching. A less restrictive approach to deterministic linking is the rule-based approach, where a set of rules is established to determine whether a pair of records constitutes a match. The primary benefits of this approach include the flexibility to define and incorporate rules, speed, interpretability, and simplicity. On the negative side, defining the rules may require considerable time and dataset-related domain knowledge. Moreover, as the datasets increase in complexity and vary in quality, you might end up with a large number of rules that can impact maintainability and performance.

A simple rule-based approach involves computing the similarity between records and classifying a pair as a match if it exceeds a given threshold (e.g., if the similarity is > 0.8, then it's classified as a match; otherwise, it's a non-match). This method offers a good alternative to exact matching as it accommodates minor variations in the data attributes.

Probabilistic linkage

When a unique identifier is missing or the data contains errors and missing values, deterministic record linkage may deliver poor results. *Probabilistic linkage*, also known as *fuzzy matching*, was developed to overcome this issue. Probabilistic methods have demonstrated superior linkage quality compared to deterministic approaches.

Probabilistic linkage takes a statistical approach to data matching by computing probability distributions and weights of the different attributes in the data. For example, assuming there are many fewer people with the surname "Bloomberg" than there are people with the surname "Smith" in any two datasets, the weight given for the agreement of values should be smaller when two records have the surname value "Smith" than when two records have the surname value "Bloomberg." This is because it is considerably more likely that two randomly selected records will have the surname value "Smith" than it is that they will have the surname value "Bloomberg."

To formalize these concepts, a variety of probabilistic linkage techniques have been developed.[12] However, to illustrate the main idea, let's take as an example the

---

12 For an overview on this topic, have a look at Olivier Binette and Rebecca C. Steorts' "(Almost) All of Entity Resolution" (*https://oreil.ly/_1fbt*), *Science Advances* 8, no. 12 (March 2022): eabi8021.

well-known framework of Fellegi-Sunter (a theory of record linkage) (*https://oreil.ly/7bWIA*). Fellegi and Sunter proposed a decision-theoretic linkage theory that classifies a candidate comparison pair into one of three categories: link, non-link, and possible link. Pairs are analyzed independently. In their analysis, Fellegi and Sunter demonstrated that optimal matching can be achieved via a threshold-based strategy of likelihood ratios under the assumption that the attributes are independent of each other. To illustrate the main idea, let's first define what the likelihood ratio is.

Let λ represent the agreement/disagreement pattern between two records in a given pair. Agreement can be expressed as a binary value (0 or 1) or, if needed, using more specific values. Using a binary agreement scale, if we have three attributes, then λ can be (1,1,1) if both records agree on all attributes, (1,1,0) if they agree on the first two but not the third, and so on. Let's denote the set of all possible agreement patterns by δ. For example, our three attributes can be represented in $\delta = 8$ ($2 \times 2 \times 2$) agreement patterns.

Let's assume we have two datasets we want to match, A and B. We create the product space as A $\times$B to obtain all possible comparison pairs (assume we don't do indexing, for the sake of simplicity). Then, we partition the product space into two sets: matches (M) and non-matches (U).

Denote by $P(\lambda \in \delta \mid s \in M)$ the probability of observing the agreement pattern λ for a pair of records that are actually a match, and $P(\lambda \in \delta \mid s \in U)$ the probability of observing λ for a pair of records that is not a match. The likelihood ratio is then defined as:

$$R = \frac{P(\lambda \in \delta \mid s \in M)}{P(\lambda \in \delta \mid s \in U)}$$

For example, if we consider our three attributes to be market capitalization, exchange market, and name, then the likelihood of a pair in full agreement can be written as:

$$R = \frac{P(agree \ on \ capitalization, agree \ on \ name, agree \ on \ exchange \mid s \in M)}{P(agree \ on \ capitalization, agree \ on \ name, agree \ on \ exchange \mid s \in U)}.$$

If they agree on all attributes but the exchange, then the likelihood is:

$$R = \frac{P(agree \ on \ capitalization, agree \ on \ name, disagree \ on \ exchange \mid s \in M)}{P(agree \ on \ capitalization, agree \ on \ name, disagree \ on \ exchange \mid s \in U)}$$

The ratio R is referred to as *matching weight*. Based on likelihood ratios, Fellegi and Sunter proposed the following decision rule:

- If $R \geqslant t_{upper}$, then call the pair a link (match).

- If $R \leqslant t_{lower}$, then call the pair a non-link (non-match).
- If $t_{lower} < R < t_{upper}$, then call the pair a potential link.

For details on how to calculate the probabilities and thresholds, I refer the reader to the seminal work of Thomas N. Herzog, Fritz J. Scheuren, and William E. Winkler, *Data Quality and Record Linkage Techniques* (Springer).

Supervised machine learning approach

A limitation of deterministic and probabilistic approaches is that they tend to be specific to the datasets at hand and fail when there are complex relationships between the data attributes. Machine learning approaches excel in this area, as they are mainly focused on generalization and pattern recognition.

The supervised machine learning approach to record linkage trains a binary classification model to predict and classify matches in the datasets. As a supervised technique, it requires training data containing the true match status (match or non-match). Once trained on the labeled data, the model can be used to predict new matches for unlabelled data. Tree-based models,[13] support vector machines,[14] and deep learning[15] techniques are among the most popular machine learning approaches used in ER.

Developing a supervised machine learning model for ER can be quite challenging. First, the model needs to consider the imbalanced nature of the data-matching problem, where most pairs correspond to true non-matches, while only a small fraction are true matches. Second, obtaining labeled training data can be quite challenging and time-consuming, especially for large datasets. Third, labeled data may not be available or accessible due to privacy issues. To solve this issue, a special type of ER, called privacy-preserving record linkage, has been proposed.[16] Finally, an ML-based

---

13 A good example is Kunho Kim and C. Lee Giles' "Financial Entity Record Linkage with Random Forests" (*https://oreil.ly/7GWUI*), in *Proceedings of the Second International Workshop on Data Science for Macro-Modeling* (June 2016): 1–2.

14 A good example is Peter Christen's "Automatic Record Linkage Using Seeded Nearest Neighbour and Support Vector Machine Classification" (*https://oreil.ly/Xy4_8*), in *Proceedings of the 14th ACM SIGKDD International Conference on Knowledge Discovery and Data Mining* (August 2008): 151–159.

15 A good read on deep learning for ER is Nihel Kooli, Robin Allesiardo, and Erwan Pigneul's "Deep Learning Based Approach for Entity Resolution in Databases" (*https://oreil.ly/-wlbG*), in *Asian Conference on Intelligent Information and Database Systems (ACIIDS 2018)*, Lecture Notes in Computer Science, vol. 10752 (Springer, 2018): 3–12.

16 For a good overview on this topic, I recommend Aris Gkoulalas-Divanis, Dinusha Vatsalan, Dimitrios Karapiperis, and Murat Kantarcioglu's "Modern Privacy-Preserving Record Linkage Techniques: An Overview" (*https://oreil.ly/AGFbg*), *IEEE Transactions on Information Forensics and Security* 16 (September 2021): 4966–4987.

approach to ER might present interpretability and explainability challenges, especially when employing advanced techniques such as deep learning and boosted trees.[17]

Entity Resolution Software Libraries

Entity resolution is a well-known problem with a lengthy history of development and application. Many software programs for ER have been developed by individuals and organizations. As of the time of writing this book, there are open source tools like fastLink, Dedupe, Splink, JedAI, RecordLinkage, Zingg, Ditto, and DeepMatcher. Additionally, on the commercial side, several vendors offer ER tools and solutions such as TigerGraph, Tamr, DataWalk, Senzing, Hightouch, and Quantexa.

Summary

In this chapter, you learned about two primary challenges commonly encountered by financial institutions: named entity recognition (NER) and entity resolution (ER). NER entails extracting and identifying financial entities from both structured and unstructured financial datasets. Conversely, ER focuses on the critical task of matching data pertaining to the same entity across multiple financial datasets.

The landscape of challenges and solutions in financial NER and ER is dynamic, evolving alongside data, technologies, and changing market requirements. To excel at these tasks and gain a competitive edge, it's essential that you stay current with the latest updates, methodologies, technologies, and industry best practices around financial NER and ER. Consider exploring machine learning techniques and natural language processing tools, and enrich your financial domain knowledge to enhance the accuracy and efficiency of your NER and ER systems.

Looking ahead, the next chapter will present and discuss the critical problem of financial data governance, exploring concepts and best practices for ensuring data quality, integrity, security, and privacy in the financial domain.

---

17 Some effort has been made in this direction, for example Amr Ebaid, Saravanan Thirumuruganathan, Walid G. Aref, Ahmed Elmagarmid, and Mourad Ouzzani's "Explainer: Entity Resolution Explanations" (*https://oreil.ly/kge1X*), in the *2019 IEEE 35th International Conference on Data Engineering (ICDE)* (IEEE, 2019): 2000–2003.

## CHAPTER 5

Financial Data Governance

As financial markets expand, so do the methods and use cases for how financial data is collected, stored, and used. This has generated concerns within the financial industry as well as broader governing bodies that are pushing for solid data controls, quality assurance, privacy rules, and increased security measures. As a result, data governance frameworks have emerged as a promising approach to defining and implementing rules and principles for guiding data practices within financial institutions.

This chapter will provide a practical framework for financial data governance based on three key components: data quality, data integrity, and data security and privacy. First, I'll cover the basics of financial data governance. Then, I'll go into depth about each of the three components in the sections that follow.

Financial Data Governance

Data governance is critical to securing financial data, ensuring regulatory compliance, and fostering trust among stakeholders. By implementing robust data governance practices, financial institutions can safeguard sensitive information, adhere to legal requirements, and maintain the integrity of their financial operations.

Financial Data Governance Defined

Before defining what financial data governance is, let's examine a few existing definitions. For example:

> Data governance is everything you do to ensure data is secure, private, accurate, available, and usable. It includes the actions people must take, the processes they must follow, and the technology that supports them throughout the data life cycle.
>
> — Google Cloud (*https://oreil.ly/NUcA2*)

> Data governance is, first and foremost, a data management function to ensure the quality, integrity, security, and usability of the data collected by an organization.
>
> — Eryurek et al., *Data Governance: The Definitive Guide* (O'Reilly, 2021)

As you can see, data governance can be considered a data management function, a process, or simply a set of technological and cultural practices. Interestingly, all the above definitions share a common purpose, that of ensuring data quality, security, integrity, availability, and usability. Building on these ingredients, I define financial data governance as follows:

> Financial data governance is a technical and cultural framework that establishes a set of rules, roles, practices, controls, and implementation guidelines to ensure the quality, integrity, security, and privacy of financial data in compliance with both general and financial domain–specific internal and external policies, standards, requirements, and regulations.

There isn't a one-size-fits-all solution for financial data governance frameworks. Two financial institutions may follow the same set of principles to establish financial data governance; however, the final implementations are very likely to be unique to each institution. The reason has to do with the nature of the issues that different financial institutions might face in terms of data quality, security, privacy, integrity, and more. It also depends on the financial institution's internal organizational structure, culture, process standardization and harmonization, senior management support, and participation.

Financial Data Governance Justified

Defining and enforcing an effective financial data governance framework requires a nonnegligible investment. On the one hand, a concrete and functional data governance framework needs to be defined, implemented, and integrated within the financial institution's data infrastructure. On the other hand, employees and data users need to be trained and prepared to adhere to the established data governance principles in their daily work. As such, it is important to first understand the value proposition of a financial data governance framework for your institution.

Importantly, financial organizations are among those that require and benefit from data governance the most. This can be explained by two main factors: performance and risk management.

Financial data governance impacts performance in several ways. First, data governance drives high data quality standards, which is a major input to most financial operations and decisions. Brian Buzzelli attributes *operational inefficiency* (inefficient use of input to produce output) in the financial industry to poor data quality (*https://oreil.ly/x6-md*). It impacts financial institutions' ability to conduct business efficiently, gain insights into market activity, make informed investment decisions, respond on time to new events, and communicate accurate figures to stakeholders. Second, financial data governance saves employees the nuisance of constantly checking and rechecking data quality, integrity, privacy, and security. Third, with solid data governance principles in place, developers and business teams feel more confident in the quality and compliance of their applications and products.

Another critical reason for implementing data governance in financial institutions is to effectively manage risks associated with data, which can have significant implications for these institutions. Such risks include the following:

- Cyberattacks intended to steal data, damage organizational resources, or interfere with the operation of confidential systems
- Data breaches where sensitive data falls into the hands of unauthorized persons or organizations
- Discriminatory biases built into financial applications
- Erratic data injected in models that distorts the results
- Data loss due to lack of backups, snapshots, or archives
- Absence of firm-level risk oversight due to decentralized data processes
- Lack of visibility into the data processing steps
- Privacy risks when sharing data with third parties
- Impact on model prediction quality due to bad data
- Financial and reputational risks due to nonconformance with legal and regulatory requirements

Regulators around the world have put forth substantial efforts toward creating and enforcing laws and regulations that address the above risks. Some examples are listed here:

- Sarbanes–Oxley Act
- Bank Secrecy Act
- Basel Committee on Banking Supervision's standard number 239 (BCBS 239)
- European Union's (EU's) Solvency II Directive
- California Consumer Privacy Act (CCPA)
- EU's General Data Protection Regulation (GDPR)

In order to adhere to these regulations, financial institutions must now establish and implement robust data governance frameworks. Consequently, compliance has emerged as the primary driver for the adoption of data governance within the financial sector.

The topic of data governance is quite vast and can be complex to navigate. Practitioners, researchers, financial institutions, and consulting firms regularly publish data governance studies and guidelines. In this chapter, I will present a practical data governance framework centered on three major areas that are common to all financial institutions: data quality, data integrity, and data security and privacy.

Data Quality

Data quality measures how well a dataset satisfies its intended use in various operational and analytical applications. For financial institutions, data has a primary role as input in the decision-making and product development process. Consequently, the problem of financial data quality needs to be handled with care by financial data engineers, analysts, and machine learning experts. Some use the term *data downtime* to refer to periods during which data is not accessible or is unusable due to quality-related issues. In a data-driven financial institution, prolonged or frequent data downtimes can severely impact efficiency, erode customer trust, interrupt research endeavors, and influence management and investment decisions.

A *Data Quality Framework* (DQF) is required to ensure financial data quality. The definition and specifications of a DQF may vary from one institution to another based on internal and external factors.[1] In this chapter, I will share the main ingredients that you, as a financial data engineer, can leverage to define and build a DQF. Such ingredients are often called *data quality dimensions* (DQDs). A DQD refers to those attributes or indicators of data quality that, if measured correctly, can convey information about the overall quality of financial data.

There isn't a fixed list of DQDs. As new requirements and data issues emerge, various DQDs can be identified and measured. Furthermore, the relevance of particular quality dimensions can vary depending on the specific problem being addressed and the needs of data consumers.[2] For example, certain aspects of data quality can have a greater influence on the performance of machine learning models.[3]

Therefore, educating your team on defining DQDs can greatly benefit your financial institution. To establish a baseline, in the following sections, I will present nine DQDs

---

1 For an overview of data quality frameworks, see Corinna Cichy and Stefan Rass' "An Overview of Data Quality Frameworks" (*https://oreil.ly/IoVPH*), *IEEE Access* 7 (2019): 24634–24648.

2 This approach of defining data quality attributes based on the needs of data consumers, rather than on theoretical findings, is brilliantly illustrated in the work of Richard Y. Wang and Diane M. Strong in their paper "Beyond Accuracy: What Data Quality Means to Data Consumers" (*https://oreil.ly/iYXyQ*), *Journal of Management Information Systems* 12, no. 4, (1996): 5–33.

3 For a good read on this, see Lukas Budach, Moritz Feuerpfeil, Nina Ihde, Andrea Nathansen, Nele Noack, Hendrik Patzlaff, Felix Naumann, and Hazar Harmouch, "The Effects of Data Quality on Machine Learning Performance" (*https://oreil.ly/VP3h5*), *arXiv* preprint arXiv:2207.14529 (July 2022).

that are particularly relevant to financial data: errors, outliers, biases, granularity, duplicates, availability and completeness, timeliness, constraints, and relevance. Note that while the needs of your organization are unique and may vary, these DQDs are fairly universal and likely to apply to your business.

Dimension 1: Data Errors

Data errors are digital records that have been recorded erroneously, and therefore reflect invalid or incorrect values. The presence of data errors can compromise the value, accuracy, and reliability of the data and negatively impact reporting, analysis, and decision-making.

Data errors are quite common in financial data and represent the most frequent data quality issue for financial institutions. A global survey (*https://oreil.ly/xTpLA*) of over 1,100 financial executives and professionals conducted by BlackLine in 2018 revealed that 55% of respondents were not completely confident in their institution's ability to spot financial data errors before reporting results. The survey shows that 7 in 10 respondents believe that their institution made important decisions based on inaccurate or out-of-date financial data. The majority of C-level respondents agreed that there would be a negative impact if financial inaccuracies were not detected before reporting. The negative impacts included harm to the company's image, trouble obtaining new investments, rising debt levels, penalties, and even jail time.

There isn't a fixed list of financial data error types; rather, they materialize with the introduction of data sources, products, pipelines, and various manipulation and transformation operations. But to give a few examples, financial data errors can involve the following issues:

- Random measurement errors (e.g., $9.345 instead of $9.335)
- Wrong decimal places (e.g., a price of $111.34 instead off $11.134)
- Decimal precision (e.g., an exchange rate of 1.345 instead of 1.3458)
- Negative prices (e.g., one Apple stock is worth $-200)
- Dummy and test quotes (submitted to test latency or other technical specifications)[4]
- Extra or removed digits (e.g., $10000 instead of $1000)
- Invalid date (e.g., option maturity on 01-01-1345)
- Inverted exchange rates (e.g., 1 dollar equals 1.27 pounds instead of 1 pound equals 1.27 dollars)

---

4 If you want to learn more about this issue, I recommend Ramazan Gençay, Michel Dacorogna, Ulrich A. Muller, Olivier Pictet, and Richard Olsen's *An Introduction to High-Frequency Finance* (Elsevier, 2001).

- Rounding (e.g., price of $1.01 rounded to $1)
- Misspelled entity names (e.g., Bnk of America)
- Typos (e.g., $0900)
- Invalid formatting (e.g., 01-2022-01)

Let's walk through an example. Suppose you want to convert one billion euros to dollars. Let's assume that the Forex quote you are supposed to use is 1 EUR = 1.07291 USD. Using this exchange rate, the converted sum is $1,072,910,000. Now, assume that the exchange rate is slightly different due to a data error, say 1.07191. In this case, the newly converted sum is $1,071,909,999, which is $1,000,000 less! Similarly, if a decimal precision error happens, say the exchange rate is 1.072, the converted sum would be $1,072,000,000, leading to a loss of $910,000.

 An important aspect to keep in mind about financial data is the nature of its correctness or trueness. While certain financial variables possess an absolute and indisputable value in specific scenarios—like the number of shares sold in a market transaction—others, such as derivative prices or Forex quotes, are subject to estimates, averages, or provider-specific values. For instance, a EUR/USD quote may differ among Forex brokers, with no universal market quote for reference. Therefore, it's vital to assess financial data errors against the appropriate reference value.

Data errors can also significantly impact the robustness of financial analysis. For instance, a research article from the *Journal of Fixed Income* (*https://oreil.ly/46tEh*) estimates that around 7.7% of transaction reports in the Trade Reporting and Compliance Engine (TRACE) database are erroneous records. If these errors are not considered, liquidity measurements based on this data may be skewed toward indicating a more liquid market than is the case.

To handle financial data errors, a few steps are required. In the first step, you need to identify and detect data errors. Error detection in financial data can occur at either the single-record or dataset level, with the former focusing on individual data points (e.g., an error with a single transaction) and the latter analyzing multiple records simultaneously, often producing aggregated error metrics like the error ratio (e.g., for statistical analysis purposes).

Crucially, financial data errors vary in complexity, making detection difficult at times. For example, a computer algorithm can easily detect an intraday price jump from $100 to $0.100. However, a more subtle error might require a more in-depth investigation, such as an intraday price of $50, followed by three prices of $40 and then a fifth price of $50. For simple errors, rule-based approaches are often used (e.g., if the price is negative → error). For more complex errors, statistical and data mining techniques have been traditionally employed, such as Pearson correlation, z-score, percentile analysis, and Mahalanobis distance.[5] A more advanced technique involves the computation of the value of the erroneous record using theoretical or quantitative models such as financial asset pricing.

Once detected, errors need to be checked against business-defined tolerance and impact levels. A tolerance level can be something like an error ratio < 0.01%. Once the error is checked against the tolerance ratio, the next action depends on its business priority. An error with a Forex exchange rate may significantly impact the business if it converts large sums of money and, therefore, it needs to be given high priority.

A challenging situation arises when the data containing errors comes from a third party and is not produced by the final data consumer. In this case, detecting and correcting the errors might be difficult as there is no valid ground truth to compare the data against. When this happens, a useful approach is cross-dataset validation, which consists of comparing data from one source against an alternative data source that records similar but high-quality data. In a research article from the *Journal of Finance* (*https://oreil.ly/eW2ec*), the authors analyzed error rates in CRSP (a stock price dataset) and Compustat (a company fundamentals dataset) and found that errors happen with a very low frequency, but the impact of existing errors is substantial. In the same paper, the authors suggest that their methodology could be generalized as a means of data quality assessment for competing databases.

Dimension 2: Data Outliers

In basic terms, a data outlier is a data observation that differs significantly from the others. For example, consider a stock price time series with 100 observations, 99 of which have a value less than 1000, but one record has a value of 1,000,000. It is typical to refer to this last observation as an outlier. The presence of outliers in financial data may adversely affect the robustness of statistical analysis and bias machine learning models.

Outliers within financial data might arise due to various factors. In market and transaction time series, outliers commonly result from the inherent high noise level in the data. Additionally, outliers may signal fraudulent or anomalous financial activities like money laundering and credit card fraud. Furthermore, some records may seem like outliers due to systematic issues (e.g., data transmission errors), structural breaks (sudden shifts in market conditions), poorly formatted or unadjusted data, or measurement errors (e.g., errors in price quoting).

---

5 For a good introduction to this topic, I recommend reading Chapter 9 of Pang-Ning Tan, Michael Steinbach, Vipin Kumar, and Anuj Karpatne's *Introduction to Data Mining*, 2nd ed. (Pearson Education, 2019).

To identify financial data outliers, researchers have proposed several methods. Some use statistical techniques such as principal component analysis, z-score, percentile analysis, and kurtosis, while others use machine learning techniques such as clustering, classification, and anomaly detection.[6] Keep in mind that financial outlier detection might be a challenging task whose difficulty depends on the type and structure of the data. For example, outliers in financial time series data are different in terms of detection and treatment than in cross-section data.[7]

Once detected, outliers need to be treated following a specific method. The most common outlier treatment methods among financial researchers are *winsorization* and *trimming*. Trimming is the simplest approach, which works by removing outliers from the dataset. The main challenge with trimming is that if you trim too much, you risk altering the statistical properties or coverage of the dataset, while if you trim too little, you might still end up with an unstable and noisy dataset.[8]

Winsorization, on the other hand, involves limiting extreme values in the data to a specified percentile. In a 90% winsorization, for instance, all observations above the 95th percentile are set to equal the value of the 95th percentile, and all observations below the 5th percentile are set to equal the value of the 5th percentile.[9]

Another popular and reliable technique is *scaling*. This can be performed by taking a dataset's logarithm or square root value. Scaling helps to normalize the data distribution and reduce the impact of extreme values. For instance, consider a dataset containing stock prices where some stocks have significantly higher prices than others. By applying logarithmic scaling to the stock prices, the dataset's range can be compressed, making it easier to compare and analyze percentage changes or returns across different stocks. This normalization step helps in recognizing trends and patterns without being heavily impacted by the extreme values of high-priced stocks.

Another technique involves trimmed estimators, which are statistical measures created by excluding a portion of the extreme values from the dataset through

---

6 For more on this topic, see Carson Kai-Sang Leung, Ruppa K. Thulasiram, and Dmitri A. Bondarenko's "An Efficient System for Detecting Outliers from Financial Time Series" (*https://oreil.ly/6Os2f*), in *Flexible and Efficient Information Handling: Proceedings of the 23rd British National Conference on Databases, BNCOD '06*, Belfast, Northern Ireland, UK, July 18–20, 2006. (Springer Berlin Heidelberg, 2006): 190–198.

7 For more on this topic, see Kangbok Lee, Yeasung Jeong, Sunghoon Joo, Yeo Song Yoon, Sumin Han, and Hyeoncheol Baik's "Outliers in Financial Time Series Data: Outliers, Margin Debt, and Economic Recession" (*https://oreil.ly/Tlrdm*), *Machine Learning with Applications* 10 (December 2022): 100420.

8 For a good read on this topic, see Christian T. Brownlees and Giampiero M. Gallo's "Financial Econometric Analysis at Ultra-High Frequency: Data Handling Concerns" (*https://oreil.ly/5WgP1*), *Computational Statistics & Data Analysis* 51, no. 4 (December 2006): 2232–2245.

9 For more on this topic, I highly recommend John Adams, Darren Hayunga, Sattar Mansi, David Reeb, and Vincenzo Verardi's "Identifying and Treating Outliers in Finance" (*https://oreil.ly/cEJoe*), *Financial Management* 48, no. 2 (March 2019): 345–384.

---

truncation. For instance, the 5% trimmed mean is computed by averaging the values within the 5% to 95% range, removing the lowest and highest 5% of the data.

Dimension 3: Data Biases

Data biases refer to inherent distortions that impact the representation of the subjects/entities that constitute the data. These biases can result in erroneous conclusions, skewed patterns, biased decisions, and discrimination.

A large number of biases may emerge in financial data. To illustrate with an example, let's say you want to analyze the performance of fund managers (a common area of study in finance) and get a dataset for your study from a data provider. Interestingly, many commercial fund datasets are collected via a voluntary reporting mechanism. In this setting, fund managers may or may not decide to report their performance highlights to the data vendor.

For instance, when a fund performs well, and the manager aims to attract more capital, they may disclose its figures to draw market attention. Conversely, if the fund underperforms or the manager prefers not to attract new investors, they might opt not to report the performance figures. This kind of behavior might lead to self-selection bias. Such bias will distort the dataset and give the impression that some funds are always outperforming.

As institutional investors, hedge funds are exposed to a number of risks, and in some cases, this might lead to failure/bankruptcy. If a hedge fund dataset systematically excludes/removes failed or poorly performing funds from its archive, this could lead to a type of bias called *survivorship bias,* where only the successful funds appear in the dataset. Similar to self-selection bias, survivorship bias may convey an over-optimistic image of the fund industry's performance.

In some cases, a new hedge fund could be added to the dataset together with its full history. Even though it looks natural, this behavior might lead to *backfilling* bias, also known as *instant history bias.* This bias can be relevant if only funds with a strong track record choose to join the database, which would distort historical performance statistics for the hedge fund industry.

Another significant bias in financial data is *look-ahead bias,* which occurs when conducting historical studies using information that would not have been accessible during the analyzed period. For instance, consider a scenario where a company releases its annual report for the year 2019 in March 2020, as is typically the case. Suppose you're a financial analyst conducting backtesting to evaluate your investment strategy's performance. In that case, it's crucial to avoid assuming that the company's annual report was available before March 2020 (e.g., December 31, 2019), even if you're analyzing data from a later date.

Detecting and correcting biases in financial data is a challenging task. As a financial data engineer or analyst, make sure you understand how the data was generated and recorded. Consider collecting more data to adjust for possible biases. Furthermore, if you are extracting a data sample from a large dataset, design a methodology that proactively prevents biases, for example, by assessing the data sample representation. Another good practice is to compare two datasets to check for potential bias that exists in one but not the other.[10] Finally, I highly recommend keeping an eye on the latest research on bias and fairness in data analysis and machine learning.[11]

On the data vendors' side, efforts have been made to detect and correct biases in their products. For example, among the most reputable hedge fund data sources is LSEG's Lipper Fund Data (*https://oreil.ly/N0eMI*), formerly known as the *Trading Advisor Selection System* (TASS) database. Lipper tracks and publishes fund-related information such as its profile, performance, and investment strategies. Funds report to Lipper voluntarily, which, as we saw earlier in this section, can lead to various biases. To account for this issue, Lipper keeps two separate databases: the *graveyard* database, which records data on defunct funds or funds that haven't been reported for a long time, and the *live* database, which records data for actively reporting funds.[12]

Dimension 4: Data Granularity

Data granularity describes the level of detail within a dataset, with highly granular data offering detailed observations about individual entities, while low-granularity data typically provides summarized or aggregated information at a higher level. To better illustrate the concept within the finance domain, let's consider a few examples:

Financial portfolios
A financial portfolio is a collection of investments created to achieve a specific financial goal, considering elements such as diversification, risk appetite, and expected returns. Portfolio data can be available either in aggregated form, providing an overview of portfolio performance, risk, and investment strategy, or in a more detailed form, including details about individual portfolio constituents

---

10 For more on this topic, see Sagar P. Kothari, Jay Shanken, and Richard G. Sloan's "Another Look at the Cross-Section of Expected Stock Returns" (*https://oreil.ly/mDCB5*), *The Journal of Finance* 50, no. 1 (March 1995): 185–224.

11 For a good read, start with Ninareh Mehrabi, Fred Morstatter, Nripsuta Saxena, Kristina Lerman, and Aram Galstyan, "A Survey on Bias and Fairness in Machine Learning" (*https://oreil.ly/BbZkM*), *ACM Computing Surveys (CSUR)* 54, no. 6 (July 2021): 1–35.

12 For more on the Lipper database, see Mila Getmansky, Andrew W. Lo, and Shauna X. Mei's chapter, "Sifting Through the Wreckage: Lessons from Recent Hedge-Fund Liquidations" (*https://oreil.ly/waZYV*), in *The World of Hedge Funds: Characteristics and Analysis*, H Gifford Fong, ed. (World Scientific Publishing Company, 2005): 7–47.

and their respective allocations, such as Apple stock at 5%, US government bonds at 20%, and so on.

Financial indices

A financial index is a single aggregated metric constructed to represent and track the performance of a specific category of financial assets. For example, the S&P 500 index offers an aggregated metric of the top 500 public companies in the United States by market capitalization. Index data may be available at the index level (single metric) or at the constituent level (the individual assets included in the index and their corresponding weights).

Financial exposures

Financial institutions hold assets with each other, such as interbank loans, securities, and cash. A financial institution might disclose its total exposure to another institution at the aggregated level (Bank A holds $1bln assets with the rest of the system) or at the individual institution level (e.g., Bank A holds $1mln at Bank B, $33mln at Bank C, and so on).

Financial time series

These can be recorded with high temporal accuracy, such as every second, minute, or hour, or with lower granularity, such as daily, weekly, or monthly aggregates.

Financial transactions

These can be stored at the individual transaction level or as summaries, such as monthly purchases.

The level of data granularity is an essential factor in determining the type of analysis that can be performed on the data. Highly granular data enables deeper insights and the identification of meaningful patterns utilizing advanced analytical approaches. Importantly, granular data comes with increased storage requirements, processing time, and the potential for privacy concerns. Therefore, it is recommended to keep in mind the challenges and tradeoffs associated with managing and analyzing highly granular data.

Granular financial data may not always be available. Portfolio composition data, for example, may not be disclosed since it would reveal the firm's investment strategy, which might harm its competitive position. Another reason this information may be withheld is data confidentiality, like with customer transaction details. In some cases, detailed data may not be collected in the first place, for example, in noncentralized markets such as OTC markets.

To overcome the issue of data granularity, you can try to collect detailed data. Alternatively, aggregated data may be decomposed into its constituent elements using statistical and machine learning techniques. For example, network scientists who analyze financial networks are often limited by privacy issues when collecting data about the topology of a financial network. As mentioned earlier, the best example is banks' exposures to each other, where data is available at the aggregate level only. To overcome this issue, researchers have proposed network reconstruction (*https://oreil.ly/vXWdd*) and link prediction (*https://oreil.ly/avoq0*) methods to infer and construct the network structure at the bank-to-bank level.

Dimension 5: Data Duplicates

Data duplicates are repeated records that represent the same data observation. Duplicate data is a widespread issue in finance, and its consequences can range from negligible to severe. For example, a duplicate record in a data sample used in a financial study may not lead to serious consequences; however, if a financial transaction appears multiple times on a user account, then it might impact the available balance.

Data duplicates may occur for a variety of reasons. First, there are human errors, which happen when a person adds the same data entry into a system multiple times. Second, duplicates may be inserted automatically by a machine when the system is not properly built to ensure data uniqueness. For example, a household submits a loan application twice. Third, data duplicates might emerge when merging multiple data sources improperly, for example, using nonunique identifiers.

Crucially, despite the apparent simplicity of the problem, detecting duplicates may be quite challenging. In the simplest case, a data record is considered duplicate if the values of all its fields exactly match those of another record. For example, two financial accounts are considered duplicates if they match the account holder's first name, last name, social security number, and account number. In a more complex scenario, two duplicate records may be recorded differently, thus making it harder to identify. For example, if names are recorded with different formatting (e.g., J.P. Morgan versus JPMorgan), then the duplicate records would have a nonperfect match. In other cases, the presence of exact duplicates may be due to inconsistency in the data recording mechanism. For example, an investment of $10,000 in stock A may be recorded as an investment of $5,000 in stock A twice, while an investment of $10,000 in stock B is recorded only once.

Detecting and treating duplicate records can also vary in complexity. The best strategy is to always think in advance about the duplicate generation mechanism and add the necessary checks, constraints, and validations to prevent duplication. For example, having a well-defined unique identifier for each record is a good practice. If the unique identifier is not sufficient, then it is possible to add constraints on a subset of data fields that ensure no two records share the same set of values. Let's walk through an example of how to prevent duplicates before data insertion in PostgreSQL:[13]

---

13 To test the code quickly online, you can use OneCompiler (*https://oreil.ly/Pc9d5*).

```
-- PostgreSQL
CREATE EXTENSION btree_gist;
CREATE TABLE company(
    record_key INT PRIMARY KEY,
    company_id VARCHAR NOT NULL,
    company_name VARCHAR NOT NULL,
    dividend_date DATE NOT NULL,
    dividend_amount DECIMAL(10,2) NOT NULL,
    EXCLUDE USING gist (company_id WITH =, company_name WITH <>)
);
INSERT INTO company VALUES(1, 'JPM', 'JP Morgan', '2020-11-20', 10);
INSERT INTO company VALUES(2, 'BOA', 'Bank of America', '2022-01-08', 5);
INSERT INTO company VALUES(1, 'JPM', 'JP Morgan', '2019-05-01', 8);
INSERT INTO company VALUES(3, 'JPM', 'J.P. Morgan', '2023-06-01', 3);

psql:commands.sql:12: ERROR:  duplicate key value violates unique constraint
"company_pkey" DETAIL:  Key (record_key)=(1) already exists.
psql:commands.sql:12: ERROR:  conflicting key value violates exclusion con-
straint "company_company_id_company_name_excl"
DETAIL:  Key (company_id, company_name)=(JPM, J.P. Morgan) conflicts with exist-
ing key (company_id, company_name)=(JPM, JP Morgan).
```

In this example, we created a table that stores data on company dividend distributions. Each company has a unique ID and a human-readable name, while each record has a unique record key. We want to avoid having two records with the same record key or the same company ID but with a different company name. To achieve this, we can add a primary key constraint on the record key field and an *exclusion constraint* on the company ID and company name. After that, we test the implementation by trying to make four inserts, two of which violate the two constraints.

The first two insert statements will execute successfully, and two records will be created. However, for the third statement, we will get an error that says the uniqueness constraint was violated as they share the same record key (= 1). For the fourth insert, we will get an error saying that you are trying to insert a record with a new format (J.P. Morgan and JP Morgan).

If data has already been generated and stored with potential duplicates, then a variety of solutions are possible. In the simplest case, duplicates share the same field values. To identify them, we can use aggregation or analytical queries. Let's consider the following example:

```
-- PostgreSQL
-- create
CREATE TABLE company (
  company_id INTEGER PRIMARY KEY,
  company_name VARCHAR,
  company_headquarters VARCHAR
);
```

```
-- insert
INSERT INTO company VALUES (1, 'Company A', 'New York');
INSERT INTO company VALUES (2, 'Company B', 'California');
INSERT INTO company VALUES (3, 'Company A', 'New York');

-- fetch
SELECT company_name, company_headquarters, count(company_id) AS record_count
FROM company
GROUP BY company_name, company_headquarters

 company_name | company_headquarters | record_count
--------------+----------------------+--------------
 Company B    | California           |            1
 Company A    | New York             |            2
```

In the above table, two duplicates store the same data for Company B. To detect these duplicates, we used a GROUP BY statement that counts the number of records that share the same company name and company headquarters.

The GROUP BY is an aggregation tool that reduces the number of rows to summary groups. If we want to keep the original data without aggregation, we can use a window function such as ROW_NUMBER() (*https://oreil.ly/SJLSW*) to assign an ordered sequential number to each record in a group. This way, deduplication can be performed by taking the records with row_num = 1 and discarding those with higher row numbers. Here is an illustrative example:

```
SELECT company.*,
ROW_NUMBER() OVER (PARTITION BY company_name, company_headquarters) AS row_num
FROM company
ORDER BY company_name, company_headquarters, row_num

 company_id | company_name | company_headquarters | row_num
------------+--------------+----------------------+---------
          1 | Company A    | New York             |       1
          3 | Company A    | New York             |       2
          2 | Company B    | California           |       1
```

A more challenging scenario occurs when a dataset contains duplicates, but they cannot be directly identified due to data quality issues. For example, we might know the subset of columns that could identify duplicates, but the data may be recorded differently, so it won't be detected via an exact match. In this case, the data deduplication process becomes an entity resolution (data matching) task. We discussed entity resolution systems in Chapter 4. One thing to keep in mind is that data deduplication is a special type of entity resolution (*https://oreil.ly/Bf64q*), as it involves only one dataset that is matched against itself to resolve similar entities.

Another subtle scenario with duplicates happens when two records look the same, but they are not duplicates because a distinguishing field is missing. Examples include transaction data where the date of the transaction is available but the time is missing; multiple data at the security level (e.g., company stocks) that look like duplicates but, in reality, refer to different security issues (e.g., different stock issues) that are missing issue IDs; or a financial option is available twice, but one is a call (buy-side), and another is a put (sell-side).

Dimension 6: Data Availability and Completeness

A crucial dimension of data quality is the completeness of a dataset, indicating whether it contains all necessary information required for its intended analytical or operational purposes. A dataset is considered incomplete or unavailable when essential data attributes or observations are missing. In finance, issues of data availability and incompleteness are quite common (*https://oreil.ly/EMS9m*). This happens for a variety of reasons, such as the following:

Voluntary data reporting
> If the data collection process involves a voluntary data reporting mechanism, e.g., survey data, then it is likely that some respondents will decline to report their data for one reason or another, e.g., to hide bad performance. Additionally, respondents might report data with different frequencies (e.g., Firm A responds to all surveys, while Firm B responds to some and skips others).

Security and confidentiality concerns
> Unless enforced by law, financial firms might have a number of concerns about the security and confidentiality of their data. This might generate a high level of risk aversion toward data sharing.

Market factors
> Market factors such as liquidity, sentiment, and risk might impact the data generation process. For example, a liquid stock that trades frequently will have a large number of price observations per day, while an illiquid instrument might trade once every six hours and have a few daily records. This type of behavior is called nonsynchronous trading (*https://oreil.ly/CEymv*).

Technological reasons
> If a financial firm or the market lacks adequate data collection infrastructure, it can lead to data collection gaps. For instance, a considerable amount of data on over-the-counter (OTC) market transactions remains unrecorded due to the absence of a centralized entity responsible for collecting and aggregating such data.

Publication delay
> If there is a latency between the time data is created and the time it is published, it could be considered unavailable. This might happen with company fundamental data, created at the end of the fiscal year but released a few months later.

Data Time to Live (TTL)

TTL is a database mechanism that sets a period of time after which data will be considered expired and no longer visible to queries and database statistics. TTL doesn't necessarily mean that the data was deleted, as this might happen at a later point in time.

In certain circumstances, the existence of a specific type of data may be optional; in these situations, the consequences of missing data are minor and may not require any correction effort. However, in many cases, incomplete or missing data can cause a number of problems for financial institutions. For example, missing data may lead to biased and unreliable financial models, which in turn can impact investment decisions and product development. Incomplete data may also mean less visibility and insight into market activities and patterns, thus foregoing potentially profitable opportunities and reducing trust in the data within a financial institution. Gaps in customer-related data may impact the business and sales teams' ability to understand consumer segments and offer personalized services. Moreover, missing data may delay reporting and releases, which can impact market sentiment and expert estimations.

To effectively deal with missing financial data, it is crucial to understand the mechanisms that cause data missingness. Following the existing literature (*https://oreil.ly/5xfqc*), three forms of missing data are often discussed:

Missing Completely at Random

Data on variable X is said to be Missing Completely at Random (MCAR) if the mechanism that leads to observations of X being missing is independent of X itself and any other variable in the dataset, whether observable or missing. The missingness happens randomly and without any systematic pattern. For example, a hedge fund that reports its performance data to a data provider might incur a technical issue preventing some of its data from being submitted.

Missing at Random

If data on variable X is Missing at Random (MAR), then the missingness mechanism is independent of X itself but is systematically related to one or more features in the dataset. For instance, a hedge fund firm might opt not to disclose performance data due to confidentiality concerns surrounding its investment strategy. Here, the missingness is unrelated to the fund's performance but rather to its investment secrets.

Missing Not at Random

This happens when observations on variable X are missing for reasons related to X itself. To continue with our example, a hedge fund might decide not to report its performance data because it had a bad performance and wants to hide it from investors or because they are doing very well and they don't want to attract more investors or media coverage.

A variety of techniques have been developed for treating missing financial data (*https://oreil.ly/6lGnq*). The simplest and most common technique is *likewise deletion*, where observations with missing data are removed from the dataset. Another technique is the *omitted variable approach*, which drops the variable with missing values from the dataset. In some cases, dropping observations or variables might lead to biased or sparse datasets. A family of techniques called *imputation* is often used to overcome this issue. Imputation aims to estimate the missing values in a dataset using a specific method. One basic imputation technique is the *mean substitution*, which replaces missing values for variable X with the average value of X. Another imputation technique is filling in a missing value in one dataset with another value in another dataset, e.g., via entity resolution. Last but not least, a practical approach to data imputation is regression, where a model is used to produce an estimate of the missing value. Models can be machine learning based (e.g., linear regression) or financial models (e.g., Capital Asset Pricing Model, Value at Risk, etc.).

Dimension 7: Data Timeliness

Timeliness of data is a critical dimension of data quality within financial institutions. This section will discuss two key aspects related to data timeliness:

- Is the data available and accessible at the time it is expected to be?
- Does the data reflect the most recent observations?

Many financial datasets are used in a time-critical context, e.g., algorithmic trading, and if data is not available in the expected window, then the data is of no use. On the other hand, if the available data does not reflect the latest facts, e.g., the latest Forex quote or the latest analyst estimate, then it might lead to wrong business decisions and lost revenues. Financial markets use the term *stale price* to describe an outdated or no longer accurate quoted value of a financial asset or instrument.

A variety of factors may influence financial data timeliness. The most common factors are latency, market closure, time lags, or lengthy processes in the data generation, ingestion, and transformation mechanisms. For example, complex data pipelines are likely to be time-consuming and delay data availability. Another factor is the data *refresh rate*, which is the frequency with which data is refetched and updated to reflect the latest observations. Refresh frequencies may vary from real time to regular schedules.

Furthermore, many applications rely on *data caching*, a strategy where a copy of the data is stored in a temporary storage location that allows fast access. However, cached data can become outdated over time, requiring periodic updates or replacements to ensure alignment with the most recent data. This problem, known as *cache invalidation*, poses one of the most common challenges in software development (*https://oreil.ly/jCOIG*).

Dimension 8: Data Constraints

The data constraints dimension reflects the degree to which data conforms to predefined technical and business rules and limitations. Examples of such constraints include the following:

Extension constraint
> Data is stored in allowed formats only (e.g., CSV files).

Schema constraint
> Data follows a predefined schema structure that defines the mandatory fields and their data type.

Non-null constraint
> A data field does not contain null values.

Range constraint
> A data field contains values that fall within a given range (e.g., price >=0, year >=1990).

Value choice constraint
> A field can assume values from a fixed list of choices (e.g., country names).

Uniqueness constraint
> A record must be unique across a dataset.

Referential integrity constraint
> Values in one field are allowed only if they exist in another referenced field. For example, an online purchase transaction cannot be stored if it contains a nonexistent product.

Regular expression patterns
> A field contains values that match a given string pattern (e.g., an email pattern, a financial identifier pattern).

Cross-field validation
> This ensures that a field satisfies a certain condition in relation to one or more fields. For example, the date of issuance of a derivative contract cannot be earlier than the date of expiry.

Based on your business needs, additional constraints may be defined. An important thing to remember is that violating a given constraint may not always signal a bad data quality issue. For example, a schema change that involves adding or deleting a given field might be done to enrich data quality and correct existing errors. As another example, a value choice constraint may be violated if the list of allowed options is outdated.

Dimension 9: Data Relevance

Data relevance is an important data quality dimension, determining the degree to which available data aligns with the specific problem or purpose it aims to address. Relevance ensures that the data is actionable and contributes effectively to gaining insights and understanding the problem at hand. For example, in his interesting analysis published in *Getting It Wrong: How Faulty Monetary Statistics Undermine the Fed, the Financial System, and the Economy* (MIT Press, 2011), William Barnett illustrates how the lack of adequate financial data to assess financial systemic risks has been identified as one of the main factors leading to the great financial crisis of 2007–2008.

In the following years, several initiatives have been launched to review and enhance the data collection processes in financial markets. For example, in 2020 the Bank of England conducted a Data Collection review (*https://oreil.ly/3XLLR*) to identify the challenges the industry faces in providing data, the issues the bank encounters in receiving and using it, and the necessary steps to address these problems. As another example, in response to the significant impact of swaps, especially credit default swaps, during the 2007–2008 financial crisis, the Dodd-Frank Wall Street Reform and Consumer Protection Act (Dodd-Frank Act) established *swap data repositories (SDRs)* (*https://oreil.ly/4gtMz*) to serve as entities responsible for swap data reporting and recordkeeping. According to the Dodd-Frank Act, all swaps, whether cleared or uncleared, must be reported to registered SDRs.

In recent years, the importance of data relevance has increased alongside the rise of machine learning and generative AI. If the available data features (variables) are not pertinent to the analytical problem or do not provide insights into the patterns analysts aim to capture, developing accurate models becomes challenging.[14] Similarly, fine-tuning a language model requires contextual data that matches the specific requirements and conditions of the task or problem at hand.

The question of what data is relevant is ultimately a function of the problem at hand. For example, investment firms may employ a range of trading strategies, each of which requires different types of data. For instance, *day trading* demands real-time intraday price, volume, volatility, and market liquidity data. *Swing trading* relies on technical and fundamental indicators, market sentiment, and medium-term price trends. *Trend trading* depends on moving averages, trend lines, and momentum indicators. *Arbitrage trading* needs data on order books, market liquidity, transaction costs, trading fees, real-time price discrepancies, and Forex rates. *Mean reversion trading* uses data on moving averages, Relative Strength Index (RSI), Bollinger Bands, and Moving Average Convergence Divergence (MACD); *systematic trading* requires

---

14 For a good read on this topic, see Pat Langley's "Selection of Relevant Features in Machine Learning" (*https://oreil.ly/b65da*), in *Proceedings of the AAAI Fall Symposium on Relevance (1994),* vol. 184 (AAAI Press, 1994): 245–271.

time series data for transactions (price and volume), orders, and news (economic releases and events).[15]

Data Integrity

Throughout its lifecycle, data goes through a number of transformations, movements, and adjustments as well as aggregation, matching, and more. In this context, the concept of *data integrity* is often used to indicate a set of principles established to ensure consistent, traceable, usable, and reliable data. Depending on the institution type and business requirements, there may be a number of ways data integrity could be ensured. To offer a general overview, this section outlines nine key data integrity principles—standards, backups, archiving, aggregation, lineage, catalogs, ownership, contracts, and reconciliation—all of which hold significant relevance within the financial sector.

Principle 1: Data Standards

As financial markets have grown in size and complexity, the terms *standard* and *standardization* have become keywords. According to authors Spivak and Brenner in their book *Standardization Essentials* (CRC Press, 2001), the term standard "denotes a uniform set of measures, agreements, conditions, or specifications between parties." The process of formulating, developing, and implementing standards is called standardization. Standards differ in their nature, function, and acceptance. Spivak and Brenner provide a general framework by categorizing standards into the following taxonomy:

- Physical standards or units of measure
- Terms, definitions, classes, grades, ratings, or symbols
- Test methods, recommended practices, guides, and other applications to products and processes
- Standards for systems and services, in particular, quality standardization and related aspects of management system standards for quality and the environment
- Standards for health, safety, consumers, and the environment

Financial industry participants have made several calls for standardization (*https://oreil.ly/ZoCQI*), acknowledging its role in increasing market efficiency, confidence, and stability and reducing costs. For example, research conducted by McKinsey (*https://oreil.ly/PYotd*) found that the adoption of the Legal Entity Identifier standard

---

15 To learn more about trading strategies and their data requirements, I recommend Eugene A. Durenard's *Professional Automated Trading: Theory and Practice* (Wiley, 2013).

(which we discussed in detail in Chapter 3) could save the global banking industry around USD $2–4 billion annually in client onboarding costs.

Furthermore, standards play a crucial role in financial markets by promoting consistency across key aspects of processes, products, and services, including quality, compatibility, interoperability, comparability, and reliability. For instance, the ISO 21586 standard (*https://oreil.ly/c6FeC*), which specifies the description of banking products or services, was introduced to ensure uniformity in descriptions of banking products and services (BPoS) across various financial institutions, enabling customers to understand and compare them effectively.

Furthermore, as domain experts develop standards, they distill best practices and codify the most recent technologies and expertise, which saves market participants the effort of reinventing the wheel. A few great examples of this are accounting standards (e.g., *generally accepted accounting principles*, or GAAP), risk management standards (e.g., value at risk, or VAR), and data quality standards (e.g., ISO 8000: Data Quality).

Principle 2: Data Backups

One of the primary operational risks faced by financial institutions is the loss of data, which can occur for various reasons. For example, data may be destroyed by accident, corrupted, converted incorrectly, overwritten with a later version, mixed with the incorrect sort of data, lost during a hardware failure, or simply buried in a large pile of log files where it is hard to detect.

Data backups are an effective method for mitigating the risk of data loss. A data backup is a copy of the original data stored in a different place that can be recovered in a case of a data loss accident.

A number of factors need to be considered when building a data backup strategy. I recommend approaching the problem through a *data backup lifecycle*. This includes defining data backup steps and elements such as when to back up (e.g., scheduled, on demand, or event driven), what data to back up (operational, analytical, client), the number of backups to create, backup security (e.g., through encryption), backup storage locations (multizones, geographies, data centers), recovery tests and plans, retention time, and deletion.

Principle 3: Data Archiving

A variety of data within financial institutions may reach a point where they are no longer actively utilized but are still necessary for future reference, reviews, audits, electronic discovery, litigation, and compliance purposes. Examples include financial transactions, customer information, and regulatory reports.

In addition, regulatory frameworks such as the Bank Secrecy Act (BSA), Federal Deposit Insurance Corporation Improvement Act (FDICIA), and General Data Protection Regulation (GDPR) have established several data retention requirements that financial institutions need to comply with.

To manage this data retention challenge, a common approach is *data archiving*, which refers to the process of moving data that is no longer actively used out of production systems and onto a separate long-term storage system.

 Data archives should not be confused with data backups. Although both are concerned with keeping data in secondary storage, they serve different purposes. Data backups are part of a disaster recovery strategy and are meant to manage data loss accidents. Data archives, on the other hand, serve a data retention purpose.

In addition to compliance and risk management, data archiving lowers storage costs by moving data from more costly high-performance primary storage to significantly less expensive secondary storage (e.g., hard disk drives [HDDs]).

A *data archival policy* is often established to manage data archival. It comprises elements such as a data retention policy (*https://oreil.ly/S9p9A*), data archival software, and data access and discovery functionalities.

Principle 4: Data Aggregation

Financial institutions engage in diverse operations, including lending, payments, investments, risk management, insurance, proprietary trading, portfolio management, and more. Often, a single institution performs multiple activities simultaneously. For instance, a commercial bank may accept deposits, offer loans, market financial investment products, and provide insurance.

In traditional settings, individual activities within a financial institution are often overseen within distinct organizational silos, each maintaining data about its operations using separate systems. An inherent challenge with such silos is the complexity involved in consolidating data across a large number of business units, legal entities, and disparate data storage systems. This, in turn, may jeopardize a financial institution's capacity to generate an aggregated view of its activities and risks. Such constraints were one of the primary reasons that banks could not adequately assess their risk exposures and concentration before and during the 2007–2008 financial crisis.

 One thing to keep in mind is that data aggregation is a capability of a data infrastructure, and it doesn't necessarily mean having all data in the same place.

In response, the Basel Committee published a set of 13 principles (*https://oreil.ly/dSCF7*) for designing and implementing data aggregation capabilities in financial institutions, primarily banks. Logically, the final implementation of these principles will vary from one financial institution to another. In addition, variations in internal structures among banks may facilitate or hinder the complete implementation of all 13 principles. Indeed, in assessing the adherence to the guidelines, the Basel Committee observed that banks were not fully compliant (*https://oreil.ly/jWYFT*), mainly due to the complexity of their internal IT infrastructure.

Several other practices in financial markets emphasize the aggregation of data. For instance, asset and fund managers typically maintain an *Investment Book of Record* (IBOR), a centralized database consolidating investment-related information like transactions, positions, and holdings. Another example is the *Accounting Book of Records* (ABOR), which aggregates accounting-related data on assets, liabilities, transactions, costs, net asset value, and charts of accounts. Another good example are *consolidated tapes*, which refer to systems that aggregate data from different trading venues, offering a unified source of information on trading activity across multiple markets.

Principle 5: Data Lineage

As a financial data engineer, a practical way to think about data is through the *data lifecycle* approach, also called the *information lifecycle*. The term data lifecycle is frequently used in industry (*https://oreil.ly/8_t-B*) to indicate the different phases that data goes through from the initial creation, or ingestion, onward. Based on each financial institution's particular context, the data lifecycle's phases and complexity may vary. At a high level, there are five main phases: extraction, transformation, storage, usage, and archiving. However, this process can quickly evolve into a complex chain of steps involving a multitude of actions and operations. Consequently, maintaining visibility into the data lifecycle becomes increasingly challenging, potentially exposing financial institutions to costly risks and errors.

To gain visibility into the data lifecycle, financial institutions need to develop a *data lineage* framework. The term data lineage is used to describe the discrete steps involved in the generation, movement, transformation, storage, delivery, and archiving of data. In other words, it is a feature of the data infrastructure that allows users and engineers to track a given data object throughout its lifecycle. Knowing how the data was generated and what actions were applied to it at each step builds confidence in the data infrastructure, pipelines, and lifecycle. Nowadays, the visibility of data lineage is a valuable feature that is top of mind for consumers, managers, and regulators.

Data lineage can be implemented in a number of ways. The most appealing and user-friendly approach is *lineage graphs*, which display a graphical visualization of data processing history. Importantly, visualization tools may not be performant when the processing logic becomes more complex and intricate. In such cases, detailed step-by-step descriptions of the processing logic are required.

> ## Audit Trails: A Financial Data Lineage Approach
>
> When working in finance, a common term that you might frequently encounter is *audit trail* (*https://oreil.ly/YmtR4*). An audit trail is a special implementation of data lineage that builds a chronological step-by-step data recording system that tracks financial activities such as accounting transactions, financial transactions, trades, buy and sell quote submissions, and any financial activity that can be tracked from its origination onward. An audit trail is often used when an auditor or regulator wants to examine the origin of a certain figure (e.g., earnings per share) or a given financial activity (e.g., quote to sell a specific number of securities). The importance of audit trails has increased remarkably after the flash crash of 2010, where a trader intentionally submitted an exceptional set of orders (a practice called *spoofing*) (*https://oreil.ly/XSfca*) in order to manipulate the market in their favor. Thanks to audit trails, regulators were able to identify the person responsible for the orders. Systems such as the Order Audit Trail System (OATS) and Consolidated Audit Trail (CAT) were established to automate the recording of information on orders, quotes, and other trade-related data from all shares traded on the National Market System (NMS). Such systems streamline the lifecycle of an order from reception through execution or cancellation for simple tracking and auditing.

Principle 6: Data Catalogs

Financial institutions produce and consume vast quantities and varieties of financial, economic, operational, and business data. To create an efficient and reliable data-driven culture, data producers and consumers must be able to search and find all the data they need quickly.

In this context, the idea of *data catalogs* has received particular attention. In simple terms, a data catalog is a set of metadata (i.e., data that describes or summarizes other data) combined with search and data management tools that allow a data producer or consumer to find and document a data asset within a financial institution. In other words, you can think of a data catalog as a central and searchable inventory of all data assets.

Data catalogs can be implemented in a variety of ways based on your data consumption needs and the complexity of your data assets. For instance, it can be a database where you store and search the metadata directly or a full-fledged application with features such as a UI, search and discovery, metadata management, user permission, and API integration. For a practical example of such tools, have a look at the open-source Python-based library Comprehensive Knowledge Archive Network (CKAN) (*https://oreil.ly/uQ7Xn*). To see a minimal data catalog in action, check the online data catalog of LSEG Data & Analytics (*https://oreil.ly/Vpu9W*).

Crucially, the more advanced and complex a data catalog, the higher the maintenance and curation burden. Conversely, having a sparse or out-of-date data catalog may lead to higher resource use and more wasted time than not having any.[16]

Principle 7: Data Ownership

Data ownership is one of the most valuable data governance practices for data-driven organizations. It's important to note that the term data ownership is used in two different contexts. On the one hand, it can refer to the legal owner of a given data asset. This topic emerged following the considerable increase in data collection practices and the adoption of third-party storage solutions such as the cloud. As more and more data is collected about people and organizations, concerns have emerged regarding who the final owner of the data is. Similarly, with the widespread adoption of public cloud storage solutions, questions have emerged regarding who owns the data stored in the cloud.[17]

Looking at it differently, data ownership involves designating an individual or team with the task of overseeing the collection, cleansing, maintenance, sharing, and management of a particular data asset within a financial institution. These individuals are often known as *data owners* and are typically selected for their domain expertise. The rationale is that data owners, being subject matter experts, are better equipped and motivated to maintain and manage a specific data asset compared to a centralized team that may lack the requisite domain knowledge to comprehend the data fully.[18]

Principle 8: Data Contracts

One of the main factors that can significantly impact the quality of data within organizations is the communication structure. A well-known adage, called *Conway's law* (*https://oreil.ly/ckLje*), is often cited in this context. It states that "organizations which design systems are constrained to produce designs which are copies of the communication structures of these organizations." Following this principle, the term *data contract* has recently emerged as a promising approach to organizing requirements and expectations around data. Let's consider how industry experts define data contracts:

---

16 For an excellent treatment of data catalogs, I recommend Ole Olesen-Bagneux's *The Enterprise Data Catalog* (O'Reilly, 2023).

17 For more on this topic, see Ali M. Al-Khouri's "Data Ownership: Who Owns "My Data?" (*https://oreil.ly/H5yAJ*), *International Journal of Management & Information Technology* 2, no. 1 (November 2012): 1-8.

18 For a detailed study on this topic, I recommend Marshall Van Alstyne, Erik Brynjolfsson, and Stuart Madnick's "Why Not One Big Database? Principles for Data Ownership" (*https://oreil.ly/Hce45*), *Decision Support Systems* 15, no. 4 (December 1995): 267-284.

> Data contracts are API-like agreements between Software Engineers who own services and Data Consumers that understand how the business works in order to generate well-modeled, high-quality, trusted, real-time data.
>
> — Chad Sanderson, "The Rise of Data Contracts" (*https://oreil.ly/9i_TG*)

> A data contract is an agreed interface between the generators of data and its consumers. It sets the expectations around that data, defines how it should be governed and facilitates the explicit generation of quality data that meets the business requirements.
>
> — Andrew Jones, *Driving Data Quality with Data Contracts* (Packt, 2023)

With a data contract, data consumers can define their data-related needs (e.g., structure, semantics, relations, formatting, fields, frequency, typing, rounding, privacy, and terms of use) and establish an agreement with data engineers to receive data that matches their expectations. This allows data consumers to concentrate on analysis and product development rather than worrying about data generation and engineering. Data engineers, on the other hand, do not need to be concerned about making modifications to the database or data model that may lead to production issues. This is why it is called a contract: both sides agree to it and each needs to hold their end of the deal. Naturally, a data contract can be revised and changed (e.g., a new field is required, a new owner is assigned, etc.) which would result in a new modified agreement.

Currently, general guidelines for implementing data contracts don't exist. Depending on the institution and its data strategy, different data contract definitions may be established.[19] To give an illustrative example, assume that the analytics team needs daily price data for the top 100 US stocks by market capitalization, with no null prices, a price range of 0–1000000 and no missing observations, and the data must be ready by 10:00 a.m. on each working day. In this case, following the data contract specification proposed by Jochen Christ and Simon Harre (*https://oreil.ly/-Rgzk*), we can build a basic contract as follows:

```
dataContractSpecification: 0.0.1
id: stock-price-extraction
info:
  title: Daily Adjusted Stock Price Extraction
  version: 0.0.1
  description: daily extraction of the adjusted stock price of the top 100 U.S
               stocks by market capitalization.
  owner: Analytics Team
  contact:
    name: John Smith (Analytics Team Lead)
    email: john.smith@example.com
```

---

[19] For a good read on data contracts, I highly recommend the book by Andrew Jones, *Driving Data Quality with Data Contracts: A Comprehensive Guide to Building Reliable, Trusted, and Effective Data Platforms* (Packt, 2023).

```
servers:
  production:
    type: Snowflake
    project: daily_adjusted_prices_prod
    dataset: snowflake_adjusted_prices_top_100_latest_v1
terms:
  usage: Data can be used for financial analysis, backtesting, and machine
         learning use cases.
  sla: 10:00 AM of each working day.
  daily_record_count: 100 observations
  limitations: >
    Not suitable for intra-day financial time series analysis.
    Data may be missing some identifiers such as ISIN.
    Max data processing per day: 10 Gigabytes.
    Max instrument requests per day: 1000 instruments.
  cost: 0.01$ per instrument request
schema:
  type: json-schema
  specification:
    adjusted_prices_top_100:
      description: One record per instrument and date.
      type: object
      fields:
        price_date:
          type: timestamp
          format: date-time
          nullable: false
          description: time of the price observation
        adjusted_price:
          type: numeric
          precision: 4 decimals
          range: 0-1000000
          nullable: false
          description: The adjusted price value.
        instrument_ticker:
          type: string
          description: The ticker identifier of the stock
          nullable: false
```

It's important to note that data contracts are not about specs or tools, but rather are a design pattern that emphasizes automating data quality and governance across various systems. The final specifications and the tools you will employ depend on your specific business requirements.

Principle 9: Data Reconciliation

In financial markets, the same financial record often appears across different systems owned by various counterparties, posing challenges for maintaining consistent records. This issue is addressed through data reconciliation, which involves aligning diverse sets of records to create a unified view of financial transactions and balances.

This process helps minimize errors and discrepancies, thereby ensuring operational integrity, financial stability, compliance, and customer trust.

A typical data reconciliation process in financial markets is portfolio reconciliation, where records of holdings, transactions, and positions are compared and verified between two or more counterparties, such as financial institutions or investment managers. The International Swaps and Derivatives Association (ISDA) has identified portfolio reconciliation as one of the most advantageous practices in mitigating operational and credit risks in OTC markets.[20]

For instance, in the fund industry, multiple entities may hold the same portfolio exposure data for a specific fund, such as a management company and a custodian. For instance, suppose a mutual fund is managed by Management Company A, and its assets are held in custody by Custodian B. Management Company A reports a $50 million exposure in technology stocks for the fund, while Custodian B, responsible for safekeeping and reporting the fund's assets, shows a $49.5 million exposure in the same sector. To ensure consistency and accuracy, portfolio reconciliation is necessary. This process involves comparing the data from both Management Company A and Custodian B to resolve any discrepancies and provide a unified view of the fund's holdings.

Similarly, in payment processes, multiple entities are involved in storing ledger records, often resulting in discrepancies in ledger balances among banks, FinTech companies, and service providers like BaaS providers. These discrepancies can stem from data duplication, incomplete or inaccurate record-keeping practices, delays or errors during system upgrades, and the inherent complexity of reconciling multiple systems of record.[21]

Data Security and Privacy

Financial institutions deal with highly sensitive and valuable data such as customer financial data, money transfers, transactions, investment strategies, and credit card numbers. Consequently, the financial industry has traditionally been a primary target for cyberattacks. To give a few examples, according to a report by Capgemini (*https://oreil.ly/FEpjo*), Citigroup US suffered a data breach in 2011 that resulted in data on more than 360K customers being leaked. Citigroup Japan reported a similar breach that affected around 92K customers. Again in 2011, Bank of America suffered a data breach that cost the bank around $10mln.

---

20 To read more about portfolio reconciliation and the technological side of it, I recommend the ISDA's paper, "Portfolio Reconciliation in Practice" (*https://oreil.ly/sp57g*).

21 For more on payment reconciliation, see "Payment Reconciliation 101: How It Works and Best Practices for Businesses" (*https://oreil.ly/kFLb4*), by Stripe.

Additionally, certain aspects of the financial industry make it particularly vulnerable to security threats. First, safeguarding intellectual property through patents and copyrights has been shown to be more challenging and ambiguous (*https://oreil.ly/I4Xfb*) in the financial industry than in other industries such as manufacturing. Second, due to the complex interdependencies of financial systems, a security breach in one financial institution may cause a cascading shock that affects the entire system. Third, the monetary impact of a security breach at a financial institution can be consequential, given that financial data is directly connected to client funds.

Given these considerations, data security and privacy have traditionally been regarded as a top priority by financial institutions and regulatory bodies. If you have worked at a financial institution, you must have noticed that security is given significant weight in practically all discussions. Importantly, while the terms privacy and security may be used interchangeably, they actually refer to distinct problems. To illustrate the difference, I will rely on international standards developed specifically for information security and privacy.

In terms of data security, standard ISO 27001—*Information Security Management Systems* (ISMS) (*https://oreil.ly/1SWTc*) is the primary worldwide reference. It specifies a set of guidelines for developing an ISMS system that protects data from cyber threats. The standard guides organizations through the stages required for ISMS development, such as assessing vulnerability risks, developing policies and procedures for data protection, training employees, and managing incidents.

On the other hand, standard ISO 27701 on developing a *Privacy Information Management System* (PIMS) (*https://oreil.ly/kk9xJ*) builds on top of ISO 27001 to ensure that a system is in place to ensure that *personally identifiable information* (PII) is handled in accordance with data legislation and regulations (we discuss PII in detail in the "Data Privacy" on page 201 section). The standard guides organizations through the steps needed to ensure the protection of PII, compliance with data regulations, and transparency about how organizations handle personal data.

From the two standards presented above, we can deduce that in designing for security and privacy, we consider different risks. When designing for security, we presume that an adversary may launch a cyberattack against our organization. When designing for privacy, we assume that personal data is not being handled in accordance with the law.

What Types of Cyberattacks Are Committed Against Financial Institutions?

Financial institutions can be exposed to a variety of cyberattacks. These include but are not limited to the following:

Malware
> Malicious software installed on a device connected to the internal institution system. It can be a virus, spyware, Trojan, or other. If installed successfully, malware can enable the hacker to access sensitive data and compromise critical systems.

Ransomware
> A special type of malware where the hacker gains access to the institution's data and holds it hostage in exchange for the payment of a ransom.

Spoofing
> When a cybercriminal manages to impersonate and replicate the website of a financial institution (often banks) that looks and functions the same way. If users are not careful, they may end up providing their personal information to the fake website.

Spam and phishing
> An email-based cybercrime where a person sends emails to random people soliciting them to send banking or credit card details.

Distributed denial-of-service attack (DDoS)
> This occurs when a cybercriminal floods a financial institution's server with internet requests.

Corporate account takeover
> When a cybercriminal gains access to a corporate account associated with a financial institution. This may allow the attacker to initiate fraudulent money transfers and other transactions.

Brute force attacks
> When a hacker tries to guess the access credentials of a user via trial and error. Although it might seem outdated, it might still work if passwords are not strong enough.

SQL injection
> A code injection technique where malicious SQL statements are inserted into a specific part of the application accessible to the user in order to manipulate the final query submitted to the backend database. A successful SQL injection attack might lead to data loss, a breach, or corruption.

An important thing to keep in mind is that cybercriminals are creative (newer ways of conducting cyberattacks are continuously being invented) and adaptive (work-arounds are developed to circumvent existing security measures). For this reason, ensuring data security at financial institutions requires continuous monitoring, testing, and reinforcement.

The literature and practices surrounding data security and privacy are vast. Different financial organizations may confront different security issues and approach privacy in various ways. Furthermore, planning for security and privacy frequently involves a large number of individuals, including managers, chief information officers, chief security officers, chief technology officers, security experts, network experts, infrastructure engineers, software engineers, data engineers, data architects, and data analysts. This book will concentrate on four major issues of interest to financial data engineers: data privacy regulations, data anonymization, data encryption, and access control.

Data Privacy

Data privacy is a data governance practice that ensures data is collected, stored, processed, and shared in accordance with data protection laws and regulations, as well as the data subject's general interests. Data privacy guarantees that sensitive information is not used for reasons other than those consented to by the data subject or established by law. *Personally identifiable information* (PII) is possibly the most sensitive sort of information. PII refers to any data that can be used either alone or in combination with other data to identify an individual. This can include direct identifiers such as a person's name, address, social security number, or email address, as well as indirect identifiers like birth date, phone number, IP address, or biometric data. In the context of financial markets, financial PII may refer to bank account details, credit card numbers, investment account information, and any other identifiers that could potentially reveal an individual's financial identity.

A number of data regulations and laws have been devised and put into effect internationally in recent years. The most prominent and comprehensive framework is the European Union's *General Data Protection Regulation* (GDPR) (*https://oreil.ly/ VRxDM*).[22] In a nutshell, GDPR's main goal is to give EU citizens more control over their personal data. It applies to all EU citizens as well as the entities that do business with them, including those not based in EU countries. GDPR distinguishes between two types of data processing entities: a *data controller* and a *data processor*. A data controller is an entity that collects personal data and determines the purposes (why)

---

22 For a practical introduction to GDPR, I strongly recommend Paul Voigt and Axel von dem Bussche's *The ER General Data Protection Regulation (GDPR): A Practical Guide*, 1st ed. (Springer, 2017).

for which and the means (how) by which personal data is processed. If multiple data controllers are involved, then the entity is called a *joint controller*. On the other hand, a data processor is an entity that processes data on behalf of the controller. In most cases, the data processor is an external third-party entity (e.g., a payroll company).

Individual rights defined in GDPR relate mostly to the collection, usage, sharing, transfer, and deletion of personal data. Such rights can be grouped into three categories that you are likely to encounter:

Right to access
EU individuals have the right to access and request a copy of their personal data, as well as clarifications on how their data is processed, stored, and used.

Right to be forgotten
EU individuals have the right to request the deletion of their personal data or reject having their data processed.

Data portability
When feasible, EU individuals should have the right to have their personal data transmitted from one data controller to another.

A variety of similar data protection laws have been introduced worldwide, such as:

- The California Consumer Privacy Act (CCPA) in the US
- The Gramm–Leach–Bliley Act
- Canada's Personal Information Protection and Electronic Documents Act (PIPEDA)
- Japan's Act on Protection of Personal Information (APPI)
- Brazil's General Data Protection Law

With the adoption of these regulations, the demand for privacy-preserving features in system design has increased considerably. As a financial data engineer, your responsibility within this context is related to data collection, visibility, and utilization. For example, if a user consents to the usage of their data for marketing purposes only, then such a restriction needs to be taken into account in the data pipeline(s) that process customer data. A good approach to enforcing data privacy is through data contracts, where all privacy-related requirements are established and agreed upon by both data producers and consumers.

When integrating data privacy elements into system design, a tradeoff might emerge between data confidentiality and data sharing. While limiting data sharing might increase data security and confidentiality, it can also limit prospects for meaningful innovation, both within the financial institution and with external partners. On the other side, enabling excessive data sharing exposes the company to security breaches, legal penalties, and reputational risks.

Ensuring privacy requires having a culture of privacy in the first place. Explaining the impact that privacy infringement can have on the employees is an essential first step. This encourages a due diligence mindset when handling data. Additionally, having management support and interest in enforcing data privacy plays a crucial role. Depending on these and other factors, various financial institutions may invest differently in data privacy standards.[23]

On the methodological side, a variety of data privacy techniques exist. The most effective of such techniques is data anonymization, which I explain in detail in the next section.

Data Anonymization

Data anonymization is a data governance practice that ensures both data security and privacy via transformations that obscure the identifiability of the data. If data is properly anonymized, then it loses its essential identification elements and cannot be linked to specific data objects. This in turn makes it useless if it falls into the wrong hands. In financial institutions, anonymization can be adopted as a good data practice, but it may also be mandated by law. For example, GDPR states (*https://oreil.ly/Kb-ff*) that for data to be exempt from certain GRPD privacy restrictions, it needs to be anonymized.[24]

---

23 For a comparative study on this topic, I recommend Lorrie Faith Cranor, Kelly Idouchi, Pedro Giovanni Leon, Manya Sleeper, and Blase Ur's "Are They Actually Any Different? Comparing Thousands of Financial Institutions' Privacy Practices" (*https://oreil.ly/s6pSA*), presented at the 12th Annual Workshop on the Economics of Information Security (WEIS 2013).

24 A key distinction to remember under GDPR is the difference between anonymization and pseudonymization. According to GDPR, anonymization refers to the process of irreversibly removing personal identifiers from data so that individuals can no longer be identified, making the data completely anonymous and not subject to GDPR. Pseudonymization, on the other hand, involves processing data in such a way that individuals cannot be identified without additional information, which is kept separately and protected. Unlike anonymized data, pseudonymized data is still considered personal data under GDPR and remains subject to its regulations, as the potential to reidentify individuals exists if the additional information is accessed.

Anonymization strategy

Interestingly, if you check any reference about data anonymization, you will notice that there exists a large discrepancy in the presentation and categorization of data anonymization techniques. Consequently, to establish a baseline, I will initially outline the key factors to consider when devising or choosing a data anonymization approach.

The first element of an anonymization strategy is the *identifiability spectrum*. At one end of the identifiability spectrum, data is completely identifiable. One way to achieve full identifiability is via *direct identifiers*, which refer to values in a dataset that can directly identify a data object without additional information. Examples of direct identifiers could be client name, social security number, financial security identifier, company name, and credit card number. For example, if you know that the ISIN of a company is US5949181045, then you can easily find out that this is Microsoft Corporation. On the other hand, *indirect identifiers or quasi-identifiers* are values that, when combined with other variables in the data, can identify a data object. Examples of indirect identifiers include company domiciliation, market capitalization, price, and the name of the CEO. If your data has information about a company whose CEO in 2023 is Satya Nadella, then it is very likely that we are talking about Microsoft Corporation. Following this logic, we can place direct identifiers on one extreme of the spectrum followed by indirect identifiers. As you obscure or remove data identifiers, you anonymize the data more and more, and it becomes more difficult to identify data objects. At the other end of the spectrum, data is completely anonymized and it is not possible to distinguish one data object from another. To decide where to be on the spectrum of identifiability, you need to consider the risks and costs of reidentification. The higher such risks and costs, the higher the threshold is on the spectrum.[25]

The second element of a data anonymization strategy is *analytical integrity*. Suppose that a financial institution agrees to share some of its internal data with a group of external researchers working on a specific project. To this end, the institution decides to anonymize the data. In this case, the anonymization strategy should take into account the fact that data should still be valid for analysis. For example, if the dataset encompasses certain correlations between the variables that cannot be randomly altered, then it is important to use an anonymization technique that preserves such features in the data.

Reversibility is the third element, which denotes the possibility of reversing the anonymization process by reidentifying the data. If the anonymization is done for data-sharing purposes, then it may not be necessary to reverse the process as it concerns a

---

25 For an introduction to risk-based data anonymization techniques, I highly recommend the book by Khaled El Emam and Luk Arbuckle, *Anonymizing Health Data: Case Studies and Methods to Get You Started* (O'Reilly, 2013).

copy of the data intended for external use. However, if anonymization is done for internal purposes, e.g., credit card numbers, then it may be necessary to introduce reversibility into the anonymization strategy.

The fourth element is *simplicity*. A large number of anonymization techniques are available and they differ in their implementation complexity and interpretability. Simple methods are easy to implement and reverse, while complex techniques require more time and effort.

Fifth, anonymization can be performed statically or dynamically. In static anonymization, data is anonymized and then stored in the final destination for safe future use. Dynamic anonymization, also called interactive anonymization, applies anonymization on the fly to the result of a query or request and not to the entire dataset. When dynamic anonymization is used, an important variable that needs to be taken into account is performance and the speed at which data gets anonymized.

Finally, anonymization can be applied in a deterministic or nondeterministic way. In deterministic anonymization, the outcome of anonymization is always the same even if repeated multiple times. For example, if the name John Smith gets replaced by XXYREQ12, then repeating the process again would replace John Smith with XXYREQ12. In a nondeterministic anonymization, this is not a requirement. For example, the name John Smith can be replaced by a randomly generated string that can change every time you implement the anonymization.

 Data anonymization is an investment that requires effort, expertise, and integration into your financial data infrastructure. For efficiency reasons, I recommend that you first classify your data based on its sensitivity/confidentiality (e.g., Class A is public data, Class B is for internal use, Class G is strictly confidential, etc.) and then anonymize just the most critical data classes.

Anonymization techniques

After outlining your anonymization needs, you can employ a range of techniques for implementation. But before moving forward, it's important to differentiate between an anonymization technique and a measure of its effectiveness.

An anonymization technique takes a raw dataset as input and returns an anonymized dataset as output. An anonymization effectiveness measure evaluates the level of anonymity of an anonymized dataset. Examples of anonymization effectiveness techniques include *k-anonymity*, *l-diversity*, and *t-closeness*. To illustrate the idea, *k*-anonymity, for example, checks whether the information for each data object contained in the dataset cannot be distinguished from at least $k - 1$ data objects whose information also appears in the dataset.[26]

The rest of this section will focus on five common anonymization techniques: generalization, suppression, distortion, swapping, and masking. To illustrate each of these, let's take an initial data sample (Table 5-1) and see how each technique applies to it.

 You can always implement your own anonymization technique. However, before crafting your own solution, you should first consider the available solutions and their use cases. Data anonymization is a major field of study, and you are very likely going to find what you need in the literature.

Table 5-1. Original data before anonymization

ID	Company name	CEO	Headquarters	Revenues	Market capitalization
XYA12F	Standard Steel Corporation	John Smith	New York	$45 mln	$400 mln
BFG76D	Northwest Bank	Lesly Charles	Las Vegas	$5.5 bln	$50 bln
M47GK	General Bicycles Corporation	Mary Jackson	Chicago	$650 mln	$10 bln

Using the generalization technique involves substituting values with less specific yet consistent alternatives. For example, instead of indicating the exact numbers for revenues and market capitalization, we can use ranges. Table 5-2 illustrates the outcome of this generalization strategy.

Table 5-2. Anonymized data after generalization

ID	Company name	CEO	Headquarters	Revenues	Market capitalization
XYA12F	Standard Steel Corporation	John Smith	New York	$0–100 mln	$0–1 bln
BFG76D	Northwest Bank	Lesly Charles	Las Vegas	$5–10 bln	$0–100 bln
M47GK	General Bicycles Corporation	Mary Jackson	Chicago	$0–1 bln	$0–50 bln

Another technique is *suppression*, which simply removes or drops an entire field from a dataset. For example, in our data sample, we may want to suppress the direct identifiers ID and company name by replacing all values with ********. Table 5-3 illustrates the outcome of suppression.

---

26 To learn more about these measures, I highly recommend the publication by Ninghui Li, Tiancheng Li, and Suresh Venkatasubramanian, "t-Closeness: Privacy Beyond k-Anonymity and l-Diversity" (*https://oreil.ly/_Vd92*), in the *2007 IEEE 23rd International Conference on Data Engineering* (IEEE, 2006): 106-115.

Table 5-3. Anonymized data after suppression

ID	Company name	CEO	Headquarters	Revenues	Market capitalization
********	********	John Smith	New York	$45 mln	$400 mln
********	********	Lesly Charles	Las Vegas	$5.5 bln	$50 bln
********	********	Mary Jackson	Chicago	$650 mln	$10 bln

Another effective technique is *distortion*, which applies mostly to numerical fields and works by adding a certain noise to the values to alter their true value. For example, one can simply generate a random number from a given probability distribution and add it to the value of each record in the column. A large number of formulas can be used for distortion. For illustrative purposes, let's assume that we want to alter the values for revenues by multiplying each number by 1.1, and market capitalization by 1.3. The outcome of this anonymization process is shown in Table 5-4.

Table 5-4. Anonymized data after distortion

ID	Company name	CEO	Headquarters	Revenues	Market capitalization
XYA12F	Standard Steel Corporation	John Smith	New York	$49.5 mln	$520 mln
BFG76D	Northwest Bank	Lesly Charles	Las Vegas	$6.05 bln	$65 bln
M47GK	General Bicycles Corporation	Mary Jackson	Chicago	$715 mln	$13 bln

The next technique is swapping, which works by shuffling the data within one or more fields. For example, in our original data, we could shuffle the company and CEO names as illustrated in Table 5-5.

Table 5-5. Anonymized data after swapping

ID	Company name	CEO	Headquarters	Revenues	Market capitalization
XYA12F	Northwest Bank	John Smith	New York	$45 mln	$400 mln
BFG76D	General Bicycles Corporation	Lesly Charles	Las Vegas	$5.5 bln	$50 bln
M47GK	Standard Steel Corporation	Mary Jackson	Chicago	$650 mln	$10 bln

One of the more popular techniques is masking, which obfuscates sensitive data by using a modified version with modified characters. For example, the ID field in our data sample can be masked by keeping the first character and replacing numbers with 0 and alphabetic characters with 1, as shown in Table 5-6.

Table 5-6. Anonymized data after masking

ID	Company name	CEO	Headquarters	Revenues	Market capitalization
X11001	Standard Steel Corporation	John Smith	New York	$45 mln	$400 mln
B11001	Northwest Bank	Lesly Charles	Las Vegas	$5.5 bln	$50 bln
M0011	General Bicycles Corporation	Mary Jackson	Chicago	$650 mln	$10 bln

In addition to these basic techniques, a variety of more advanced options are available. One prominent example is *differential privacy*, a mathematically rigorous technique that has proven to be quite reliable.[27] Another special technique that has found applications in finance, and in particular financial machine learning, is synthetic data (*https://oreil.ly/UkZIy*). Synthetic data is machine-generated data that mirrors the properties of original sensitive data. For example, if we are able to infer the probability distribution of a sensitive dataset (e.g., user account balance), then we can use such probability distribution to generate a synthetic sample that preserves the same statistical properties of the original dataset.

Payment Tokenization

One of the most important applications of data anonymization in finance is payment tokenization. This is a security technique that uses cryptographic algorithms to convert sensitive payment information such as credit card and bank account data into a unique, random string of characters called a "token." Successively, when conducting payment transactions, the token is used instead of the real payment details. If an unauthorized party gets their hands on a token, they won't be able to do anything with it.

Within the payment industry, several participants provide tokenization services, including payment processors and third-party tokenization vendors. Some payment services providers, such as Stripe (*https://oreil.ly/4sMcX*), provide tokenization-enabled payment hardware or software as part of their service. Once payment tokens are generated, they are stored and secured in a secure vault managed by the tokenization service provider.

With payment tokenization, a business only needs to store the tokens of their customers. When processing client transactions, the business can send the token to the tokenization service provider, which in turn maps the token to the original payment data securely. This technique can be quite useful for businesses that process recurring transactions such as subscriptions or store customer profile details.

Various methods can be employed to generate tokens in payment tokenization. The simplest approach is Random Number Generation (RNG), where tokens are generated using a random number generator to produce a string of numbers or alphanumeric characters. For added security, mathematical algorithms such as hashing or encryption can be employed. A technique called Format-Preserving Encryption (FPE) can be used to encrypt the card number in such a way that the resulting token retains the format of the original card number (e.g., same length and structure).

---

[27] See for example Cynthia Dwork's "Differential Privacy: A Survey of Results" (*https://oreil.ly/IM4s1*), in the *Proceedings of the 5th International Conference on the Theory and Applications of Models of Computation* (Springer, 2008): 1–19.

Don't take it for granted that anonymization is bulletproof. Always keep in mind that reidentification risks are present and can change and evolve as a result of multiple factors. For example, in 2006, Netflix launched a one-million-dollar open competition to enhance its movie recommender engine. To this end, Netflix publicly disclosed one hundred million records exposing hundreds of thousands of user ratings from 1999 to 2005. Although the released dataset contained no direct identifiers, two researchers were able to reidentify a subset of people in the data by cross-referencing Netflix data with *IMDB.com* ratings (*https://oreil.ly/k2aus*).

Data Encryption

Data encryption is a fundamental practice in information security and privacy. It involves converting data into an unreadable format, rendering it meaningless to unauthorized individuals. Essentially, encryption transforms plain-text (unencrypted) data into ciphertext (encrypted) using a cryptographic algorithm. This process utilizes an encryption key to encode the data and a decryption key to decode it back to plain text. This way, if encrypted data falls into the wrong hands, then without the decryption key, they will simply see gibberish text. However, this assumes that the decryption key is kept safe!

Data can be encrypted in different states: at rest, in transit, and in use. Data at rest refers to data residing in a storage location such as a hard disk or cloud storage. Data in transit refers to data that is being transferred from one location to another over a network. Data in use is any data that is being processed or data that is temporarily held in memory.

The field of cryptography is quite vast, and a full discussion of encryption methods and techniques is beyond the scope of this book.[28] Nevertheless, to ensure the security of a financial data infrastructure, financial data engineers will benefit from having a basic understanding of the essential concepts and principles of data encryption.

An important distinction to understand is between *symmetric* and *asymmetric* encryption. In symmetric encryption, only one (symmetric) key is used to encrypt and decrypt the data. Symmetric keys are often considered more efficient to generate and faster at data encryption/decryption. However, they need to be shared and stored carefully. This might occasionally necessitate encrypting the key itself using a different encryption key, which could result in a cycle of dependency. The most popular symmetric encryption method is the Advanced Encryption Standard (AES), developed by the US National Institute of Standards and Technology (NIST).

---

28 Interested readers are encouraged to read Jonathan Katz and Yehuda Lindell's *Introduction to Modern Cryptography: Principles and Protocols* (Chapman and Hall/CRC, 2021).

Notably, companies like Google utilize the AES to encrypt their data at the storage level (*https://oreil.ly/tHwxx*).

On the other hand, *asymmetric encryption* uses a pair of keys, called public and private, to encrypt and decrypt the data. Anyone with the public key can encrypt and send data; however, only the private key can decrypt the data. Due to this double-key feature, asymmetric encryption is often considered more secure. However, asymmetric encryption could be more computationally expensive, especially for large data packets, as it relies on large encryption keys.

The most popular asymmetric encryption technique is *Rivest–Shamir–Adleman* (RSA). RSA generates the keys via a factorization operation of two prime numbers. The public RSA can be used to encrypt the data, but only the person who knows the prime numbers can decrypt the data. RSA keys can be very large (e.g., 2,048 or 4,096 bits are typical sizes), and thus their usage might have an impact on performance.

Nowadays, the use of data encryption has become a default and recommended practice both for data security and compliance purposes. This goes without saying for the financial sector. To give an example, let's take the well-known standard, ISO 9564—Personal Identification Number (PIN) management and security (*https://oreil.ly/14uGr*). ISO 9564 specifies principles and requirements for reliable and secure management of cardholder Personal Identification Numbers (PINs). PIN codes are used in many places such as automated teller machine (ATM) systems, point-of-sale (POS) terminals, and vending machines. When inserting the PIN, it needs to be transmitted to the issuer for verification. To secure PIN transmission, ISO 9564 requires that the PIN be encrypted, and specifies a list of approved encryption algorithms (*https://oreil.ly/YjxnA*): Triple Data Encryption Algorithm (TDEA), RSA, and Advanced Encryption Standard (AES).

Access Control

Access control is a data security practice that allows firms to manage access to their data and related resources. A secure access control policy defines who has access to what, what type of access privileges are assigned, and a disaster management strategy to deal with access anomalies or incidents.

The two main components of access control are *authentication* and *authorization*. Authentication is an identity verification process that checks who is making the access request. Once a user has been authenticated, authorization verifies which resources the user has access to and what access privileges they have.

Access control management is a continuous and primary function within any financial institution. The typical approach to access control involves creating and enforcing a set of guidelines and protocols to be followed when granting access and privileges, as well as a monitoring system to alert against unauthorized access or excessive rights. Although such procedures might differ from one institution to another, a number of best practices have emerged over the years. For example, a quite effective principle is that of *least privileges (https://oreil.ly/26NAp)*, which states that a user or application should be granted the minimal amount of permissions required to perform their tasks. Excess privileges can be quite dangerous and lead to consequential incidents, especially if the user is not aware of them. For example, if a new user is given access and read/write/update/delete privileges to the production database, then data is exposed to deletion or corruption risk.

Another best practice is *multifactor authentication (https://oreil.ly/f2TKO)*, which requires going through separate factors to log in—for example, logging in via email plus entering a code that is sent to a linked mobile device. Of similar importance is the practice of access control audit logs *(https://oreil.ly/YKVTN)*, which involves monitoring and collecting information on user activities to detect anomalous or unexpected privileges.

Case Study: Payment Card Industry Data Security Standard

To give an empirical overview of how the financial industry formulates data security requirements and policies, let's illustrate the widely used Payment Card Industry Data Security Standard, or for short, PCI DSS.

PCI DSS is a set of policies and procedures intended to ensure the security of payment card transactions and associated data. PCI DSS is defined by the PCI Security Standards Council (SSC). Compliance with PCI DSS is not mandatory by law or regulation. However, it is highly recommended for any institution that stores, processes, and transmits cardholder data. In some cases, such institutions might be required to comply with PCI DSS due to a contractual clause. Furthermore, businesses that demonstrate compliance with PCI DSS are more likely to be trusted in the market.

Cardholder data can be identification data such as PAN, cardholder name, expiry date, and service code, as well as authentication data such as the magnetic stripe data, card verification code (CVC), and PIN code.

To comply with PCI DSS, 12 requirements have been established, which can be grouped into 6 major goals:

- Build and maintain secure networks for conducting card transactions. The recommended approach suggests installing reliable firewalls to block and prevent unauthorized access to the network.

- Protect cardholder data. The standard recommends storing only what's necessary for business operations. Card authentication data should never be stored. When transmitting card data over a network, it should be encrypted.

- Maintain a vulnerability management program to protect against attacks, and perform regular updates and patches of antivirus and operating systems.

- Implement strong access measures via access policies, authentication, and authorization, and ensure the physical security of data.

- Regularly monitor and test networks by tracking all access to network resources and cardholder data and testing security systems.

- Maintain an information security policy that highlights the duties and responsibilities of the personnel and the potential consequences of noncompliance.

For more details on the standard specifications, consult the PCI DSS Quick Reference Guide available on the official PCI DSS web page (*https://oreil.ly/H5RcF*).

Ongoing efforts are continuously improving security within financial markets. For instance, the European Union is planning to introduce the Digital Operational Resilience Act (DORA) (*https://oreil.ly/uoEzk*) to enhance the digital operational resilience of financial institutions. DORA sets requirements for ICT risk management, incident reporting, and testing to ensure firms can withstand, respond to, and recover from all types of ICT-related disruptions.

Summary

This chapter provided an overview of financial data governance, which we can summarize as follows:

- Defining financial data governance and illustrating its critical importance within the financial domain

- Introduction to data quality, with a discussion of nine dimensions relevant to financial data

- Examination of data integrity through the lens of nine fundamental principles pertinent to financial data

- Illustration of primary security and privacy challenges and best practices affecting most financial institutions

Financial data governance can apply to any aspect of your institutions' data infrastructure, strategy, and business operations. As you read further in this book, you will observe how the different practices and principles discussed in this chapter are employed.

Over the next five chapters, we will go through the financial data engineering lifecycle, where you will learn about the different layers you will need to implement when designing a financial data infrastructure.

## PART II

The Financial Data Engineering Lifecycle

In the first part of this book, we explored the major ideas and problems around the management of financial data, including the complexity of the financial data landscape, the diversity and nonuniversality of financial data identifiers, the problems of financial entity recognition and resolution, and financial data governance.

In the second part of this book, spanning Chapters 6 through 12, the focus shifts to the technological aspects of financial data engineering. This includes the models, tools, frameworks, software systems, hardware components, libraries, design patterns, and networking systems needed to design and implement a financial data infrastructure.

Chapter 6 will begin by introducing the financial data engineering lifecycle (FDEL), a conceptual framework that will be used to organize the many components of a financial data infrastructure into four structured layers: ingestion, storage, transformation and delivery, and monitoring. Subsequently, Chapters 7 through 10 will cover each of these layers in detail. After that, Chapter 11 will discuss the various workflow architectures that are commonly used to implement the FDEL. Chapter 12 concludes with four hands-on projects designed to familiarize you with key practices and technologies in financial data engineering.

## CHAPTER 6

Overview of the Financial Data Engineering Lifecycle

As a financial data engineer, navigating the multitude, diversity, and complexity of available technological options can be overwhelming. Without a systematic approach in mind, this complexity may lead to chaotic situations and accumulating costly technical debt. Therefore, this chapter introduces a structured approach to financial data engineering, organizing its components into a layered architecture called the *financial data engineering lifecycle* (FDEL). This framework draws inspiration from the foundational work of Joe Reis and Matt Housley on data engineering lifecycles.

In this chapter, I will introduce the FDEL and outline its four layers: ingestion, storage, transformation and delivery, and monitoring. Following this, I will discuss specific criteria that financial data engineers can consider when selecting technologies to support the FDEL. Please note that since there is so much information to cover, I'll save the details of each FDEL layer for Chapters 7 through 10.

Financial Data Engineering Lifecycle Defined

Data engineering is a fast-moving and continuously evolving field. However, if there is one constant that characterizes and defines the job of a data engineer, it is the fact that it revolves around systems that perform a series of actions for the extraction, transformation, storage, and consumption of data.

To move beyond the simple view of data engineering as merely a series of data-related tasks, authors Joe Reis and Matt Housley introduced the *Data Engineering Lifecycle* (DEL). This concept offers a structured framework that formalizes the various stages of data engineering. According to the authors, the DEL "comprises stages that turn raw data ingredients into a useful end product, ready for consumption by analysts, data scientists, ML engineers, and others."

 It is essential to differentiate between the data lifecycle and the data engineering lifecycle. While they are related, the data lifecycle is a conceptual model that describes the stages data goes through from creation to archival or deletion. On the other hand, the data engineering lifecycle is a practical framework that outlines the processes, patterns, and tools used to manage data throughout its lifecycle, ultimately delivering a final product to data consumers.

The DEL can be adapted to incorporate several processes or stages depending on how complicated the data lifecycle and business needs are. In their original work, Joe Reis and Matt Housley divided the DEL into five stages: data generation, storage, ingestion, transformation, and serving.

When applied to the financial domain, the data engineering lifecycle needs to be adapted to account for a number of domain-specific elements. These originate from the strict data governance and regulatory requirements for financial institutions, legal and content licensing constraints, the complexity of the financial data landscape, industry-specific software standards and protocols, and the unique demands for low latency, high throughput, and other performance constraints that characterize financial operations.

To offer a domain-focused perspective that incorporates these considerations, this book introduces the *financial data engineering lifecycle* (FDEL), a layered framework[1] consisting of four layers: *ingestion layer, storage layer, transformation and delivery layer,* and *monitoring layer.* Figure 6-1 illustrates this framework.

In the ingestion layer, data engineers design and implement an infrastructure for handling the generation and reception of data coming from different sources and in different formats, volumes, and frequencies. This layer is quite critical, as errors or performance bottlenecks in ingestion are likely to propagate downstream and impact the entire FDEL. In Chapter 7, we will explore the ingestion layer in depth, covering various ingestion processes, patterns, technologies, and formats.

Following is the storage layer, where the focus is on selecting and optimizing data storage models and technologies to meet various business requirements. Choosing the right data storage system for a given problem is one of the most important decisions throughout the FDEL. A poor data storage choice can very easily translate into

---

1 Layered architectures are quite common in software engineering. Their main advantages include simplicity, maintainability, familiarity, and cost. To learn more about this topic, I recommend Mark Richards and Neal Ford's *Fundamentals of Software Architecture: An Engineering Approach* (O'Reilly, 2020).

bottlenecks, degraded performance, and rocketing costs, which in turn can jeopardize product development and analytical capabilities. Chapter 8 will detail the varieties of data storage models and illustrate their data modeling principles, internal features, and financial use cases.

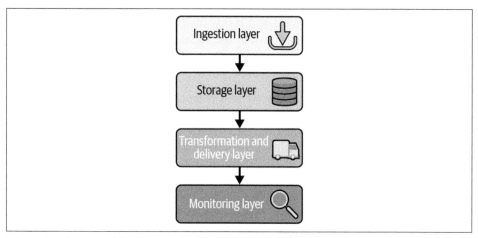

Figure 6-1. Layers of the financial data engineering lifecycle

Next is the transformation and delivery layer, which performs a number of business-defined transformations and computations that produce high-quality data that is ready for consumption by its intended data consumers. In Chapter 9, I will thoroughly explore this layer, examining the key types of transformations applicable to financial data, the computational demands of different transformation processes, and the various mechanisms for data delivery.

Finally, the monitoring layer is there to make sure that issues related to data processing, data quality, performance, costs, bugs, and analytical errors are all monitored and tracked to allow efficient and timely fixes. Chapter 10 will be dedicated to this layer.

The FDEL framework will provide several advantages if correctly applied. You may benefit greatly, for instance, in terms of modularity and separation of responsibility. The larger the firm is, the larger and more complex its data engineering processes are going to become. This suggests that, from an organizational perspective, it could be feasible to assign distinct teams to each FDEL layer. For example, a team may be dedicated to optimizing and securing the ingestion layer, another for ensuring the performance, scalability, and security of the storage layer, and so on. It is important to note that the FDEL is an *iterative* process where feedback and requirements from one layer may impact the design, constraints, and implementation of another layer.

Over the next four chapters, I will detail these layers, highlighting the domain-specific challenges they present in financial markets, and offering concrete examples to provide deeper insights.

Criteria for Building the Financial Data Engineering Stack

When implementing the FDEL, it's essential to choose the best tools and technologies to design and architect each layer, i.e., the technological stack. This is no small feat. If you want to learn about data engineering technologies and you do a quick search, you will find hundreds of different tools and frameworks. This makes it hard to know where to start since there is practically a jungle of tools to choose from. To make it more complex, these diverse tools can be used together and sometimes compete to process financial data throughout its lifecycle.

In this section, I will outline six criteria that financial institutions can employ to inform their technological decisions. These criteria serve as a fundamental and general guideline but are not exhaustive. Depending on your organization's unique needs, you may need to identify additional criteria. Furthermore, in the following five chapters, I will discuss more granular criteria that are tailored to each layer of the FDEL.

Criterion 1: Open Source Versus Commercial Software

A crucial and highly debated decision in financial institutions concerns the choice between proprietary commercial software and open source software. Proprietary commercial software is distributed under a purchased license that restricts user access to the source code. On the other hand, open source software is typically distributed with a license to access, use, modify, sell, and distribute the source code.

The main advantages of commercial software include the following:

Vendor accountability
> The software provider ensures frequent updates, bug fixes, security, and customer support. This is typically ensured via a *Service-Level Agreement* (SLA), which is a guarantee by the vendor to commit to a certain level of quality, availability, and performance of the offered service. Vendors might need to pay a penalty if their SLA is not met. SLAs and security are two of the most important factors behind the widespread reliance on proprietary software by the financial sector, given the risk aversion culture in financial markets that is driven by regulatory and security concerns. Vendor accountability and SLAs can help financial institutions measure and manage their operational risks, which is a regulatory requirement under frameworks such as Basel III.[2]

---

2 According to the Basel framework (*https://oreil.ly/i1WO6*), operational risk is defined as "the risk of loss resulting from inadequate or failed internal processes, people and systems or from external events."

Product integrations

The vendor guarantees seamless integration between different commercial products, which in turn can be a major cost-saving factor. Financial institutions rely heavily on trust when conducting a new activity or project. Therefore, they are more likely to adopt a new product or service that integrates with their current offerings if it is offered by a reliable software provider.

Enterprise-grade features

The vendor offers specific features for large corporations, including scalability, security, and compliance. This is particularly relevant for financial institutions operating on a large scale, with stringent requirements of audit and monitoring.

User-friendly experience

Commercial products are often offered with an easy-to-use interface and offer rich documentation and guides. Employees at financial institutions are often users rather than developers; therefore, a user-friendly interface is likely to be more welcomed than a complex one.

On the negative side, commercial software may come with disadvantages such as the following:

Cost

Commercial software licenses can be very expensive and include a variable part that is hard to predict (e.g., support fees, hidden features). For large financial institutions that have critical applications, the risks can easily outweigh the costs.

Bulky products

Many commercial software tools come in a single package that includes a large number of features. Some financial institutions (e.g., FinTech firms) may not need all of these features and end up using only a fraction of what the tool offers.

Vendor lock-in

The more a company relies on commercial tools, the harder it is to switch to other options, including open source. Vendor lock-in gets stronger for factors such as network effect (where product value increases with its user base), and risk aversion (uncertainty from switching to another solution).

Lack of customization

Commercial software is proprietary, meaning that financial clients may not able to adapt or modify the product to their unique needs or client expectations.

Traditionally, financial institutions have been skewed toward proprietary software because internal control rules, policies, standards, procedures, and IT audit checklists all lay out strict requirements for support agreements. The top financial services software vendors include Microsoft, FIS Global, SAP, Oracle, IBM, and NCR Corporation.

The Oracle Database: Why Is It Widely Used by Banks?

To illustrate why financial institutions have traditionally preferred commercial software, let's take as an example the Oracle Database. If you have ever wondered what type of database systems big banks use for their core operations, the answer is likely to include a mention of Oracle. It is perhaps the most popular enterprise-level database system among financial institutions. Interestingly, according to the DB-Engines ranking (*https://oreil.ly/P7VQJ*), as of 2024, Oracle is considered the most popular database system in the world.

The Oracle Database, a commercial SQL database management system by Oracle Corporation, is predominantly used by financial institutions for online transaction processing (OLTP) purposes. It is used to store and manage core business data encompassing credit, accounts, loans, and transactions.

Over time, new database systems have emerged in the market, and some are gaining traction. However, to date, Oracle remains the gold standard for financial services.

First of all, Oracle has been in the market since 1979; therefore, it is considered a mature and reliable product. Throughout its history, Oracle has consistently added features to its flagship products (*https://oreil.ly/Mdv-a*), placing the company at the forefront of database technology. By offering many features, the Oracle database could fit the many applications, requirements, and use cases that have emerged in the financial sector.

Second, the Oracle Database is flexible because it can run on Windows and various flavors of Unix. Additionally, a variety of Oracle database editions are available (*https://oreil.ly/IQvIY*), ranging from large-scale editions such as the Oracle Database Enterprise Edition to single-user editions like the Oracle Database Personal Edition. Oracle Database products are available on Oracle hardware as well as being offered by several service providers on premises, on cloud, or as a hybrid cloud installation.

Third, Oracle clients can access Oracle support services through the company's own support team or third-party consultants. This allows financial institutions to develop a feeling of trust and security as they have a reliable partner to call when needed.

In conclusion, maturity, stability, and support offer reliability against failures and risks, which is essential for critical applications such as finance. This explains the high popularity of Oracle among financial institutions and in the market in general.

The main alternative to commercial financial software is open source software. Unlike proprietary solutions, open source is typically licensed for free, and its development and maintenance is led by the public and/or by associations such as the Apache Foundation. The most popular type of open source license is the Apache 2.0 license (*https://oreil.ly/gsFzS*), which allows users to obtain, modify, distribute, sublicense, and patent the software as well as use it for commercial purposes that can include proprietary software.

A large number of open source software options are available. Examples include Linux, PostgreSQL, Firefox, Kubernetes, PyTorch, Apache Spark, Apache Cassandra, Apache Airflow, and many more.

The main advantages of open source include the following:

Cost
    Open source software is often available under free licensing. Nevertheless, compared to commercial software, open source might entail indirect costs such as maintenance, upgrades, and feature development costs.

Customization
    Because the source code is available to anyone to use and modify, companies can introduce new features that accommodate their business needs.

Community
    Open source software tends to have a large community of developers who actively add new features and fix existing bugs. The main advantage of community contributions is that they aggregate the skills and knowledge of multiple people from different backgrounds and experiences. This, in turn, can guarantee that the final solution is very likely the best in the market.

Transparency
    Because the entire codebase is available to the public, open source software tends to offer more transparency into its internal workings, unlike proprietary software, which is a black box.

On the other hand, open source software could face the following drawbacks:

Support
    Users can freely report a bug or ask for a new feature in open source software, but this usually takes time as contributors tend to dedicate a variable amount of time to maintain the software. For mission-critical applications such as financial payments, this may not be acceptable.

Documentation
    Open source projects may lack up-to-date, detailed documentation and usage instructions.

Complexity
    The evolution of open source projects is characterized by frequent updates to address bugs and introduce new functionalities. Consequently, as the codebase grows with additional features, it may become increasingly complex to comprehend.

Compatibility
    A major issue with open source software is compatibility with other software applications, which can jeopardize product development and integration efforts.

Security
    With open source software, malicious actors and cybercriminals find and exploit code vulnerabilities more easily.

Confidentiality
    Open source is based on the idea of community-driven collaboration and knowledge sharing. For financial institutions, sharing their codebase might be impossible if it becomes confidential or provides a competitive advantage that the institution wants to protect.

The use of open source software in financial services has significantly increased in the last few years. According to a report published by the Fintech Open Source Foundation (FINOS) (*https://oreil.ly/Kz3sU*), 2022 saw a 43% increase in the number of GitHub repositories with code contributors from the financial services industry. The report indicates that most of the contributions financial institutions make to open source projects are related to web development, cloud and containerization software, AI/ML, and continuous integration/continuous delivery (CI/CD).

Having said all of this, how would you choose between open source and proprietary software?

First, the pros and cons of open source and proprietary software can vary depending on the specific business problem and context; therefore, no single solution can fit all circumstances. In some cases, certain problems can have a well-accepted solution among market participants. For example, if your application requires high standards of security and reliable 24/7 customer support, then commercial software might be the right choice. On the other hand, if you are exploring the possibility of employing AI to build new product features, you might want to use open source libraries. Nowadays, it is common for the same financial institution to use both commercial and open source software.

 Some commercial software products are based on open source frameworks. These frameworks can either be provided as managed services by vendors or form the foundation for distinct solutions. For instance, PostgreSQL, an open source database management system, serves as the basis for Amazon's Relational Database Service (RDS) for PostgreSQL, a managed service offered by AWS. Conversely, Amazon Redshift, a proprietary data warehousing service, is built on top of PostgreSQL but is a separate product offered by AWS.

Second, consider your budget. If you are a small startup developing cutting-edge financial technology, you will likely be limited in your budget. In this case, using open source might be the best option. On the other hand, if you are a large multinational financial institution with big teams and departments, spending the money on commercial software might be more efficient as it will save the team time and effort when fixing bugs and dealing with security issues. Large corporations prefer to use commercial products as they offer a solution that standardizes internal operations across departments and teams.

Third, the level of technical expertise is a crucial factor. If you are planning on developing software that managers and accountants will use, then unless there is a big IT department, these professionals are likely to have limited expertise in software development to understand and interact with the codebase. In this case, vendor software is likely to cause fewer headaches. On the other hand, if your institution is well-equipped with software engineers who can support and help users, it would be possible to take advantage of the flexibility and developmental freedom that open source software offers.

Fourth, consider the urgency and impact on the competitive advantage of adopting a given software tool. If a financial institution feels behind compared to the market with open source adoption, then it might need to accelerate the adoption process. However, if the company is currently experimenting with open source for potential uses, then it might be possible to do it slowly.

In-House Proprietary Financial Software

A lot of innovative financial institutions create their own in-house software, mainly in response to customer demand and changing client expectations, which can be challenging to fulfill by relying on third-party software vendors. For example, to boost the time-to-market of its new financial products, the US financial institution JPMorgan Chase developed Kapital (*https://oreil.ly/bfOBV*), an advanced financial risk management and pricing software system. More recently, JPMorgan Chase leveraged the Python ecosystem to build Athena, a cross-asset platform for trading, risk management, and analytics used internally as well as by external clients. According to a presentation given by Misha Tselman (*https://oreil.ly/eLLz5*), executive director at JPMorgan Chase, at PyData 2017, Athena has thousands of users, more than 1,500 Python developers contributing to it, and uses over 150,000 Python modules.

Another prominent example is Aladdin (*https://oreil.ly/S3wGr*), an end-to-end portfolio and investment management platform developed by the largest asset manager in the world, BlackRock. Given its significant success and reliability, the Aladdin platform is no longer only an internal tool; rather, it is significantly influencing the way the financial sector works. Scholars use the term *platform economy* to describe such a scenario, where platforms play a major role in facilitating market activities.

If you are interested in learning more about this topic, I highly recommend the paper by Dirk A. Zetzsche, William A. Birdthistle, Douglas W. Arner, and Ross P. Buckley, "Digital Finance Platforms: Toward a New Regulatory Paradigm" (*https://oreil.ly/ZuO0F*), European Banking Institute (EBI) Working Paper Series No. 58 (2020): 273.

Criterion 2: Ease of Use Versus Performance

When choosing software or data technology, a frequent tradeoff arises between complexity and performance. Software technology can be complex if it has a steep learning curve: it may be difficult to understand or master the syntax, many elements must be managed in the code, it is demanding to set up and use, hard to debug, challenging to rerun on other machines, difficult to integrate with other software, and hard to extend with new features, deploy, or share with others. On the other hand, software is performant if it optimizes dimensions such as execution time, latency, throughput, I/O access, memory usage/footprint, carbon footprint, dependency and package management, scalability, security, or other custom metrics specific to the business operations.

The reason why there is a tradeoff between complexity and performance is that performance optimization often requires low-level interaction and configuration of the technology. Consider, for example, the difference between driving a manual versus an automatic car. To make a more concrete example, let's think about programming languages. A programming language such as C can be considered by many as a challenging language to work with due to its strict syntax requirements, exposure to low-level details, manual garbage collection, static typing, and memory management. Once you learn how to work with languages like C, your performance advantages could be substantial.

On the other hand, programming languages such as Python are well-known for their friendly syntax, usability, automatic garbage collection, and ease of integration. However, a number of features of Python make it less performant in terms of speed than C, such as the reliance on dynamic typing and the multistep compilation process to machine code.

The same logic applies to hardware. For example, engineers can leverage different computer processors and accelerators such as Central Processing Units (CPUs), Graphical Processing Units (GPUs), and Field Programmable Gate Arrays (FPGAs) to perform various tasks.[3] The CPU is the computer's main processor, and it excels in performing a wide range of tasks. However, certain applications might require custom optimizations (e.g., high parallelism or low latency), which can be achieved through the use of specialized processors such as a GPU and FPGA. Crucially, using a GPU and FPGA is more complex and requires good knowledge of their internals, cost, and implementation principles.

When comparing hardware and software technologies, pay close attention. Not everything is as easy as it looks on the surface. For instance, it's not unusual to come across articles that claim something like a GPU outperforms a CPU, or C# is superior to Python, and so forth. Even though they could have some truth to them, these generalizations have three problems. First, it might be challenging to compare technologies that are created according to different design principles. Second, technologies and the concepts behind their design change throughout time, and as a result, a technology that was once superior to another may not be any longer. Third, depending on the task that they are assessed against, technologies may perform differently. What I recommend in this case is to find a trusted reference from literature that you can rely on to derive a solid foundation for comparison.

Traditionally, financial market participants and researchers have thoroughly tested and benchmarked a number of technologies to certain business and technological requirements. For example, with time-critical or large-scale financial applications such as algorithmic trading, Monte Carlo simulations, asset pricing, and fraud

---

3 For a high-level introduction to the CPU, GPU, and FPGA, I recommend Intel's article "Compare Benefits of CPUs, GPUs, and FPGAs for Different oneAPI Compute Workloads" (*https://oreil.ly/S1Z6h*).

detection, financial institutions might prefer to use performant languages such as C, C++, Rust, and Java.[4] However, for less critical or small applications or situations where users are not highly skilled in software engineering internals, a more user-friendly language such as Python, R, or Julia might be a better choice.

The Quest for Low Latency in Financial Markets

Low latency is a key differentiator when it comes to performance in financial markets. Generally speaking, the notion of latency is often used to describe the time it takes for a request to travel over a network to its destination and receive a response back from it. In many financial domains, a firm's ability to grasp market opportunities or otherwise lose money is largely dependent on how quickly it reacts to market events. This is particularly the case in electronic trading systems, and more specifically, high-frequency and algorithmic trading.

There are several aspects to latency. First, it may concern the speed at which financial data is harvested and distributed to the many players involved in the trading system. The faster a financial institution can access market data and make trading choices, the more probable it is to capitalize on important short-term opportunities. The second aspect relates to the speed of the order execution flow. The faster an order reaches its destination, the more likely it is that the firm will make profits out of it. A millisecond difference in data access and trade processing time can equate to millions of dollars of gain or loss. For example, when executing an arbitrage strategy to profit from tiny differences in asset prices in two or more markets, the investing firm will have a tiny temporal window before the market reaches parity.

What markets consider "low" latency is not well defined but rather an evolving paradigm. Different financial market segments may operate and make improvements at different orders of time magnitude, such as the second, millisecond (thousandth of a second), microsecond (millionth of a second), and nanosecond (billionth of a second). For example, real-time payments may be considered fast at the second or millisecond level, while high-frequency traders are chasing the microsecond and nanosecond.

Numerous variables can influence latency in the financial markets. For example, a trading firm that speculates on short-term market opportunities will be impacted by the distance between its trading system and the trading venue, the distance between trading venues (in case of arbitrage), the choice of the programming language (e.g., C++ or Rust), hardware (e.g., CPU or FPGA), the efficiency of the trading program (e.g., time complexity), and cabling (e.g., copper versus fiber versus microwave).

---

4 For a benchmark study, I recommend S. Borağan Aruoba and Jesús Fernández-Villaverde's "A Comparison of Programming Languages in Macroeconomics" (*https://oreil.ly/cTLy8*), *Journal of Economic Dynamics and Control* 58 (September 2015): 265-273.

Due to the potential for large returns, low-latency trading firms constantly invest a great deal of resources and effort to accelerate their trading systems. One approach is called *Direct Market Access* (DMA), a trading arrangement that allows traders and investors to place orders directly into the order book of an exchange, bypassing intermediaries such as brokers.

Standardized communication protocols, such as FIX, are essential for DMA, as they allow traders, brokers, and exchanges to exchange trade-related data using a unified language (we discuss FIX in Chapter 7). DMA usually involves a sophisticated and costly technology setup. Consequently, it is commonly offered as a service by sell-side firms and specialized technology providers.

In addition, to provide markets with the opportunity to gain a speed advantage, stock exchanges started providing trading firms with the option to position their trading servers in close proximity to, or even within the same data center as, the exchange servers.

This strategy, called *colocation*, allows trading firms to access financial data through data feeds that stream data right from the source as soon as it appears in the exchange server. Colocation has raised some issues of fairness in financial markets (*https:// oreil.ly/OpInR*), as the average investor or market maker will get the information at a later date, when they will have less advantage to react.

Another direction toward low latency in financial markets relies on the use of specialized hardware such as a field-programmable gate array (FPGA). An FPGA is a configurable type of integrated circuit that can be programmed after manufacturing to suit whatever purpose and needs you want. As such, FPGAs have been widely adopted by financial markets to build systems that react to market events and process orders in nanoseconds, as well as to perform complex/parallel computations efficiently.

Criterion 3: Cloud Versus On Premises

In today's technological landscape, a major and critical technological choice often emerges between cloud-based and on-premises infrastructures. In an on-premises server infrastructure, the firm owns, controls, and maintains a group of servers (often called commodity servers) for its storage and computing purposes. Alternatively, a firm can use the cloud to host or lease servers at a third-party cloud provider or use the vendor's managed servers and services directly.

There are pros and cons to using either on premises or the cloud, and making the right decision may be quite challenging. Generally speaking, on premises is viewed by many as the traditional (or legacy) way of managing server infrastructure, while the cloud represents the modern and user-friendly approach. This, however, doesn't mean that on premises is bad and the cloud is good. Let's explore in more detail the main differences and features of both solutions.

On premises

In an on-premises setting, the financial institution is fully responsible for its servers and data infrastructure. This means that the institution owns, configures, and manages its servers, computing environments, networking, security, scalability policies, logs, and user access.

As you might have guessed, the main advantage of this infrastructure choice is that you have full control of your digital assets. If managed properly, an on-premises infrastructure can guarantee maximum security. Having all your data and software reside within your organization's premises provides a feeling of safety and peace. Security is a major concern for highly regulated businesses like finance; hence, on premises is a very typical choice.

Nevertheless, the on-premises approach has a number of potential downsides. Cost is perhaps the main issue. To maintain an on-premises infrastructure, institutions need to have a dedicated IT department responsible for software and hardware maintenance, availability, updates, security, license purchases, and user support. Such costs might rise exponentially, especially in large institutions or in the presence of poor management and usage practices.

 Keep in mind that cost is not always a downside to on-premises solutions. In some cases, it might be the best cost-efficient solution if configured and managed with high quality standards as well as software-aware and hardware-aware best practices. For example, in 2023, X (formerly known as Twitter) announced that it implemented a cloud exit strategy (*https://oreil.ly/JWqKY*) by moving data and workload out from the cloud and onto its own on-premises servers. The move resulted in a 60% decrease in cloud data storage size and a 75% decrease in cloud data processing costs.

The second downside is scalability. In an on-premises setting, institutions have a certain number of servers that they manage. As long as the infrastructure can handle the load, there should be no problems. However, if the load increases much more than the current server infrastructure can handle, then either the system will experience downtime issues or more servers need to be added. Adding more servers can be costly and time-consuming; and once added, they can't simply be removed and returned. One solution to this issue is to overprovision by having extra server capacity all the time. However, this strategy can lead to extra costs due to unused resources.

The third drawback is that institutions may find themselves spending less time on product and feature development and more time on server maintenance and time-consuming technical, bureaucratic processes. Large financial institutions may tolerate this; however, for smaller institutions such as FinTech firms, the burden may not be sustainable.

Mainframe Architecture

As far as the financial sector is concerned, it is hard to avoid mentioning *mainframes*. In a few words, a mainframe is a highly performant, scalable, and resilient computer endowed with large amounts of memory and processing power. The main advantage of mainframe computers is their ability to handle massive volumes of simultaneous transactions and requests while at the same time ensuring reliability, security, availability, high throughput, and low latency.

This feature makes mainframes well-suited for core financial applications such as banking, customer order processing, payment processing, and various mission-critical tasks that process billions of transactions on a daily basis. If you have ever interacted with an automated teller machine (ATM) or point-of-sale terminal at a retail shop, your request likely involved a mainframe at some point.

The market pioneer in mainframes is IBM (*https://oreil.ly/XEeAp*), which has been producing mainframe computers since 1952. IBM mainframes have evolved over time to meet the diverse requirements of resilience, security, and performance. The primary mainframe system offered by IBM is the IBM Z System, which includes various generations such as the IBM z15, IBM z14, and IBM z13. Complementing these mainframes are a range of related IBM offerings, including IBM's proprietary operating system, known as IBM z/OS; IBM's transaction processing system, known as the Customer Information Control System (CICS); IBM's relational database management system DB2; and the middleware communication system IBM MQ. This integrated and secure ecosystem has enabled IBM to maintain a significant market share within the financial sector, particularly for payment and transaction processing.

Cloud computing

A major alternative and competitor of the on-premises model is the cloud. In this book, we define the cloud as:

> A general-purpose technology that enables the development and delivery of computing and storage services over a networked system.

In this definition, the term *general-purpose technology* refers to a technology whose adoption and impact span many sectors within the economy, substantially impacting preexisting social and economic structures. The best examples of general-purpose technologies are electricity, the internet, and artificial intelligence. The cloud is already a general-purpose technology, given its wide range of applications and adoption in businesses, governments, hospitals, research centers, financial institutions, educational institutions, the military, and many more.[5]

The most important thing about the cloud is how it's delivered, not just the services it delivers. Many of the underlying technologies powering the cloud already exist and are utilized in various applications. This includes, for example, software and hardware virtualization technologies, multicore technologies, networking (network computing, software-defined networking, software-defined security, WAN), data centers, database management systems, file storage systems, open source tools, machine learning, and DevOps, to name a few. However, with the cloud, such technologies have been abstracted and architectured in a novel way that allows for the delivery of scalable, highly available, managed, and pay-as-you-go services through a networked system. The public internet is the primary delivery network, but it is also possible to establish a private cloud that operates on premises or in a data center managed by a cloud provider. In the next section, we will explore in detail the differences among public, private, and hybrid clouds.

Cloud products can be classified into three main categories:

Software-as-a-service (SaaS)
> SaaS products are delivered to customers via the internet and are entirely managed and maintained by the cloud provider. With a SaaS solution, users can easily get started with the product, often instantly upon confirming a subscription plan, and they do not need to worry about configuration, software licensing, installation, or upgrades. Users might still need to confirm who can access their SaaS and what privileges they have. Examples of SaaS products include Gmail, GDrive, BigQuery, Dropbox, Snowflake, and many more. Sometimes, SaaS solutions get assigned more precise names, such as database-as-a-service and AI-as-a-service.

Platforms-as-a-service (PaaS)
> PaaS provides online platforms for developing applications via APIs and operating system services. Consumers of PaaS control the settings of the hosting environment, the application, and access policies but not the infrastructure, storage, and networking. SaaS apps are typical users of PaaS. Examples of PaaS include the Google App Engine and DigitalOcean App Platform.

Infrastructure-as-a-service (IaaS)
> IaaS is the lowest level of cloud offering and provides raw physical resources (CPU, RAM, storage, and networking) as a service, with the user having nearly complete control over the configuration of the instances. The majority of SaaS

---

5 For a detailed study on the cloud as a general-purpose technology, I recommend Federico Etro's "The Economic Impact of Cloud Computing on Business Creation, Employment and Output in Europe" (*https://oreil.ly/55cZq*), *Review of Business and Economics* no. 2 (January 2009): 179–208.

and PaaS apps are based on IaaS. Examples of IaaS include AWS EC2 and Google Compute Engine.

 The cloud market is growing into a complex landscape of providers, services, and products. It is important to keep in mind that there are differences between a cloud provider and a cloud-based service provider. Cloud providers own and provide a large number of data centers distributed all over the world. These providers are called hyperscalers (*https://oreil.ly/KjHx1*) and include major players such as AWS, Microsoft, and Google. On the other hand, there exist a large number of cloud-based service providers that develop and offer services through the cloud. The best example is Snowflake, which offers a cloud-based data warehouse solution that runs on AWS, Google, or Microsoft.

In the financial sector, cloud computing has drawn a lot of interest, especially as a means to boost innovation and save expenses. According to a 2022 report by McKinsey (*https://oreil.ly/KrOKg*), the adoption of the cloud is on most financial institutions' agendas. A large number of strategic partnerships have been announced between major cloud providers/service providers and financial institutions. For example, BlackRock, the largest asset manager in the world, has partnered with Snowflake (*https://oreil.ly/khbtY*), a cloud data warehouse provider, to offer a cloud-based version of its investment platform Aladdin; Goldman Sachs established a collaboration with AWS (*https://oreil.ly/KhXXg*) to create cloud-based data management and analytics solutions for the financial sector; JPMorgan Chase established Fusion (*https://oreil.ly/wuqCb*), and State Street created Alpha (*https://oreil.ly/0ryAI*), both cloud-based integrated platforms for investment and financial data management.

Migrating to the cloud can bring a large number of benefits for financial institutions. These include the following:

- Quicker time to market, facilitated by the ease with which resources can be provisioned and managed.

- More innovation as developers can test and experiment with new ideas without having to buy hardware and incur unnecessary costs.

- Continuous access to novel technologies developed by cloud providers, which would otherwise be very costly to develop in-house.

- Cost savings due to the pay-as-you-go model, where users pay only for what they use. This shifts the cost structure from fixed IT capital expenditure to variable operating costs based on demand.

- Scalability, where users can scale resources up and down based on their current and planned needs without having to purchase physical servers.

- Better collaboration as the cloud allows for easy and quick sharing of resources, files, and proof-of-concept demonstrations.

- Advanced security and data protection features such as Identity and Access Management (IAM), backups, encryption, centralized management, and audit logs.

- Cloud providers offer multiregion options for data storage and resource provisioning. This increases operational resilience as it reinforces availability. Such a feature is quite crucial for financial applications. For example, for a digital banking firm that is *branchless,* online services must always be on and available at any time of the day.

- Compliance: cloud computing's multiregion feature allows financial institutions to pin their customer data to a specific region to meet the data privacy requirements of that location.

Logically, as with most technologies, cloud computing has its drawbacks. Examples include the following:

- Internet access, which raises the risk of access loss in case of internet or service downtime

- Lack of full control over the underlying infrastructure and data

- Security and privacy concerns

- Regulatory constraints

- Integration challenges with existing systems

- Vendor lock-in

- Unforeseen costs and consumption patterns that defy the original migration goals

---

Is the Cloud Secure?

One of the major perceptions about cloud technologies is their lower degree of security compared to hosting data in-house on an on-premises infrastructure. The fundamental justification for this opinion is that shifting data to a third-party location entails giving up complete ownership and control of that data as well as opening it to the public since you are likely to access it via the internet.

Even though such concerns are rational, cloud computing isn't that insecure. Cloud service providers make significant investments in cloud security, regularly hire security professionals, and use cutting-edge security measures. For example, in August 2023, Google blocked a massive denial-of-service attack (DoS) on its infrastructure (*https://oreil.ly/aCui1*) that reached 398 million requests per second (rps). To put

---

things in perspective, this two-minute attack generated more requests than the total amount of Wikipedia page views during the entire month of September 2023.

Nevertheless, cloud security should be carefully examined and assessed before making any major decision. I highly recommend checking the cloud vendor certifications and compliance with the different security regulations and standards for different sectors. Examples of security certifications include the following:

ISO/IEC 27001:2022 (https://oreil.ly/1SWTc)
  Information security, cybersecurity, and privacy protection

ISO/IEC 27017:2015 (https://oreil.ly/CesIB)
  Guidelines for information security controls applicable to the provision and use of cloud services

ISO/IEC 27018:2019 (https://oreil.ly/9qMpk)
  Code of practice for protection of personally identifiable information (PII) in public clouds acting as PII processors

Cloud providers often include a comprehensive list of their compliance offerings grouped by country, sector, region, and more. Examples include the following:

- Google compliance offerings for financial services (*https://oreil.ly/wf8w2*)
- AWS compliance programs and certifications (*https://oreil.ly/8vtR8*)
- Microsoft compliance offerings (*https://oreil.ly/QZv90*)

Additionally, most cloud providers have offerings tailored to the needs of the financial sector. Examples include IBM's Cloud for Financial Services (*https://oreil.ly/6M6FM*), Google's Cloud for Financial Services (*https://oreil.ly/HnZ3k*), AWS's Cloud Solutions for Financial Services (*https://oreil.ly/S8hVs*), Microsoft Cloud for Financial Services (*https://oreil.ly/0nkv6*), and Snowflake's AI Data Cloud for Financial Services (*https://oreil.ly/woB82*). What distinguishes these cloud offerings is the focus on data protection, privacy, security, fraud detection, and several other features that financial institutions require.

To evaluate the suitability of cloud services for highly confidential financial data, Ilya Epshteyn from AWS proposed a framework consisting of five key factors (*https://oreil.ly/xMNi-*), which I recommend as an example of a general guideline.

When considering a cloud migration decision, keep in mind that it must be done through a cloud migration strategy that matches your institution's goals and requirements with what the cloud offers. Otherwise, migration efforts might easily run into unexpected issues such as excessive costs, technological limitations, security and compliance issues, scalability, and control.

A full treatment of cloud migration strategies is beyond the scope of the book.[6] However, from a high-level view, a cloud strategy is, in the first place, an economic strategy.[7] If moving to the cloud is going to increase your costs or not have a major impact on your costs or revenues, then it might not be worth it. Consider calculating your cloud strategy's return on investment (ROI) (*https://oreil.ly/Qm9o2*) and proceed gradually based on your analysis. For example, it might initially seem more appealing to migrate your analytical data to a cloud-based managed data warehouse service for machine learning purposes. Successively, other types of data can be migrated to a data lake, NoSQL database, and other data stores. Should this be beneficial, you might consider migrating your virtual machines and gradually the rest (or a significant part) of your infrastructure.[8]

Second, consider analyzing the potential impact of cloud migration on your business models and the value creation logic. For example, businesses need to get used to the idea of web-based services and delivery mechanisms, pay-per-use expenditure models, managed services, and the shared responsibility model.[9]

Third, consider the technological limitations of the cloud and their impact on your business needs. Cloud technologies are very powerful, but they have limitations. Some of these limitations are inherently derived from the technology itself (e.g., the connection limit in a PostgreSQL database) or cloud-related limitations, such as the shared resources model of the cloud, which might limit the amount of RAM or CPU dedicated to a virtual machine.

Fourth, your strategy must carefully assess your company's data governance and compliance requirements to ensure you keep your system resilient and secure. Cloud services are user-friendly and relatively easy to use. But with such ease comes a challenge, which is the risk of misusing cloud services and creating chaotic architectures. This, in turn, might impact the level of control and quality of the data and infrastructure you host in the cloud.

---

6 For a good introduction, see Jamil Mina, Armin Warda, Rafael Marins, and Russ Miles' *Digitalization of Financial Services in the Age of Cloud* (O'Reilly, 2022).

7 An excellent reference on cloud economics is Joe Weinman's *Cloudonomics: The Business Value of Cloud Computing, + Website* (Wiley Online Library, 2012).

8 To learn more about cloud migration strategies, see "What Is a Cloud Migration Strategy?" (*https://oreil.ly/PfGKC*) by VMware.

9 For an interesting read on this topic, I recommend Thomas Boillat and Christine Legner's "From On-Premise Software to Cloud Services: The Impact of Cloud Computing on Enterprise Software Vendors' Business Models" (*https://oreil.ly/3bFI9*), *Journal of Theoretical and Applied Electronic Commerce Research* 8, no. 3 (December 2013): 39–58.

Criterion 4: Public Versus Private Versus Hybrid Cloud

With the adoption of cloud computing worldwide, three cloud models have emerged: public, private, and hybrid. In this section, we will explore the main features of each model and illustrate their relevance to financial institutions.

Public cloud

In a public cloud model, the underlying infrastructure (compute, storage, networks, etc.) is owned and managed by a third-party vendor and accessible by users over the public internet. Examples of public cloud providers include Amazon Web Services, Google Cloud, Microsoft Azure, IBM Cloud, and Oracle. The public cloud is the most popular model and is often the default choice.

A key feature of the public cloud is *multitenancy (https://oreil.ly/T0Y0_)*, meaning that cloud service users share the underlying infrastructure while remaining isolated through virtualized environments. Multitenancy allows the cloud vendor to optimize the use of resources and reduce costs.

Due to multitenancy, the public cloud model advocates the *shared responsibility principle*, wherein both the cloud provider and users assume distinct yet overlapping responsibilities to safeguard the security of services and data hosted in the public cloud. The cloud provider oversees physical infrastructure security and maintains a logical separation between client data and resources. Simultaneously, clients are responsible for ensuring application-level security, such as user access and permissions, data encryption, backups, and multifactor authentication.

The main advantages of the public cloud include the following:

Simplicity
Public cloud providers focus on making their services user-friendly to cater to the diverse needs of all sectors and clients they serve.

Flexible pricing
Public cloud users can pay on demand while also capitalizing on discounts offered for committed usage, where they reserve a resource for a predetermined duration.

Scalability
Cloud providers strategically plan and provision their infrastructure to accommodate variable resource needs, ensuring clients can access the necessary resources whenever needed.

Minimal configuration and maintenance burden
The cloud provider manages and maintains the data centers hosting the physical servers.

On the negative side, the public cloud may not be ideal for the following reasons:

- Data confidentiality and security, as data is stored at a third-party location and accessed through the public internet
- Excessive costs, which may arise with large-scale applications, miscalculated resource needs, or unexpected spikes in demand
- Limited infrastructure control

Given their security and confidentiality requirements, financial institutions looking to adopt the cloud might find the public cloud the most risky option. However, the public cloud might be a good solution if used for less confidential types of data, e.g., machine learning. Among financial institutions, FinTech firms are major public cloud users, given the extra features it provides in terms of products and flexibility, which are ideal for innovation.

Misconfiguration Risk in Public Clouds: The Capital One Data Breach Case

The most critical security threat when using public cloud services is cloud misconfiguration (*https://oreil.ly/XdBYd*). Since the public cloud is built on the shared responsibility principle, customers may incorrectly set access to their resources, leaving them vulnerable to cybercriminals' attacks. For example, a common misconfiguration happens when a resource is accidentally made public or given excessive permissions that can be easily exploited to gain access to sensitive data.

In 2019, over 100,000 social security numbers, credit card details, and client financial information were stolen as a consequence of a cloud data breach at the US financial company Capital One (*https://oreil.ly/LMLpt*). The breach was possible thanks to a misconfiguration in permission settings that allowed one resource to access data stored in the storage service AWS S3 that Capital One used to store its client data. The misconfigured resource was attacked and used to gain access to client data in S3.

Cloud providers have implemented measures to help users detect and mitigate cloud misconfiguration issues (*https://oreil.ly/Ujadc*). Nevertheless, if you use a public cloud service, I highly recommend that you assign primary importance to cloud misconfiguration and vulnerability risks.

Private cloud

In the private cloud model, an organization has a dedicated cloud infrastructure that is not shared with others. The dedicated infrastructure can be owned and hosted by the organization itself, owned by the organization and hosted at a third-party vendor, or owned by the vendor and rented by the organization. The rise of the private cloud primarily stemmed from large corporations with data centers seeking to replicate the public cloud model internally.

The private cloud's main advantages are control and security, which makes it an ideal solution for many regulated industries, such as financial services. If a financial institution builds and deploys a private cloud on its data centers, then security is the full responsibility of the institution. If a private cloud is deployed at a third-party data center, then the servers' physical security is the cloud provider's responsibility. In both cases, the security of the data and user access management is the responsibility of the institution.

As a main downside of the private cloud, it is considerably harder to set up and deploy, especially if managed fully by the institution in-house. The private cloud might require significant up-front investment in infrastructure and IT talent and lead to ongoing costs in terms of maintenance and personnel.

The private cloud has received considerable attention among financial institutions, which tend to favor security and compliance over other features. Large financial institutions already owning big data centers might benefit greatly from switching or adapting to a private cloud setting. For example, Bank of America invested heavily in building an internal private cloud, which, according to a *Business Insider* article (*https://oreil.ly/p-dNZ*), helped save $2 billion in annual infrastructure expenditure and reduced the number of servers from 200,000 to 70,000 and its data centers from 60 to 23. This reduction was possible through the use of virtualization technologies, which led to a reduced need for servers.

As a viable and more practical alternative, cloud providers offer the option to deploy a *Virtual Private Cloud* (VPC) (*https://oreil.ly/wUnFN*), which is deployed within a public cloud infrastructure. A VPC offers the best of both worlds: the private cloud's security and reliability and the public cloud's scalability and convenience. A VPC can allow a financial institution to isolate compute resources and network traffic for customers' workloads that involve highly confidential data.

Hybrid cloud

The hybrid cloud model combines public and private clouds to take advantage of both. In a hybrid setting, a private cloud is often used for operations that involve confidential data, such as client transactions and financial reporting, while the public cloud is used for high-volume and less sensitive operations, such as log analysis, machine learning, and web-based applications. The public cloud can also be dedicated to handle occasional spikes in workload from the applications running in a private cloud, a technique known as *cloud bursting*.

A hybrid cloud can be an ideal solution for financial institutions, offering the flexibility and scalability of the public cloud while ensuring regulatory compliance and security through the private cloud. Moreover, the hybrid cloud model allows for cost optimization by allocating resources and workload between public and private cloud based on demand and circumstances.

The main disadvantages of a hybrid cloud are the cost involved in building and maintaining it and the additional operational complexity that derives from the need to coordinate and orchestrate two clouds. Alternatively, a company can build a hybrid cloud via a combination of a VPC and public cloud. In this case, the maintenance burden of the private cloud is lower as the cloud vendor maintains the underlying infrastructure.

Criterion 5: Single Versus Multi-Cloud

Multi-cloud is a cloud strategy whereby an organization uses services from multiple cloud providers.

Starting with a single cloud provider is often the default and simplest solution. This is because most cloud providers offer similar products, e.g., virtual machines, managed SQL databases, file storage, and access management. However, as new business requirements and features get added, limitations might emerge in the cloud offerings of the trusted cloud provider. A company that uses cloud provider A might discover that a database service from provider B aligns more closely with the technical and cost prerequisites of the business, thus making it a more favorable option.

The choice of a public cloud provider may depend on factors that are not necessarily technology related. For example, among large financial institutions, it is common to see a preference for Microsoft Azure cloud services. This is due to the long-standing relationship of trust and security that many companies have developed with Microsoft. When formulating a cloud migration strategy, consider an approach that encompasses trust and relationships, as well as considerations regarding offerings, technology, features, and pricing.

A multi-cloud strategy can also be more economical. For example, Google's warehouse solution BigQuery charges the user based on the amount of bytes that their queries fetch. On the other hand, Snowflake's data warehouse solution charges based on the duration of the query. If your queries are data-intensive but fast, then Snowflake might be more economical, while if your queries take some time but don't fetch large amounts of data, then BigQuery might be more appealing.

Cloud pricing can be tricky and hard to understand. Before making your choice, consider carefully all costs involved in purchasing a cloud service, particularly managed database services. A large number of factors might impact costs other than the single-unit on-demand price reported on the vendor's website. Even though the individual cost might seem low, if you can't predict your scaling needs, costs can easily accumulate to a large sum. Additionally, pay careful attention if you decide to use cloud cost benchmarking, as it might be misleading (*https://oreil.ly/7NNOh*) or biased if you don't understand the settings or context in which they were conducted.

In some cases, multi-cloud can be a feature of a cloud-based product itself. For example, Snowflake cloud-based data warehousing relies on the principle of separation between storage and computing. This means that data can be stored and managed independently of the compute resources that are required to interact with the data. Snowflake allows clients to choose the cloud platform (Azure, AWS, or Google) on which to deploy the Snowflake service (*https://oreil.ly/nAR99*). This strategy makes it more appealing for clients to use Snowflake, as their data doesn't need to leave their cloud infrastructure of choice.

A multi-cloud strategy can mitigate the risk of vendor lock-in. The term *vendor lock-in* refers to a situation where the cost and effort needed to switch from one cloud provider to another is so high that the client is essentially stuck with the current cloud provider. Vendor lock-in may be disadvantageous in case the provider makes changes to their services, increases price, or incurs downtime issues. By adopting a multi-cloud strategy, you maintain your flexibility to adapt to changes introduced by a given provider and make use of each provider's best features.

The main drawback of the multi-cloud strategy is the additional management and operational burden needed to maintain the resources hosted on different cloud platforms. Using two clouds means securing both and making sure access is coordinated and managed properly. Establishing a secure and private connection between multiple clouds can be both complex and expensive, often requiring intricate VPN configurations or other advanced networking solutions. Additionally, consistency and reliability checks must be implemented if data needs to be moved between clouds. Moreover, if resources hosted on different clouds become tightly coupled, this may easily increase costs, impact performance, and jeopardize maintainability.

Case Study: Multi-Cloud Strategy at Wells Fargo

In 2021, Wells Fargo, a US multinational financial services company, announced a new digital infrastructure strategy (*https://oreil.ly/hbdy3*) that uses services from two public cloud providers as well as third-party-owned data centers for private cloud and traditional hosting services.

Wells Fargo's strategy relies predominantly on Microsoft Azure's public cloud to drive innovation across all departments and ensure a secure and trusted environment for strategic business workloads. It uses Azure Cloud as the main foundation for most day-to-day data and analytical needs and to empower employee collaboration. However, it also leverages the Google Cloud platform for more advanced data and analytical workloads, such as artificial intelligence, and to develop personalized customer solutions.

Furthermore, Wells Fargo's digital strategy complements its public cloud infrastructure with third-party-owned data centers, leveraging private cloud and traditional hosting services to create a secure, reliable, and flexible digital foundation.

In general, Wells Fargo's hybrid multi-cloud architecture is viewed as a promising future trend in cloud computing since it provides the greatest flexibility for meeting business demands in terms of performance, security, cost, scalability, and innovation. To explore this trend in detail, I highly recommend the excellent work of Paul Zikopoulos, Christopher Bienko, Chris Backer, Chris Konarski, and Sai Vennam, *Cloud Without Compromise* (O'Reilly, 2021).

Criterion 6: Monolithic Versus Modular Codebase

A major decision that companies have to make when building a data infrastructure is the organizational style of the codebase and application assets. Codebase organization style is not concerned with how the software works but rather how it is structured, linked, and deployed. Code structure can be crucial in determining the application's readability, scalability, and reliability. To this end, two main codebase styles are often proposed, primarily *monolithic* and *modular,* which I briefly illustrate in this section.

Monolith architecture

In a monolith architecture, the codebase is typically organized in a single location and is characterized by tight coupling between its constituent elements. As a consequence, when making a change to a monolith, it is very likely that you will have to deploy the entire application and not just the part that you changed. In its simplest state, you can think of a monolith as a single GitHub repository that stores the entire application codebase.

It is also possible to have a distributed monolith, which organizes the codebase in multiple locations, but due to tight coupling, a change in one place requires changes and redeployment of all or several of the other locations.

Monolith architectures may provide a number of advantages, such as the following:

- Ease of deployment, as you don't deal with the pitfalls of distributed systems
- High levels of cohesion and consistency
- Simpler development workflow, as all components of the code are visible to the developer
- Easier to monitor
- Easier to test (e.g., end-to-end)
- High throughput and performance (no need to communicate with many other services)

- Simplifies code reusability (all code is in one place; use what you need!)

The monolith architecture may be ideal for simple and lightweight financial applications, both for developers and for the application's extensibility and performance.

Nevertheless, monolith architectures may lead to a very complex and hard-to-predict application codebase, making it quite challenging to scale, extend, understand, and debug. The more components and dependencies an application has, the harder it is to understand the impact of a local change on the system's overall behavior.

Monolith architectures tend to be seen as a bad thing by default. This, however, is not necessarily true. A monolith architecture is a choice. It can be pretty good in some contexts but should be treated carefully and on a case-by-case basis to avoid its pitfalls. In 2023, Amazon Prime Video decided to switch back to a monolith architecture from a distributed microservices architecture (*https:// oreil.ly/-QaAT*). The move to a monolith architecture helped achieve higher scalability and resilience, and reduced infrastructure costs by 90%.

Modular architecture

In a modular architecture, an application is split into smaller modules that can be developed, deployed, tested, and scaled separately. Different teams may own different modules and manage the resource and feature requirements of each separately.

The most popular modular architecture pattern is the *microservices*, a term used to describe small, autonomous applications that work together to achieve a common goal. In many cases, a microservice architecture is produced from refactoring a complex monolith codebase that has reached the limits of scalability and performance. In Chapter 11, we will talk about microservice workflows, where you will learn more about microservice-related concepts and design patterns.

If you are considering a refactoring project of your monolith to a microservice architecture, make sure you plan the migration ahead of time and produce the necessary software architecture metrics and evaluations. A number of best practices exist in this regard. For example, software architecture evaluation techniques (*https:// oreil.ly/cMF9R*) can be used to assess the quality and reliability requirements of a proposed/chosen software architecture. Moreover, tools such as the Modularity Maturity Index (MMI), fitness functions, and software metrics (*https://oreil.ly/ZwSYY*) can be used to assess which components of the system need to be refactored, replaced, or left as they are.

Summary

This chapter provided a general overview of the technical implementation aspects of financial data engineering. It covered the financial data engineering lifecycle as a framework for organizing the various layers of a financial data infrastructure: ingestion, storage, transformation and delivery, and monitoring.

Following that, the chapter outlined a set of six criteria intended to assist financial institutions in making informed decisions when evaluating technological alternatives for the FDEL stack. These criteria serve as a general guideline applicable to all layers of the FDEL. In the next chapters, you will learn about additional criteria specific to each layer within the FDEL.

The next four chapters will cover each of the four FDEL layers in depth to provide more technical details. More specifically, Chapter 7 will cover the ingestion layer, Chapter 8 the storage layer, Chapter 9 the transformation and delivery layer, and Chapter 10 the monitoring layer.

Data Ingestion Layer

In Chapter 2, we learned about the different sources and mechanisms that generate financial data. This included public, market, alternative, and internal sources. Once data is generated at the source, its lifecycle within a financial data infrastructure begins with ingestion. As this chapter will show, data ingestion isn't as simple as the term may sound. In today's complex financial data landscape, data ingestion has expanded to encompass a large variety of data transmission and arrival processes as well as ingestion technologies, mechanisms, and formats.

Data ingestion serves as the foundational layer for information exchange in financial market operations. It facilitates communication among financial institutions and market participants for initiating transactions like payments, settlements, and trades. It also supports the exchange of inquiries and notifications between financial entities. Furthermore, compliance with regulatory requirements relies on efficient data ingestion practices, enabling financial firms and brokers to transmit various financial details and compliance reports to regulatory bodies. In addition, data ingestion is essential for disseminating market data and delivering real-time updates, critical for maintaining liquidity and operational efficiency throughout financial markets.

This chapter will examine the data ingestion layer as the primary entry point for receiving transmitted data and as a crucial bridge facilitating communication and information exchange among financial institutions and other entities.

Data Transmission and Arrival Processes

Data ingestion is a process wherein data gets transmitted from a given source, travels over a network, and arrives at its destination. Understanding the details of such a process is critical for designing a reliable financial data infrastructure that meets different business and technical requirements. With such knowledge, financial data engineers can optimize time and mission-critical financial applications, design cost-effective and efficient data pipelines, anticipate scalability needs, manage security, and guide technology choices such as database management systems.

In this section I'll explain the standard transmission protocols that enable most data transactions worldwide and will provide an examination of the many types of data arrival patterns.

Data Transmission Protocols

When designing a system that transmits and receives data, transmission protocols, also known as communication protocols or network protocols, are an essential component. Simply put, a transmission protocol is a set of rules, techniques, and definitions that allow two or more agents or machines to exchange data over a network such as the internet.

Understanding industry transmission protocols is crucial to mastering the art of data ingestion. A data infrastructure is reliable only if it can access, deliver, and ingest data over a network. This is particularly relevant to the financial industry, which relies substantially on data transfers due to the large volume of financial transactions.

Various communication protocols and standards are employed throughout the data transmission lifecycle, each serving specific purposes. A variety of models have been developed to establish a reference framework. Such models rely on the idea of organizing network protocols and the technologies used to implement them into distinct layers. In such a design, each protocol belongs to one layer, and each layer is interested in the services that it offers to the layer above. This defines the *service model* of the layer. In this architecture, each service performs certain actions that belong to it, uses input/instructions from the service below, and conforms to the requirements of the service above. For example, the service model of layer N might involve encrypted message delivery between systems. This could be realized by implementing nonencrypted message delivery at layer N-1 and incorporating layer N functionality to encrypt messages.

The most popular internet protocol model is the seven-layer *Open Systems Interconnection* (OSI) model, defined in standard ISO/IEC 7498 (*https://oreil.ly/H4hHw*), and the four-layer internet protocol suite known as the *TCP/IP*, developed by the Department of Defense (DoD). Both models are illustrated in Figure 7-1.

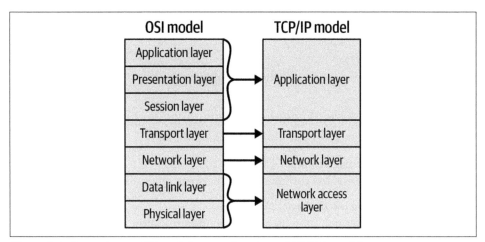

Figure 7-1. Seven-layer OSI model versus four-layer TCP/IP model

 Keep in mind that communication layer models such as OSI and TCP/IP are conceptual frameworks intended to discuss networking in a structured way. Reality may be more complex than a model. For example, some protocols or functionalities might be hard to place in one single layer and multiple layers may duplicate the same functionality. Additionally, layers might have dependencies that could blur the line between them. Nevertheless, reference models are very useful for thinking about such a complex topic.

In the following sections, I will briefly discuss the various network layers of the TCP/IP model. I chose to illustrate the TCP/IP model rather than OSI due to its simplicity and popularity among engineers.

Application layer

This is the topmost layer, where network applications and their protocols reside. Applications in this layer are distributed over multiple end systems, and they exchange packets of information via the service protocols. Such protocols include the following:

Hypertext Transfer Protocol (HTTP)
    Used to serve web page requests

Simple Mail Transfer Protocol (SMTP)
    Used to send and exchange emails

File Transfer Protocol (FTP)
  Used to transfer files between two systems

Domain Name System (DNS)
  Used to resolve web page names into their address

Secure Shell (SSH)
  Used to secure login to remote servers and execute commands, or secure file transfer through the *Secure File Transfer Protocol* (SFPT)

Advanced Message Queuing Protocol (AMQP)
  Used for message-oriented communication between applications

Message Queuing Telemetry Transport (MQTT)
  Designed for lightweight, message-oriented communication

Transport layer

This layer is responsible for transferring application layer packets between application endpoints in a reliable, optimized, and guaranteed way. Transport layer messages are commonly called *segments*. The most important transport layer protocols include the *Transmission Control Protocol* (TCP) and *User Datagram Protocol* (UDP). TCP is a *connection-oriented* protocol, meaning that the sender and receiver must establish a continuous connection before exchanging data segments. This feature makes TCP a reliable protocol, as it acknowledges message reception and resends data again in case it doesn't arrive. TCP breaks down an information packet from the application layer into a small set of segments and submits it for delivery to the next layer, the network layer. In the network layer, segments are represented as datagrams.

Additionally, TCP offers functionalities such as flow and congestion control, which regulate the data transmission rate and dynamically adapt to network congestion through message segmentation and breakdown. Furthermore, TCP ensures secure delivery by keeping track of all transmitted segments and confirming their successful delivery.

On the other hand, UDP is a faster but less reliable protocol than TCP. UDP is a *connectionless* protocol, meaning that data transmission happens via a fire-and-forget mechanism without establishing a continuous connection. This means that it offers fewer delivery guarantees compared to TCP.

A significant improvement over TCP is the *Transport Layer Security* (TLS) protocol, also referred to as TLS/SSL, which is designed to facilitate secure communication across insecure networks. TLS can be positioned between the application and transport layers. It encrypts data before transmission via TCP and decrypts it upon arrival at the transport layer of the receiving end. In addition to encryption, TLS also manages identity verification (authentication), facilitates the exchange of encryption keys between hosts, and mitigates Man-in-the-Middle (MITM) attacks through the TLS handshake process (*https://oreil.ly/gqnmF*).

TLS is very important to understand because you will encounter it several times when designing a financial data infrastructure. A common use case for TLS is enabling encrypted connections to a database engine.[1] Similarly, when using HTTPS instead of HTTP to serve web requests and design APIs, you are adding a TLS/SSL layer for encryption.

Electronic Banking Internet Communication Standard

Internet protocols are essential in developing financial communication protocols. A good example in this context is the *Electronic Banking Internet Communication Standard* (EBICS), developed in Germany and adopted by France, Switzerland, and other countries to exchange instructions between financial institutions and corporations over the internet. The EBICS standard has been primarily used to initiate *Single Euro Payments Area* (SEPA) exchanges over the internet, such as SEPA Direct Debits and SEPA Credit Transfers.

According to the official technical specifications (*https://oreil.ly/9MIgQ*), the TCP/IP internet protocol suite had a decisive influence on the design of EBICS. Data is transmitted as packages via IP addresses or URLs that get resolved to IPs. Package transfer and delivery are monitored and guaranteed via the TCP protocol. The client and the EBICS server communicate using the HTTP protocol at the application layer. The XML file format has been selected as the protocol language at the application layer. To ensure security and data encryption, EBICS relies on TLS to secure communications via HTTPS.

Network layer

This layer moves information units known as *datagrams* between two hosts. When a source host wants to send data to a target host, it includes a transport layer segment along with the target host's address. Upon reception, the network layer ensures the segment is delivered to the transport layer on the target host.

---

[1] For more on this topic, I recommend reading this blog post by Google Cloud: "Authorize with SSL/TLS Certificates" (*https://oreil.ly/acqDy*).

The most prominent network layer protocol is the *internet protocol* (IP), with its version 4 (IPv4) being the most prevalent. IPv6 serves as its successor and has been progressively integrated into the public internet infrastructure since around 2006. To add an extra encryption layer on top of the IP protocol, the *IPsec* can be used. IPsec is commonly used with Virtual Private Networks (VPNs).

The IP protocol submits datagrams independently to the receiving host. A datagram might include several fields about its content, destination, and relevant details for the receiving end. Once received by the host, the datagrams are assembled again through the TCP protocol at the transport layer.

Understanding IP addressing is of primary importance for financial data engineers, particularly in the context of designing distributed systems such as Apache Cassandra for distributed databases or Apache Spark for distributed computing environments. In these setups, a typical strategy involves provisioning a defined number of nodes (machines) and linking them to form a cluster. Each node in the cluster is uniquely identified by an IP address, which can be used by the cluster manager and the worker nodes to establish connections and communicate with each other.

Another interesting use case of IP addressing is with Virtual Private Clouds (VPCs). One of the main concepts behind VPCs is the *subnet*, which refers to a range of IP addresses assigned to the VPC. IP addresses within a subnet are private, meaning they are inaccessible via the public internet but solely accessible through the VPC's internal network. When you provision and launch an instance of a given resource into a VPC, a primary private IP address from the subnet range is assigned to the instance.[2]

Network access layer

In this layer, datagrams coming from the network layer get routed through a network of routers that connect the network layer interfaces of the source and target. Datagrams are moved from one node (router) to the next until they reach their destination. Examples of network interface protocols include the Ethernet, WiFi, and Data Over Cable Service Interface Specification (DOCSIS) protocols employed in cable access networks.

The physical transmission of the individual data bits through the network happens via hardware devices that directly interface with a network, such as coaxial, optical, fiber, or twisted pair cables.

---

2 To learn more about VPCs and subnets, I recommend checking the documentation of AWS on IP addressing for your VPCs and subnets (*https://oreil.ly/4doEy*).

Speed Physics in Financial Markets

You might wonder how the physical networking layer is relevant to financial markets. Interestingly, it holds significant relevance and has been transforming certain market infrastructures, such as trading.

An illustrative example is the establishment of the transatlantic fiber-optic line Hibernia Express (*https://oreil.ly/m8oFR*), designed to link London and New York with ultra-low latency in response to demand from banks, exchanges, and trading firms. Thanks to Hibernia Express, London and New York experienced a five-millisecond reduction in latency compared to existing high-speed network services. In the era of automated trading, even a five-millisecond difference holds substantial importance to computers.

High-frequency traders, who have been engaged in a technical arms race to accelerate trade execution time, are speculating on an experimental form of fiber-optic cable (*https://oreil.ly/sKaY5*), called *hollow-core fiber*, to speed up their trades by billionths of a second.

Data Arrival Processes

Data may arrive at the ingestion layer with different temporal and structural patterns. In this section, I will use the *data arrival process* (DAP) concept to identify and describe the characteristics of a certain data ingestion pattern. A variety of DAPs may exist. Let's examine six that are particularly relevant to financial data engineering.

Scheduled data arrival process

In a scheduled DAP, data is ingested into the system according to a predetermined schedule and ingestion specifications. This process is generally more manageable as it follows a predictable pattern, with known details such as the arrival time, data type, format, volume, and ingestion method.

Scheduled DAPs are quite common in financial markets. For example, they may be used in the following circumstances:

- Arrival of company annual report filings at specific intervals such as by the end of the year, the end of March of each year, or at a future announced date

- Arrival of historical financial data snapshots from a financial data vendor on a daily, weekly, monthly, or yearly basis

- Arrival of financial institutions' required regulatory filings on a predefined date
- Arrival of data from continuous model training, stress testing, scenario analysis, and other financial quantitative analysis

Knowing when the data is expected to arrive can greatly enhance financial data engineers' jobs. This is because they can plan data ingestion jobs, anticipate the capacity and computational needs of the data infrastructure, and provision the necessary resources on a predictable basis (e.g., on a specific day of the week).

The main drawback of scheduled DAPs is the delay between data generation and arrival, which can impact data timeliness. Additionally, if scheduled jobs run without fetching any data, it can waste resources.

Event-driven data arrival process

When the arrival of data is contingent upon the occurrence of an event that cannot be predicted in advance, the DAP becomes event-driven. Event-driven DAPs are very common in financial markets. These include the arrival of the following types of data:

- Trade and quote data upon submission and execution in the market
- Financial information messages
- Transaction data upon the execution of a financial operation, such as payments, transfers, and others
- Client files for loan and credit card applications
- Data streams from financial data vendors
- News data
- Company updates and announcements
- Social media posts

The primary advantage of event-driven DAPs is that data is available shortly (or immediately) after its generation. This allows financial institutions to act promptly in response to new information and have the most recent, up-to-date market and operational insights. For this reason, event-driven systems are often associated with real-time systems. A system is considered real-time if its response time—typically set at a very low value—is essential to its proper functioning. Moreover, event-driven DAPs can save costs and optimize resource allocation as they switch resource utilization from a fixed to an on-demand pattern.

What Exactly Is a Real-Time System?

The term *real-time* is used widely in a variety of contexts. To many people, real-time would mean "instantaneously" or "immediately." For software and system engineers, real-time may refer to time-related characteristics of a system or application, such as processing time, response time, or latency. Given the significance of real-time systems in finance, I will provide a detailed description to clear up any misconceptions. To do so, I will draw a summary from the seminal work of Seppo J. Ovaska and Philip A. Laplante, *Real-Time Systems Design and Analysis: Tools for the Practitioner* (Wiley-IEEE Press, 2011).

Authors Laplante and Ovaska define a real-time system as "a mapping of a set of inputs into a set of outputs." The time between a system's reception of input and the generation of the final output is called the system's response time. The nature and speed of the response time depend on the system's features and purpose.

Building on this, the authors define a real-time system as a "computer system that must satisfy bounded response-time constraints or risk severe consequences, including failure." Failure, in this case, means that the system is not able to function or meet one of the requirements of its design specifications. More specifically, a failed real-time system is one that cannot satisfy timing or deadline constraints established in its specifications. In short, a system does not necessarily need to respond instantaneously to be considered real-time; it must simply define and meet response time criteria in its specifications.

At this point, however, all systems may be considered real-time as there is always some sort of time constraint. To further clarify this point, Laplante and Ovaska classify real-time systems into three categories:

Soft real-time systems
  A failure to meet a response time constraint leads to performance degradation but not system failure.

Hard real-time systems
  A failure to meet a single deadline can lead to complete or major system failure.

Firm real-time systems
  Missing a few deadlines may not be consequential, but missing more than a few may lead to complete or major system failure.

According to business and operational considerations, real-time systems can be categorized as soft, hard, or firm. For instance, if an ATM machine occasionally fails to respond to requests within its internal time limit (e.g., 10 seconds), it might lead to some customer dissatisfaction, but it remains tolerable, thus qualifying as a soft real-time system.

Conversely, in the context of a hedge fund engaged in high-frequency trading, delays in receiving data beyond expected deadlines could result in significant financial losses, necessitating the classification of the system as hard or firm. Another example is financial systems that involve Forex currency conversions. This process frequently includes a *Request for Quote* (RFQ), where a market participant requests a price quote from a liquidity provider or Forex broker to either buy or sell a specified amount in a particular currency pair. RFQs include an expiry time, during which the liquidity provider commits to honoring the quoted price. Failing to settle a Forex transaction within the RFQ's expiry time can expose the requesting institution to market risks, potentially resulting in financial losses.

Importantly, it is still common for people (even engineers) to think of real-time systems as being "instantaneous." To understand why, let's take the technological concept of *real-time payments* (RTPs). According to Stripe (*https://oreil.ly/T9K7B*), RTPs are "instant payments that are processed immediately and continuously, 24/7." In this context, instant refers to the fact that money is moved between bank accounts in seconds instead of hours or days (as is the case with traditional payment systems). For humans, several seconds may feel instantaneous, thus the use of the term instant in this context.

Nonetheless, I highly recommend following a systematic approach similar to the one outlined above when creating real-time financial systems. Software and data engineers must carefully understand and incorporate time constraints and limitations into their systems and investigate potential ways to change a soft real-time system into a hard or firm one, or vice versa.

With the emergence of cloud computing, event-driven data processing technologies have remarkably increased in popularity. These include message brokers (detailed in Chapter 8), such as Amazon Simple Notification Service (SNS), Amazon Managed Streaming for Apache Kafka (MSK), and Google Pub/Sub, as well as event-driven serverless computing platforms (illustrated in Chapter 9), such as AWS Lambda and Google Cloud Functions.

As event-driven DAPs are unpredictable, designing an event-driven financial data infrastructure requires careful attention. One essential feature to focus on concerns the ability of the infrastructure to scale to accommodate varying workloads and occasional spikes. Moreover, due to the data-intensive nature of event-driven DAPs, data quality issues such as errors, outliers, and timeliness may easily arise. Furthermore, event-driven DAPs may incur the issue of duplicate or concurrent ingestions, which happens when the same data or file gets ingested twice or more. This requires careful attention when designing the data infrastructure, as it might impact data consistency and potentially cause system failures.[3]

---

3 Systems that can handle duplicate ingestions reliably are often called *idempotent*. To learn more about this topic, I recommend the article "Idempotency and Ordering in Event-Driven Systems" (*https://oreil.ly/4NBlF*), by Wade Waldron.

Homogeneous data arrival process

In a homogenous DAP, the ingested data has predetermined consistent properties. For example, if you purchase a subscription to a dataset provided by a financial data provider, you are likely to know the kind of data, the schema, the ingestion format, and other details.

A homogeneous DAP is simpler to manage and maintain, and it helps ensure data integrity and consistency. In the financial industry, a number of projects have been underway to standardize and universalize data input and exchange formats. The section "Data Ingestion Formats" on page 256 will illustrate examples of standardized financial data formats.

Importantly, you should avoid overfitting your financial data architecture to handle only one type or format of data. This may cause problems if a data attribute changes or a new data type is ingested.

Heterogeneous data arrival process

In a heterogeneous DAP, ingested data may possess variable attributes such as extension, format, type, content, schema, and others. Heterogeneous DAPs are quite common in finance. For example, financial data vendors provide their data in different formats and structures. In addition, for optimization purposes, different types of data may be stored and transmitted in specific formats (a topic that will be covered in the section "Data Ingestion Formats" on page 256 in this chapter). Furthermore, different internal systems within financial institutions may generate data with their unique formats and structures.[4]

When designing for heterogeneous DAPs, the financial data infrastructure must account for various ingestible data types and possess the necessary capability to handle each. This complexity makes optimizing the infrastructure more challenging, but it also increases the financial institution's flexibility to ingest and accommodate new data sources.

Such flexibility is critical in today's fast-changing financial data landscape, where new data sources emerge regularly, and the amount and speed with which data is generated has grown significantly. Being able to accommodate a new data source means adding new analytical capabilities, developing new products, and gaining comprehensive insights into market trends, sales, customers, and operations.

---

4 For a detailed study on this topic, I recommend Sunila Gollapudi's "Aggregating Financial Services Data Without Assumptions: A Semantic Data Reference Architecture" (*https://oreil.ly/w_D42*), in the *Proceedings of the 2015 IEEE 9th International Conference on Semantic Computing* (IEEE, 2015): 312–315.

Single-item data arrival process

In a single-item DAP, data is ingested either on a record-at-a-time or file-at-a-time basis. Think, for example, about the arrival of information related to a payment transaction, bank loan application, market order, analytical report, or piece of news.

The main advantages of single-item DAPs are traceability and transactional guarantee. When the ingestion process concerns a single data item, it is typically easier to trace its lifecycle through system logs. Moreover, inserting one record at a time allows for easier data integrity and constraint checks.

As an illustration, let's say we have a database that stores customer financial transactions. A simple SQL-based single-item ingestion into this table would look like this:

```
-- PostgreSQL
INSERT INTO customer_transactions (
  user_id,
  transaction_id,
  time,
  transaction_type,
  amount,
  communication
) VALUES (
  195,
  'XT4h4Y453',
  '2024-01-20 10:09:42',
  '1985-02-10',
  'Credit Transfer',
  'online course subscription fees'
)
```

In some circumstances, single-item DAPs may lead to performance bottlenecks. For example, if the number of data ingestions is remarkably high, then it may jeopardize the system's ability to handle all incoming requests. This can happen due to a max connection limit on the database side (discussed in Chapter 8) or quota limit on an API side (covered in section "Data Ingestion Technologies" on page 269 in this chapter). Additionally, ingesting a large number of records one at a time can be very slow, which in turn can impact data quality dimensions such as timeliness.

Bulk data arrival process

In a bulk DAP, data is ingested in large chunks. Rather than processing one record at a time, a bulk DAP handles blocks of data or files that may contain hundreds or even millions of records simultaneously.

Bulk DAP offers performance advantages by processing large data volumes in a single request, saving overhead costs. This is ideal for tasks like bulk data loading, migration between storage systems, data archival processes, and regulatory reporting. For instance, when switching database systems, dumping data in a format compatible with the new system is far more efficient than copying records individually.

To give an example, let's consider how Snowflake's bulk loading works.[5] Assume you have a bunch of CSV files stored in the Amazon cloud storage service AWS S3, and you are using Snowflake as a data warehouse. You wish to upload the data from your CSV files into your Snowflake table.

The first thing to do is to create a FILE FORMAT object in Snowflake that describes the type and format of the data to be loaded. Let's say that our CSVs use the semicolon, ";", as a field delimiter, and we want to inform Snowflake to skip the first line in each file as it represents the header. The following command creates the desired format object:

```
-- Snowflake SQL
CREATE OR REPLACE FILE FORMAT s3csvformat
    TYPE = 'CSV'
    FIELD_DELIMITER = ';'
    SKIP_HEADER = 1;
```

Next, we want to create the so-called stage object, which tells Snowflake the location where the files are stored (staged). Snowflake provides several types of stage objects (*https://oreil.ly/IQ79x*), but in this example, we will use the recommended Named stage,[6] which may be created as follows:

```
-- Snowflake SQL
CREATE OR REPLACE STAGE s3_csv_stage
    FILE_FORMAT = s3csvformat
    URL = 's3://snowflake-docs';
```

Finally, to load the data from the stage location into the Snowflake table, we can execute the following command:

```
-- Snowflake SQL
COPY INTO destination_table
    FROM @s3_csv_stage/myfiles/
    PATTERN='.*daily_prices.csv'
    ON_ERROR = 'skip_file';
```

The PATTERN clause specifies that the command should load data from any file that matches the specified regular expression .*daily_prices.csv, which matches any file that ends with daily_prices.csv. Furthermore, the command specifies that if an error occurs when loading a specific file, skip it and proceed with the remaining files.

---

5 The full guide is available on Snowflake's website (*https://oreil.ly/WCto4*) and it assumes you have satisfied all the necessary requisites such as granting roles and permissions between Snowflake and AWS S3, creating the Snowflake table, and other tasks.

6 To upload files into a stage location, you need to use the Snowflake PUT command (*https://oreil.ly/S1shG*).

Now that we've covered the various data transmission and arrival processes, let's explore the different types of data formats that can be ingested into a financial data infrastructure.

Data Ingestion Formats

Data can be ingested in a variety of formats. A data format is used to indicate the extension or encoding used to store the data on a machine. In general, there is no standardized classification of the many data formats that a financial data infrastructure may support. To establish a baseline, this section will illustrate the most common types of data formats that financial data engineers might encounter when working with financial data.

General-Purpose Formats

General-purpose formats are widely used data formats with broad applicability and extensive adoption within the financial markets. Examples include the following:

- Comma-separated values (CSV) files are text files with comma-separated values (,).
- Tab-separated values (TSV) files are text files with tab-separated values (\t).
- Text files (TXT) are text files with lines delimited by a line separator (\n).
- JavaScript Object Notation (JSON) files are structured as a collection of name/value pairs.
- Extensible Markup Language (XML) files structure and store data in a hierarchical format using custom tags.
- Microsoft Excel files work with Microsoft Excel (e.g., XLSX and XLS) (*https://oreil.ly/lcybD*).
- Compressed files are compressed using a compression algorithm such as GZip or Zip.

Financial markets use these formats for a variety of reasons and purposes. For example, Microsoft Excel files are quite popular (*https://oreil.ly/03GEu*) among financial professionals and accountants due to their reliability (Microsoft as maintainer), simplicity, and advanced analytical capabilities. CSV and TSV formats are widely used for storing and sharing financial time series and tabular data. TXT files are used to store textual financial content such as reports, news, entity and reference data, and many more. JSON and XML are widely used for programmatic and web-based financial data exchange due to their user-friendly nature and dependable technical specifications. Consequently, they frequently form the basis for financial data standards.[7]

The downside of using general-purpose formats is that their flexibility increases the chance of data errors or quality issues. Moreover, these formats may not be efficient when dealing with large data volumes. To address this concern, more specialized formats can be employed, which will be discussed in the following sections.

Big Data Formats

General-purpose formats such as CSV and XML can easily encounter performance issues when ingesting and exchanging large amounts of data. To solve this issue, several big data formats have been developed, including Apache Parquet, Apache Avro, and ORC.

Apache Parquet is an open source, column-oriented data file format that supports efficient and economical data storage and retrieval. Parquet offers efficient data compression, decompression, schema evolution, and encoding algorithms to handle complex and large data. Parquet is accessible in several languages, including Python, C++, and Java. Parquet files are widely used. For example, the leading cloud data warehouse provider, Snowflake, reports that Parquet is the file format most often used by its customers (*https://oreil.ly/k8YFb*) to upload data to the Snowflake platform.

Column-Oriented Versus Row-Oriented File Formats

When dealing with file formats, it's important to understand the difference between column-oriented and row-oriented formats. In row-oriented formats (e.g., PostgreSQL's internal data format), data is stored on disk row by row. These formats are preferable for small datasets, strict data consistency requirements, or applications with heavy write/update operations, such as financial systems handling transactions like payments and clearing.

In contrast, column-oriented formats like Parquet store data on disk column by column. This format is highly advantageous for read-intensive and big data applications. Queries are more efficient and economical because read-intensive applications often retrieve only a subset of columns, avoiding unnecessary querying of other columns. Additionally, column-wise storage enhances compression efficiency as it optimally compresses data of the same type within a single column, unlike row-oriented formats, which compress heterogeneous data within a single row.

---

7 XML's popularity has remarkably increased in recent years. To read more about this topic, see "Making Life Easier in an XML World" (*https://oreil.ly/rDSVR*), by Denise Warzel.

Apache Avro is another common big data format known for its row-oriented structure and compact binary encoding, which helps reduce file storage size. Avro stores data definitions, types, and protocols in an easily readable JSON format, while the actual data is stored in a highly optimized binary format. Avro is schema dependent, meaning that the data and its schema are stored and transmitted together in the same file. As a result, Avro is preferred over Parquet when frequent schema changes occur, as merging schemas from multiple files can be quite costly.[8]

A third common big data format is Optimized Row Columnar (ORC), a column-oriented, binary format primarily used for storing Hive data in Hadoop environments. ORC is renowned for its exceptional performance (*https://oreil.ly/61P0Y*) in terms of data processing speed and storage efficiency, making it well-suited for handling large volumes of data.

In-Memory Formats

In many applications, data is frequently read and processed in memory. Crucially, different software programs may store data in memory using different formats. If data moves from one application to another during a data processing pipeline, then each application needs to convert the data to its in-memory format before processing it. This is a costly operation as it often involves data serialization and deserialization, which in turn can impact performance.

To solve this issue, a variety of in-memory data formats have been developed. A prominent example is Apache Arrow (*https://oreil.ly/4Vf72*), a standardized, column-oriented, language-agnostic data format for structuring and representing tabular datasets in memory. Apache Arrow can be used to develop a data infrastructure that processes data across multiple systems using an out-of-the-box standardized format.

Another noteworthy example is the Resilient Distributed Dataset (RDD) abstraction (*https://oreil.ly/THRcv*) created for Apache Spark to enable reliable, fault-tolerant, and parallel computations in memory.

Standardized Financial Formats

Market participants can exchange financial information in any of the formats covered thus far, such as CSV, JSON, TXT, and XML. However, if each financial institution employs its own convention to structure its financial messages and communications, markets will incur significant costs in understanding and extracting information from each and every format. For instance, imagine a network of one thousand trading firms where each firm submits trade request messages using its own JSON or

---

8 For a comparison of Avro and Parquet formats, see "AVRO vs. PARQUET" by Snowflake (*https://oreil.ly/ m7AU9*).

XML structure. This scenario would result in hundreds of different message formats that every trader would need to understand.

To address this challenge, financial market participants have been working on creating standardized formats for financial information. This effort is often described by industry experts as establishing a "common financial language" for data exchange.[9] Several initiatives have been proposed, leading to the development and adoption of multiple standards. Examples include the following:

- Financial products Markup Language (FpML)
- Financial Information eXchange (FIX)
- Interactive Financial eXchange (IFX)
- Market Data Definition Language (MDDL)
- Financial Electronic Data Interchange (FEDI)
- Open Financial Exchange (OFX)
- eXtensible Business Reporting Language (XBRL)
- Financial transaction card-originated messages (ISO 8583)
- Securities—Scheme for messages (ISO 15022)
- Universal Financial Industry Message Scheme (ISO 20022)
- SWIFT proprietary messages

In the following sections, we will go over some of these financial data standards in depth.

Financial Information eXchange (FIX)

Financial Information eXchange (FIX) (*https://oreil.ly/LDBs7*) is an electronic communication protocol widely used to exchange financial transaction information between financial institutions such as banks, trading firms, brokers/dealers, security exchanges, and even regulators. FIX is a nonproprietary open standard owned and maintained by the FIX Trading Community member firms. FIX was originally developed to exchange pre-trade and trade equities trading messages. Over time, its scope has expanded to include support for post-trade activities, as well as transactions in fixed income, foreign exchange, and listed derivatives markets.

A full account of the technical specifications of the FIX infrastructure (*https://oreil.ly/gY00B*) is beyond the scope of this section. However, the FIX system can be broken

---

9 See, for example, Aldane Haldane, Robleh D. Ali and Paul Nahai-Williamson's "Towards a Common Financial Language" (*https://oreil.ly/Xy3id*), presented at the Securities Industry and Financial Markets Association Symposium on "Building a Global Legal Entity Identifier Framework," New York, 2012.

down into (1) a standardized message format, (2) a FIX order routing network, and (3) a FIX engine necessary to submit and receive FIX messages. The classical encoding of FIX messages is called *tagvalue encoding*, which structures a message as a chain of tag/value pairs. Tags are integers that identify the field, followed by the "=" character (hexadecimal 0x3D), and finally, the value of that field, encoded in the ISO 8859-1 character set. Each tag/value pair is separated by the ISO 6429:1992 Start of Heading control character <SOH> (hexadecimal value 0x01). Other encodings include FIXML, which leverages XML and JSON to format the message.

For example, a single buy order FIX message looks like this:[10]

```
8=FIX.4.2^A 9=145^A 35=D^A 34=4^A 49=ABC_DEFG01^A 52=20090323-15:40:29^A
56=CCG^A 115=XYZ^A 11=NF 0542/03232009^A 54=1^A 38=100^A 55=CVS^A 40=1^A 59=0^A
47=A^A 60=20090323-15:40:29^A 21=1^A 207=N^A 10=139^A
```

The fields can be broken down as follows:

```
8=FIX.4.2 FIX version number
9=145 Body Length: 145 bytes
35=D Message Type: New Order - Single
34=4 Message Sequence Number: 4
49=ABC_DEFG01 Sender Company ID: ABC_DEFG01
52=20090323-15:40:29 Sending Time: March 23, 2009, 15:40:29
56=CCG Target Company ID: CCG
115=XYZ On Behalf Of Company ID: XYZ
11=NF 0542/03232009 Client Order ID: NF 0542/03232009
54=1 Side: Buy
38=100 Order Quantity: 100 shares
55=CVS Symbol: CVS
40=1 Order Type: Market
59=0 Time In Force: Day
47=A Special Instructions: Agency single order
60=20090323-15:40:29 Transaction Time: March 23, 2009, 15:40:29
21=1 Handling Instructions: Automated execution
207=N Security Exchange: NASD OTC
10=139 Checksum: 139
```

According to the FIX protocol, to exchange FIX messages between two financial institutions, both must have a FIX engine that communicates over a FIX routing network. Several FIX network routing options are available, including the internet, leased lines, point-to-point VPNs, and Hub-and-Spoke. The FIX engine needs to be implemented and connected to the selected routing network to exchange messages.[11]

---

10 The sample message was taken from the "Sample Messages Document" (*https://oreil.ly/2_9YW*), by NYSE. A dictionary of all FIX tags and their meaning is available online (*https://oreil.ly/ykUfo*).

11 Detailed technical specifications on FIX networks and engines are available at the FIX community website (*https://oreil.ly/wt8SS*).

eXtensible Business Reporting Language (XBRL)

eXtensible Business Reporting Language (XBRL) (*https://oreil.ly/y9Tp6*) is an XML-based open international standard for digital business and financial reporting. XBRL is managed and maintained by XBRL International, a nonprofit consortium. In a nutshell, XBRL provides a standardized, accurate, and reliable way to represent and exchange business and accounting data in both human-readable and machine-readable formats. XBRL is widely used by regulators, companies, governments, data providers, investors, analysts, and accountants.

The main building block of XBRL is an XBRL *instance*, which refers to the collection of business facts that an XBRL document contains. More technically, an XBRL is an XML file whose root element is <xbrli:xbrl>.

Another important element is XBRL *facts*, which represent individual pieces of information in an XBRL instance. For example, a fact may say that Heckler & Brothers Inc.'s 2018 revenues were $5 billion. The fact is reported as a value of 5b against a corresponding concept representing "Revenues," in addition to associated contextual information for the units (dollars), the period (2018), and the entity ("Heckler & Brothers Inc."). Technically, facts are represented by elements in an XBRL document.

Additionally, there are XBRL *concepts*, which can be used to describe the meaning of facts. For instance, "Assets," "Liabilities," and "Net Income" are examples of these concepts. Technically, concepts are represented as element definitions in an XML schema.

Finally, XBRL *taxonomies* correspond to collections of concept definitions. Taxonomies are typically created to represent a given reporting regime, such as international financial reporting standards (IFRS) and generally accepted accounting principles (GAAP) standards, as well as for reporting requirements of various regulators and government agencies. A taxonomy is used to define what needs to be reported clearly. At a technical level, a taxonomy is an XML schema document containing element definitions and a collection of XML documents with additional information associated with concept definitions.

XBRL allows for defining business rules that can constrain and verify what kind of data can be reported. Rules can be logical or mathematical, and they are often used to control the data quality of XBRL documents.[12]

---

12 For more details, check the official XBRL Essentials guide (*https://oreil.ly/PeX4W*).

Financial products Markup Language (FpML)

Financial products Markup Language (FpML) (*https://oreil.ly/9ozTa*) is an open source, XML-based information exchange standard designed for the electronic trading and processing of financial derivatives instruments. The standard is defined and maintained by the FpML Standards Committee.

Among the most distinguishing aspects of derivative markets is the flexibility in defining and shaping derivative contracts to meet specific client requirements. Moreover, a large portion of derivative trading happens over the counter (OTC), meaning that such transactions are conducted business-to-business and not through a centralized trading venue.

With such flexibility comes a large variety of data communication and representation styles. On the one hand, this has been considered necessary as it allows two parties to customize a derivative product to meet specific client needs. Consequently, attempts to standardize OTC derivative communications have not gained much traction, as they were doomed to become obsolete quite fast once new requirements emerged. This situation has led to a manual data exchange process between trading parties, which is prone to errors.

However, with the increase in derivative trading volume and the establishment of new requirements for derivative trade processing, standardization became more appealing. In this regard, FpML was introduced to automate the flow of information across the entire derivative trading network (of partners and clients), independent of the underlying software or hardware infrastructure supporting the related activities. The standard was initially developed for interest rate derivatives such as swaps, but it has been extended to other classes of derivatives, structured products, bonds, and commercial loans since then. Moreover, FpML has evolved to cover the different stages of a derivative transaction, such as pre-trade, trade, and post-trade.

An FpML message is encoded using Unicode Transformation Format (UTF)-8 or UTF-16 and uses XML as the file format. FpML may include a number of elements whose values are restricted to a limited set of values (e.g., currencies). Such restricted sets are called *domains*. FpML relies on two types of domain codings. First are domains that don't change frequently throughout the life of the specification, which are coded using XML schema enumerations. The second type is domains coded using a strategy defined by the Architecture Working Group, referred to as *schemes*. A scheme is associated with a Uniform Resource Identifier (URI). Three categories of coding schemes exist:

- External coding scheme with a URI assigned by an external body such as an open standards organization or a market participant
- External coding scheme without a URI; in such a case, FpML assigns a URI

- An FpML-defined coding scheme, defined and versioned by FpML, which also assigns the URI

For example, an FpML-defined scheme is *actionTypeScheme,* which codes the action types as defined by the European Securities and Markets Authority (ESMA).[13] As of the time this book was written, the URI for this scheme is *http://www.fpml.org/coding-scheme/action-type-1-0,* and its coding scheme is shown in Table 7-1.

Table 7-1. FpML-defined action type scheme

Code	Description
C	Cancel (a termination of an existing contract)
E	Error (a cancellation of a wrongly submitted report)
M	Modify (a modification of details of a previously reported derivative contract)
N	New (a derivative contract reported for the first time)
O	Other (any other amendment to the report)
V	Valuation update (an update of a contract valuation)
Z	Compression (a compression of the reported contract)
C	Cancel (a termination of an existing contract)

FpML's flexibility, enabled by its use of schemes, makes it well-suited for handling custom exchange definitions and requirements in the derivatives markets. Those interested in exploring the specifics of these schemes can refer to the comprehensive FpML Coding Schemes documentation (*https://oreil.ly/RjvBJ*).

Open Financial Exchange (OFX)

Open Financial Exchange (OFX) (*https://oreil.ly/S8-Uu*) is a widely adopted open standard for the electronic exchange of financial data and instructions between financial institutions, businesses, and customers. OFX allows direct connection between customers and institutions without requiring an intermediary.

Open Financial Exchange relies on open specifications that anyone can implement (e.g., financial institution, software development firm, transaction processor, or other party). A client-server model is used to design the OFX system. The client submits a request (e.g., HTTP) to an OFX server, and the server replies with a response to the client. OFX defines the request/response message structure and provides guidelines for building the infrastructure for supporting message exchange. OFX uses widely accepted open standards for networking (such as TCP/IP and HTTP), data formatting (such as XML), and TLS.

---

13 The source of this example is the official FpML Coding Schemes documentation (*https://oreil.ly/RjvBJ*).

OFX is widely utilized by financial institutions for a variety of applications and use cases. Since 1997, it has been the leading direct API standard (*https://oreil.ly/yrM2p*) for banks to provide data to financial applications. It is currently in use at over 7,000 financial institutions. OFX can be implemented and adapted across a wide range of frontend applications and platforms. Moreover, it is an extensible standard, allowing for the straightforward addition of new services as needed.

Readers are encouraged to check the official documentation (*https://oreil.ly/-UqIZ*) for more details on OFX's technical implementation and message structure.

Universal Financial Industry Message Scheme (ISO 20022)

As messaging standards increased in scale, sophistication, and variety, financial market participants, in collaboration with the ISO, initiated discussions to make uniform the message standardization process. This resulted in the introduction of the highly celebrated ISO 20022—Universal Financial Industry Message Scheme (*https://oreil.ly/Z2k6L*).

ISO 20022 is an open and global standard that aims to streamline financial market communication and messaging using a common language. Its general-purpose design makes it suitable for the majority of use cases, irrespective of the business domain, communication network, or counterparty.

A distinguishing feature of ISO 20022 is its model-based approach. When you use ISO 20022 to develop a new message, the outcome is a model that defines and describes all parts of the message exchange and communication protocol between participants. The modeling method consists of four levels: scope, conceptual, logical, and physical. These levels are developed as one progresses from the business process and its associated features and components to the development of the final instance of the message model in a given syntax (typically XML).

Having said this, it is important to remember that ISO 20022 is not a single communication standard in and of itself but rather a standard that describes a development methodology for creating financial message models.

ISO 20022 models and their related message components are available online via a central repository (*https://oreil.ly/e-bhU*) organized into two areas:

The Data Dictionary
Contains industry model elements such as business concepts, message concepts, and data types. These elements are called dictionary items and serve as reusable components for future models.

The Business Process Catalog
Contains model message definitions and syntax implementations.

According to the official ISO documentation (*https://oreil.ly/vIenF*), the modeling methodology of ISO 20022 consists of eight parts:

ISO 20022-1
Metamodel for all models and the repository

ISO 20022-2
UML profile to create models that conform to the ISO 20022-1 Metamodel

ISO 20022-3
Modeling method to produce models

ISO 20022-4
XML schema generation rules to transform a logical-level model into a physical-level implementation

ISO 20022-5
Reverse engineering guidelines to extract relevant information from existing messages

ISO 20022-6
Message transport characteristics

ISO 20022-7
Registration process description

ISO 20022-8
Abstract Syntax Notation One (ASN.1) generation rules to transform a logical model into an ASN.1-based physical level

ISO 20022 messages follow a four-block convention for naming. For instance, a well-known message is the "FinancialInstitutionToFinancialInstitutionCustomerCredit-Transfer" message, represented in the ISO 20022 convention, as shown in Figure 7-2. In this example, "PACS" denotes "Payment Clearing and Settlement," indicating the message's business domain of payment and settlement instructions. The "008" segment serves as the message type identifier, specifying the type of transaction—in this case, a financial institution to financial institution customer credit transfer. The "001" designation represents the variant number, indicating the global message definition. Lastly, "12" identifies the message version within the ISO system.

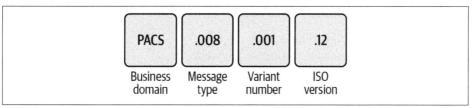

Figure 7-2. Structure of an ISO 20022 message

ISO 20022 Variants

Variants (*https://oreil.ly/9Z9Fe*) and versions are pivotal aspects of ISO 20022, allowing for the creation of simplified and purpose-specific versions of the global message to suit specific requirements.

One of ISO 20022's nicest features is the concept of a variant. Each ISO 20022 message has a *global message definition*, typically represented with variant number 001. Other variants (>001) can be created to produce restricted versions of a global message definition. For example, a straight-through processing (STP) variant of a global message definition may exclude all the options that would require manual processing of the message instance, and thus ensures the STP of the messages.

Each variant can have multiple versions, which is the last component you see in the message identifier shown in Figure 7-2. Versions are independent of the variant; for example, variant 001 can have versions 001.001 and 001.002, while variant 002 may have versions 002.001, 002.002, and 002.003.

ISO 20022 variants play a crucial role by enabling customization of global message definitions to align with specific operational and processing needs in financial transactions. In addition, they simplify the adoption of ISO 20022 message definitions by reducing complexity and providing clarity on how to apply message definitions in specific contexts.

Examples of some of the most used ISO 20022 messages include the following:

pain.001—Credit Transfer
  Customer-initiated credit transfers to banks

pain.013—Request to Pay
  Requests payment from a payer

pain.002—Payment Status Report
  Status updates on initiated payments

pacs.008—FI to FI Customer Credit Transfer
  Customer credit transfers between banks

pacs.003—FI to FI Customer Direct Debit
  Direct debit transactions between banks

pacs.002—FI to FI Payment Status Report
  Status updates on financial institution payments

camt.05x

Various account reporting messages (e.g., *camt.054—Bank to Customer Debit/ Credit* can be used to notify an account holder of debit and/or credit entries reported to their account)

Here is a simple XML snippet that illustrates a PACS.008.001 message. Each tag within the message has been annotated with a comment detailing its meaning or purpose:[14]

```
<FIToFICstmrCdtTrf>  Financial Institution Credit Transfer
    <GrpHdr>  Group Header
     <MsgId>123456789</MsgId>  Message Identification
     <CreDtTm>2022-05-20T14:30:00</CreDtTm>  Creation Date and Time
     <NbOfTxs>1</NbOfTxs>  Number of Transactions
     <CtrlSum>1000.00</CtrlSum>  Control Sum (Total Amount)
    </GrpHdr>
    <CdtTrfTxInf>  Credit Transfer Transaction Information
     <PmtId>  Payment Identification
      <EndToEndId>00001</EndToEndId>  End-to-End Identification
     </PmtId>
     <Amt>  Amount
      <InstdAmt Ccy="USD">1000.00</InstdAmt>  Instructed Amount
     </Amt>
     <Cdtr>  Creditor
      <Nm>John Smith</Nm>  Name of the Creditor
     </Cdtr>
     <CdtrAcct>  Creditor Account
      <Id>  Identification
       <IBAN>GB29NWBK60161331926819</IBAN>  IBAN Number
      </Id>
     </CdtrAcct>
     <RmtInf>  Remittance Information
      <Ustrd>Invoice payment for services rendered.</Ustrd>
     </RmtInf>
    </CdtTrfTxInf>
   </FIToFICstmrCdtTrf>
```

Any community user or organization can use the ISO 20022 modeling methodology to develop and submit a proposal for a new model or a modification of an existing model. Candidate models are reviewed and approved by three registration bodies: the Registration Management Group (RMG), the Registration Authority (RA), and the Standards Evaluation Groups (SEGs).[15]

---

14 To see the full message body and have a more detailed idea about the meaning of the tags, download the full message data online (*https://oreil.ly/ZEQIf*).

15 To learn more about the ISO 20022 registration process, see the official web page on the development of new ISO 20022 message definitions (*https://oreil.ly/zkMX3*).

ISO 20022 has seen remarkable adoption and acceptance among market participants. This includes all domains where financial data is exchanged, including payments, securities trading and settlement, credit and debit card transactions, foreign exchange transactions, and many more.[16] For example, SWIFT introduced ISO 20022 in March 2023 and established a migration plan (*https://oreil.ly/6EtRB*) in which both SWIFT proprietary MT (message type/text) messages and ISO 20022 will coexist until November 2025. After that, SWIFT messages will be completely based on ISO 20022.

Case Study: Society for Worldwide Interbank Financial Telecommunication (SWIFT)

A good example demonstrating the use of messages in financial markets is the Society for Worldwide Interbank Financial Telecommunication (SWIFT). SWIFT is a Belgium-based cooperative that provides a secure and reliable messaging system for financial transactions worldwide. SWIFT does not hold or manage financial assets. Instead, it offers a platform for exchanging financial messages, such as money and securities transfer instructions. Over 11,000 financial institutions globally are connected to the SWIFT system.

SWIFT provides different messaging formats and schemas. The most common is the FIN message, which follows a store-and-forward mode: messages sent from the source are stored at a central intermediary location before being transmitted to the recipient. Another format is InterAct, which is XML-based and offers features such as real-time messaging and query-and-response capabilities. Finally, FileAct messages are used to transfer files, such as large batches of messages or other payment-related files. Many of SWIFT's messaging formats are based on ISO standards, such as ISO 15022 and, more recently, ISO 20022.

SWIFT messages are categorized using the convention MT (message type/text) (*https://oreil.ly/7v4oO*), followed by three digits that indicate the message category, group, and type (e.g., MTxxx). There are nine message categories in the SWIFT system; for example, MT1xx is for customer payments and checks, and MT5xx is for securities market transactions.

Consider a scenario where Corporation A wants to send $500,000 to Corporation B. Corporation A initiates the transaction by submitting payment instructions to its bank (Bank 1) using an MT101 message (or ISO 20022 pain.001). Upon receiving the message, Bank 1 issues a credit transfer request to Corporation B's bank (Bank 2) using an MT103 message (or ISO 20022 pacs.008). Figure 7-3 illustrates the flow.

---

16 For a detailed analysis, I recommend checking the implications of ISO 20022 on the payment industry. For this reason, I highly recommend the paper by Steve Goswell, "ISO 20022: The Implications for Payments Processing and Requirements for Its Successful Use" (*https://oreil.ly/PQ4k-*), *Journal of Payments Strategy & Systems* 1, no. 1 (Autumn 2006): 42–50.

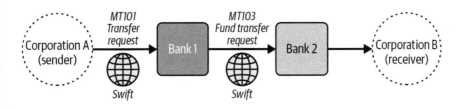

Figure 7-3. A SWIFT transfer

In this example, it was assumed that Bank 1 and Bank 2 have a corresponding banking relationship, which allows them to directly exchange messages such as MT101 and MT103. However, if they do not have a corresponding banking relationship (*https://oreil.ly/UJ8wM*), the payment process would involve one or more intermediary or correspondent banks. Recently, SWIFT launched SWIFT GPI (Global Payments Innovation) to enhance the cross-border payment experience, addressing the industry's demands for greater speed, traceability, and transparency.

Now that you have an understanding of data ingestion processes and formats, let's explore the various technological options for integrating a data ingestion mechanism into a financial data infrastructure.

Data Ingestion Technologies

To enable and integrate data ingestion capabilities into a financial data infrastructure, one or more ingestion mechanisms need to be implemented. To this end, a number of technological options are available to meet varying business and technical needs. In this section, I will discuss six of the most common ingestion technologies used in financial markets.

Financial APIs

API stands for *application programming interface,* and it refers to a wide range of software implementations that allow one software component to interact with another. An API defines the rules, protocols, and methods for interacting between two software types.

At the highest level, an API can be described in terms of a client and a server. A client using one application sends a request to a server operating in another application. The server processes the request and returns a response to the client. For instance, when you open a social media application to upload a new image, you (the client) interact with the app provider's server via an API.

Technically, there are several approaches to designing and implementing APIs. These include SOAP APIs, RPC APIs, GraphQL, WebSocket APIs, and REST APIs. Among these, REST APIs, which stands for Representational State Transfer, are the most popular. REST APIs primarily use the HTTP protocol for communication. They can implement various HTTP request methods such as GET (to retrieve data, e.g., account balance or transaction history), POST (to initiate a backend process), and PUT (to create or update a resource on the backend).

 Although both PUT and POST can be used to create or update a resource, the main difference is that PUT is *idempotent*. This means that making the same PUT request multiple times will produce the same result each time. For example, if you submit a request through your banking application to pay an electricity bill, submitting the same request again should not result in the bill being paid twice.

APIs can be written in most programming languages, including Java, C, C++, Node.js, and Python. Java and Python APIs are quite common among data engineers. Within the Python ecosystem, frameworks such as Flask, FastAPI, and Django are widely used to program web-based APIs. To provide a short example, consider the following statement:

```Bash
# Bash
curl -X POST \
    -H "Content-Type: application/json" \
    -d '[{"idType": "TICKER", "idValue": "AAPL", "exchCode": "UN"}]' \
    https://api.openfigi.com/v2/mapping
```

This `curl` command is making a POST request to the OpenFIGI API (`https://api.openfigi.com/v2/mapping`) to fetch mapping information for the financial instrument with the ticker symbol AAPL (Apple Inc.) on the exchange with code UN (New York Stock Exchange). To test this API request, open a terminal or command line window on your computer, paste the command, and press Enter. The response is expected to have a structure similar to this:

```
[
  {
    "data": [
      {
        "figi": "BBG000B9XVV8",
        "name": "APPLE INC",
        "ticker": "AAPL",
        "exchCode": "UN",
        "compositeFIGI": "BBG000B9XRY4",
```

```
        "uniqueID": null,
        "securityType": "Common Stock",
        "marketSector": "Equity",
        "shareClassFIGI": "BBG001S5N8V8",
        "uniqueIDFutOpt": null,
        "securityType2": "Common Stock",
        "securityDescription": "AAPL"
      }
    ]
  }
]
```

APIs are everywhere. In finance, they are extensively used for all kinds of purposes. Payment APIs, often known as payment gateway APIs, are a major application field. In simple terms, a payment gateway is a technology that facilitates the acceptance and processing of electronic payments between merchants and financial institutions. This includes credit and debit card payments, digital wallets, and bank transfers. At the core of a payment gateway technology is an API that handles all the payment lifecycle phases and allows the involved entities (merchant, processor, gateway, financial institution, etc.) to talk to each other. Among the most known payment gateway APIs are Square, Stripe, PayPal, Authorize.Net, and Adyen.

APIs play a pivotal role in accessing data from financial data vendors. These APIs are designed to allow clients to retrieve and import data programmatically, enabling the development of data-driven financial applications. For instance, Bloomberg offers the Server API (SAPI) (*https://oreil.ly/HwBFO*) to allow customers to access Bloomberg Terminal data through both proprietary and third-party applications. Similarly, LSEG (formerly Refinitiv) provides the Eikon Data API (*https://oreil.ly/Dd94Z*), a Python-based library that enables users to access Eikon data using Python.

> When ingesting financial data from external sources, check if the data provider has an API in place. Using the API can be quite convenient and accelerate development. At the same time, make sure you check any vendor-specific API limitations that might impact your application, such as a single-request size limit (e.g., 100 prices per request), request rate limits (e.g., 1K requests/day), request timeout, and maximum concurrent requests. If you'd like to learn more, check the FactSet's Formula API limitations available on the vendor's official web page (*https://oreil.ly/fpfkn*).

Financial Data Sharing with Open Finance, Open Banking, and Financial APIs

Recently, there has been growing interest (*https://oreil.ly/Srug5*) among financial market participants in open finance initiatives. These initiatives seek to establish a digital ecosystem that enables seamless sharing of financial data between financial institutions and third-party service providers. The primary driver of this new paradigm is to foster collaboration among market participants to produce better goods and services driven by financial data.

The most popular example of an open finance initiative is commonly referred to as *open banking* (*https://oreil.ly/X5d0V*), in which traditional banking institutions and third-party service providers such as FinTech firms collaborate to provide innovative financial products. To facilitate collaboration, banks and FinTechs share data using ad hoc financial APIs.

Various regulatory frameworks have been developed to promote open finance. For example, the second Payment Services Directive (PSD2) (*https://oreil.ly/v3G1E*), adopted in 2015 by the EU, imposed an obligation on banks to facilitate access to payment data for third-party service providers via a secure interface. To promote a wider open finance ecosystem that goes beyond payment account data, the EU proposed the Financial Data Access legislation (*https://oreil.ly/t0Ai6*), whose main goal is "to establish a framework governing access to and use of customer data in finance."

Special types of open banking enablers, regulated under frameworks such as PSD2 in Europe, include *Account Information Service Providers* (AISPs) and *Payment Initiation Service Providers* (PISPs). An AISP, or a company with an AIS license, collects, aggregates, and facilitates access to a user's financial information across accounts held with various institutions. PISPs, on the other hand, facilitate direct payments from the consumer's bank account to online merchants.

Various enablers have emerged to offer platforms for open banking. For instance, Tink, a Swedish company later acquired by Visa, facilitates connections to over 6,000 banks throughout Europe. Another example is Powens, a French company that connects over 1,800 institutions across numerous European countries, providing an open finance platform to its clients.

Crucially, it is important to keep in mind that financial APIs are not simply a bunch of FastAPI or Flask methods. Instead, APIs should be designed with business, user, and application requirements in mind. For example, JPMorgan Chase classifies financial APIs into data and service APIs (*https://oreil.ly/UbV9U*). Data APIs are mainly used to request financial data, but they can be designed in a way that they can be essential tools for building applications, enable external collaborations, and be reusable across multiple departments, channels, and product lines. Service APIs, on the other hand, are used to create and trigger an instance of a service, such as initiating a payment, a balance inquiry, or requesting a change from the bank. Many firms use the term *API integration* to denote a strategy where applications are connected via their APIs. The goal is to create an infrastructure in which data exchange and communication occur seamlessly through APIs, facilitating creativity and innovation.

When designing a financial API, the two most important elements to consider are performance and security. API performance is often measured by the ability of the system to scale to a large number of concurrent requests, as well as its request response time. Measures such as "hits per sec and "requests per sec" are often used for this purpose. The idea is to measure the ability of an API to handle a large number of requests/hits in one second. Common API performance optimization techniques involve load balancing, caching, rate limiting, and throttling, among others.[17]

As for security, the primary elements to consider are authentication and authorization to control how and who can interact with the API. Tools such as firewalls, authentication tokens, OAuth 2.0, API keys, and API gateways are often used for this purpose.[18] In addition, APIs need to be protected against advanced malicious attacks such as SQL injection (SQLi). In SQLi, a cybercriminal exploits application vulnerabilities to inject malicious input into an API request that alters the behavior of a backend SQL query. For example, let's take a naive scenario where the user is required to insert their user ID to access their account balance. Upon providing such credential (e.g., user ID: 267), an API request is sent to the backend, which then executes the following SQL query:

```
-- SQL
SELECT first_name, last_name, account_balance
FROM user_accounts
WHERE user_id = 267
```

Now, if the API doesn't handle SQL injection properly, then it is possible to provide input such as user ID "267 OR 1=1". In this case, your backend may end up executing the following query:

```
-- SQL
SELECT first_name, last_name, account_balance
FROM user_accounts
WHERE user_id = 267 OR 1=1
```

---

17 To learn more about these and other API optimization topics, I highly recommend the book by De Brajesh, *API Management: An Architect's Guide to Developing and Managing APIs for Your Organization* (APress, 2017).

18 For a good reference on API security, see Neil Madden's *API Security in Action* (Manning, 2020).

Because the SQL condition 1=1 always evaluates to TRUE, the entire WHERE statement will be true, regardless of whether the provided user ID is correct. In this case, the entire list of users and their account balances will be queried, which may lead to major data breaches.[19]

Financial Data Feeds

In the financial industry, the term "data feed" refers to a mechanism designed to deliver the latest financial data and updates to traders, investment firms, and financial institutions. The main sources of data feeds include stock exchanges, financial news providers, and market data vendors.

Financial data feeds can be designed to transmit data either as historical snapshots or, more commonly, in live mode. When provided in live mode, a data feed offers a continuous stream of real-time data, essential in scenarios where timely data access is critical. Moreover, data feeds often include features that allow users to configure the timing, location, and specific data they want to receive. Financial data feeds may vary in terms of latency, throughput, and delivery guarantees.

Examples of financial data feeds include S&P Global's Xpressfeed (*https://oreil.ly/YSXP4*), which offers access to over 200 datasets and allows users to customize data extraction and delivery locations. LSEG's Real-Time – Ultra Direct (*https://oreil.ly/5b6MT*) is another example, providing a high-performance, low-latency real-time market data feed. In addition, Bloomberg provides the Bloomberg Market Data Feed (B-PIPE) (*https://oreil.ly/sPpaE*). Exchange venues also offer market data feeds, such as the NYSE Trades Data Feed (*https://oreil.ly/bqaDN*) and NASDAQ Market Data Feeds (*https://oreil.ly/h3pK6*), which stream trading data as it happens and often provide the lowest latency due to being the original data source. Finally, news feeds, like those from MT Newswires (*https://oreil.ly/Yx7Vk*), are a common type of data feed, delivering real-time news headlines and text.

One challenge when dealing with financial data feeds is information overload. This happens when a large volume of data from one or more feeds overwhelms the existing financial data infrastructure. The adoption of cloud technology has alleviated this issue by allowing financial institutions to store and retrieve data at any scale without the need to manage and maintain the underlying infrastructure.[20]

---

19 For a detailed analysis of SQL injection, I recommend the seminal paper by William G. Halfond, Jeremy Viegas, and Alessandro Orso, "A Classification of SQL Injection Attacks and Countermeasures" (*https://oreil.ly/OEjX1*), in the *Proceedings of the International Symposium on Secure Software Engineering*, vol. 1, (March 2006): 13–15.

20 For an overview of this issue, see "The Relentless Rise of Real-Time Data" (*https://oreil.ly/YbMMX*), by LSEG.

Secure File Transfer

File transfer is one of the most frequent and regular operations in the financial sector. Banks, for example, transfer files for loan applications, transaction history, and account information; investment firms transfer trade data, portfolio composition, and intellectual property files like investment strategy or trading algorithms; insurance companies transfer client policy and personal information files; and regulated financial institutions must submit various filings to comply with regulatory reporting requirements.

Importantly, files transferred by financial institutions often contain sensitive information. As a result, file sharing needs to be secured to meet the financial sector's security and privacy requirements. To this end, a widely used technology is the *Secure File Transfer Protocol* (SFTP), which leverages the SSH protocol to encrypt data and commands that one machine submits to another. SFTP is secure, reliable, and platform independent.

File transfer via SFTP is a good solution for bulk and large file transfers. It is also often used when there isn't an API available for data exchange. Crucially, SFTP may not be the best option for all use cases. For example, it may not be ideal in high-speed and large-volume data-driven systems characterized by demanding workloads. Furthermore, SFTP may require a security policy to manage passwords, keys, and user access, which can increase the complexity of file transfer.

Various alternatives have been proposed to address these issues. For instance, managed SFTP solutions, like Managed File Transfer (MFT) (*https://oreil.ly/wehCT*), provide enhanced enterprise-level functionality for security, performance, compliance, and reporting beyond what standard SFTP offers. Additionally, protocols such as FTPS (a more secure form of FTP), SCP (Secure Copy Protocol), and WebDAV (Web Distributed Authoring and Versioning) can be utilized depending on the specific business requirements.

Cloud Access

With the widespread adoption of cloud computing across nearly every sector, cloud-based data sharing and access has emerged as a reliable and convenient way to exchange data. In its simplest setup, a data provider creates a storage bucket or cloud database within a dedicated and isolated cloud environment. It then uploads the data and authorizes the target user to access and manipulate it. Subsequently, whenever new data updates are available, the provider uploads them to the storage location, enabling immediate access for the user.

One convenient aspect of this access method is that users can leverage various cloud-based features when working with the data, including user interfaces, querying capabilities, data management, search functions, and more. Furthermore, there are cost-saving benefits and seamless integration experience with other cloud services, particularly for clients already utilizing the cloud. For instance, if your data pipelines are already processed in the cloud, having a new data source accessible directly through the cloud simplifies workflow management. Additionally, data updates occur continuously with minimal intervention required on the user's part.

Here are a few examples. In 2022, Bloomberg and Google announced a new partnership (*https://oreil.ly/4s0DX*) that will allow mutual customers to easily access B-PIPE, Bloomberg's real-time market data feed, through Google Cloud. Similarly, CME Group, the world's leading derivatives marketplace, partnered with Google Cloud (*https://oreil.ly/g71UV*) to provide fast and reliable market data access to their customers.

> ## Case Study: FactSet Integration with AWS Redshift and Snowflake
>
> FactSet is a well-known financial data vendor that provides content to more than 160,000 investment professionals worldwide. FactSet has expanded its data delivery options in the past few years to include cloud-based access. For example, it is now possible to access 100+ FactSet proprietary and third-party financial datasets through popular cloud data warehouse services such as AWS Redshift (*https://oreil.ly/li3AQ*) and Snowflake (*https://oreil.ly/zdMKq*).
>
> With this cloud-based delivery, FactSet saves its clients the need to clean, model, and normalize the data. It is already populated in SQL tables and is ready for users to query. Data is constantly updated and added to existing tables. In addition, if the user relies on both FactSet proprietary data and third-party vendor data offered via FactSet, cloud delivery allows centralization and integration of disparate data sources into a single platform such as Redshift or Snowflake.

Cloud providers have recently increased their market competition in the financial data market. This is expressed by the emergence of the so-called financial data marketplaces. These managed cloud solutions allow financial data providers to distribute and share their data through a single cloud interface. This may be convenient for financial data providers as it eliminates the need to build and maintain an infrastructure for data storage, distribution, billing, and user management. Examples include AWS Data Exchange for Financial Services (*https://oreil.ly/d2clm*) and Google Cloud Datashare for financial services (*https://oreil.ly/dFU-K*). Cloud marketplace data can be delivered in a variety of ways. For example, Google Datashare distributes data in batches through its managed warehouse solution BigQuery and in real time through its managed messaging service Pub/Sub.

Web Access

A user-friendly and straightforward way to access financial data is through a dedicated web page provided by a financial institution or data vendor. In this web access mode, financial data can be downloaded in file format, queried and visualized using a query builder, or quickly parsed and analyzed by the user.

This mode is convenient for handling small datasets or when speed is not critical, such as for scheduled data extractions. However, for faster data access or bulk file downloads, alternative data ingestion technologies like SFTP, API, or cloud-based solutions are more suitable.

Specialized Financial Software

In certain financial data exchange settings, specialized or dedicated software is implemented. This is particularly common when setting up standardized systems for secure financial messaging, payments, transactions, and other market operations.

An example of specialized financial software is FIX engines (*https://oreil.ly/wt8SS*), which are software applications that enable two institutions to exchange FIX messages (discussed in the previous section). The FIX engine handles the network connection, transmits and receives FIX messages, and validates the submitted messages against the FIX protocol and format.

Data Ingestion Best Practices

When building a data ingestion layer, it is important to make sure it is rock solid. A poorly designed data ingestion layer may easily become the bottleneck of your infrastructure and impact the entire financial data engineering lifecycle. Adhering to best practices can help ensure the resilience of this layer. This section discusses a few.

Meet Business Requirements

First of all, the data ingestion layer needs to meet the business requirements established by your financial institution. Don't overcomplicate the ingestion layer; if your organization wants to work and exchange CSV and Excel files, then build a simple ingestion layer that can process these formats. If an API is not going to bring great benefits, don't build one and instead use a simple filesystem or cloud storage solution. However, if your company has complex data ingestion needs, consider building an extensible and flexible layer that can handle new types of formats and ingestion mechanisms.

Design for Change

Change is a constant in financial markets. New practices, standards, and regulations are continually taking place across the industry. For example, it is not unusual for markets to begin migrating to a newly published standard, and, in the meantime, a new standard emerges to replace it.[21] For this reason, always consider the change dynamics that might affect your data ingestion layer. There isn't a fixed recipe for managing change, but you can consider best practices such as the following:

Incremental change
> Make small and gradual changes.

Isolated change
> Make sure you develop and test your changes in isolation and avoid release incompatibility.

Documented change
> Make sure you describe the what, how, and why of your changes so others can understand what will change.

Zero downtime
> Roll out changes using a reliable technique with a rollback option to ensure zero downtime and avoid disruption to end users. Examples include Blue/Green, Canary, and Rolling deployment techniques.[22]

Enforce Data Governance

Enforcing data governance at the ingestion layer is recommended in financial applications. Examples of good practices include the following:

Data validation
> Add validators to check the conformity of ingested data to defined acceptance criteria. For example, you can validate if a file format is CSV or XML, validate an ingested message against standard requirements (e.g., FIX or XBRL), or validate ingested data against errors and quality issues.

---

21 For a good reference on this problem, I recommend Chris Pickles' "Securities Standards Migration: ISO 15022 vs ISO 20022" (*https://oreil.ly/s9Rcc*), *Journal of Securities Operations & Custody* 1, no. 3 (Spring 2008): 289–300.

22 To learn about these techniques, I suggest Chaitanya K. Rudrabhatla's "Comparison of Zero Downtime Based Deployment Techniques in Public Cloud Infrastructure" (*https://oreil.ly/G_3aC*), in the *2020 Fourth International Conference on I-SMAC (IoT in Social, Mobile, Analytics and Cloud)* (IEEE, 2020): 1082–1086.

Logging and reporting

Consider having an audit log that records all ingestion events. This is useful for tracking wrongful or malicious ingestions and for regulatory reporting.

Lineage and visibility

Implement a mechanism that allows ingested data to be traced back to its origin. The goal is to determine when, how, and where a particular piece of data entered the system.

Security

The data ingestion layer is the entry point for your financial data infrastructure. This means that it can be exploited by cybercriminals to ingest malicious data or software. To this end, ensuring the security of your data ingestion needs to be a top priority. Malicious data can be ingested in different ways, such as malware files, SQL ingestion, and data poisoning.[23] Security can be ensured via proper authentication and authorization policies, user permission management, virus scanning, allowed file formats (e.g., you may want to discard zip or pickled files), API security, and more.

Perform Benchmarking and Stress Testing

A good practice when building a data ingestion layer is performing a stress test to check the infrastructure's ability to handle variable workloads and ingestion scenarios. This is particularly essential when designing an event-driven or real-time data ingestion layer. A useful testing technique is benchmarking, which can be useful when choosing between different ingestion technologies. A benchmarking tool can be used for assessing the performance of a given ingestion technology by simulating a realistic workload scenario.[24]

Summary

In this chapter, you explored the first layer of the FDEL: ingestion. This layer acts as the entry point to a financial data infrastructure, enabling data to be ingested through various arrival processes, transmission protocols, formats, and technologies. This

---

23 Data poisoning is a type of attack where data is intentionally ingested to alter the performance or behavior of a machine learning model. For more on this topic, I recommend Antonio Emanuele Cinà, Kathrin Grosse, Ambra Demontis, Sebastiano Vascon, Werner Zellinger, Bernhard A. Moser, Alina Oprea, Battista Biggio, Marcello Pelillo, and Fabio Roli's "Wild Patterns Reloaded: A Survey of Machine Learning Security Against Training Data Poisoning" (*https://oreil.ly/BZzlz*), *ACM Computing Surveys* 55, no. 13s (July 2023): 1–39.

24 For a reference on benchmarking financial data ingestion, I recommend Manuel Coenen, Christoph Wagner, Alexander Echler, and Sebastian Frischbier's "Benchmarking Financial Data Feed Systems" (*https://oreil.ly/gw2JN*), in the *Proceedings of the 13th ACM International Conference on Distributed and Event-based Systems* (June 2019): 252–253.

chapter covered various aspects of ingestion specific to financial data, focusing on the unique requirements and preferences of market participants.

The ingestion layer should be regarded as a vital component of your FDEL. Bottlenecks at this stage can lead to performance issues further downstream. Additionally, a robust ingestion system is becoming increasingly essential for financial institutions due to the growing trends in data sharing, the expanding variety of data formats and arrival processes, and the increasing volumes of ingested data.

At this point, you may be asking yourself, "Where does the ingested data go?" This takes us to the next layer, storage, which will be covered in Chapter 8. In this layer, a data storage system is used to store and retrieve data according to specific business and technical requirements. As you might have guessed, this is the layer where you implement the most popular technology in data engineering: a database.

Let's continue!

Data Storage Layer

In the previous chapter, you learned how the data ingestion layer works, including the mechanisms, technologies, and formats used to ingest data into a financial data infrastructure. Once ingested, data must be stored and persisted in a storage location for further processing and querying. This is where the data storage layer comes into the picture.

To help you understand how to build a robust storage layer, this chapter will provide you with the necessary fundamentals and concepts, along with illustrations of technologies and their applications in finance. First, you'll learn how to approach the design of a data storage system (DSS) using appropriate criteria. Next, the concept of a data storage model (DSM) and its categorization criteria will be introduced. Then, I will present a comprehensive list of DMSs relevant to the financial industry, highlighting each DMS's key features, data modeling concepts, technical implementations, and financial applications.

Principles of Data Storage System Design

Throughout this book, I use the term *data storage system* (DSS) to denote a software implementation that enables the storage and retrieval of data. In many cases, people use the term "database" to refer to a storage solution. However, databases are only one type of DSS, albeit a popular one.

As a financial data engineer, knowing how to assess, choose, design, and implement a DSS should be one of your primary skills and areas of knowledge. The DSS is a core component in several financial applications, such as trading, payment, and messaging platforms. Making the wrong DSS choice can be quite costly and lead to a notable impact on the performance and reliability of your infrastructure. If a change is required later, you might find yourself dealing with a complex and expensive data migration project that wastes resources and time. This is particularly true when other applications and layers have already been built on top of the existing DSS.

Designing the appropriate DSS may look overwhelming at first glance. This is because of the vast number of technologies, patterns, constraints, business requirements, and marketing materials that affect the decisions around a DSS. To address this challenge, this section will provide a set of universally applicable principles that can guide your DSS design and implementation strategy.

Principle 1: Business Requirements

Although data engineering appears to be a strictly technological discipline, the truth is that it is highly driven by business requirements and customer needs. I highly recommend that you do not proceed with the design of a DSS without first including the business team's feedback into your decision-making process. As a financial data engineer, you don't necessarily need to be a business expert, but by knowing just enough to understand business expectations, you are likely to make the best design choices.

Business requirements can vary in terms of complexity (e.g., what and how many features are required?), flexibility (are they strict requirements?), technical feasibility (are there technical limitations?), predictability (can you anticipate the requirements in advance?), timing (have the requirements already been formulated?), and stability (do requirements change with time?).

Examples of data-related business requirements include the following:

- Ease of data access (e.g., a user interface)
- Schema flexibility (e.g., a new feature requires a new field in the data schema)
- User scalability (e.g., a high number of concurrent users)
- Speed of data access (e.g., for high-frequency trading)
- Querying capabilities (e.g., complex analytical queries and filters)
- Storage needs (e.g., storing a massive dataset such as market transactions)
- Data sharing (e.g., to collaborate with external companies)
- Data aggregation (e.g., for regulatory reporting)

DSS design and business requirements are matched through an iterative and collaborative approach. To succeed in this process, financial data engineers need to communicate in business terms and translate the requirements into technical implementation. Along the way, they need to spot all possible bottlenecks or technical limitations and reach an agreement with the business team to achieve feasibility.

Principle 2: Data Modeling

Data modeling is a crucial, yet often underestimated, practice in DSS design. In general, data modeling focuses on how data is organized, connected, and stored to meet both technical and business requirements. Importantly, the data engineering community still lacks a widely recognized data modeling framework. Nevertheless, market practitioners have typically relied on a popular approach that breaks down data modeling into three sequential phases: *conceptual*, *logical*, and *physical*. These phases are developed as one progresses from business needs to a comprehensive data storage specification, which is the desired end state.

The conceptual phase is technology independent and involves a communicative process where data engineers and stakeholders together discuss all their data needs. Think of the conceptual phase as a whiteboard session where various members of your team meet to discuss the initial data requirements. The main outcome of this phase is identifying a model for data, relationships, constraints, and querying needs that are essential to the business application. At this stage, no decisions are made about how the data will be stored or which DSS will be used for this purpose.

Subsequently, during the logical phase, the conceptual model is mapped to a blueprint of structured and technical constructs such as rows, columns, tables, and documents that a DSS can implement. At the end of the logical phase, you still haven't picked a specific DSS, but you should clearly know how the data will appear in the DSS and what DSM to use (for example, relational or document models). Later in this chapter, we will discuss DMSs in detail.

Finally, the physical phase translates the logical model into the DSS language, which is often known as *Data Definition Language* (DDL). This stage's main outcome involves choosing a specific DSS (e.g., a relational database management system) and developing a clear understanding of how data is stored (e.g., on disk, in memory, or hybrid), and how data is replicated, sharded, partitioned, or distributed.

Data Modeling Use Case in Finance: Reference Data and Financial Standards

In Chapter 2, we discussed the well-known problem of financial reference data, i.e., metadata used to describe financial instruments. The main challenge with reference data is the lack of a universally accepted framework for its representation and formatting, especially for complex financial instruments like derivatives. This issue is an excellent example of a financial domain problem that can be addressed through data modeling. Data modeling offers a robust solution by providing structured and standardized conceptual models for representing, collecting, and storing reference data. For an excellent treatment of this topic, I recommend Robert Mamayev's book *Data Modeling of Financial Derivatives: A Conceptual Approach* (Apress, 2013), in which he illustrates how to structure and describe derivatives such as futures, forwards, options, swaps, and forward rate agreements using advanced data modeling techniques.

Similarly, the development and formulation of financial standards like ISO 20022 can be viewed through the lens of data modeling. As discussed in Chapter 7, creating an ISO 20022 message model involves conceptual, logical, and physical stages, mirroring the methodology outlined in this section.

An important thing to keep in mind is that data modeling is an iterative process. Data engineers and business teams may continually reorganize, restructure, and optimize data models to fit new or revised business needs.[1]

Principle 3: Transactional Guarantee

One of the most important features of a DSS is its ability to ensure data consistency and reliability. In other words, the data must always accurately reflect its true state. For example, if you have $10,000 in your bank account and purchase a book for $50, your new balance should be $9,950, not $9,000. Similarly, if you purchase a book for $50 and at the same time you also purchase a car for $10,000, then you either end up with $9,950 or $0 but not –$50.

This feature is known as a *transactional guarantee*. Here, "transaction" describes an internal DSS mechanism that allows the bundling together of multiple instructions into a single, all-or-nothing operation.[2] In the data technology landscape, transactional guarantees are commonly implemented using two main models: *ACID* and *BASE*.

ACID is the most popular model,[3] and it stands for:

Atomicity
> A DSS transaction either succeeds completely (gets committed) or, in case of a fault, gets entirely aborted, reverting the DSS to the state before the transaction started. In our previous book and car example, atomicity would mean that either both items are bought (a book and a car) or neither is bought and the account balance remains intact. A violation of atomicity would occur if we attempted to

---

1 For a comprehensive overview of data modeling, I highly recommend Graeme Simsion and Graham Witt's *Data Modeling Essentials*, 3rd ed. (Morgan Kaufmann, 2004).

2 This definition is derived from the one provided by PostgreSQL documentation (*https://oreil.ly/Q5cDP*).

3 The acronym ACID was coined in 1983 by Andreas Reuter and Theo Härder in their seminal work, "Principles of Transaction-Oriented Database Recovery" (*https://oreil.ly/rKOKj*), *ACM Computing Surveys (CSUR)* 15, no. 4 (December 1983): 287–317.

purchase both the book and the car in a single transaction, where the purchase of the book succeeds but the car purchase fails.

Consistency

DSS transactions need to preserve structural integrity and enforce defined constraints. Consider again our previous example of a $10,050 transaction with an available balance of $10,000. Assume that the account balance has a non-negative constraint. In this scenario, the transaction should fail to prevent the balance from becoming negative, ensuring consistency. Maintaining this consistency is typically the responsibility of DSS engineers, who establish and implement data consistency checks, constraints, and validations based on business requirements, both at the DSS level as well as within the applications that interact with it.

Isolation

Concurrent DSS transactions get executed in isolation from one another while ensuring integrity and resolving conflicts. For instance, if you attempt two separate transactions—one to buy a book and another to buy a car—and only one can succeed, the DSS identifies this conflict and ensures proper resolution. Maintaining isolation is primarily the responsibility of the DSS. A notable strategy is *snapshot isolation*, where each transaction within the DSS perceives a consistent snapshot of data that includes all committed changes up to the transaction's initiation.[4]

Durability

The DSS preserves and persists the committed transactions even in case of a system failure (e.g., a power outage or crash). In our example, suppose you just completed the book purchase for $50. If the transaction is completed and you receive a notification of success, then the DSS must ensure that your purchase has been recorded in nonvolatile storage such as a hard drive or SSD. One of the most reliable techniques for ensuring durability is *Write-Ahead-Logging* (WAL), whose main idea is to first "log" all changes to be applied to the data before persisting them to disk.

ACID properties are of primary importance for the design of financial DSSs. Examples include financial transaction processing, where money or ownership of financial instruments is transferred between customer accounts, and order matching systems that execute buy and sell orders. In all of these applications, it's critical to maintain a consistent state of the data by ensuring that transactions either complete entirely or

---

4 The definition I present for snapshot isolation is provided in an operational way, which is done for the sake of simplicity. This concept can be further explored from a more rigorous, mathematical point of view; for example, see Andrea Cerone and Alexey Gotsman's "Analysing Snapshot Isolation" (*https://oreil.ly/5TxT-*), *Journal of the ACM (JACM)* 65, no. 2 (January 2018): 1–41.

not at all. Throughout this chapter, I will provide detailed technical illustrations of how various DSSs implement and ensure ACID properties.

 Many data storage solution providers make the ACID compliance promise. However, they don't all implement it in the same manner. Some may use a portion of the ACID properties (e.g., atomicity) or develop their own version of ACID. When designing a financial application with strict requirements in terms of data consistency and a transactional guarantee, ensure you thoroughly comprehend the ACID features of the chosen solution. If not, this might influence your product's market reputation.

In some cases, enforcing ACID compliance may impact performance or may not even be that necessary. In other cases, ACID might even be impractical to achieve. This is where a lighter version of ACID, called BASE, has been introduced.

BASE stands for:

Basically available
Instead of enforcing immediate consistency, BASE-modeled DSSs focus on ensuring availability by distributing and replicating data across a set of nodes in a data storage cluster. In the event of a failure in one node, data would still be available through another node that holds a replica of the data.

Soft state
As the requirement of immediate consistency is relaxed, the BASE model delegates the responsibility of achieving data consistency to the engineer instead of the DSS itself. In other words, it is the developer's problem to ensure data consistency, and it is no longer a feature of the DSS itself.

Eventually consistent
Even though BASE does not aim for immediate consistency, this does not mean that it never achieves it: it is eventually achieved, meaning that data will converge to a consistent state at some point in the future. No guarantee is made, however, about when consistency will be achieved.

The BASE model is quite useful for designing distributed and big data storage solutions, especially for analytical purposes where speed and scalability are more important than strict consistency. For instance, a trading platform might analyze vast amounts of data to provide traders with insights and market trends. In this scenario, the BASE model could be suitable, as it prioritizes processing large datasets quickly, even if some data might be slightly outdated.

Principle 4: Consistency Tradeoffs

A distributed DSS consists of several machines, or nodes, working together to store and manage data collectively. Designing and building such systems can be highly complex. Several consistency tradeoff theorems have been formalized to assist engineers with this challenge. The most prominent is the CAP theorem, which stands for consistency, availability, and partition tolerance. According to the CAP theorem, if a *network partition* occurs, where some nodes in a distributed DSS are unable to communicate due to a network failure, the system can guarantee at most two out of the following features:

Consistency
    All users always see the same latest version of the data, regardless of which node they interact with.

Availability
    The DSS responds to all user requests at all times, though it may not always provide the most recent data.

Partition tolerance
    The data storage system continues to operate even when there is a network partition.

 Keep in mind that consistency in ACID is different from consistency in the CAP theorem. In the CAP theorem, consistency means that all nodes maintain a consistent view of the data. Conversely, in the context of ACID, consistency ensures that the database remains in a valid and correct state.

To illustrate the CAP theorem with an example, suppose we have a bank with two ATMs connected over a network.[5] Assume the bank requires that customer balances never drop below zero, but there is no central database system to ensure this condition. Instead, a copy of the database is stored on both ATM instances, and as users carry out their operations on their accounts, the two ATMs communicate over the network to ensure consistency.

Now, suppose that a network partition happens, and the two ATMs can no longer communicate. In such a case, you, as the designer of the DSS, need to decide whether to prioritize consistency or availability. If you prioritize consistency, you are likely to refuse all ATM operations (withdrawal, deposit, balance checks) until the partition is

---

5 This example was inspired by the excellent illustration of the CAP theorem by ByteByteGo on YouTube (*https://oreil.ly/mUNyi*).

resolved. This guarantees balance consistency, but the ATM services will not be available to customers. If, on the other hand, you favor availability, then you may allow each ATM to perform deposit and withdrawal operations but at the risk of ending in an inconsistent state until the partition is resolved (e.g., withdrawing the entire balance from both ATMs, ending up with a negative balance).

Keep in mind that the CAP theorem is quite simplistic and basic. In real applications, tradeoffs might be more complex than just 100% availability or 100% consistency. For example, in our ATM example, rather than completely blocking or allowing all ATM operations, the bank may still allow for balance inquiry or small money withdrawals during a partition and only refuse large withdrawals and deposits.

As an extension of the CAP theorem, the PACELC theorem was introduced. PACELC considers two system scenarios: first, if the system has a network partition, it must decide how to trade off consistency and availability; second, if the system is running normally without a network partition, it must still decide how to trade off consistency and latency. The latency/consistency tradeoff exists only if the distributed DSS replicates data.[6]

When working with distributed DSSs, several of them offer the option to tune the consistency level. For example, Azure Cosmos DB offers five levels of consistency guarantees (*https://oreil.ly/8wo-0*), which, from strongest to weakest, are strong, bounded staleness, session, consistent prefix, and eventual; Amazon DynamoDB offers either strong or eventual consistency levels; and Cassandra offers several consistency levels (*https://oreil.ly/pRt15*) that also range from weak to strong.

Principle 4: Scalability

Scalability is a highly desired property of DSSs. Generally, a system is considered scalable if it can effectively handle varying or increasing amounts of workload. Importantly, scalability can be achieved differently depending on the component or layer of the DSS. To simplify, we can categorize DSS scalability into two main aspects: storage scalability and compute scalability.

A DSS achieves storage scalability if it can seamlessly store increasing volumes of data without hitting a space limitation. In more practical terms, storage scalability means that the system can store data at any scale: gigabytes, terabytes, or even petabytes.

---

6 To learn more about consistency tradeoffs, I highly recommend Daniel Abadi's "Consistency Tradeoffs in Modern Distributed Database System Design: CAP Is Only Part of the Story" (*https://oreil.ly/td_3V*), *Computer* 45, no. 2 (February 2012): 37–42.

Conversely, compute scalability in a DSS refers to its ability to efficiently handle varying data read and write requests. A common measure of compute scalability is the maximum number of concurrent read/write requests that the DSS can accommodate.

Scalability can be achieved in multiple ways. One approach is vertical scalability, where a single machine is replaced with a bigger one that has more storage, CPU, and RAM. On the other hand, horizontal scalability requires a distributed system that scales by adding a new node to an existing cluster of connected nodes.

When designing a DSS, it is crucial to evaluate its capability to handle anticipated workloads. This is often done via stress testing and benchmarking. A database stress test works by simulating the generation of a large amount of data, queries, and concurrent requests while observing how the DSS behaves in terms of response time, errors, and reliability. The goal, in lay terms, is to stress the DSS to identify its operational limits and where it may encounter system failures or breakpoints.

A *database benchmark* is a special type of database stress test that relies on well-defined and industry-accepted testing methodology. Examples include Transaction Processing Performance Council (TPC) standards (*https://oreil.ly/f1hUS*) such as TPC-C and TPC-E.[7] TPC-C simulates an order-entry environment where a population of users concurrently submit a variety of transactions against a database. Transactions may vary in complexity and include placing and fulfilling orders, keeping track of payments, confirming order status, and checking the level of stock in the warehouse. TPC-C evaluates performance based on the number of new-order transactions processed per minute.

TPC-E is a more sophisticated benchmark that simulates a brokerage firm receiving and fulfilling various customer transactions related to trades, account inquiries, and market research. To execute client requests, the brokerage firm interacts with financial markets and updates account information. Performance is measured using the transactions per second (TPS) metric.

A best practice is to conduct both industry benchmark tests and internally defined ad hoc tests to gain insights into specific behaviors of the DSS that may not be fully addressed by standardized benchmarks. Commercial database vendors frequently employ this dual approach to showcase the robustness and reliability of their products.[8]

---

7 To learn more about database stress testing, see Bert Scalzo's *Database Benchmarking and Stress Testing: An Evidence-Based Approach to Decisions on Architecture and Technology* (Apress, 2018).

8 See, for example, "How We Stress Test and Benchmark CockroachDB for Global Scale" (*https://oreil.ly/oOGNN*), by Stan Rosenberg, Alexander Shraer, William Kulju, and Alex Lunev.

Principle 5: Security

Ensuring strong database security is crucial in financial applications. When designing for security, a variety of processes, tools, and controls can be put in place to protect a DSS against malicious or accidental threats. These include, for example, the following:

- Data encryption at rest (e.g., customer account information residing in a database)
- Data encryption in transit (e.g., when transmitting payment information over a network)
- Database access permissions and roles
- Separation of database servers from other application servers
- Backups and data recovery plans
- Real-time security information and event monitoring

Data security features vary across different DSSs. Therefore, it's essential to stay informed about your institution's specific security requirements and ensure that the chosen DSS can effectively meet them.

Data Storage Modeling

To implement a DSS, a large number of technological choices are available. However, comparing such technologies is not trivial. Some technologies share several features, yet others may be based on noncomparable design principles. Additionally, on occasion, even the lines between the different data technologies might become blurry as they introduce more of the same features. To this end, this book will take a different approach by relying on the concept of *data storage models* (DSMs) rather than data storage technologies.

A DSM refers to the logical design and structure of a DSS, which determines the manner in which data can be stored, modeled, optimized, accessed, and manipulated. The concept of a DSM is closely related to the general practice of data modeling discussed earlier. To better contextualize things, consider a DSM as a focused subset within data modeling that specifically addresses the logical data modeling phase.

DSMs are technology agnostic, allowing them to be implemented using a variety of technologies, with the possibility of employing the same technology for implementing different DSMs. As a result, conceptualizing in terms of DSM is considerably easier and less susceptible to technology-specific limitations.

In today's data engineering landscape, a variety of DSMs are available. In the following sections, I will cover eight DSMs in depth, highlighting their main features and applications in finance. But first, let's illustrate a number of popular criteria that are often used to categorize DSMs.

SQL Versus NoSQL

If you are part of the data engineering community, you often hear discussions comparing NoSQL and SQL. However, many argue that the SQL versus NoSQL comparison lacks a clear technical basis. But to illustrate the main idea, I will briefly explain its origin.

In data engineering, the most trusted type of DSSs have traditionally been relational database management systems, or more simply, SQL databases (illustrated in detail in the section "The Relational Model" on page 301). With the massive increase in data volume, variety, and velocity, traditional SQL databases hit scalability and performance limitations. In a nutshell, SQL databases could only scale vertically, which is a limited scaling strategy since it is constrained by the maximum capacity of a single server.

To overcome this issue, people began exploring more scalable and high-performance alternatives. This led to the development of a new family of database technologies such as document, graph, key-value, and wide-column databases. To distinguish these database technologies from traditional SQL databases, they were grouped under the label NoSQL, which stands for "Not only SQL." NoSQL databases tackled the issue of scalability by adopting a horizontal scaling approach that relies on distributed systems and partitioning principles.

Importantly, SQL databases adhere to internationally recognized SQL standards, which have contributed to their reliability and trust within the data engineering community. In contrast, NoSQL databases are diverse and lack standardized behavior or common standards. Moreover, to ensure high performance, some NoSQL databases sacrifice several of the core features that gained SQL popularity, such as integrity constraints, ACID transactions, and advanced querying capabilities. Keep in mind, however, that NoSQL is not always more performant than SQL; it mostly depends on the function for which it is used.[9] Additionally, it is worth noting that later developments in database technologies made it possible for SQL databases to scale horizontally, thus reducing the gap between SQL and NoSQL.[10]

---

9 For more on this topic, read Yishan Li and Sathiamoorthy Manoharan's "A Performance Comparison of SQL and NoSQL Databases" (*https://oreil.ly/4Y1ps*), in the *2013 IEEE Pacific Rim Conference on Communications, Computers and Signal Processing (PACRIM)* (IEEE, 2013): 15–19.

10 For more details, see Rick Cattell's "Scalable SQL and NoSQL Data Stores" (*https://oreil.ly/Pq3l8*), ACM SIGMOID Record 39, no. 4 (May 2011): 12–27.

Primary Versus Secondary

A primary DSS is designed to act as the secure and permanent repository for data storage.

Think of the primary DSS as the stronghold of your data. But in many cases, the primary DSS may not have all the features needed to interact with the data. This is where a secondary DSS comes into the scene. A secondary DSS reads and stores a copy of data from a primary database and allows users to perform more advanced data querying and filtering operations.

A secondary DSS may not maintain the same level of data consistency as the primary DSS, but it is generally intended for use cases where this discrepancy does not cause significant issues.

A secondary DSS is typically utilized in situations where the primary DSS stores massive amounts of log or text data, which might be valuable if analyzed using sophisticated search queries. In this scenario, a search engine-like secondary DSS (e.g., Elasticsearch) may be implemented to regularly fetch and index log data from the primary DSS (more on Elasticsearch in "The Document Model" on page 314). Every time you see an additional monitoring dashboard bundled with an application such as an orchestration engine or a managed database, it's very likely that a secondary database is used for this purpose.[11]

Operational Versus Analytical

A DSS can be designed to handle different types of business processes. In data engineering, a distinction is often made between operational and analytical processes. Operational processes refer to the day-to-day operations and transactions within a business. Examples may include the following:

- Find customer account details.
- Update the account balance.
- Record and track financial transactions.
- Execute a payment or fund transfer orders.

Analytical processes, on the other hand, are concerned with understanding what is going on within a business; for example:

---

11 For example, Netflix created an orchestration engine called Conductor which uses Dynomite for primary persistence storage. On top of that, Elasticsearch is used as a secondary indexing database to allow workflow search and discovery. For more on Conductor, read the official documentation (*https://oreil.ly/jbjHG*).

- Assess the performance of the trading desk.
- Monitor the effect of different investment strategies.
- Understand the main cost and profit drivers.

DSSs intended to handle operational processes are often called *online transaction processing* (OLTP), while those designed for analytical processes are known as *online analytical processing* (OLAP). Generally speaking, OLTPs prioritize reliability and transactional guarantee, while OLAPs favor speed and advanced querying capabilities. A typical scenario involves the use of OLTP as a primary DSS for business transactions and an OLAP as a secondary DSS that stores a copy of OLTP data for analytical purposes.

Native Versus Non-Native

A DSS can serve a single function or a variety of functions. For instance, it might be designed for storing and querying tabular data exclusively, or it could handle document, graph, and key-value data as well. Crucially, various types of design optimizations may be required for supporting each function. This is where a relevant distinction is often drawn between *native* and *non-native* DSSs.

To illustrate the difference, let's say we want a DSS to store and query graph data. A DSS that is specifically designed and optimized for graph data (e.g., Neo4j) is called *native*, whereas a DSS that is capable of handling graph data but was not primarily designed for graphs in mind (e.g., PostgreSQL) is called non-native.[12]

Choose a native DSS when your application's core functionality relies on an optimized DSS tailored for specific tasks (for example, choosing a native graph DSS for a network analysis application).

Multi-Model Versus Polyglot Persistence

Having in mind the difference between native and non-native DSSs, another important distinction is often made between multi-model and polyglot persistence DSS patterns. Polyglot persistence uses different native DSSs for each function. For instance, you can use PostgreSQL for storing user account information data, Neo4j for managing social network data and graph-based queries, MongoDB for storing and querying user-generated content and posts, and Redis for caching frequently accessed data for improved performance.

---

12 Example inspired by the excellent article "Native vs. Non-Native Graph Database" (*https://oreil.ly/swtye*), by John Stegeman.

Alternatively, a multi-model DSS supports multiple DSMs within a single integrated environment. Such a system may offer support for different DSMs either natively or through extensions. For example, PostgreSQL is a native relational DSS, but it also offers extensions for geospatial data (PostGIS) and image data (PostPic). On the other hand, solutions such as Microsoft Azure Cosmos DB offer native support for document, graph, and key-value data models.

The polyglot persistence approach offers better performance, but it may add significant overhead. In contrast, the multi-model is much simpler but may end up behaving like the proverbial "Jack of all trades, master of none," which means that while it can accomplish a lot, it won't provide outstanding performance at any one function.

 Keep in mind that data storage technologies are continuously evolving and adding new features and functionalities. If a given data storage technology doesn't support a specific feature today, it doesn't mean it won't tomorrow. A missing feature is often an optimization choice that can be changed in a future release.

Data Storage Models

Now that you understand what a DSM is, let's explore the various types of DSMs you might encounter when building a DSS for financial data. Remember, these models are not mutually exclusive. Financial institutions often use a mix of DSMs to construct DSSs for a range of operational and analytical purposes.

The Data Lake Model

A data lake serves as a centralized repository capable of storing massive amounts of data in raw, unprocessed formats. Data lakes are the most flexible type of DSS since they allow for reliable and cheap storage of any type of data: big or small, structured or unstructured, static or stream. In a typical scenario, data lakes are used to store large amounts of miscellaneous data, including files, news text, documents, logs, data snapshots, archives, and backups.

Why data lakes?

Data lakes provide several features that financial institutions often seek. These include the following:

Data variety and agility
> Data lakes offer a flexible storage solution to ingest, store, and analyze any type of data without the need to define a schema or enforce a structure. Data lakes are said to implement *schema on read*, meaning that the data schema is generated on

the fly during data query. This is in contrast to *schema on write,* where data is first modeled and structured before being stored.

Simple data ingestion
Data ingestion into a data lake is simple and cost-effective because it does not necessitate transformations or harmonization, thereby lowering data ingestion expenses.

Data integration
Data lakes are useful for organizations that want to consolidate all their data in one central place. This can be practical for purposes such as compliance, data aggregation, risk management, and customer analysis, as well as experimenting with new ideas and datasets. Moreover, it eliminates data silos within the organization.

Data archiving
Data lakes offer a cost-effective solution for data archiving and retention.

Data analysis and insights
Data lakes store data in their original raw format. This allows organizations to perform ad hoc data querying and transformation and access historical snapshots of data.

Data governance
Data lakes can be designed with data governance practices, including access control, cataloging, auditing, reporting, and compliance.

Separation of storage and compute
Data lakes can scale to accommodate large volumes of data and access patterns. If you implement a computation layer on top of a data lake, this means that you have a separation of storage and compute layers. With such separation, you can scale and manage storage and computation independently.

It's important to remember, however, that data lakes are not query-optimized in the same manner as relational databases or data warehouses. Furthermore, performance may be impacted by a data lake's growing size or deeply nested hierarchical structure.

Technological implementations of data lakes

As a DSM, a data lake is an abstract idea that conceptualizes a centralized repository for storing raw data, independent of any specific technology. If a data lake aligns with your use case, the next step would involve selecting a technology to implement it. The classical solution has traditionally been the *Hadoop Distributed File System* (HDFS) (*https://oreil.ly/HMySV*). HDFS is a part of the Hadoop ecosystem, which is extensively used to build big data applications. It is an open source, distributed, scalable, and fault-tolerant file storage solution for working with large amounts of data. It runs on commodity servers (mostly on premises), thus making it a cost-effective solution. It is written in Java and has several configuration options that can match various business needs. In addition to HDFS, other prominent open source data lake solutions include MooseFS, Ceph, and GlusterFS.

With the emergence of the cloud, a major preference shift occurred toward building data lakes using managed cloud storage solutions. Examples include AWS's Simple Storage Service (S3), Azure Blob Storage, Google Cloud Storage, and DigitalOcean Spaces. Cloud-based data lakes are considerably easier to build and use; they scale seamlessly and require minimal configuration and maintenance. You can even create a basic cloud data lake in less than a minute if you already have an account!

Nevertheless, don't get overexcited with the simplicity of cloud storage solutions. When designing an enterprise-wide data lake solution, quite a few challenges and factors need to be considered to avoid building a monster. Two things worth discussing in this regard are data modeling and data governance, which I will cover in more detail in the next two sections.

Data modeling with data lakes

When designing data lakes, data modeling is rarely a major discussion point. The reason is that data lakes are not assumed to enforce a specific schema or structure on the ingested data. Even though this might be a valid point, data lakes can still have their own data models and architecture. To illustrate how data modeling works for data lakes, let's take a cloud-based data lake solution such as AWS S3 as our desired technological implementation.

To start with data lake data modeling, bucket architecture is the first thing to consider. Buckets are the main containers of objects stored in S3. Think of buckets as the logical data model for your data lake, which are distinguished based on your business requirements and can be assigned user permissions independently of the other buckets. For example, one bucket may be dedicated to storing log data, another for financial vendor data, and a third for analytics data. Alternatively, it is common to organize buckets into zones (*https://oreil.ly/xzDhh*), such as landing zones for raw files, staging zones for enriched files, business zones for analytics and research data, and trusted zones for anonymized and analysis-ready data.[13]

---

13 For more details on this data lake architecture pattern, I recommend reading Franck Ravat and Yan Zhao's "Data Lakes: Trends and Perspectives" (*https://oreil.ly/fl7Fu*), in *Database and Expert Systems Applications: 30th International Conference, DEXA 2019, Proceedings*, Part I (August 2019): 304–313.

There is no single recipe for how and how many buckets to create, but I can recommend keeping in mind architecture simplicity: don't create too many buckets such that you won't know which data is where, and don't create one huge bucket to store all kinds of data.

The second element of data lake modeling is a folder structure that organizes data items based on their categories and relationships. The most common folder structure is the tree-like hierarchical structure where parent folders contain subfolders, which in turn may contain other subfolders and so on. A simplistic zone-based folder structure might look like this:

Landing zone
Stores files at the second level, e.g., */landing_bucket/year/month/day/hour/minute/second*

Staging zone
Cleans and aggregates the data at the daily level, e.g., */staging_bucket/year/month/day*

Business zone
Splits daily data based on business areas, e.g., */business_bucket/business_area/year/month/day*

In the landing zone, raw files have schema on read rather than schema on write. This is because they are stored as they arrive without any modification. As data gets transformed in the staging and business zones, it is a good practice to implement schema on write, meaning that you enforce data schema into the files. If you want to apply anonymization to the data, you may want to create a trusted zone where you store data that has been anonymized for safe use and analysis.

A good practice when organizing your data lake folder structure is to avoid having different file formats within the same folder. For example, assume that the ingestion layer loads files in gzip, CSV, and TXT formats. To model this properly, consider a landing zone structure like the following:

- gzip files: */landing_bucket/gzip/year/month/day/hour/minute/second*
- CSV files: */landing_bucket/csv/year/month/day/hour/minute/second*
- TXT files: */landing_bucket/txt/year/month/day/hour/minute/second*

By design, a data lake may accommodate any type of data from any source. All you have to do is specify a bucket name and drop data in it. However, this simplicity can potentially lead to several issues. Think of the *Downloads* folder on your PC; if you are like me, then it is simply a big dump of files of all types and formats; you don't know what's in there, whether it is in the right place, and how to navigate and search for files. Similarly, without the right controls in place, data lakes can easily turn into *data swamps*: an out-of-control place for dumping any data from any source without any checks or validation rules. To avoid this issue, you need to implement a data governance layer on top of a data lake. Let's discuss this topic in more detail.

Data governance

Creating and using a data lake might sound very easy: (1) log in to AWS, (2) select S3, (3) create a bucket, (4) drop files there! This works, and I did it many times. However, architecting a reliable and scalable enterprise-wide data lake is a much more challenging task than this. Large data lakes, in particular, are likely to pose significant issues to users, especially when it comes to understanding things like the following:

- Metadata (information about the data)
- Sources and movements of the data
- Transformations and changes applied to the data
- The architecture of the data (buckets, folders, formats, etc.)
- The level of data quality, consistency, and integrity
- Data access and retrieval methods, which are less intuitive than just using SQL

To address these issues, it is recommended to implement a data governance layer on top of the data lake. Common considerations to keep in mind include the following:

Privacy
> Data coming from various sources may include sensitive user information, such as personally identifiable information (PII). Therefore, the data lake should be designed to anonymize and store this data in compliance with predefined privacy rules. For instance, you can separate buckets that store sensitive data from those that store anonymized data.

Security
> Data lakes must be protected against malicious attacks, data loss, and unauthorized access. This is especially important given the extensive use of cloud-based data lakes, which are vulnerable to the risks associated with cloud misconfiguration, i.e., the improper or incorrect setup of cloud resources, services, or settings. Policies to achieve this include encrypting data both at rest and in transit, implementing access controls to specify who can read, upload, and delete files, and establishing data retention rules, such as security locks, to ensure that archived data is never deleted.

Quality controls
> Data must be checked for quality issues as it gets ingested into the data lake. Note, however, that quality controls may not be needed for all types of data. For

instance, while log data generally does not require quality checks, business and financial data do benefit from them.

Data cataloging
A data catalog is a valuable tool that provides users of a data lake with functionalities to search for data, metadata, versions, ingestion history, and other attributes associated with the data stored within the data lake.

Importantly, there is no one-size-fits-all approach to implementing a data governance layer on top of a data lake. I suggest beginning with the four elements previously mentioned (privacy, security, quality control, and data cataloging). Keep in mind that for complex data lakes, data governance might be a substantial investment. Some cloud services, such as AWS Lake Formation, provide data lake solutions that include built-in data governance capabilities.

Continuous technological advancements are consistently enhancing the reliability of data lakes. For example, the *data lakehouse* model was created to introduce more structure into data lakes. The main idea of a data lakehouse is to create an integrated data architecture that combines a data lake, data warehouse (covered later in this chapter), and related analytics and processing services.

For example, using AWS, you can build an architecture where you upload and store raw CSV files in an S3 bucket (data lake) and query them with SQL queries using services such as Amazon Athena or Amazon Redshift Spectrum. Another example is Snowflake, which allows users to interact with data stored in a data lake of choice using the Snowflake compute layer. A recommended approach to achieve this is by storing the data in Apache Iceberg tables (*https://oreil.ly/mT5RP*) that use the Apache Parquet format. Apache Iceberg is an open source table format for massive analytic datasets, supporting features such as ACID transactions, schema evolution, partitioning, and table snapshots. Similarly, technologies such as Apache Hudi (*https://oreil.ly/jdFMy*) were introduced to bring database and data warehouse capabilities such as ACID transactions and record-level data updates/deletes to data lakes.

Financial use cases of data lakes

Data lakes have attracted significant attention within the financial industry (*https://oreil.ly/FmW_g*). Many financial institutions are increasingly investing in building their own data lakes, often leveraging managed cloud storage solutions.

Several reasons can explain the financial sector's excitement for data lakes. An important factor is cloud migration. As many financial institutions are moving to the cloud, data lake solutions such as AWS S3 appear to be particularly appealing because they are simple to set up and can store any type or size of data.

Second, financial institutions process a large amount of unstructured data, such as reports, prospectuses, client files, news data, logs, and more. Data lakes offer an efficient and reliable solution for storing, sharing, and archiving such data.

The third factor is data aggregation, which is both a regulatory requirement and an enabler of innovation. By consolidating data in one location, financial institutions can quickly respond to regulatory inquiries that demand aggregated information, such as total risk exposure. Moreover, emerging trends in data-driven product development and analytics require data from diverse sources, often scattered across decentralized silos within financial institutions. Data lakes enable these institutions to seamlessly consolidate and aggregate data from various sources and silos into a centralized, accessible, and scalable repository.

Fourth is compliance. Financial institutions have a lot of compliance requirements that relate to data privacy, security, retention, and protection. Data lakes may offer a number of desired compliance-related features. For example, AWS S3 offers *Write-Once-Read-Many* (WORM) storage features (*https://oreil.ly/abujc*) such as S3 Glacier Vaults and S3 Object Lock to ensure the integrity of archived data in accordance with US SEC and FINRA rules (*https://oreil.ly/DadEH*). A number of features are also available to ensure security. For example, S3 provides the *Block Public Access* feature, which simply blocks all public access to S3 buckets. In this case, financial institutions deploy their S3 data lake within a VPC and enable access through VPC endpoints for Amazon (*https://oreil.ly/Iamsb*).

Case Study: NASDAQ Data Lakehouse with AWS S3 and Redshift Spectrum

NASDAQ is a multinational financial services firm operating several financial market platforms worldwide, particularly the NASDAQ Stock Exchange. NASDAQ manages the matching of buy and sell operations on a massive scale and at a rapid speed while providing data-feeding services for its prices and quotes. As a result, a large number of daily records are generated, including orders, quotes, trades, and cancellations. By 2020, NASDAQ was processing around 70,000 records on a daily basis. These records need to be loaded for reporting and billing purposes before the market opens the following day.

To support its large-scale data needs, NASDAQ invested in a data lake solution leveraging AWS S3 (*https://oreil.ly/fYya9*). This strategic decision enabled NASDAQ to decouple the compute layer from the storage layer, allowing independent scaling of each component. Using S3, NASDAQ gained the capability to manage numerous concurrent read and write operations on large datasets seamlessly, without encountering contention issues.

Using AWS Identity and Access Management (AWS IAM), NASDAQ established a comprehensive access control policy for data stored on S3. Additionally, NASDAQ took advantage of the lower costs of archival storage offered through Amazon S3 Glacier. Moreover, NASDAQ leveraged the Amazon S3 Object Lock feature (*https://oreil.ly/fBX6P*) to protect objects from deletion or modification, ensuring compliance.

For the compute layer, NASDAQ chose Amazon Redshift Spectrum (*https://oreil.ly/IpoxH*), a service that allows users to perform SQL queries on data stored in Amazon S3 buckets. The resulting architecture is a data lakehouse that combines a data lake (S3) with a data warehouse (Redshift Spectrum), each scalable independently to support various levels of storage and computing.

The Relational Model

The popular and highly trusted DSSs are built on the relational DSM, which organizes data in rows and columns, forming a table or relation. These tables can be related to each other through a common attribute (column), hence the term "relational." Figure 8-1 illustrates the concept.

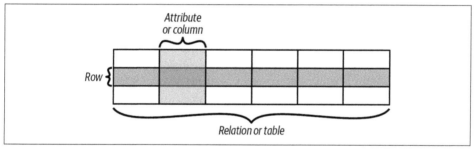

Figure 8-1. Components of the relational DSM

A collection of tables, along with other objects such as views, indexes, stored procedures, and functions, within a relational model is often referred to as a *schema*. Multiple schemas can coexist within the same *database*. For this reason, it is common to refer to a relational DSS as a *relational database management system* (RDMS) or relational database.

Interaction with a relational database happens through a *declarative* language known as *Structured Query Language*, or more commonly SQL. For this reason, relational databases are also commonly called SQL databases.

The relational DSM foundations were laid out by IBM's expert Edgar Codd in the 1970s. After extensive research on the relational model, Codd proposed a list of 12 rules (*https://oreil.ly/Z_l3f*) that must be observed to develop a true relational database.

Why relational databases?

Relational databases are widely trusted and heavily relied upon by financial market participants, often serving as the default choice for data storage. Let's explore the reasons behind this preference.

SQL standards. The origins of the SQL language go back to 1974 when Donald Chamberlin and Raymond Boyce from IBM released the essay "SEQUEL: A Structured English Query Language." Chamberlin and Boyce relied on Codd's framework to develop an intuitive and user-friendly language to interface with relational databases.[14]

As the language gained wide popularity and a strong reputation among market participants, the *American National Standards Institute* (ANSI) intervened in 1986 to develop and promote a standard for SQL. The ANSI Database Technical Committee (ANSI X3H2) within the Accredited Standards Committee (ASC) X3 developed the first SQL standard, known as ANSI X3.135-1986. In 1987, the ISO started developing an international version of SQL standards, further solidifying SQL's presence on the global stage. Since then, the standard has been defined and revised under ISO/IEC 9075 (*https://oreil.ly/duMsM*). What ISO/IEC 9075 offers is a set of features and requirements that need to be implemented in order for a database to become SQL compliant. Figure 8-2 illustrates the historical evolution of SQL standards.

Thanks to ISO/IEC 9075, the SQL language has evolved along a path of continuous improvement, resulting in a rich array of features that continue to make SQL a favored choice among engineers and financial markets to this day. One thing to keep in mind is that SQL standards are advisory, not mandatory technical specifications. It is quite possible to create an SQL database system that implements only a subset of SQL standards.

---

14 To learn more about the history of SQL, I highly recommend Donald D. Chamberlin's "Early History of SQL" (*https://oreil.ly/fwBZj*), *IEEE Annals of the History of Computing* 34, no. 4 (October–December 2012): 78–82.

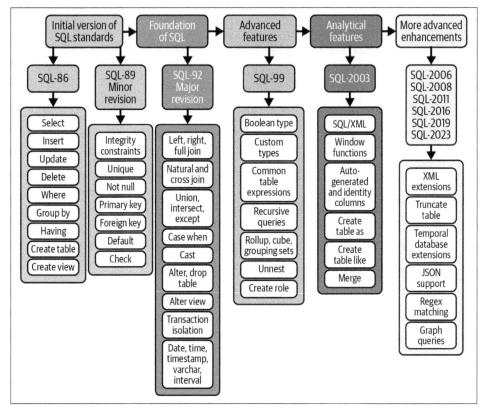

Figure 8-2. Overview of SQL standards

ACID transactions. By design, relational databases offer the strongest ACID transactional guarantee among all DSSs.

Atomicity is guaranteed by executing each statement or block of statements within a single transaction. A transaction either succeeds completely or is aborted without leaving partial or incomplete results. This is possible thanks to a transaction log mechanism known as *Write-Ahead-Logging* (WAL). Before a transaction is executed, it is logged into the WAL log. The database system may utilize the WAL to roll back changes and return the database to its initial state if a transaction fails or is interrupted. Otherwise, the transaction is marked as committed.

Consistency is primarily achieved via the use of constraints such as uniqueness, non-null values, primary key, foreign keys, and checks. Foreign key constraints are a distinguished feature in SQL used to ensure *referential integrity* (*https://oreil.ly/ebw9S*). This integrity ensures that references are valid, i.e., if the presence of one value in table A requires the presence of a specific referenced value in table B, then the value in table B must exist. For example, within a customer order table, a foreign key constraint would prevent recording an order for a product referenced from another table (such as the products table) if that product does not exist in the referenced products table.

Consistency is also guaranteed via concurrency control mechanisms that handle the concurrent execution of transactions. Among the most popular concurrency control mechanisms is *Multi-Version Concurrency Control* (MVCC), a snapshot-based mechanism that allows each transaction to see a snapshot of the data (data version) at the time of the transaction initiation, regardless of what changes take place later. This way, transactions are protected against data inconsistencies that might emerge from the actions of other concurrent transactions.

Isolation is guaranteed via mechanisms such as locking, snapshot isolation (e.g., MVCC), and isolation levels. Database locks are a mechanism that allows a given transaction to place a flag on a database object (e.g., table or row) to prevent others from concurrently performing specific actions on the same object. Locking is termed *implicit* when performed automatically by the database and *explicit* when intentionally initiated by the user. Furthermore, locking is called *pessimistic* if the lock is placed while changing a DB object and *optimistic* if placed only when the changes are being committed to the DB.

 Explicit locking may be complex and may affect your application's reliability. Key concerns in this area include lock contention, suspension, timeouts, and deadlocks. Deadlocks, where two transactions are waiting on one another to release locks, are particularly common. Additionally, locks differ in terms of the set of lock modes with which they conflict; therefore, make sure you understand the side effects of using a specific lock.

Isolation levels are used to control the visibility of concurrent transactions. The SQL standard defines four isolation levels: *Read Uncommitted, Read Committed, Repeatable Read,* and *Serializable*. These levels are defined in terms of four phenomena: *dirty read, nonrepeatable read, phantom read,* and *serialization anomaly*. As this topic is a bit long to illustrate in detail, I refer the reader to the excellent documentation page of PostgreSQL on transaction isolation (*https://oreil.ly/-jRyE*).

Finally, durability is ensured via mechanisms such as WAL. By first logging transaction steps into the WAL log, there is a guarantee that once a transaction is committed, its results will not be lost even in the event of subsequent failures.

Analytical querying. One of the strongest arguments in favor of using SQL databases is their advanced querying capabilities. This includes table joins, aggregations, window functions, common table expressions, subqueries, stored procedures, functions, views, and many more. One major advantage of such querying features is the flexibility they provide in terms of data modeling. This is because you don't need to guess all your queries in advance before designing and creating an SQL database. Other types of DSM, such as the document model, require queries to be defined in advance in order to obtain good performance.

Schema enforcement. Relational databases require and enforce a data schema, which defines table structure, column names, data types, constraints, and more. This is an essential feature if data needs to adhere to a predefined structure. Schema enforcement improves data quality and integrity by ensuring consistency in how data is stored and accessed.

Keep in mind, however, that in many real-world applications, schemas can change quite often due to changing business needs. This is an important factor to consider when assessing the suitability of the relational model to your business problem.

With later revisions of the SQL standard, new data types such as JSON (*https://oreil.ly/bQ8sT*) were added, which introduced some sort of schema flexibility into SQL databases. By creating a column of type JSON, an SQL database allows users to store data with variable structures, just like a JSON file.

Data modeling with relational databases

Data modeling is predominantly used in SQL databases. This is because of their standardized design principles and features, the flexibility they offer in terms of table organization, and the business and technical intuitiveness of the relational DSM.

As we discussed earlier in this chapter, data modeling is a technique used to define and assess the data requirements necessary to support various business operations within the corresponding data infrastructure of financial institutions. That said, data modeling needs to always start with a business discussion (conceptual phase) that you later translate into an actual database design (logical and physical phases). We can discuss a lot about how to define and fulfill each of these three phases. However, to keep things simple and within scope, I will limit my treatment of SQL data modeling to the following techniques: normalization, constraints, and indexing. For each technique, I will briefly illustrate a few business use cases.

Normalization. Normalization is the most popular SQL data modeling technique. It defines a table structure following several so-called *normal forms*. Normalization ensures that the following conditions are met:

- Data redundancy and repetition are minimized
- Data is organized in small tables instead of one large table
- Tables have well-defined relationships and references
- Updating or adding data will be done in as few places as possible
- Ability to add and remove data without altering or refactoring the tables
- Tables are neutral to queries (i.e., your table design is not constrained by the queries you want to perform)
- Tables offer clear and informative data for business users
- You avoid the problem of insertion, update, and delete anomalies[15]

There are several types of normal forms; however, most databases are normalized using the following three forms:[16]

First normal form (1NF)
> This form ensures that all columns are single valued. A field may not contain composite values or nested records. If such nested values exist, they should be expanded to multiple rows. An example is illustrated in Figure 8-3. The table on the left is not in 1NF as it contains a multivalued column (transaction_id), while the table on the right is in 1NF as it contains no multivalued records.

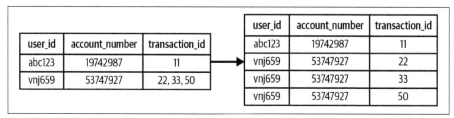

Figure 8-3. First normal form conversion

Second normal form (2NF)
> This form eliminates *partial dependency*. If a table has a composite primary key with two or more columns, then all the columns (not included in the primary key) must depend on the entire composite primary key and not on a part of it. A

---

15 For a good read on this topic, see "Anomalies in Relational Model" (*https://oreil.ly/sS4HR*) by GeeksForGeeks.

16 For an excellent illustration of these normal forms with examples, I suggest checking the article "Normalization in DBMS" (*https://oreil.ly/uNOel*) by Study Tonight.

table exhibits partial dependency when a nonprimary key column depends on only a portion of the primary key. Figure 8-4 shows an example. The right table has a composite primary key including account_id and account_type_id. In this case, the column account_type_description depends only on account_type_id, hence generating a partial dependency. To normalize in 2NF, the account_type_id should be stored in a separate table, as illustrated on the right side of the figure.

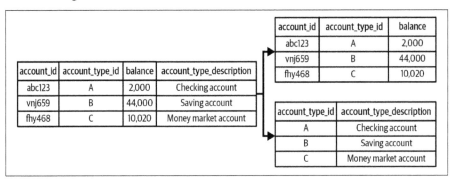

Figure 8-4. Second normal form conversion

Third normal form (3NF)

This form eliminates *transitive dependency*. All columns should only depend on the primary key, not on any nonprimary key columns. If a nonprimary key column depends on another nonprimary key column, the table is said to have a transitive dependency. See Figure 8-5 for an example. The table on the left side of the figure has a single-column primary key defined for transaction_id. Both account_id and amount depend on transaction_id, but max_transaction_limit depends on account_id, which is not a primary key. This generates transitive dependency. To normalize in 3NF, we need to create a separate table that stores the max_transaction_limit, as illustrated on the right side of the figure.

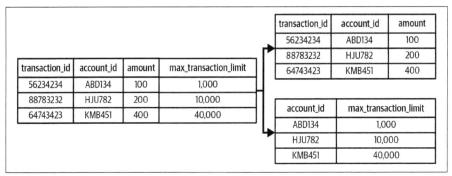

Figure 8-5. Third normal form conversion

Relational database systems often prioritize normalization as their main modeling strategy. By eliminating redundancy, normalization ensures data integrity by minimizing the number of places that store the same piece of data and establishing reliable relationships between the tables. Think of this from a compliance perspective. For example, if a client of a financial institution requests that their personal data be updated or erased, the institution will only need to check one or a few tables (e.g., a client table) to find all of the individual's information. If data was not normalized, the same personal information may be duplicated in many places, making it difficult to find, aggregate, update, or delete.

Constraints. Constraints are a crucial feature of relational databases. They enforce data integrity and consistency during insert, update, and delete operations. The main advantage of defining constraints at the database level is that it decouples the constraint checks and management from the application that interacts with and manipulates the database.

Examples of SQL constraints include the following:

- The not-null constraint ensures that values in a given column are never null.
- The uniqueness constraint ensures that values in a given column are unique.
- The check constraint ensures that values in a given column satisfy a given value condition (e.g., >=0).
- The primary key constraint ensures that values in one or more columns can be used as the primary unique identifier in the table.
- The foreign key constraint ensures that values in one or more columns in one table match the values in a given column in another table.

For a comprehensive overview of these constraints and how to create them, I recommend the official PostgreSQL documentation on constraints (*https://oreil.ly/4uXHE*). Keep in mind that constraints may have an impact on performance as they add additional work for the DB to do. The best way to approach DB constraints is by mapping them to business constraints during data modeling. For example, a check constraint may be added to ensure that the account balance never goes below zero, while a foreign key constraint may be added to guarantee that a product is not sold if it's not in the inventory, and so on.

Indexing of relational databases. If you are going to work with relational databases, indexing is a must-have strategy. SQL databases physically organize data on disk in *data files*, with each row called a *record* and each column within a row called a *field*. To search for a specific record, an SQL database can perform a full scan of all data files. However, this is an expensive operation, especially when the data size gets very large. This is where indexing is needed.

An index is a specialized data structure stored separately from data files in index files. It is optimized to enable rapid search and retrieval of specific data records. Indexing is typically applied to the column(s) that you will use in your filtering statement. For example, suppose you are tasked with the creation of a bank transactions table that stores the transaction_id, user_id, transaction type, transaction_time, and transaction_amount. Your business team tells you that they want to query this transaction table by filtering on the user_id. Without an index, a query will scan the entire transaction table, which may be extremely slow and costly. To overcome this issue, you can add an index on the user_id column. If the business team tells you that they want instead to query user_id for a given time interval, then consider adding a *composite* index on both the user_id and transaction_time columns.

Relational databases offer a variety of indexes, and you can add as many indexes as you want.[17] However, it is important to keep in mind that indexes get regularly updated when you add, modify, or delete records. If such operations are quite frequent, then index updates might impact performance. Additionally, be careful how you define composite indexes. For example, if you create a composite index on columns A, B, and C, then a query that filters by B only, or C only, or B and C, is likely to not benefit from the index. Furthermore, if you create an index on a column of one type (e.g., integer) and then cast the column to another type during a query (e.g., string), then the index is likely to be useless. A recommended practice is to monitor index usage to see if it's being utilized by the DSS.

Technological implementations of relational databases

A large number of database technologies have been developed following the relational DSM. These include commercial solutions such as Oracle Database, Microsoft SQL Server, IBM Db2, IBM Informix, and MySQL Enterprise Edition as well as open source alternatives such as PostgreSQL, MySQL, and MariaDB.

A full account of the differences between all these technologies is beyond the scope of this book. A general criterion that I recommend following is the degree of compliance with the SQL standard. Some database technologies, such as PostgreSQL, are well-known for their high compliance with the SQL standard. Others, such as MySQL, may exclude some aspects of the standard (*https://oreil.ly/EOxBR*) in return for reliability or speed, as well as include features and extensions that are not necessarily part of the standard.

---

17 For a good overview of SQL database indexing, see the official PostgreSQL documentation on indexes (*https://oreil.ly/fNQpi*).

The database's technological specifications are another distinguishing criterion. One SQL database system may have a functionality that others may not have. These specifications include the following:[18]

- The operating system that the database system can run on (e.g., Linux, Windows, etc.)
- ACID properties
- Concurrency control and locking mechanisms
- Data size limits (e.g., max table size, max row size, etc.)
- Supported data types (e.g., varchar, integer, numeric, JSON, etc.)
- Supported constraints (e.g., foreign keys, etc.)
- Data connectors
- Security, roles, access control, and encryption
- Data replication and partitioning
- Backup and recovery
- Support for materialized views
- Supported index types (other than basic B-tree indexes)

An essential factor that might impact the choice of your relational database technology is scalability. Traditionally, relational databases have supported vertical scaling, where a small machine is replaced with a larger one with more RAM, CPU, and storage. This strategy has several advantages, such as simplicity and data consistency and integrity. However, it also has some drawbacks. First, it creates a single point of failure as it involves a single machine; second, it can easily hit capacity and load balancing limits if the workload grows quickly or unexpectedly; third, there are physical limitations in terms of how much CPU and RAM a single machine can have. This is where horizontal scaling comes into play.

In horizontal scaling, the database system relies on a system of connected machines/nodes to distribute the load. If the workload grows, additional nodes can be added to handle the increased demand. A typical approach for achieving SQL horizontal scaling is through *read replicas*, which are additional copies of the primary database that are regularly synchronized with it, either synchronously or asynchronously. These replicas are often dedicated to handling read operations (such as SELECT queries), while the primary database continues to handle write operations (such as INSERT, UPDATE, DELETE). It is also possible for some systems to have read/write replicas.

---

18 For a good comparison between relational database management system features, consult Wikipedia (*https://oreil.ly/mYQEJ*).

Another horizontal scaling strategy is *sharding* (*https://oreil.ly/twWdt*), which involves partitioning the database into chunks (shards) based on a shard key (e.g., date range) and distributing them across multiple machines. This way, the traffic load gets distributed among the shards. Importantly, sharding-based horizontal scalability can be difficult to manage.[19] For example, a significant amount of maintenance effort may be needed to ensure the database's integrity, involving operations such as data resharding, rebalancing, and partitioning. Furthermore, it may require incorporating complicated logic into your application's read/write methods to route requests to the relevant shard.

To overcome this issue, a new generation of horizontally scalable SQL databases emerged: *distributed SQL databases*. These databases offer native built-in scalability without the need to manually manage shards. Examples include Google Spanner, YugabyteDB, and CockroachDB. If your scalability needs are remarkably large, then such databases may be the ideal solution. For example, Deutsche Bank leveraged Google Spanner to achieve one of the biggest IT migrations (*https://oreil.ly/8UakC*) in the history of the European banking industry, involving 19 million Postbank (Deutsche Bank's retail branch) product contracts alongside the data of 12 million customers.

Financial use cases of relational databases

Relational databases are extensively used within the financial sector. This can be explained by a number of factors. First, a significant part of financial data is tabular time series and panel data, which is perfectly suited for the relational DSM.

Second, financial professionals perform a lot of analysis related to business intelligence, forecasting, pricing, risk management, and modeling. Relational databases are an ideal solution for these tasks due to their powerful and intuitive analytical querying capabilities.

Third, relational databases offer a lot of the reliability features that most financial applications require, such as data consistency, integrity, and a transactional guarantee. For example, financial payment applications require transactions to be idempotent, meaning if they are executed multiple times, the outcome should be consistent. If you purchase an item for $100 and the application processes your payment twice, idempotency ensures your account is debited only once for $100. SQL databases can achieve idempotency through mechanisms like uniqueness constraints and idempotency tokens. For instance, if each payment is assigned a unique idempotency token

---

19 A detailed account of this problem is offered in the blog post "Why Sharding Is Bad for Business" (*https://oreil.ly/bX0qM*), by Michelle Gienow.

and the column storing these tokens has a uniqueness constraint, any attempt to insert the same payment twice will be rejected by the database due to the violation of the uniqueness constraint.

Case Study: Payment Processing Applications with CockroachDB

Payments are one of the most essential operations in financial markets. A large number of players are involved in payment processing, including SaaS applications, online shops, ecommerce websites, retailers, payment gateways, card networks, payment processors, and payment service providers. Crucially, designing a payment system can be quite challenging, as it needs to ensure the following:

- Scalability (imagine how easily the volume of payments can increase)
- Data durability (people won't like it if they can't find their historical payment records)
- High availability and zero downtime (it's not a pleasant experience if you can't pay)
- Data consistency and correctness (people won't tolerate mistakes with their money)

How do you build a payment system that meets all the above requirements? First, let's try to understand how payments are processed. According to Stripe (*https://oreil.ly/_N9-W*), a typical card payment transaction involves the following steps:

1. The customer initiates a payment by providing their payment details (e.g., credit card) at the business payment channel (e.g., online shop).

2. A payment gateway receives the transmitted information, encrypts it, and passes it to the payment processor.

3. The payment processor forwards the information to the acquiring bank (the online shop's bank), which in turn forwards the information to the issuing bank (the customer bank) through the relevant card network (e.g., Visa or Mastercard).

4. The issuing bank verifies the request and responds with an approval or rejection message sent back to the payment processor via the same path (card network and acquiring bank).

5. The payment processor communicates the transaction outcome to the business, which proceeds to conclude the purchase or inform the customer of any issue.

6. If the transaction is concluded, a clearing and settlement process takes place in which the transaction amount is transferred from the issuing bank into the acquiring bank, which in turn deposits the funds into the business's account.

Importantly, when data passes through this chain of information exchange, some of the involved entities store a portion of the payment data for reasons such as transaction reviewing, reporting, reconciliation, and fraud detection. Due to the mission-critical nature of payments, a highly available, scalable, and reliable database system is required. This is where distributed SQL databases can excel.

A prominent solution in this market is CockroachDB, a cloud native, distributed database based on standard SQL and developed by Cockroach Labs (*https://oreil.ly/Xnkoe*). CockroachDB offers a number of valuable features for mission-critical applications:

- Simple horizontal scalability where users can add additional nodes as needed. Interestingly, even though it's a distributed system, CockroachDB works as a single logical database, enabling data access from any node, regardless of its location.
- Support for transaction-heavy workloads with distributed atomic transactions (*https://oreil.ly/7XDlb*).
- High availability with no downtime, achieved via a consensus algorithm (*https://oreil.ly/6Xw8O*).
- Multiactive availability (each node can serve both read and write requests).
- Support for multiregion and multi-cloud (ideal for compliance that restricts data residency to a specific region).

To give an example of the application of CockroachDB in the financial sector, let's take the case of Shipt (*https://oreil.ly/vJWLE*), an American delivery service owned by Target Corporation. As an online ecommerce company, Shipt payment services are core to its business model. The Shipt team was tasked with the creation of a distributed database system that meets the requirements of a reliable payment system, in line with what we discussed earlier in this section. In particular, Shipt wanted a multiregion payment service that could ensure correctness (*https://oreil.ly/_DZDm*) throughout the entire payment cycle.

By leveraging CockroachDB, the Shipt engineering team managed to build a reliable, correct, cloud native, multiregion, and highly available payment data management system. Regional replication allowed Shipt to achieve lower transaction latency. Furthermore, to ensure idempotency throughout the payment lifecycle, Shipt relied on idempotency tokens (*https://oreil.ly/WQpnt*). Overall, by building its system on top of CockroachDB, Shipt can now support its business growth across different regions and markets with a resilient and scalable payment architecture.

The Document Model

A highly reputable DSM is the document model, which stores information in a document format such as JSON or XML. This section will specifically focus on JSON-based DSMs, which are the predominant choice in the industry. A document looks like the following:

```
{
    "document_id": 1,
    "legal_name": "Microsoft Corporation",
    "type": "public company",
    "isin": "US5949181045",
    "symbol": "MSFT",
    "sector": "Information technology",
    "products": [
            "Software development",
            "Computer hardware",
            "Social networking",
            "Cloud computing",
            "Video games"
    ]
}
```

A DSS designed to store and query documents is called a document-oriented database, or simply a document database.

Why document databases?

Document databases are extensively used for all kinds of purposes, powering some of the world's largest applications. Among their most desired features are the following:

Schema flexibility
  A document database can store any document, regardless of its content structure. In other words, document databases do not enforce schemas natively, unlike SQL databases. This allows businesses to quickly develop an application and easily change its logic. You can add, change, or rename the document fields based on your business requirements. Make sure, however, to be aware of the potential side effects of such flexibility; if not managed properly, it might impact data integrity and consistency. At some point, you might even want to enforce a schema in the documents. This is often achieved via a schema validation mechanism implemented on the application side.

Document modeling
  Document formats such as JSON are quite familiar and might be easier to work with. Moreover, unlike relational or other types of data storage formats, documents map directly to objects such as hash tables or classes in most popular programming languages, without the need to add an *Object Relational Mapping* (ORM) layer to your application.

Horizontal scalability

Document databases are distributed by design, which means that they can scale horizontally. This makes them an ideal choice for modern data-intensive applications. Moreover, being distributed, document databases provide resiliency and availability through multinode data replication.

ACID (atomic) transactions

Document databases support ACID transactions, at least for single-document transactions, and in many cases for multidocument transactions as well. Crucially, it is often a less strict version of ACID that focuses on achieving data consistency via atomicity and an isolation guarantee (e.g., using snapshot isolation).

Performance

Document databases are quite performant when it comes to high-volume data reads/writes. This can be partly explained by the distributed architecture of document databases, which splits the load among the many nodes that make up the system. Furthermore, unlike traditional SQL databases, document databases do not necessarily enforce schema checks, standards, constraints, and ACID properties, which in turn increases query performance. Keep in mind that this is not a shortcoming, but rather a design choice.

Data modeling with document databases

In document databases, data modeling must be seen from a somewhat different viewpoint than that of the SQL DSM. Technically speaking, document databases are not designed for performing complex queries and table joins as is customary with SQL databases. This means that the range of queries that you can perform in a document database will be constrained by your data model. For this reason, the first step in document data modeling needs to be a business discussion to think and define in advance the queries and filters that users will want to perform. This is often called *query-driven data modeling*. User-defined queries should serve as the foundation for the subsequent data modeling stages. In this section, I will discuss three document data modeling techniques: document and collection structure, denormalization, and indexing.

Document and collection structure. The central concept of a document database is the *document*. You can think of documents as the equivalent of rows in the relational model. A document stores data objects as a set of key-value pairs. It can store many types of data, including strings, integers, dates, Booleans, arrays, and even subdocuments. Documents are then organized in *collections*, which are the equivalent of tables in the relational model.

Unlike SQL databases, there are no standardized rules for modeling a document database. In this case, the modeling process is mostly driven by business needs. As far as collections are concerned, the main thing to consider is that document databases do not allow for performing joins; therefore, collections should be modeled in a way that minimizes inter-collection relationships and at the same time maximizes intra-collection data cohesion. For example, a separate collection may be created for each business entity, such as users, products, transactions, subscriptions, reference data, prices, and quotes.

 Managing schema changes in a NoSQL database can be challeng-ing, especially in environments where the schema is not strictly enforced and evolves over time. A number of good practices can be adopted to mitigate this issue. One such practice is schema version-ing, which can be implemented by defining and storing your docu-ment schema in a separate location, and adding a schema_version field to your documents. Each version of the schema should have a unique identifier. Furthermore, you can implement schema valida-tion on the application side to check if your document matches the referenced schema. Make sure you document and communicate schema changes clearly within the team.

Denormalization.   To ensure intra-collection cohesion, all related data needs to be stored in the same document. This strategy is often called *denormalization*, as it involves making redundant copies of the data in multiple collections to increase per-formance and avoid data joins. As an alternative, it is possible to use *references* that link documents across collections. You can think of references as a soft version of for-eign keys in SQL databases. For example, a user ID field in the *transactions* collection can be used to find a related document in the *contacts* collection.

Indexing of document databases.   Document databases are designed for large amounts of data. As such, indexes are often used to improve query performance. An index stores a small portion of the collection data in an easy-to-traverse data structure. Without appropriate indexing, a document database will have to scan the entire col-lection when searching for a specific document.

The two primary types of indexes often supported by document databases are *single-field* indexes and *composite* indexes. Deciding which and how many indexes to create depends on your queries and it is crucial for improving the performance of your application. If a large number of your queries filter by a single field only, then it's bet-ter to create a single-field index for each of these fields. If you also have queries that repeatedly filter by multiple fields, then you can create a composite index on those fields. Other types of advanced document indexes exist. For example, multikey indexes are used to index array fields, while text indexes are used to support text search queries on string content.[20]

Importantly, there are a few factors to consider while indexing a document database. First, although indexes improve read performance, they will negatively impact write operations as they must also update the index. This is especially the case for applications with a high write-to-read ratio. Second, several document databases impose a limit on the number of indexes that a collection can have. If you run out of indexes, then you might not be able to meet your business or performance requirements anymore. Third, indexing might become more challenging if you have a highly nested or complex document structure. For this reason, consider making your documents as flat as possible to achieve optimal indexing results.

Technological implementations of document databases

There are a large number of data storage technologies that implement and support the document model. The most prominent examples include open source options such as MongoDB and Apache CouchDB, as well as managed commercial solutions such as Amazon DynamoDB, Azure Cosmos DB, and Google Cloud Firestore. Cloud-based solutions such as DynamoDB, Google Firestore, and Azure Cosmos DB are commonly preferred as they offer tight integration with other cloud services as well as reduced infrastructure and security overheads.

Moreover, a few specialized document-oriented data storage options are available. The most prominent example is *Elasticsearch*, which can be described as a distributed search and analytics engine. It is built on the Apache Lucene search software, which implements a well-known technique called inverted indexing. Elasticsearch is often used as a secondary DSS, where data from one or more primary DSSs is regularly pulled and indexed to allow easy and fast searching.

Financial use cases of document databases

Document databases have received considerable attention within the financial industry. This is particularly the case for financial applications that require scalability, latency, availability, schema flexibility, and integration capabilities, which are characteristic of document databases.

Let's take MongoDB, for example. Financial institutions have leveraged MongoDB for various business applications. A common example is the development of payment systems (*https://oreil.ly/K5fSa*). MongoDB's flexible data schema enables payment applications to accept and enrich any payment data structure and type. In addition, MongoDB may offer the necessary scalability and availability features that are

---

20 For a general overview, consult the official MongoDB page on indexing (*https://oreil.ly/IfapL*).

essential to payment systems. Moreover, MongoDB's API-based data management is an ideal fit for the payment business, which relies significantly on APIs.

Case Study: Wells Fargo's Next-Generation Card Payments System with MongoDB

Wells Fargo is a well-known financial services corporation with a remarkable global reach. To modernize its credit card payment system, Wells Fargo launched the *Cards 2.0* initiative. Based on an industry case study (*https://oreil.ly/igLCJ*), the main goals of the initiative were the following:

- Ensuring a seamless multichannel experience for credit card customers (branch, mobile, digital, etc.)
- Reusable and scalable data APIs to enable the quick rollout of changes across multiple channels
- Reduced dependency on third-party card processors

To achieve success with Cards 2.0, Wells Fargo had to reduce its reliance on mainframe infrastructures. The reason, according to the case study, is that "while mainframes hold critical System of Record (SOR) data, they often bring technical debt, dependencies, and are increasingly costly to manage—not least because there's a shortage of people with the right skills to maintain them."

While the bank is responsible for issuing the cards, the gateway that tracks all the transactions is the Fiserv mainframe system. Relying on data ingestion mechanisms based on a mainframe was not ideal for modern multichannel applications. To solve this problem, the engineering team at Wells Fargo designed a modern data infrastructure powered by MongoDB. The new solution included batch (Apache Spark) and real-time (Apache Kafka) systems that listen and pull the data from the mainframe and upload it to MongoDB. The resulting MongoDB-based DSS was an Operational Data Store (ODS) that could serve data to many business channels.

The Wells Fargo team didn't expose MongoDB collections directly to data consumers. Instead, data APIs were designed to serve various types of data (e.g., accounts, transactions, etc.). Such data APIs are then imported and used in the various microservices. Using MongoDB, Wells Fargo was able to handle over 20+ terabytes of daily data and move from a monolith architecture to a modular architecture of more than 80 microservices.

Another noteworthy example of a reliable and scalable document database technology for financial services is AWS DynamoDB. DynamoDB is a key-value and document-oriented database designed for high speed, throughput, availability, scalability, and millisecond latency. To illustrate its capabilities, on 2022 Amazon Prime

Day, Amazon DynamoDB reliably handled 105.2 million requests per second (*https://oreil.ly/gntiZ*) across trillions of API calls with single-digit millisecond performance. In addition, DynamoDB can be natively integrated with AWS Lambda to execute a data processing logic each time a DynamoDB table is updated. For example, the Amazon finance technologies (FinTech) payment transmission team, which supports and manages products for the accounts payable (AP) team, implemented a similar architecture (*https://oreil.ly/5nmM-*) to ensure the scalability and timely processing of remittances at Amazon.

The Time Series Model

In Chapter 2, we talked about time series data and illustrated its main characteristics. In essence, a time series is a sequence of measurements or observations of one or more variables tracked at increments in time. Examples include temperature, resource consumption by a computer, events, clicks, and stock prices.

Financial time series data such as stock prices are now generated in large volumes and velocities and are widely employed to analyze temporal market dynamics. This includes the analysis of historical trends, averages, variances, anomalies, correlations, stationarity, and cycles.

Moreover, as financial time series data has increased in volume, variety, and velocity, its range of application has significantly expanded. Time series analysis is now integral to financial analysis and forecasting and can be used in predicting stock prices, market risks, interest rates, foreign exchange fluctuations, and many more.

As a result, demand has emerged for a new type of a DSM to enable efficient storing, manipulating, and querying of time series data. I shall refer to this model as the *time series DSM*. A notable increase in the popularity of time series databases has been observed in recent years (*https://oreil.ly/_5sY0*). To understand why, the next section will highlight the key characteristics that distinguish time series databases.

Why time series databases?

A time series database is a specialized type of DSS designed specifically to implement the time series DSM. Time series databases offer several advantages, such as the following:

- A specialized engine designed for storing and processing time series data, providing substantial performance enhancements tailored for applications that handle large volumes of time series data, such as trading systems.
- Built-in functionalities to perform efficient time-based aggregations, such as temporal grouping of data (yearly, monthly, daily,..) and temporal transformations (e.g., simple moving average, exponential moving average, cumulative sum, percentile).

- Fast queries enabled through optimized time series indiexs and in-memory caching.
- Simple data model based on the time association of entities.
- Data immutability: time series databases are often designed for immutability and append-only behavior—i.e., once recorded, data is rarely updated.
- Efficient data lifecycle management by keeping recent data in memory, and deleting or compressing old data for efficient storage.

Keep in mind that the time series DSM is a specialized model; therefore, it should be considered only when your business and application requirements are centered around the efficient storage and processing of time series data. If the time series dimension of your application is just one of many aspects, then you might want to go for a more general-purpose DSM such as the SQL or document model.

Data modeling with time series

Data modeling in the time series DSM is as simple as the structure of time series data: a timestamp and associated data. The equivalent of a table in a time series database is often called a *measurement*. A measurement is a container of at least three main elements: time, fields, and metadata. Table 8-1 illustrates an example.

Table 8-1. A measurement in a time series database

Time	Price	Ticker	Exchange
2019-02-18T16:12:01Z	15.45	ABC	NYSE
2019-02-18T16:13:01Z	15.41	ABC	NYSE
2019-02-18T16:20:01Z	15.44	ABC	NYSE
2019-03-06T17:33:20Z	345.45	ZYK	NYSE
2019-03-06T17:33:25Z	345.47	ZYK	NYSE

In Table 8-1, the first column is time, which in a time series database must always be present. The next column, price, is a field. Field values represent the actual data in a measurement, and each measurement should have at least one field. In our example, we are observing the price of stocks over time. The final two columns, ticker and exchange, are referred to as metadata or tags. Tags are optional, although they are quite useful. Most time series databases construct indexes based on tags rather than time or field columns. A single row in a measurement is called a *point*. A set of points that share the same set of tag values is called a *series*. For example, the first three rows in the measurement shown in Table 8-1 form a series, since they hold data related to the price of the ticker ABC on the NYSE exchange.

Technological implementations of time series databases

A variety of time series database implementations have been developed in the market. These can be divided into native and non-native implementations.

A non-native implementation is not primarily designed for time series data, but it can be used for this purpose. For example, it is possible to use an SQL database such as PostgreSQL to create a time series table like the one shown in Table 8-1. To boost performance, an index like a B-tree or BRIN (Block Range Index) can be created on one or more tag columns plus the timestamp column. Furthermore, PostgreSQL supports index-based table clustering, which can enhance the efficiency of queries that filter by a given temporal interval. Similarly, a document database such as MongoDB can be used to store a time series as a set of documents in a collection indexed by time and tag keys.

Crucially, while SQL and document databases may be able to handle time series data, they are not optimized for this purpose. Two options are available to overcome this issue. First is time series extensions created on top of general-purpose databases. A prominent example is TimescaleDB, which extends PostgreSQL with time series characteristics. TimescaleDB is quite popular due to its performance, scalability, and compatibility with PostgreSQL and the SQL query language. As another example, MongoDB introduced time series collections (*https://oreil.ly/4CJmg*), which allow for optimized storage and retrieval of time series data. To do this, MongoDB time series collections use a columnar storage format and store data in time order. Moreover, upon the creation of a time series collection, MongoDB automatically creates a composite index on the time and metadata fields.

The second and most reliable option for handling time series data is native purpose-built time series databases. A good example is kdb+, developed and maintained by KX. Kdb+ is designed with high performance and scalability features in mind. It stores the data in a columnar format, allowing for efficient data compression and fast queries. In addition, it uses an in-memory compute engine for fast processing and querying in real time. Furthermore, kdb+ supports the q language, which is known for its powerful and efficient querying capabilities.

In-Memory Databases

Some database systems may frequently be referred to as in-memory databases or as having in-memory characteristics. What this means is that the database system keeps all or part of its data in memory (i.e., RAM). By storing data in memory, the database achieves very low response times (i.e., low latency) by eliminating the need to fetch the data from disk. It is well-known empirically that RAM-based access is substantially faster than disk access, precisely random disk access. In-memory data access capabilities can be crucial for time-critical applications such as trading and online stores. A common data management strategy with in-memory databases involves

---

storing the most current data in memory while keeping historical data in a separate location.

There are different types of in-memory databases. On the one hand, there are native in-memory databases such as Redis and kdb+. Among financial institutions, the Oracle TimesTen in-memory database (*https://oreil.ly/76R41*) has been widely used. Alternatively, there are in-memory extensions designed to improve the performance of existing DSSs. For example, the Amazon DynamoDB Accelerator was created to add in-memory capabilities to DynamoDB tables. To boost the performance of their primary database product, Db2, IBM introduced BLU Acceleration, which adds in-memory processing capabilities and columnar storage to enhance the speed of data analytics. Open source in-memory storage and computing frameworks such as Apache Ignite also exist.

Two things are worth noting when working with in-memory databases. First, they are not to be treated as a primary DSS as data in memory is considered volatile (if the machine is shut down, the data will be lost). Second, data stored in memory may become invalid and require a refresh. Such a practice is called cache invalidation (*https://oreil.ly/_u7PF*) and may be a challenging issue if not understood properly.

Another popular time series database is InfluxDB, developed and marketed by InfluxData. InfluxDB is a native time series database designed for high performance and intuitiveness. InfluxData uses *InfluxQL*, an SQL-like query language for querying data in InfluxDB databases. InfluxDB implements a data model that organizes data around buckets, databases, retention policies, series, measurements, tag keys, tag values, and field keys. InfluxDB's engine relies on an optimized data storage format called a Time-Structured Merge Tree (TSM) and an indexing technique called Time Series Index (TSI).[21]

Financial use cases of time series databases

Time series databases were originally developed for financial applications. As new market structures such as high-frequency and electronic trading mechanisms emerged, the volume of trades, quotes, and prices experienced a substantial increase. For example, the NYSE, which currently allows trading for all 8,000+ US securities, reports that an average of 2.4 billion shares exchange hands on a daily basis (*https://oreil.ly/grEbF*). In addition to volume, the speed of data generation has also increased. Nowadays, high-frequency trading at the NYSE occurs at the nanosecond level (i.e., one-billionth of a second). Consequently, a single second of trading can have hundreds of trades and quotes and reveal a variety of market patterns.

---

21 To learn more, read InfluxDB's documentation on the InfluxDB storage engine (*https://oreil.ly/STcKh*).

Multiple firms, in particular those involved in high-frequency and algorithmic trading, can leverage this fine-grained market view. However, to stay competitive, rapid data access is crucial. This is where highly performant DSSs, such as time series databases, are required.

Kdb+ has become a primary choice for financial markets, particularly in high-frequency trading, due to its exceptional performance and speed.[22] One of the main challenges (*https://oreil.ly/uT61x*) that firms using kdb+ face is the need for fast access and analysis of critical market data in real time.

The Message Broker Model

In distributed systems, it is common for multiple applications to need to communicate with each other to complete specific tasks. A typical scenario involves one type of application, known as *producers,* generating and storing data messages asynchronously[23] in a shared data store, and another type of application, called *consumers,* reading and processing the messages from the same store. This communication pattern is known as the *producer-consumer pattern.* Figure 8-6 provides an example.

A DSM that follows the producer-consumer pattern is called a message broker DSM, and a technology that implements the message broker DSM is simply called a *message broker.* In the next few sections, you will learn about the main features of message brokers, their data modeling principles, technological implementations, and, lastly, their use cases in the financial sector.

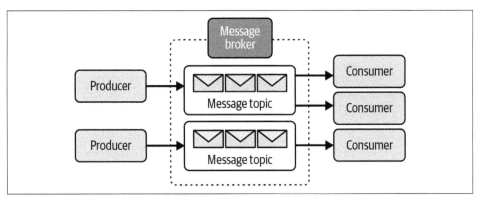

Figure 8-6. The message broker model

---

22 For a comparative study on this topic, I recommend Fazl Barez, Paul Bilokon, and Ruijie Xiong's "Benchmarking Specialized Databases for High-frequency Data" (*https://oreil.ly/KLZBD*), *arXiv* preprint; arXiv: 2301.12561 (January 2023).

23 In asynchronous communication, an application sends a request or message in a *fire-and-forget* mode, meaning that a response isn't expected from the target receiver or consumer.

Why message brokers?

Message brokers are widely used in developing data-intensive systems, particularly in event-driven, distributed, and streaming architectures. In these contexts, data is generated and consumed by various applications following different patterns and scales. To meet such requirements, message brokers offer the ideal features in terms of simplicity, speed, and scalability. Importantly, a message broker is not to be used as a primary or persistent DSS but rather as an intermediary that facilitates the exchange of messages between applications.

By decoupling data production and consumption, message brokers enable producer and consumer applications to work and scale independently. If a small number of messages are being produced, a few consumers can handle the workload. However, if the number of messages increases significantly, additional consumers can be added to handle the increased load. Moreover, producers need not worry about who the consumers of the data will be, which allows for flexibility in adding different types of consumers based on business needs.

A distinguishing feature of message brokers is their fault tolerance. Consumers and producers can be easily replaced in case of failure without impacting the state of the message broker. Moreover, message brokers are quite simple to use as applications only need to know the topic for publishing or consuming messages. Let's discuss message topics in the next section.

Data modeling with message brokers

Message broker data modeling revolves around two main concepts: topics and message schema, which I will illustrate in this section.

Topic modeling. Topics are the main building blocks of message brokers. A topic is a unique container of messages that publishers and subscribers need to specify when communicating with each other. Think of topics as the equivalent of tables in SQL databases.

Topic modeling involves defining the topics and their target consumers and producers. They can be created based on business requirements. In some cases, certain message brokers support multiple types of topics, each optimized for a specific need. For example, suppose you have an online application offering customer support for five categories of issues, each handled by a different backend system. If you decide to use a message broker, then you may want to create five topics, each handling a different type of client request. In this case, if Topic 1 handles issues of Type A, then only messages related to issue Type A will be published to that topic, and only backend systems that handle issue Type A will be able to process messages from Topic 1.

Naturally, large-scale applications can have hundreds or even thousands of topics. In this case, establishing data governance policies for topic management becomes critical. This might include the people and methods involved in creating a topic, the producer and consumer applications that are permitted to use it, the type and format of data that can be submitted to the topic, data quality checks and validations, data anonymization, encryption, and data loss management.

Message schemas.   Message brokers do not enforce a schema on message structure, offering flexibility in message definition. However, if consumers don't know what information to expect from producers, things might get out of control. This situation may force applications to manage multiple formats, which adds unnecessary complexity.

Therefore, it is a good practice to define a message schema for each topic initially and then implement validators on both the producer and consumer sides. These validators ensure that the message content is checked for correctness before it is published or consumed.

The most popular format for message definition is JSON. However, it is also possible to use XML or other formats.

Message Schema Registry

One of the best practices in designing message brokers is the establishment of a message schema registry. This consists of a centralized repository for storing, managing, versioning, and validating schemas for topic message data. Think of the schema registry as data governance practices that allow producers and consumers to communicate over a well-defined data contract in the form of a schema.

Apache Kafka, which is discussed in more detail later in this section, is a leading example of a message broker that supports a schema registry (*https://oreil.ly/d1UZx*). The schema registry in Kafka facilitates schema evolution and compatibility, enabling producers and consumers to update their schemas while preserving data integrity and cross-version compatibility. This capability is especially valuable for ensuring that data written to Kafka remains well structured and can be accurately interpreted by downstream consumers.

A technical aspect to keep in mind about message brokers is that they typically require messages to be serialized before being submitted to a topic. The message consumer then deserializes the message back into its original structure. Serialization is the process of converting a data object into a format optimized for transmission and storage, typically a byte stream. Deserialization reverses this process, converting the byte stream back into the original data object. While custom serializers and deserializers can be created, it is common to use built-in ones for formats such as JSON, Avro, and Protocol Buffers.[24]

Technological implementations of message brokers

Several technological options are available for implementing a message broker. Examples include Apache Kafka, RabbitMQ, Redis, Google Pub/Sub, Apache ActiveMQ, Amazon SQS, Amazon SNS, and Azure Service Bus. Making a full comparison between such technologies is beyond the scope of this book. However, the following criteria can be used to perform a technical assessment:

Business need
Some message brokers are designed for specific use cases, such as message queues (e.g., AWS SQS), while others are better suited for multiconsumer notifications (e.g., AWS SNS).

Performance
Message brokers differ in throughput and message read/write latency. For instance, Apache Kafka excels in throughput, whereas Redis is known for its low latency.

Delivery mode
Message brokers offer different levels of message delivery guarantees, such as "At Most Once," "At Least Once," and "Exactly Once." For more details, refer to Cloudflare's documentation page (*https://oreil.ly/-dvZz*).

Message persistence
Some message brokers purge messages from their store upon delivery to consumers (e.g., Apache ActiveMQ and RabbitMQ), while others store messages in a commit log where the same message can be consumed by multiple consumers and at a later point in time.

Scalability
Message brokers can vary in their scaling capabilities. Some excel at scaling message production, enabling the publication of a large number of messages per second, while others are more effective at scaling consumption, allowing for many concurrent consumers. For example, Apache Kafka is well-known for its scalability features. One way this can be achieved is by allowing a topic to be further divided into partitions. This way, instead of having one consumer blocking a topic, partitions allow multiple consumers to read messages from the same topic by referencing the partition ID within the topic from which they want to consume data.

---

24 For more on this topic, consult the Confluent Developer website (*https://oreil.ly/6ENFr*).

Message prioritization

Some message brokers, such as RabbitMQ and ActiveMQ, offer message prioritization features whereby high-priority messages are consumed before low-priority messages.

Message ordering

Message ordering refers to the order in which messages are consumed from a topic. While some message brokers may not enforce any specific ordering, others ensure that messages are consumed following a specific order, such as consuming the first messages received first.

When developing a cloud-based data infrastructure, managed cloud message brokers can be an excellent choice. These solutions are specifically engineered to seamlessly integrate with other cloud services. For example, you can configure topics to automatically receive messages when a file is uploaded to cloud storage. Then, a cloud function can consume that message from the same topic to perform a specific task related to that file.

Financial use cases of message brokers

Message brokers have found a variety of applications in the financial sector, particularly in the development of event-driven and real-time systems. They are extensively used for managing operations involving a continuous stream of high-volume data such as payments, credit card transactions, loan applications, ATMs, and mobile notifications. Message brokers can streamline tasks such as fraud analysis, application and transaction approvals or rejections, credit authorizations, and client notifications.

For example, At PayPal, Apache Kafka has been used extensively (*https://oreil.ly/ 3Xh7Y*) to support various critical operations such as first-party tracking, metrics streaming, database synchronization, log aggregation, batch processing, risk management, and analytics, with each of these use cases processing over 100 billion messages daily. PayPal's Kafka infrastructure includes 1,500 brokers across 85+ clusters, 20,000 topics, and nearly 2,000 Mirror Maker nodes, achieving 99.99% availability. In the 2022 Retail Friday, PayPal's Kafka processed a traffic volume of 21 million messages per second, which totaled about 1.3 trillion messages in a single day. Similarly, Cyber Monday of the same year resulted in 19 million messages per second, totaling 1.23 trillion messages in a single day.

Another significant application of message brokers in finance is the development of highly scalable and efficient applications that handle real-time financial data sharing, messaging, and streaming. For example, a financial data provider can leverage Apache Kafka to offer various types of data by organizing them into different topics. Subsequently, clients are subscribed to a specific topic based on their subscription plan. Kafka uses *Access Control Lists* (ACLs) as an authorization mechanism to determine which users are allowed to perform which actions on Kafka resources.

Moreover, within the same topic, it is possible to further categorize the data into partitions (e.g., by ticker) and offer clients the option to subscribe to a subset of the partitions. Kafka has the concept of a *consumer group*, which can be used to allow different clients to consume the same data from the same topic/partition using a Kafka consumer offset. An offset is just a pointer that indicates the position within a partition of the next message to be consumed by a consumer group.[25]

Case Study: Real-Time Fraud Detection at ING Group with Apache Kafka

ING Group is a Dutch multinational financial services corporation that provides a wide range of services such as retail and commercial banking, investment banking, and insurance services. ING, like other commercial banking firms, has a mechanism in place to identify fraud in its online banking activities. However, over time, this system became overly complex, expensive, unreliable, and challenging to scale effectively to manage the growing volume of data required for real-time fraud detection.

To overcome these issues, the ING engineering team decided to leverage Apache Kafka as the main *event bus* to support real-time fraud detection and other data streaming use cases. In a presentation given by ING experts Timor Timuri and Richard Bras in 2018 (*https://oreil.ly/9J6_3*), they illustrated the high-level use case of Apache Kafka.

To handle client-sensitive data, the ING team introduced security into the messages stored in Kafka via a symmetric end-to-end encryption module. This works by first encrypting the data before publishing it to a topic and then decrypting it upon consumption by the consumer.

The Protocol Buffers (protobuf) format was chosen for message serialization/deserialization. Before publishing, messages are serialized into protobuf, and when consumers receive the message, they deserialize it.

In addition, the ING engineering team created a number of predefined client settings to allow users who just want to use Kafka and do not care about the details (e.g., publish messages to a topic). This was provided via a simple and easy-to-use interface. Furthermore, test components were developed to simulate message publication, and monitoring was introduced to evaluate Kafka's performance. For compliance purposes, all events are persisted in a Cassandra data store.

To ensure availability, ING's team adopted a multi–data center strategy to replicate data and ensure availability in case of downtimes or disasters.

---

25 For an interesting real-world application of this idea, I highly recommend watching the presentation given by two AWS experts (*https://oreil.ly/R1Jl1*) on how to build a real-time financial data feed as a service on AWS.

Crucially, while Kafka initially served for real-time fraud detection at scale, it later expanded to become a primary development platform supporting a wide array of applications. By 2018, ING managed 200 topics, processing 1 billion messages daily with peak rates of 20,000 messages per second. Kafka is utilized across over 100 teams at ING, catering to 120 distinct use cases.

The Graph Model

In Chapter 2, we explored graph data, illustrating its structures, types, and financial applications. One of the main advantages of graph data is its ability to reveal complex patterns and mechanisms that simpler data types (e.g., time series) cannot uncover. As a result, a wide range of applications have been created, the primary functionality of which revolves around the storing and processing of graph data. The graph DSM is intended for such use cases. A technology that implements the graph DSM is known as a graph DSS or, more commonly, a *graph database*.

In the following sections, we will examine the key aspects of the graph DSM, graph databases, graph data modeling principles, technological implementations, and, finally, financial use cases.

Why a graph model?

The graph DSM is used when designing graph-oriented applications that prioritize the storing and analysis of data relationships. Examples of such requirements include the following:

Centrality analysis
> This aims at identifying the most important nodes in a network. For instance, it can be applied to identify *Systemically Important Financial Institutions* (SIFIs), whose failure could potentially disrupt the entire financial system, or market participants who play major roles as intermediaries, facilitating various transactions.

Search and pathfinding
> This aims at locating nodes with specific attributes or determining the most efficient path between two nodes within a graph. A widely used approach is shortest path analysis, which identifies the path between nodes with the fewest edges or minimal weights.

Community detection
> This aims at finding cohesive regions or subgraphs of connected nodes within a graph. Such subgraphs are called communities. Examples include stock market clusters (stocks that move together), interbank lending clusters (e.g., banks that frequently transact with each other), and fraud detection (e.g., groups of transactions that might be linked to fraud rings).

Contagion analysis

   This examines how a shock impacting one or a set of nodes propagates throughout the rest of the network. Applications include financial stress testing, cascade
   failures, and systematic risk analysis.

Link prediction

   This aims at identifying pairs of nodes that are likely to establish a link in the
   future (e.g., two financial institutions establishing a correspondence banking
   relationship).

It's important to remember that the graph data element must be crucial to your application to justify using a graph DSM. If your application needs to store graph data but
does not require specialized graph capabilities, then a general-purpose model such as
SQL may suffice.

For instance, consider a financial graph where nodes represent banks and links represent asset exposure (e.g., how many assets bank A holds at bank B). If bank A is primarily concerned with its direct exposure to the network, an SQL DSM can handle
this efficiently. You can create a table with three columns: source_bank, target_bank,
and exposure. To get your bank's total exposure, you simply run `SELECT tar
get_bank, exposure WHERE source_bank = "YOUR_BANK_NAME"`. However, if you
need to calculate the exposure of a bank to which your bank is exposed (similar to
finding the friends of your friend), the SQL model would require complex joins and
recursive operations to achieve this. This is where the graph DSM excels, as its storage and processing logic is specifically designed for such tasks.

Data modeling with graph databases

Graph data modeling is quite intuitive and flexible. It involves defining a *domain* that
consists of nodes and links (*https://oreil.ly/XyquJ*), each with their own attributes and
labels. Graph data modeling is often called whiteboard friendly, as it can be visually
drawn on a whiteboard.

Graph data modeling involves two primary aspects: node modeling and link modeling. In node modeling, you define the different categories of nodes that can exist in
the graph, such as persons, organizations, countries, or assets. Each node category is
characterized by specific attributes that provide descriptive information, including
category labels and additional fields for unique identification.

In link modeling, the focus shifts to defining the relationships or connections
between different node categories. This involves specifying the types of links that can
exist and assigning link attributes that describe the characteristics of these connections. Figure 8-7 provides an example of graph data modeling.

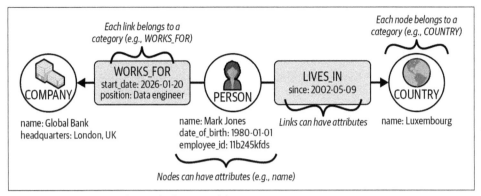

Figure 8-7. An example graph data model

Keep in mind that the graph DSM does not enforce a rigid schema, as is the case with the SQL model. New types of nodes and links can be easily added by defining their label and attributes, and existing nodes and links can be adapted to reflect new business requirements.

To enhance performance, graph data modeling may include the definition of indexes on nodes and links. These indexes are typically based on attributes associated with nodes or links.

Technological implementations of graph databases

The graph DSM can be implemented using a variety of technological options. The simplest but least performant approach involves the use of multi-model non-native DSSs such as relational databases. In this case, nodes, links, and their attributes are defined in normalized tables, and indexes can be added to improve search performance. If you recall the section on graph data in Chapter 2, this would be similar to the *edge list* graph representation. This solution is recommended if your application doesn't prioritize graph data processing or if you want to perform basic graph queries.

Some relational databases have ad hoc extensions that provide graph database functionalities. The best example is Apache AGE (*https://oreil.ly/jHh9D*), a PostgreSQL extension developed to provide graph processing and analytics capabilities. AGE provides users with the capability to compose graph queries using a hybrid query language that integrates SQL with openCypher, an open source implementation of the Cypher graph query language originally developed by Neo4j.

Non-native graph implementations have several limitations. In particular, relational databases are built on the assumption of independence between the records, which explains their good performance when querying a set of rows. However, graph data revolves around relationships between data points. This led to the development of native graph databases designed specifically to handle such interconnected data structures.

Neo4j, created by Neo4j, Inc., is the leading native graph DSS, known for its extensive feature set that supports diverse graph-based applications. Neo4j uses a proprietary querying language called *Cypher* to query data stored in a Neo4j database. To boost performance, Neo4j's processing engine relies on a special indexing strategy called *index-free adjacency* (*https://oreil.ly/-ZhlJ*). It works by assigning each node a direct reference to its adjacent nodes, which implies that accessing relationships and associated data is as simple as a memory pointer lookup. In addition, Neo4j supports simple and composite node and link attributes indexes, constraints, and atomic transactions, as well as functions, subqueries, patterns, and clauses.[26] For more advanced graph algorithms and machine learning tasks, the Neo4j Graph Data Science library (*https://oreil.ly/H7Yd1*) is available.

A major challenge with graph DSSs is scalability. Solutions such as Neo4j can scale to handle billions of nodes and links, which is more than enough for the vast majority of use cases. However, sharding is not native to graph databases. Unlike relational databases, where rows are independent, graph data is interconnected, making it difficult to partition efficiently as graph density increases. Mathematically speaking, the problem of partitioning a graph dataset across a set of nodes is near impossible (NP-complete) to perform for large graphs.[27] Nevertheless, several graph database technologies (e.g., TigerGraph) have made progress along this way and offer distributed graph processing capabilities.

Another implementation of graph storage systems is managed services. One example is *Amazon Neptune*, which offers a scalable, secure, and cost-efficient managed graph database. Neptune allows users to query data using the popular graph query languages Apache TinkerPop Gremlin, W3C's SPARQL, and openCypher. Another prominent example is *TigerGraph*, which provides a rich platform for native graph data storage and analysis at scale.

Financial use cases of graph databases

Graph databases have been applied to solve a variety of problems in the financial sector. One prominent use case is fraud detection. Many forms of financial fraud exist: credit card fraud, loan fraud, wire fraud, tax fraud, identity theft, insurance fraud, and

---

26 For more details on these features, consult the official Neoo4j documentation page (*https://oreil.ly/KSpxm*).

27 To learn more about this topic, see David Montag's "Understanding Neo4j Scalability" (*https://oreil.ly/63X8H*) white paper, *Neotechnology* (January 2013).

money laundering. In simple scenarios, fraud is easy to detect with traditional tools and databases. However, in today's environment, fraudsters use sophisticated techniques and tricks to commit their crimes and hide their actions and identities.

The best way to detect such complex patterns is by designing a framework that combines network analysis with a graph database to build a fraud graph (*https://oreil.ly/ WCTUL*). Such a graph records the connections between the actors, transactions, and other pertinent data to help experts capture anomalous trends in the data and create applications that can identify fraudulent activity. Figure 8-8 naively illustrates the concept. In this example, the real account holder is associated with a unique set of information such as address, email, phone number, SSN, etc. A fraudster, however, might use a variety of addresses, phone numbers, and other pieces of information and combine them in complex ways to hide their activities. When represented as a graph, such hidden relationships can be detected more easily. This task can be represented as an entity resolution problem where the goal is to match nodes that represent the same entity.

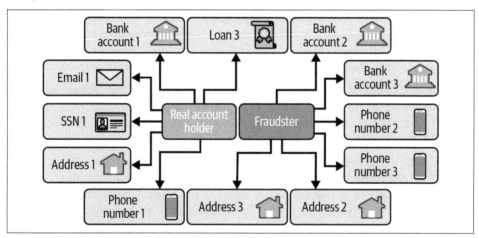

Figure 8-8. Graph-based fraud detection

Graph databases also find applications in financial risk analysis. For instance, financial assets can be structured hierarchically, bundled into new assets, segmented into tranches, and distributed across complex networks of ownership and transactions. This complicates the task of risk management and reduces regulatory oversight. One approach to address this challenge involves constructing a financial assets graph (*https://oreil.ly/Vp-Lk*). This graph models and stores the relationships among different types of financial assets, enabling financial institutions to track their assets and account for dependencies in their pricing models. Additionally, graph databases are useful for simulating various shocks and scenarios to test the stability of correlated asset portfolios, interbank networks, and various types of systemic risks.[28]

Case Study: Anti–Money Laundering at Banking Circle with Neo4j

Banking Circle (BC) (*https://oreil.ly/exb5l*) is a banking-as-a-service (BaaS) company that offers real-time and low-cost payment services by providing the clients with direct access to clearing in multiple jurisdictions. BC serves a large client base, including over 250 regulated businesses, financial institutions, and marketplaces. It allows clients to move and convert money in real time securely and compliantly. In 2021, BC processed over 250 billion euros in payment volume. Importantly, as the volume of payments that BC processed increased, so did the number of fraud attempts.

To detect fraud, BC initially relied on a traditional rule-based approach (*https://oreil.ly/HhmvY*), which worked by assigning risk scores by searching and catching certain words, amounts, and locations and sending them to fraud analysts for manual review. However, the company realized that this approach was slow, expensive, and generated a high level of false positives. As a result, it decided to adopt a data-driven AML approach that leverages graph and machine learning techniques. The outcome was a modern framework called SCAM, or System for Catching Attempted Money-laundering, which consisted of an ensemble of different machine learning models.

To capture complex relationships, SCAM relies on multiple network representations of various data features (e.g., accounts, payments, entities, countries, etc.). Using Neo4j's Graph Data Science (GDS) framework (*https://oreil.ly/m-fYF*), BC was able to conduct various types of advanced graph analysis.

For example, community detection algorithms were used to generate features that detect high-risk clusters within the network. A community detection algorithm works by finding clusters of similar nodes; for example, if a fraudster uses similar profile attributes, they are likely to fall within the same cluster. This technique, combined with other network features such as risk scores of neighboring nodes and distances to tax havens and known fraudsters, has significantly improved the reliability of SCAM.

BC was able to transform a laborious, sluggish procedure into a data-driven, scalable, flexible solution that leverages cutting-edge technology. False negatives were reduced by 10–25% and the number of overall alerts escalated for manual review was halved. BC continues to experiment with Neo4j algorithms and plans to add more graph features to tune their model further.

---

28 An example of a company that offers such services is Financial Network Analysis (FNA) (*https://oreil.ly/uJC55*).

The Warehouse Model

One of the most common business needs in data-driven organizations is an enterprise-wide system for integrated and structured data storage, access, analytics, and reporting. The most popular solution to this need is *data warehousing*, a concept that has been around since the 1970s. Bill Inmon and Ralph Kimball, the two pioneers of this field, define a data warehouse as:

> A data warehouse is a subject-oriented, integrated, nonvolatile, and time-variant collection of data in support of management's decisions.
>
> —Bill Inmon

> A data warehouse is a copy of transaction data specifically structured for query and analysis.
>
> —Ralph Kimball

I will use the term *warehouse DSM* to describe a system that periodically gathers, consolidates, and structures data from various sources within a company into a central repository intended for various analytical purposes. A DSS system used to implement the warehouse DSM is called a warehouse DSS or data warehouse. Figure 8-9 illustrates a typical data warehouse architecture. As the figure shows, data from heterogeneous sources (left side) get organized into a central data warehouse (middle) which then serves a variety of analytical data needs (right side).

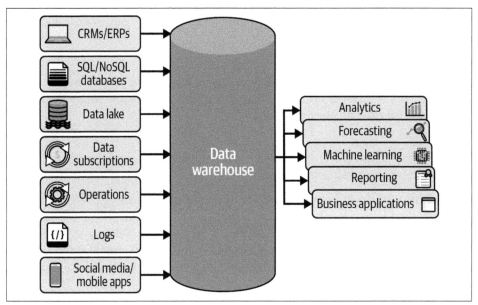

Figure 8-9. A data warehouse architecture

Why data warehouses?

The warehouse DSM offers several advantages, including the following:

Structure
> Data warehouses introduce a consistent structure to data, regardless of the original formats provided by the source systems.

Advanced analytics
> Performing advanced data queries for business intelligence and reporting is a fundamental and frequent activity within organizations. Data warehouses provide intuitive SQL-like querying capabilities that enable a wide range of data queries.

Scalability
> Data warehouses can scale to handle large volumes of data and complex read/write operations.

Subject-oriented
> Data warehouses are often designed to allow users to query and analyze data about a particular subject or functional area (such as sales, customers, payments, etc.)

Integrated
> Data warehouses consolidate, structure, and harmonize data from different sources (e.g., departments or business units) while ensuring consistency and data quality.

Nonvolatile
> Once data is uploaded to a data warehouse, it remains stable and does not change. If any changes occur to a data record, a new record is added instead of updating the existing ones.

Time-variant
> Data warehouses record data with a timestamp, allowing users to perform accurate point-in-time historical analysis.

At this point, you might be wondering about the difference between the warehouse DSM and other models that have similar features, such as the data lake or SQL DSMs. Similar to data warehouses, data lakes can also be used to consolidate data into a central location. Data lakes lack default mechanisms to ensure data structure consistency and homogeneity, and they do not offer advanced querying capabilities like a data warehouse does.

The primary difference between a relational DSM and a data warehouse DSM can be understood through the distinction between OLAP and OLTP. The relational DSM is primarily meant for OLAP-oriented applications, emphasizing transactional guarantees and single-row lookups/inserts/updates (often called *Data Manipulation Language*, or DML). The data warehouse DSM is instead aimed toward OLAP-oriented applications that require complex analytical read/write operations with less focus on point lookups and DML. However, it's important to note that both the relational and warehouse models can coexist. In many cases, a significant portion of the data ingested into a data warehouse originates from relational databases that support day-to-day business operations.

Data modeling with data warehouses

When building a data warehouse, data modeling is critical. Over the years, two competing approaches to data modeling have emerged for data warehouses: the *subject modeling approach* of Bill Inmon and the *dimensional modeling approach* of Ralph Kimball.[29]

In the Inmon approach, data is sourced from various operational systems across the organization and integrated into a centralized data warehouse. Subsequently, based on the specific needs of individual departments or business units, dedicated data marts are derived from the data warehouse. In this model, the data warehouse and the data marts are physically separate entities, each with its own storage and characteristics. Data within the data marts is considered consistent and reliable, as it originates from the centralized source of truth—the data warehouse itself. Users from different departments typically employ specialized tools to access and analyze the data within their respective data marts. Figure 8-10 offers an illustration of the Inmon architecture. The main advantage of this approach is flexibility, as new data marts can be created to meet new business needs. On the negative side, such an architecture introduces a maintenance burden due to the physical separation between the data warehouse and the data marts.

The Kimball approach takes a different perspective. Instead of isolating the data warehouse from the data marts, Kimball suggested a user requirement-driven approach that defines the data marts in advance and integrates them within the data warehouse itself. Figure 8-11 illustrates the concept.

---

29 For a comprehensive comparative study of the difference between Inmon and Kimball models, see Lamia Yessad and Aissa Labiod's "Comparative Study of Data Warehouses Modeling Approaches: Inmon, Kimball and Data Vault" (*https://oreil.ly/Bmsi5*), in *2016 International Conference on System Reliability and Science (ICSRS)* (IEEE, 2016): 95–99.

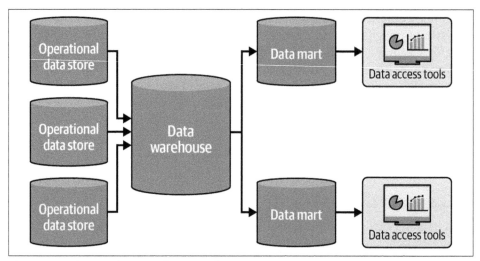

Figure 8-10. Inmon data warehouse architecture

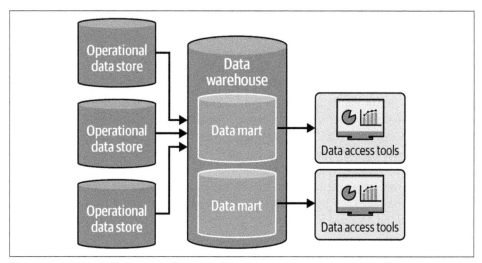

Figure 8-11. Kimball data warehouse architecture

The definition of data marts is done via a technique called *dimensional modeling*. Its main idea is to divide data into *fact* and *dimension* tables. A fact table contains data on quantifiable business entities or events, while a dimension table stores data related to the context of the events. Examples of facts include financial payments, monetary transfers, and online sales. Dimensions may be information such as product, user, and country details. Facts and dimensions may be used to categorize data into data mart–specific tables based on various business processes such as revenues, products, sales, employees, suppliers, and branches.

In dimensional modeling, two primary types of data warehouse schemas are prevalent: the star schema and the snowflake schema. The star schema features a central fact table connected directly to multiple dimension tables, resembling a star-shaped architecture. On the other hand, the snowflake schema is a normalized version of the star schema that has a single fact table and several direct and indirect dimension tables. Figure 8-12 illustrates the difference.

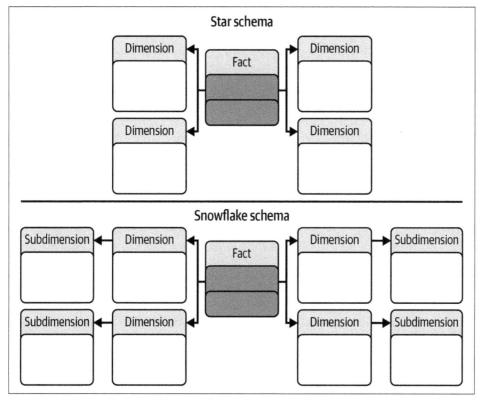

Figure 8-12. Star schema versus snowflake schema

Star schemas are generally easier to understand and simpler to query because they involve fewer table JOIN operations. Snowflake schemas, on the other hand, can be more effective at ensuring data integrity and consistency as they remove redundancy through data normalization.[30]

---

30 For an excellent reference on dimensional modeling, I recommend Ralph Kimball and Margy Ross's *The Data Warehouse Toolkit: The Definitive Guide to Dimensional Modeling*, 3rd ed. (Wiley, 2013).

Technological implementations of data warehousing

Due to the high demand for data warehousing, numerous technological implementations have been developed. As data warehouses emphasize structured data and advanced querying capabilities, most technologies in this domain support SQL and relational data modeling. Leading commercial solutions include high-performance integrated systems like IBM Netezza, IBM Integrated Analytics System (IAS), Db2, Teradata, Oracle Exadata, and Micro Focus Vertica Enterprise. Financial institutions often rely on these solutions for high-performance processing of large datasets.[31]

In recent years, cloud-based data warehousing solutions have seen a notable increase in popularity. Examples include Amazon Redshift, Snowflake, Google BigQuery, and Azure Synapse Analytics. This surge is largely attributed to the convenient features that the cloud offers in terms of scalability, managed infrastructure, on-demand pricing, reliability, and seamless integration with other cloud services. For example, with a data warehousing service such as Google BigQuery, you can easily create a database and begin writing and reading data to it in a matter of minutes. As a serverless platform, BigQuery handles all infrastructure management, so you don't have to worry about provisioning or scaling resources.

Cloud-based data warehouses commonly adopt column-oriented storage, enhancing query performance and reducing costs by retrieving only the columns requested by users. This storage method also benefits from efficiency gains through compression and deduplication techniques, optimizing data storage on disk.[32]

Cloud data warehouses achieve scalability by decoupling the compute and storage layers. For example, using Snowflake as a data warehouse, your data will be stored and managed in separate persistence storage (e.g., AWS S3) (*https://oreil.ly/6UHJF*). In contrast, compute resources are virtualized and can be independently scaled up or down by the user, separate from storage.

To enhance storage efficiency and query performance, cloud warehouses leverage the concept of data *partitioning* and *clustering*. The idea is to split a table into a set of storage units called partitions that can be managed and queried separately. With clustering, data within each partition is physically ordered into small blocks of data. When a query is executed against a table, the database engine will first filter the partitions to scan (partition pruning) and then apply block filtering (pruning) to each partition. This way, only the minimum amount of data is queried, thus increasing performance and reducing query cost. BigQuery requires the user to configure the partitioning

---

31 For instance, the NYSE transitioned to IBM Netezza to manage its growing data volumes, which traditional SQL databases were unable to handle effectively. Read more in "At NYSE, the Data Deluge Overwhelms Traditional Databases" (*https://oreil.ly/pcP2w*), by Tom Groenfeldt.

32 For a deeper understanding of how and why columnar formats are used in data warehouses, I highly recommend reading about Google BigQuery's columnar storage format Capacitor (*https://oreil.ly/1Mq_3*).

and clustering keys (from existing columns) (*https://oreil.ly/caYnO*), while Snowflake implements a more dynamic and managed approach to partitioning and clustering called *micro-partitioning* (*https://oreil.ly/A_h2H*).

> When using cloud data warehouses, it's crucial to consider vendor-specific limits, quotas, and usage guidelines. For instance, as OLAP systems, data warehouses are optimized for running complex analytical queries with moderate frequency. Attempting to support thousands of concurrent users may exceed maximum connection limits. For example, BigQuery allows up to 100 concurrent connections for interactive queries, while Snowflake, with auto-scaling, supports up to 80 concurrent connections. Furthermore, while data warehouses do support data updates and DML operations, they are not primarily designed for these tasks.

Financial use cases of data warehouses

Data warehouses are extensively used in the financial sector to address various business needs. One major use case is the consolidation of data from diverse business silos (e.g., risk, revenue, loans) into a unified data warehouse that serves as the primary source for analytics. This consolidation facilitates the extraction of valuable business insights from the vast volumes of data generated through daily operations within financial institutions. For instance, this enables business teams to effectively understand and manage different types of risks such as credit, financial, operational, and compliance risks. In Chapter 5 on financial data governance, we discussed how data aggregation and consolidation capabilities have become a regulatory requirement for banks following the crisis of 2007–2008.

Data warehouses can enable financial institutions to track financial, operational, and data quality indicators over time. Maintaining point-in-time historical data is a common business requirement in financial markets. A well-designed data warehouse may ensure this by enforcing an append-only policy, which allows new data to be written while maintaining the immutability of existing data. This principle also applies to externally sourced financial data. For instance, financial vendor data is intended for reading and analysis rather than modification, making a data warehouse an ideal solution for such use cases.

Furthermore, data warehouses are widely used in financial markets for facilitating data sharing. For example, various financial data vendors now offer the option to deliver their data to clients via the cloud. This delivery mechanism is particularly convenient with cloud-based data warehouses. Refer to the section "Data Ingestion Technologies" on page 269 to learn more about this topic.

Case Study: BlackRock's Aladdin Data Cloud Powered by Snowflake

BlackRock is the world's largest and leading investment management firm and a provider of financial technology. As of 2023, BlackRock's assets under management reached around 8.5 trillion US dollars (*https://oreil.ly/4j0fV*). BlackRock's jewel technology is known as *Aladdin*, an integrated solution that combines sophisticated risk analysis features with portfolio management, trading, and operations tools in a single platform. Aladdin has established itself as one of the most prominent examples of financial technologies. In particular, during the 2008 financial crisis, Aladdin showed its remarkable capabilities by allowing companies like Microsoft to aggregate their risk exposures to different banks (a feature that many financial institutions lacked at the time) (*https://oreil.ly/c0AZe*).

To enhance Aladdin's data-driven capabilities, BlackRock launched *Aladdin Data Cloud*, a managed data solution that allows users to combine Aladdin portfolio data with non-Aladdin data, perform timely analysis, and develop custom dashboards and applications using Aladdin Studio—BlackRock's platform for developers. To this goal, BlackRock decided to partner with the cloud-based data warehousing company Snowflake (*https://oreil.ly/WaUHG*). The main reasons for choosing Snowflake were performance, scalability, and concurrency management.

By bringing together Aladdin, a leader in investment management technology, and Snowflake's Data Cloud, the Aladdin Data Cloud is set to allow its clients to expand the range of data-driven applications across their organizations. Each Aladdin Data Cloud client receives an independent, centrally managed data store preloaded with rich front-to-back Aladdin datasets, which can then be supplemented with proprietary and other third-party data sources, allowing organizations to access and query their business-critical data on a single, cloud-based platform.

Snowflake has several features that make it attractive for building data applications. For example, it isolates work environments via virtual warehouses (*https://oreil.ly/oBrcL*), which are clusters with dedicated CPU, memory, and temporary storage. In a simple setup, each client can be dedicated to a separate virtual warehouse. Virtual warehouses offer the flexibility to scale resources up and down, thus customizing work environments for different client needs. In addition, Snowflake has advanced and secure data-sharing functionalities (*https://oreil.ly/jBDj3*), making it ideal for working with a large base of users and accounts. Moreover, Snowflake developed its own SQL language (*https://oreil.ly/Ai-zH*) with rich command features and SQL standard-compliant syntax. Additionally, Snowflake provides a list of configurable parameters (*https://oreil.ly/CrTk_*) that can be tuned to control the behavior of a user account, queries, sessions, and objects.

The Blockchain Model

Blockchain is one of the most promising technological trends in today's financial services landscape. It is the underlying technology that enables the so-called *cryptocurrencies,* such as Bitcoin and Ethereum.[33] In this section, I will briefly walk through the basic idea behind blockchain and its applicability as a data storage system for financial data.[34]

At the most basic level, a blockchain is a data structure that stores data as a chain of linked information blocks. The most prominent application of blockchain technology is in the creation of *digital ledgers.* A digital ledger is a record-keeping book of accounts that keeps track of a business's financial transactions. Think, for example, of when you deposit or withdraw money from your bank account. As per common sense, you trust that your bank will maintain a correct and truthful ledger and not modify it by deleting or updating book records.

A blockchain data ledger performs a similar function and guarantees data immutability, but following different design principles. To illustrate the idea, let's represent a blockchain as a linked list of information blocks, as illustrated in Figure 8-13. The first block in a blockchain is called the *genesis block.* Each subsequent block contains its own data (e.g., transaction records) as well as a *hash pointer* that stores both a pointer to the previous block and a hash of that older block. A hashing function, H(), is used to create a cryptographic hash of each block's data. A block hash serves as a unique identifier of each block.

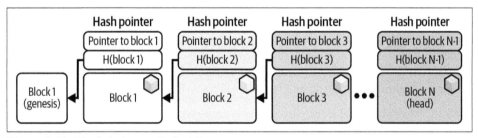

Figure 8-13. Blockchain as a linked list

To illustrate why this structure is tamper resistant, consider an adversary attempting to manipulate the blockchain by altering data entries in block 2. This will automatically update the block's hash. As a result, the hash pointer in block 3 will no longer

---

33 For a good introduction to cryptocurrencies, I highly recommend Arvind Narayanan, Joseph Bonneau, Edward Felten, Andrew Miller, and Steven Goldfeder's *Bitcoin and Cryptocurrency Technologies: A Comprehensive Introduction* (Princeton University Press, 2016).

34 For a deeper introduction to blockchain databases, I highly recommend Chapter 26 of Avi Silberschatz, Henry F. Korth, and S. Sudarshan's 2019 *Database Systems Concepts,* 7th ed. (McGraw Hill, 2019).

correspond to the updated hash of block 2. To conduct a successful attack, the adversary must alter all hash pointers up to the most recent block in the list (i.e., the head).

In addition to data immutability, blockchain-based data ledgers have shown high reliability when implemented as a distributed system. The term *distributed ledger technology* (DLT) is often used to describe these systems. In a DLT, a decentralized network of nodes cooperatively maintains the integrity of the ledger. Each node keeps a copy of the blockchain and can verify and validate any operation that alters the blockchain. For example, if a node wants to add a new block to the chain, the other nodes in the network need to agree and reach a consensus on such an operation. The same applies to our earlier example of the adversary attack: even if the adversary were able to change all the hash pointers, the changes would still need to be validated and accepted by the other nodes in the network. A variety of consensus mechanisms are available, including Proof of Work, Proof of Stake, and Byzantine Consensus.

As a financial data engineer, you might be wondering if blockchain is a good solution as a data storage system. Technically speaking, a blockchain can be used to store financial transaction data, but it comes with a price. First, blockchains have very limited data querying capabilities. Second, as more nodes are added to the network, performance may get worse in terms of throughput, latency, or capacity.[35] For example, the decentralized nature of blockchain introduces latency in both storing and retrieving data. In applications requiring fast data access, the time taken for reaching consensus, propagating blocks, and verifying transactions can lead to slower response times.

To overcome these issues, blockchain-based databases (or blockchain databases for short) were introduced. The main idea behind a blockchain database is to combine the best of both worlds: the performance and power of a traditional database system (e.g., SQL or document databases) with the immutability, cryptographic verifiability, integrity, decentralized control, and transaction traceability of a blockchain.

Crucially, when deployed internally within a financial institution, a blockchain database doesn't need to be decentralized. The institution in this case acts as the administrative authority that controls the blockchain.[36]

A few commercial solutions for blockchain databases already exist. The most prominent is BigchainDB (*https://oreil.ly/ZcpNm*), which uses MongoDB as the distributed database under the hood and offers blockchain characteristics. Another example is

---

35 For more on performance-related issues in blockchains, read Mayank Raikwar, Danilo Gligoroski, and Goran Velinov's "Trends in Development of Databases and Blockchain" (*https://oreil.ly/RfFIG*), in the *2020 Seventh International Conference on Software Defined Systems (SDS)* (IEEE, 2020): 177–182.

36 To learn more about blockchain database design patterns, I recommend MongoDB's guide "Blockchain Database: A Comprehensive Guide" (*https://oreil.ly/klrQS*).

Amazon Quantum Ledger Database (QLDP) (*https://oreil.ly/LGhUz*), a fully managed ledger database for creating an immutable, transparent, and cryptographically verifiable transaction log.

Ripple: A Blockchain-Based Global Payment Ecosystem

A successful story in the commercial implementation of blockchain technology is Ripple. Behind this is an American company called Ripple Labs, Inc. It is a unique player in this industry as it created the first financial services platform and network that leverages blockchain, tokenization, and cryptocurrency technologies for enterprises. Ripple's primary use case is to enable secure, instant, and low-cost cross-border financial transactions and settlements.

Ripple's primary offering is RippleNet, a blockchain-based infrastructure for payments. As of the end of 2024, RippleNet connects a network of over 500 participants.

XRP is Ripple Labs's native cryptocurrency (digital asset). It is used as a bridge currency in Ripple's ecosystem to facilitate liquidity for cross-border transactions. XRP is independent of RippleNet but can be utilized within the network for certain services. XRP is a bridge asset (*https://oreil.ly/_grQh*), or an asset that businesses and financial institutions can use to make a bridge transfer between two different fiat currencies. In this scenario, a financial institution can purchase an equivalent amount of XRP and send it through Ripple's network.

The underlying blockchain ledger technology that powers Ripple is called XRP Ledger (XRPL). Interestingly, XRPL differs from Bitcoin's blockchain (*https://oreil.ly/oLZhy*). Bitcoin relies on an energy-intensive Proof-of-Work (PoW) mechanism for transaction validation, while Ripple uses the faster and more efficient mechanism known as the XRP Ledger Consensus Protocol (*https://oreil.ly/KO_vH*), or XRP LCP for short. For an intuitive introduction to XRP LCP, see the CoinBrain website (*https://oreil.ly/B9SPu*). This consensus mechanism is key to XRPL's efficiency, enabling rapid transactions at low costs. XRPL has been released to the public, and it is now an open source blockchain protocol (*https://oreil.ly/3t-5j*).

To illustrate an example (sourced from the Ripple website (*https://oreil.ly/jq5-z*)), let's say that Bank A intends to transfer $10,000 to Bank B in euros using the Ripple platform. The banks agree on a Forex rate on Ripple, following which Bank A converts the USD to XRP at the agreed rate and transfers it via the XRP Ledger to Bank B. Upon receipt, which happens in a matter of seconds, Bank B converts the XRP to euros, with minimal transaction fees compared to traditional banking methods. This use of XRP as a bridge currency via RippleNet demonstrates its role in facilitating fast and cost-effective cross-border transactions.

Ripple has helped countries create their own central bank digital currencies (CBDCs) (*https://oreil.ly/Otp-V*) through its Ripple CBDC platform. Furthermore, Ripple is a member of the ISO 20022 Standards Body, becoming the first member of the ISO organization dedicated to Distributed Ledger Technology (DLT).

In conclusion, blockchain presents a complex landscape with ongoing efforts aimed at exploring its feasibility for high-storage and high-performance applications. Researchers and developers are actively investigating various approaches to enhance blockchain's capabilities, such as sharding, optimizing consensus algorithms, Layer 2 protocols, and sidechains, and are exploring hybrid architectures that combine blockchain with traditional databases.

Summary

This chapter covered the second layer of the financial data engineering lifecycle: storage. This layer facilitates the choice and implementation of various data storage models and systems, supporting the storage and retrieval of data within a financial data infrastructure.

Crucially, data is not merely ingested and stored. To unlock its full potential in driving informed decision-making and operational excellence, data must undergo a systematic transformation into structures that align with the diverse needs of stakeholders within financial institutions. This takes us to the next layer: transformation and delivery. This layer serves as the bridge between raw data ingestion and its utilization by end users.

Let's explore this critical layer further in the next chapter.

## CHAPTER 9

Data Transformation and Delivery Layer

By now, you should be familiar with the first two layers of the financial data engineering lifecycle: ingestion and storage. The next layer is the transformation and delivery layer, where two major things happen: first, the data undergoes a range of transformations, from basic preprocessing and cleaning to complex analytical calculations; second, the data is delivered to its end users following pre-established agreements. Keep in mind that all layers can impact one another based on business needs and technical limitations. As a result, the decisions you make in the ingestion and storage layers are likely to have an impact on this layer and vice versa.

Throughout this chapter, you will learn the essential concepts of data transformation and delivery and their applications in the financial domain. This includes data querying patterns, query optimization, transformations, computational requirements, data consumers, and delivery mechanisms.

Data Querying

The most common operation performed in the transformation and delivery layer is data querying. Before making any modifications, data is always queried. The performance of a financial data infrastructure is largely dependent on querying patterns and optimization. Therefore, as a financial data engineer, you will play a vital role in defining and optimizing the querying needs and patterns for your team and data consumers. Let's find out how.

Querying Patterns

A data querying pattern is a repeated request for information made by several data consumers on a regular basis. A pattern can be either detected by analyzing user requests or anticipated during an early design phase. Being able to understand and anticipate querying patterns will provide you with great input for the choice and design of your data storage model as well as optimizing the cost and execution time of your data queries.

There is no fixed catalog for querying patterns; they are primarily determined by business requirements and data consumer needs. However, in this section, I will introduce several common querying patterns that you might encounter in financial applications.

Time series queries

Time series queries are essential in finance, used to retrieve data for a specific financial entity or quantity over a given period of time. Using standard SQL pseudocode, we can express a basic time series query:

```
-- SQL
SELECT time_column, attribute_1, attribute_2
FROM financial_entity_table
WHERE entity_name = 'A'
AND date BETWEEN '2022-01-01' AND '2022-02-01'
```

Financial use cases for time series queries include the following:

- Give me the closing adjusted price for stock A from January 2022 until February 2022.
- Give me all transactions for client A for the past month.
- Give me a company's sales and revenues over the past six months.

Cross-section queries

A cross-section query is used to obtain data for a set of financial entities at a specific point in time. A simplified SQL pseudocode for a cross-section query might look something like this:

```
-- SQL
SELECT entity_name, attribute_1, attribute_2
FROM financial_entity_table
WHERE entity_name in ('A', 'B', 'C', 'D')
AND date = '2022-02-01'
```

Cross-section queries are commonly used to investigate differences between financial entities at a given point in time. Examples include the following:

- Give me the market capitalization of the top five companies listed at the NYSE for February 1, 2022.
- Give me the credit rating of all publicly traded companies in the pharmaceutical sector in the United States on January 10, 2022.

Panel queries

A panel query combines time series and cross-section dimensions. The user asks for data on multiple financial entities for a range of dates. A pseudo-SQL for a panel query may look like this:

```sql
-- SQL
SELECT time_coluumn, entity_name, attribute_1, attribute_2
FROM financial_entity_table
WHERE entity_name in ('A', 'B', 'C', 'D')
AND date BETWEEN '2022-01-01' AND '2022-02-01'
```

Panel queries are mainly used to analyze the intertemporal differences between financial entities—for example the following:

- Give me the online purchasing activities of our top 1,000 clients in the past month.
- Give me the volume of trades for stocks A, B, and C over the past month.

Analytical queries

Analytical queries are advanced statements that perform computations on the data. They are often supported and used in SQL and data warehousing systems as well as specialized databases such as time series and graph databases.

The most common type of analytical query is grouping, in which rows that have the same values are grouped into summary rows using an aggregation function such as sum, min, max, average, standard deviation, and others. For instance, if you want to find the maximum daily price for each unique combination of stock symbols and dates in your database, you would write an SQL query similar to this:

```sql
-- SQL
SELECT stock_symbol, date, MAX(price)
FROM price_table
GROUP BY stock_symbol, date
```

Grouping reduces the number of rows into a set of groups based on your aggregation fields. In some cases, you don't want the number of rows to shrink, but rather want to apply an aggregation query that spans multiple time windows. For example, suppose you want to calculate the simple moving average of the adjusted closing price for each stock in your dataset.[1] In this case, a special type of SQL method, called *window functions*, can be used. Here is how it works:[2]

---

1 A simple moving average is the average of the previous K data points. For example, take the vector [1,2,3,4,5]. The moving average over two data points becomes [1, 1.5, 3, 4.5, 6].

2 Try it yourself on CoderPad (*https://oreil.ly/ZxWWV*).

```
-- SQL
create table adjsted_price (date DATE, symbol VARCHAR(5), price NUMERIC);
insert into adjsted_price (date, symbol, price) values ('2022-02-10', 'A', 1);
insert into adjsted_price (date, symbol, price) values ('2022-02-11', 'A', 2);
insert into adjsted_price (date, symbol, price) values ('2022-02-12', 'A', 3);
insert into adjsted_price (date, symbol, price) values ('2022-02-13', 'A', 4);
insert into adjsted_price (date, symbol, price) values ('2022-02-10', 'B', 10);
insert into adjsted_price (date, symbol, price) values ('2022-02-11', 'B', 20);
insert into adjsted_price (date, symbol, price) values ('2022-02-12', 'B', 30);
insert into adjsted_price (date, symbol, price) values ('2022-02-13', 'B', 40);

SELECT symbol, date, AVG(price)
OVER (PARTITION BY symbol ORDER BY date ASC ROWS BETWEEN 2
PRECEDING AND CURRENT ROW) AS "Moving Average"
FROM adjsted_price
ORDER BY symbol, date ASC
```

A variety of data storage systems implement window and analytical functions. For example, relational DSSs like PostgreSQL implements the SQL standard window functions, while others such as Oracle implement additional functions (*https://oreil.ly/WmwMa*) on top of the standard ones. Specialized databases, such as InfluxDB time series database, offer an impressive collection of time-based analytical functions (*https://oreil.ly/IwwI4*). Similarly, graph databases such as Neo4j offer a wide range of graph-oriented functions (*https://oreil.ly/LoTnA*) that can be executed with the Cypher language, as well as a specialized library called Graph Data Science that offers advanced graph algorithms and visualization features that can be used to solve advanced business problems such as fraud detection.

Recently, cloud data warehouse solutions such BigQuery and Snowflake (*https://oreil.ly/hG3RV*) have introduced features enabling users to create and interact with machine learning models using advanced analytical SQL queries. These capabilities allow users to build various models (e.g., regression, classification, anomaly detection, etc.) and make predictions on new data, all seamlessly integrated within the data warehouse environment. Using BigQuery (*https://oreil.ly/gs-hW*), the syntax for creating a model may look like the following:

```
-- SQL
-- Create a linear regression model
CREATE MODEL `mydataset.my_model`
OPTIONS(MODEL_TYPE='LINEAR_REG') AS
SELECT
  feature_column1,
  feature_column2,
  label
FROM
  `mydataset.my_training_table_data`;
```

When calling the model, the syntax would look like this:

```sql
-- SQL
SELECT *
FROM
  ML.PREDICT(MODEL `mydataset.my_model`, (
    SELECT
      feature_column1,
      feature_column2
    FROM
      `mydataset.my_test_table_data`
  ));
```

Before moving to the next section, an essential thing to keep in mind is that data querying needs can evolve and change over time. It's impractical and costly to switch data storage systems due to query limitations. Therefore, it's essential to consider the broader context, prioritize the needs of the business and data consumers, and develop a strategy to manage both current and future query requirements effectively.

Query Optimization

Once you've identified your querying needs and patterns, the next step is to think about and implement a query optimization strategy. If queries are not optimized, their performance can be significantly impacted. For simplicity, I will define performance in terms of query speed and cost. A query optimization strategy can be approached from two perspectives: the database side and the user side. Let's explore each in detail.

Database-side query optimization

On the database side, there are three main query optimization techniques: indexing, partitioning, and clustering. Indexing is the most common technique. To understand the need for indexing, let's illustrate its main use case. Imagine you have a database that contains price data for 1,000 stocks. You want to run a time series query that fetches data for one stock (stock A). The database engine doesn't know where the data for stock A is physically located on disk. For this reason, the only way to execute the query is to read all data for all stocks and keep stock A's records only. This type of data read is called *full-scan*, as the entire table is scanned. As you can imagine, this is an expensive operation, given the time it takes to do a full scan. Can we do better? Yes, we need to add an index!

An index is an optimized data structure that holds information about the disk location of the data stored in your database. When the right index is added, the database engine will try to use it to look up the location of the data and avoid querying unnecessary records. Now you might wonder, how do I know which index to add? The answer depends on your querying patterns. A rule of thumb is to add an index on the columns that you use in your WHERE clause. For example, let's consider the following query:

```sql
-- SQL
SELECT time_column, attribute_1, attribute_2
FROM financial_entity_table
WHERE entity_name = 'A'
AND date BETWEEN '2022-01-01' AND '2022-02-01'
```

As you can see, the WHERE clause uses two columns: entity_name and date. For this reason, it makes sense to add an index on both columns. In this case, the index is called *composite* as it is created on multiple columns. If your query were to only filter by entity_name, then it's better to create a single-column index instead. Now you might ask, how do I know what type of index I need to add? There are indeed a variety of database indexes. To illustrate with an example, let's take PostgreSQL as a reference as it has a large variety of index types (*https://oreil.ly/-iaLi*).

The standard index implementation in PostgreSQL is *B-tree,* a tree-based data structure that achieves logarithmic complexity.[3] The reason behind the popularity of B-tree indexes is their ability to handle a wide range of query operators: less than (<), less than or equal to (<=), equal to (=), greater than (>), greater than or equal to (>=), and between. Other types of data storage systems, such as MongoDB and Neo4,j use B-tree as their default index implementation. Therefore, unless you have any special query needs, the B-tree is generally a good indexing strategy. Keep in mind, however, that indexes are stored on disk and grow in size as your data does. In addition, indexes get updated as you update, insert, and delete records from the database. For this reason, you must aim to create the least number of indexes when possible.

Other types of indexes are often used for more specific use cases. For example, the *Block Range Index* (BRIN) is a lightweight index that can be used with very large tables, where the indexed columns have a strong correlation with the physical order of data in the table. A typical scenario might involve a large stock price time series dataset where data is organized by date. When performing time series queries involving a wide temporal range (e.g., last month), PostgreSQL can utilize the BRIN index to quickly identify and skip over data blocks that do not contain relevant dates.

In some cases, indexes such as B-tree and BRIN are complemented with *clustering* (*https://oreil.ly/6mLiT*), which involves physically rearranging data based on one or

---

3 Logarithmic speed, denoted as O(ln(n)), is widely regarded as efficient in terms of performance. To illustrate this concept in simple terms, imagine you have a very large table and you're searching for a specific row. Now suppose that you perform your search in multiple iterations, and at each iteration, you divide the table in half and only search one half. This approach dramatically reduces the search space with each iteration. Any algorithm that operates in this manner achieves logarithmic complexity. While structures like B-trees are more complex, they share the same underlying strategy of efficiently narrowing down search areas to quickly find desired data.

more columns, often those used to create an index. This rearrangement is advantageous when your queries frequently access a range of ordered values, such as in time series queries. It's important to remember that clustering is a one-time operation. If the data is updated, re-clustering will be required.

Last but not least, a powerful database optimization technique is *partitioning*. It works by dividing the data into logical and physical partitions/tables using one or more partition keys. Queries filtering by these keys will exclusively scan relevant partitions, minimizing unnecessary data access. A partition key is often chosen to minimize the number of scanned partitions. For example, suppose you have high-frequency stock price data that arrives daily, and assume that most of your queries include a day range filter (e.g., the last three days, first 10 days of last month,...). In this case, it makes sense to partition your table by date to have one partition for each day. This way, even if you have 1,000 partitions, if you query data for one date, then only one partition will be scanned.

Query Planner

You might ask yourself, how do databases figure out the most optimal way to execute a query and choose which index and scanning strategy to perform? This is all done by the so-called query planner/optimizer.

Each database system implements its own query planner, which is responsible for figuring out the most efficient execution plan for each user query. Typically, query planners represent queries as trees, allowing for multiple execution strategies that yield identical results. These trees are typically read from the bottom up, with data being retrieved initially from one or more locations, and then aggregated as you move upwards to produce the final results. The query planner's goal is to select the optimal plan for execution, which may involve substituting the original query with one or more optimized versions to enhance performance. Some databases implement more complex techniques. For example, PostgreSQL's query planner might resort to an advanced optimization technique based on genetic algorithms when planning for complex queries (e.g., when there is a large number of join operations).

Common strategies that query planners often rely on include the following:

Sequential scan
> Scans the entire table. This is used when the table is small or if indexing is not properly done.

Index scan
> Performs an index traversal to find all matching records. The planner might perform an index scan if any index satisfies the WHERE condition.

Index-only scan
> Performed if all queried columns are part of an index, returning tuples directly from index entries.

Parallel scan
> Multiple processes fetch a subset of the requested data simultaneously, thereby speeding up query execution.

Partition pruning
> Used with partitioned database systems (e.g., BigQuery and Snowflake) to minimize the number of partitions to scan.

Block pruning
> Used mostly with clustered tables, and determines which blocks of data to read, thus saving disk access and accelerating query execution.

Many database systems offer a command called EXPLAIN, which provides a detailed breakdown of the execution plan that the query planner generates for a given query statement. To read more about query planners, I recommend having a look at PostgreSQL's Planner/Optimizer (*https://oreil.ly/926mb*), BigQuery's Dremel engine (*https://oreil.ly/rKUpU*), and Redshift's query optimizer (*https://oreil.ly/P-K5v*).

In conclusion, it is essential to remember that database optimization may be a time-consuming and challenging task (yet fun as well!). As such, give it some serious thought and include the business team to ensure that all of their demands are met. Furthermore, be sure to provide a summary of all the technical limitations that may arise along the way, and consider how they can affect future data and querying needs.

User-side query optimization

Database-side optimization is only half the story; the other half concerns optimizing the way users interact with the data. You can have the best indexing, clustering, and partitioning strategy in place, but users need to follow the right querying approach to benefit from such optimizations. There is no unique recipe for telling users how to query the data—it's all based on the querying needs and the database optimization put in place. Let me give you a few illustrative examples.

Scenario 1. If you add a single-column index on column A, try to avoid queries that do not reference column A in their search conditions. While there's no guarantee the query planner will use the index every time, doing so could potentially result in notable performance gains.

Scenario 2. If you add a composite index on columns A, B, and C, then make sure that you filter by the leading (leftmost) columns such as [A], [A, B], or [A, B, C]. Filtering by [B] or [C] or [B, C] will lead to inefficient index scans. I highly recommend that you read more about this topic, and the PostgreSQL documentation page (*https://oreil.ly/yAK5f*) is a good place to start.

Scenario 3. When querying, select only the necessary columns rather than performing `SELECT *`. This is particularly relevant when working with column-oriented databases that store data on disk column-wise. In this case, querying only a small subset of the columns will significantly improve your query speed and reduce inefficient data reads.

Scenario 4. If you use the SQL pattern matching operator `LIKE`, then try to anchor the constant string at the beginning; for example, do `column LIKE 'ABC%'`, but not `column LIKE '%ABC'`. With `ABC%`, an index such as B-tree is very likely to know which records to consider as it knows what they start with, but with `%ABC,` the index doesn't know which strings end with ABC, and it might need to scan the full index. You can read more about this topic in the PostgreSQL documentation (*https://oreil.ly/EAFTa*).

Scenario 5. When processing large amounts of data, try to modularize your queries. For example, say you have a very large stock price time series table and you want to perform a given transformation on the entire table. In this case, consider using an incremental loading and processing approach instead of applying your operation to the entire table in one run. For instance, you can query your data one day or one month at a time and apply the transformations on each batch separately. The main advantage of this approach is that in case of a failure with one batch, you don't need to query the entire dataset again.

Scenario 6. When performing complex queries that involve joins and aggregations, make sure to process a minimal amount of data. For instance, consider a scenario where you need to get monthly transaction amounts for specific customers using two tables: transactions and customers. As illustrated in Figure 9-1, one way to do this is by first joining the transaction and customer tables, then aggregating the results by month and customer, and finally filtering for the desired customers. One issue with this approach is that you might join potentially large tables, which can be a resource- and time-intensive operation. A more efficient strategy would involve delaying the join operation to a later stage and applying filtering up front to reduce the queried dataset size.

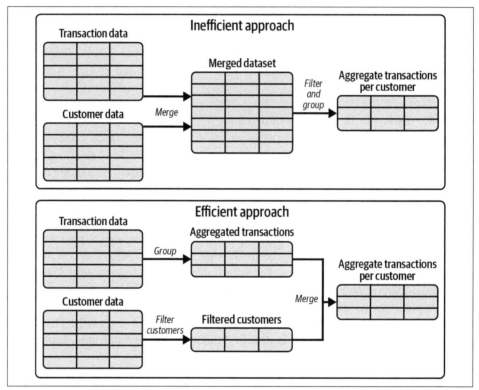

Figure 9-1. An inefficient versus efficient data processing approach

Based on your institution's requirements and the needs of data consumers, you, as a financial data engineer, should be able to anticipate and assess additional scenarios and use cases. I recommend consistently striving to understand and discover ways to improve the efficiency of your queries. Use the EXPLAIN command to analyze the query optimizer plans, try to learn about database internals and optimization strategies, and pick up some advanced SQL knowledge.[4]

Data Transformation

Once you have determined your querying strategy and optimized your database accordingly, the next step is to develop and implement your data transformations. The main purpose of data transformations is to prepare data for various use cases across your organization's departments and teams. In this section, you will learn about the different types of transformation operations and patterns commonly used in finance, along with the computational requirements essential for their implementation.

Transformation Operations

In its most basic form, a data transformation involves converting a raw, unprocessed dataset into a structured format suitable for its intended business application. Importantly, there isn't a universal list of transformations that you need to apply to your data. Therefore, as a financial data engineer, one of your key responsibilities will be to discuss and define the specific transformations to implement based on business requirements and the needs of data consumers.

Avoid applying any transformation directly to the raw data. Instead, store the raw data in an archive location and apply your transformations on a copy of the data.

I'll provide a general overview in the following sections, outlining some of the fundamental transformations typically applied to financial data.

---

4 For a good reference on database internals, I highly recommend Alex Petrov's *Database Internals: A Deep-Dive into How Distributed Data Systems Work* (O'Reilly, 2019).

Format conversion

The first transformation applied to financial data typically involves format conversion. It consists of converting the data from its source format into another format that is easier to work with. For example, you might convert data in CSV format to SQL tables, or convert data in JSON format into a collection in a document database. Once the data is converted into the desired format, subsequent transformations become easier. Figure 9-2 illustrates a common format conversion scenario in the financial industry, where raw data arriving in CSV or XLSX (Excel) formats is transformed into a tabular format within a relational database.

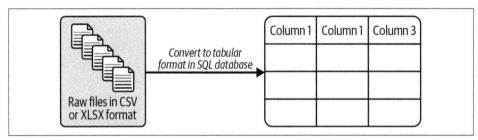

Figure 9-2. An example of format conversion

Data cleaning

Data cleaning involves the detection and correction of data quality issues such as errors, biases, duplicates, invalid formats, outliers, incorrect/corrupt values, missing data, and many others.

Data cleaning is a crucial step in the transformation layer, and it should be handled carefully. First of all, you need to make sure that all data quality issues are properly identified and understood. This assessment can vary based on your business problem; therefore, it needs to be discussed with the business team and the data consumers.[5] Once an agreement has been reached, quality checks and corrective measures need to be put in place. The nature of these remedial measures is often dependent on the severity of the data quality issue. For example, in the context of fraud detection, a data outlier might signal potentially suspicious activity that should be investigated further. But if we take intraday high-frequency price data, you could easily find outliers, but they often don't have a significant impact.

---

5 Some authors suggested adopting a data consumer-centric approach to data quality definition and management. To learn more about this topic, I highly recommend Richard Y. Wang and Diane M. Strong's "Beyond Accuracy: What Data Quality Means to Data Consumers" (*https://oreil.ly/iYXyQ*), *Journal of Management Information Systems* 12, no. 4 (1996): 5–33.

Deciding When to Clean Financial Data

Determining when and which data to clean within your financial data infrastructure is a critical aspect of data integrity. While it may seem intuitive to perform cleaning as early as possible, this approach requires careful consideration. Often, the rationale for cleaning early is that downstream systems may struggle to identify data issues originating from upstream sources, especially if they lack the necessary contextual information to diagnose the problem.

Consider high-frequency market data as an example. While academic research often highlights the importance of data cleaning and anomaly detection for such data, advances in modern data infrastructure are reducing this need. Electronic trading has greatly reduced data anomalies, and data feed providers receive quick feedback from clients—particularly trading firms that promptly test new feeds, protocols, and connections. This immediate feedback allows for quick fixes, meaning that data feeds may not always need cleaning.

However, there are exceptions. For example, if you're working with data from a redistributor that modifies the raw data, cleaning becomes essential. This is also the case for OTC markets or those with outdated systems. Additionally, data that requires manual entry or scraping (e.g., SEC filings) should be cleaned to ensure accuracy.

When data cleaning is applied only to historical data, but real-time data feeds are processed differently, discrepancies may occur, potentially undermining the reliability of your application and analysis. This issue arises because the cleaned historical data might not align with real-time data due to variations in the treatment of anomalies or errors.

Seen from a different angle, it's even more effective to delegate the identification and handling of "anomalies" to downstream consumers, such as trading units. In many cases, these anomalies represent real market behavior that convey useful information. Moreover, data errors and outliers may serve as input to incorporate within your trading strategies to adapt them to handle issues like market disruptions and trading interruption events (e.g., gateway failures and failovers, trading and regulatory halts, position limit breaches, sequence gaps, circuit breakers, and order book failures).[6]

---

6 For more on this topic, check the excellent article by Lou Lindley, "Working with High-Frequency Market Data: Data Integrity and Cleaning (Part 1)" (*https://oreil.ly/lcNBQ*).

Generally, there are three types of actions used to clean financial data:

Deletion

Low-quality records are deleted from the dataset. Examples include erroneous quotes, invalid prices, duplicate transactions, etc. When performing deletion, make sure to consider its impact on the analytical integrity and consistency of the data.

Correction

Low-quality records are replaced with their correct values. For example, a negative price is replaced with a positive one. Corrections need to be based on well-thought-out assumptions about the data (e.g., a price cannot be negative). In some instances, corrections may require notifying the entity that submitted incorrect data to resubmit it in the proper format (e.g., reporting financial data that doesn't conform to a financial messaging standard).

Enrichment

New fields are added to assist in detecting or mitigating the impact of low-quality records. This approach is useful when errors are difficult to detect, allowing the final data consumer to decide how to handle them. For example, if outlier detection is complex, a statistical model can generate an outlier probability for each record, which is then stored in a new column.

When performing data cleaning, it is important to keep in mind the two data governance principles of lineage and ownership (which we discussed in Chapter 5). Data lineage eliminates the possibility of data cleaning becoming a mystery box by guaranteeing visibility of the cleaning steps, decisions, and rules. Similarly, data ownership ensures that only the data owners have the authority to determine and implement data cleaning procedures, which makes assigning accountability for the data quality process more straightforward.

Data adjustments

Data adjustments are transformations applied to the data to account for specific data characteristics, events, and rules, or to produce more informative or analytically desired features.

In finance, the most frequently applied adjustment concerns corporate actions (*https://oreil.ly/gahJJ*). Such actions refer to important decisions made by companies that can significantly impact their stock value. The two most common types of corporate actions are *stock splits* and *dividend distributions*. A stock split involves the issuance of several new stocks for each existing stock to increase liquidity and make it more affordable for investors to buy the company's shares. For example, a 1:2 split means that each stock will be split in two, so if an investor holds 10 stocks, after the split they will end up with 20 stocks. A stock split does not change the total market capitalization of the company, but it impacts the stock price. To adjust for a split, the price of the stock needs to be divided by the split ratio. For example, if the price of a stock is $400 and a stock split of 1:2 takes place, the new stock price is $200.

Similarly, a dividend distribution event happens when a company decides to distribute part of its earnings to its shareholders. In such a case, the stock price needs to be adjusted to take into account the paid dividends. The standard approach to dividend adjustment consists of subtracting the dividend amount per share from the stock price. For example, if a company announces a dividend distribution equal to $1 per share, and the stock price is $11, the dividend-adjusted price will be 11 − 1 = $10.

When working with stock price data, pay particular attention to corporate action adjustments. First, determine whether the data source you are using incorporates these adjustments. Second, if the data is unadjusted, ensure this is clearly communicated and documented, and consider sourcing corporate action data separately. Some data sources, such as CRSP US Stock Databases (*https://oreil.ly/mCntU*), provide both stock price data and corporate actions information. There are also specialized sources for corporate actions, such as S&P's Managed Corporate Actions (*https://oreil.ly/Z8j7m*), LSEG's Equity Corporate Actions (*https://oreil.ly/i8w1K*), and NYSE's Corporate Actions (*https://oreil.ly/DmIzY*), among many others.

Another common technique is calendar adjustment (*https://oreil.ly/ugLmQ*), which modifies a financial time series to remove calendar effects. For instance, the number of working days in a month can vary each year due to holidays, making it difficult to compare total production across months. One solution is to adjust the dataset by calculating the monthly average or considering daily figures.

Data standardization

Data standardization is a critical transformation step that seeks to store and format data according to a predefined set of conventions and standards. Examples of standardizations applied to financial data include the following:

- Date and time are formatted using the ISO 8601—Date and Time Format standard (*https://oreil.ly/hYbHP*), which follows the YYYY-MM-DD convention.
- Country names are represented following the ISO 3166—Country Codes standard (*https://oreil.ly/K-_mq*) (e.g., US for the United States of America).
- Currencies are represented using the ISO 4217—Currency Codes standard (*https://oreil.ly/J4mas*) (e.g., USD for US dollars).
- Table and column names are lowercase, and spaces are replaced with an underscore (e.g., first_name).
- Monetary values are standardized (*https://oreil.ly/7ovwS*) to use one numerical format (e.g., EUR 10 million, EUR 10,000,000, or EUR 10000000).

- Monetary values are rounded off to a specified level of precision to ensure consistency and comparability across financial records.
- Standardized identifiers are used for financial instruments, such as ISIN or FIGI.

These standardizations help maintain data quality, facilitate data integration, and ensure compatibility across different financial systems and applications.

How Simple Is It to Round Financial Data?

Rounding is one of the most common transformations applied to financial data. Interestingly, despite its apparent simplicity, rounding might actually require careful consideration. First of all, a large variety of rounding algorithms exist (*https://oreil.ly/ kmwpb*), each tailored to a specific use case. Certain methods, such as *Bankers' Rounding*, are quite common in finance. This method aims to evenly distribute rounding errors, thereby reducing potential bias in the data. For example, 2.5 would be rounded to 2, while 3.5 would be rounded to 4.

Furthermore, deciding on the rounding precision might depend on the specific financial variable and accepted market practices. For example, a common practice is to set the rounding precision in line with the *Minimum Price Increment* (MPI), also called minimum tick size. This represents the smallest possible price change in a financial instrument's price. MPIs vary depending on the asset class, market regulations, and the specific trading venue. For example, in the United States, the MPI is typically $0.01 for stocks priced above $1, while for stocks priced below $1, it can be $0.0001. In Forex markets, the term *Point in Percentage* (PIP) is used to denote the smallest amount by which the quote can change. A typical PIP is equal to one basis point, or 0.0001, but it can vary among trading venues and Forex brokers depending on the currency pair and the lot size traded. Following this logic, you might decide to set the rounding precision equal to the MPI; for example, an MPI of 0.0001 means a decimal precision of 4.

In addition, rounding might depend on whether you want to round the decimal places or significant figures. To illustrate, let's consider a currency pair in which one currency has a much higher value than the other, say 0.00247839. It is possible to round this number to five decimal places, in which case it becomes 0.00248. But if we want to round to five significant figures, we would get 0.0024784.

To further explore this topic, I highly recommend the book by Brian Buzzelli, *Data Quality Engineering in Financial Services* (O'Reilly, 2022).

In today's financial markets, a key data engineering challenge is harmonizing and standardizing the diverse data formats, structures, and types from various sources. Whether it's market data, transactions, or external feeds, achieving consistency and interoperability is essential for accurate analysis and AI-driven insights. To give a recent example of how markets are approaching this problem, J.P. Morgan's Fusion, a cloud-native data platform for institutional investors, launched data containers in May 2024. These containers use a common semantic layer to model and normalize data across multiple providers, sources, and formats—giving investors a consistent, integrated view of their data.

Data filtering

Data filtering is an analytical transformation step whereby a financial dataset is examined to exclude or rearrange its records according to predefined criteria. In other words, data filtering applies a filter to a dataset, transforming it into a new dataset based on the filter criteria.

A wide range of data filters are used in finance. Here are a few examples:

Company filter
   This consists of excluding companies from a financial dataset that don't satisfy certain conditions. For instance, an article written by Priyank Gandhi and Hanno Lustig (*https://oreil.ly/88XFm*) details a study using the CRSP dataset, excluding inactive firms (legal entities without business activities) and firms incorporated outside the US to ensure a uniform regulatory regime.

Calendar filter
   This filter is used to align accounting standards across firms in a dataset. For example, in an article written by Laura Xiaolei Liu and Lu Zhang (*https://oreil.ly/nKxIK*), they excluded firms that do not have a December fiscal year-end.

Liquidity filter
   This filter is used to ensure that the securities included in a data sample have at least a certain number of active trading days during a specific time interval. In one research paper (*https://oreil.ly/F-qjO*), the authors applied a filter to exclude stocks with less than two hundred days of active trading in a year to have a sample with enough data for computing liquidity measures. Similarly, when working with option data, it is common to filter out options whose expiration falls outside a given interval (e.g., between 10 and 400 days) as such options might behave erratically near expiry due to liquidity features (the article "The Puzzle of Index Option Returns" (*https://oreil.ly/6AJQX*) provides a good example).

Size filter
   This filter excludes firms whose market capitalization is below or above a certain value, for example, when studying a specific segment of the market. In one study (*https://oreil.ly/HNhEA*), the authors excluded microcap stocks, defined at the fifth percentile of market capitalization within each country. This was done because minicap stocks often suffer from stale prices and volumes due to market

illiquidity as well as their negligible economic significance (<0.04%) on the over-all market value.

Coverage filter

This filter excludes firms that do not have enough observations in the dataset. This is often done to reduce the impact of noise generated by such observations. For example, the authors of a study on factors that drive global stock returns (*https://oreil.ly/nmn_S*) applied a similar filter by requiring a stock to have at least 12 monthly observations within the sample period to be considered for inclusion in the study.

Sector filter

This involves including entities belonging to a particular sector, market segment, industry, or subindustry. This filter is applied because certain sectors can be subject to special regulation or have different asset and investment structures. For example, in their seminal work, *The Cross-Section of Expected Stock Returns* (Wiley), Fama and French conducted their analysis by excluding financial firms, as high leverage for these firms does not indicate the same thing for nonfinancial firms, i.e., distress.

When applying data filters, it's essential to understand their purpose and the potential impact on data quality and integrity. Improper filtering can introduce biases, such as nonrepresentative sample bias or imbalanced datasets. As a financial data engineer, you should discuss these considerations with the end users of the data. Additionally, ensure that filters are applied correctly and do not modify or delete the original data. If a filtered dataset is needed, create a new table for it.

Feature engineering

Feature engineering is an advanced analytical transformation step used to extract new features from raw data to support statistical and machine learning modeling. Feature engineering is often necessary when existing features do not adequately represent the problem at hand. A feature is a variable or measurable quantity used as input in various modeling tasks. It can be numeric, categorical, binary, or text based. In database terms, a feature can be thought of as a new column in a given table. It is a well-known empirical fact that the performance of machine learning systems is heavily dependent on the feature representation of the input data (*https://oreil.ly/mggoX*).

The practice of feature engineering is quite flexible; data analysts and machine learning experts have the freedom to experiment with and derive novel features from a given dataset to represent different aspects of the data that are relevant to the situation at hand.

Feature engineering can be data driven (e.g., based on statistical correlations or patterns in the data) or domain driven (e.g., based on a financial theory). Moreover, feature engineering requirements may vary based on the type of data being analyzed. For example, there is feature engineering for text data, visual data, time series data, graph data, and stream data. A full account of these techniques is beyond the scope of this book, and for this, I recommend the excellent reference *Feature Engineering for Machine Learning and Data Analytics*, edited by Guozhu Dong and Huan Liu (CRC Press, 2018). Nevertheless, to give it a minimal treatment, let's go through some examples of feature engineering.

The most general techniques for feature engineering include the following:

Normalization
Rescaling the data to fit within a predefined range, e.g., [0–1]. This is often done to prevent some features from having a dominant impact during model training.

Scaling
Rescaling the data to have a similar scale, such as a standard deviation of 1, to ensure a model considers all features equally. Common scaling techniques include *min-max scaling* and *standard scaling*.

Encoding
Transforming a feature from categorical to numerical representation; e.g., female is 1 and male is 2. Common encoding techniques include *one-hot encoding* and *label encoding*.

Dimensionality reduction
Transforming a set of features from a high-dimensional space into a lower-dimensional one. Examples include *principal component analysis* and *t-SNE*.

Embedding
A technique used to create numerical representations of complex real-world objects that machine learning systems can use in model training. As an illustrative example, an embedding might take an image, audio, text, or a graph and convert it into multidimensional numerical representations known as vectors. Using vectors, machine learning systems can efficiently process input data and identify similarities among different data items (e.g., two similar images). A special type of database, called a vector database (*https://oreil.ly/cu6ry*), has been developed to allow ML-driven applications to store and retrieve vector datasets.

In finance, a wide range of domain-specific feature engineering techniques are often applied. For example, when conducting financial time series analysis, it is common to perform steps such as *de-trending* and *de-seasonalization*.[7] De-trending is the process of removing a trend cycle from the data. A trend cycle refers to a consistent increase

---

7 For a practical guide to this topic, I recommend reading Jason Brownlee's articles on the de-trending (*https://oreil.ly/lukxN*) and de-seasonalization (*https://oreil.ly/wRdcv*) of time series.

or decrease of a financial time series over time. On the other hand, de-seasonalization removes seasonal patterns from the time series. A seasonal pattern refers to a specific event in the time series that occurs with a fixed and known frequency such as daily, weekly, every January, etc.[8] By applying de-trending and de-seasonalization, new features are created.

Another widely used technique in finance is stationary differentiation. This involves calculating the difference between each consecutive pair of observations over time (i.e., $x_t - x_{t-1}, x_{t-1} - x_{t-2}, \ldots .$). It is commonly used to transform a non-stationary financial time series into a stationary one. In simple words, a stationary time series is a series whose statistical properties do not change over time. Stationarity is a desired property, as it makes it simpler to perform data analysis using classical statistical methods (e.g., inferential statistics). Converting a price time series to a return series is one such application of differentiation that financial analysts often perform. This is done by taking the percentage difference between two consecutive prices (i.e., $(x_t - x_{t-1})/x_{t-1}$).[9]

In addition, a popular feature engineering technique applied by financial analysts is log transformation, where each value x is replaced with log(x). Expressing data on a logarithmic scale can be helpful for analytical purposes. For example, if a price time series is expressed in a log scale, the difference between two log prices approximates the percentage change (i.e., $log(p_t) - log(p_{t-1}) \sim (p_t - p_{t-1})/p_{t-1}$). Furthermore, the log transformation is frequently used to transform skewed financial data to conform to normality, which is a desired feature in financial analysis.[10]

Finally, an advanced form of feature engineering in finance is the creation of factors. In financial investment literature, "factors" refer to common asset characteristics that explain variations in returns and risks across stocks, bonds, and other assets. They can explain why certain assets go up or down at the same time and why certain assets may yield higher returns compared to others.

There are two main types of factors: macroeconomic factors and style factors. Macroeconomic factors capture risks that affect broad segments of the financial markets and impact multiple asset classes simultaneously. Examples include interest rate (the impact of interest rate changes), inflation (the effect of price level changes), and

---

8 In financial data, several seasonal behaviors have been observed. For example, the January Effect (*https://oreil.ly/q7YdE*) refers to a seasonal pattern where prices of stocks tend to increase during the month of January of each year.

9 To read more about this topic, I recommend John Y. Campbell, Andrew W. Lo, and A. Craig MacKinlay's *The Econometrics of Financial Markets*, vol. 2. (Princeton University Press, 1997).

10 For more on this topic, see William M. Cready and Ramachandran Ramanan's "The Power of Tests Employing Log-Transformed Volume in Detecting Abnormal Trading" (*https://oreil.ly/vMZpt*), *Journal of Accounting and Economics* 14, no. 2 (June 1991): 203–214.

economic growth (variations in the business cycle). Style factors, on the other hand, explain returns and risks within individual assets or asset classes. Examples include value (assets undervalued relative to their fundamentals), momentum (assets with upward price trends), low volatility (assets with a lower risk profile), quality (assets of financially robust companies), and growth (assets or companies with strong earnings growth potential). These factors are engineered features derived from fundamental or market data to enhance portfolio returns and manage risk.[11]

Advanced analytical computations

An advanced type of data transformation may involve the computation of one or more quantities based on an algorithm or a model. Generally speaking, financial data engineers seldom perform scientific modeling or develop machine learning algorithms. However, with the rise of data products, data platforms, and analytics engineering, there are contexts where financial data engineers, particularly those with interdisciplinary backgrounds, might become involved in the modeling process.

Examples of financial applications that require advanced computations include the following:

- Algorithmic trading
- Financial recommender systems (e.g., robo advisors)
- Fraud detection
- Anti-money laundering
- Named entity recognition
- Entity resolution
- Optical character recognition (e.g., recognizing the digits on a credit card image)

To develop such systems, financial data engineers may need to handle tasks such as data collection, cleaning, quality assurance, and control checks. They are also responsible for selecting suitable DSMs and DSSs tailored to each application's requirements. Furthermore, financial data engineers may be involved in building machine learning pipelines, deploying them in production, and collecting metrics and model artifacts.

---

11 Factors are often employed in an investment strategy called factor investing. To learn more about this, I recommend David Blitz and Milan Vidojevic's "The Characteristics of Factor Investing" (*https://oreil.ly/ajjX-*), *Journal of Portfolio Management* 45, no. 3 (2019): 69–86.

Transformation Patterns

The next stage after defining your transformation operations is to design and implement your transformation patterns. A transformation pattern defines how a given data infrastructure handles and performs transformations. To illustrate the concept, let's have a look at a few examples.

Batch versus streaming transformations

In batch transformation, data is divided into discrete chunks (batches) that undergo separate processing. A data chunk can be defined in various ways. For instance, if data is received in file formats like CSV or JSON, each file can be treated as a chunk and processed individually. Alternatively, if the files can be grouped based on specific criteria (e.g., by date), a chunk might encompass all files belonging to a particular group (e.g., all files for a given day). Batch file transformation is a common practice in finance, especially when data is delivered through files. Examples include financial data vendors, which distribute their data in daily, weekly, and monthly file batches, and financial reporting, which is often done via files submitted to the regulator's data infrastructure.

Batch transformations are often used with scheduled data arrival processes, which we discussed in Chapter 7. In this case, the batch transformation is scheduled to run on a predefined interval (e.g., hourly, daily, weekly). Alternatively, a batch can be transformed once it is complete. For instance, a file batch with a maximum size of 10 will be transformed when it contains 10 files.

When data needs to be transformed as soon as it arrives, and not wait for a batch to complete, then a *streaming transformation* is used. In this case, there is no fixed schedule for data transformation; it runs continuously and processes data immediately upon its arrival. Streaming transformations are most commonly used with event-driven arrival processes, which were also covered in Chapter 7. This is the case, for example, with real-time financial applications such as payments, fraud detection, price feeds, and news. In these applications, the system needs to respond with minimum latency and, therefore, cannot wait for a batch to complete.

Streaming transformations are often performed on independent data. For instance, in a scenario where a bank allows clients to submit loan applications online, each application can be processed immediately upon submission, without the need to wait for other applications to form a batch.

In certain scenarios, data arrival may occur in real time or be event driven, yet streaming transformation may not be necessary. For instance, when bank clients fill out a questionnaire to evaluate their financial literacy, the data does not require immediate processing. Instead, it can be processed in batches at regular intervals or as soon as a batch is complete. Using batch transformation to process real-time or event-driven data is a common practice employed to handle massive volumes of data or reduce the costs of continuous monitoring for new data arrivals.

Figure 9-3 illustrates how batch and streaming transformations work. In batch transformation (top), data files arrive and get ingested into a data lake. Subsequently, files are grouped in separate batches based on date. After that, each batch is transformed separately in the transformation layer. Once transformed, the data is stored in a given target location, such as a warehouse. In the streaming transformation case (bottom), data arrives in JSON format. Each JSON gets immediately ingested into a message broker. Subsequently, each message is processed as soon as possible in the transformation layer and stored in the final data warehouse.

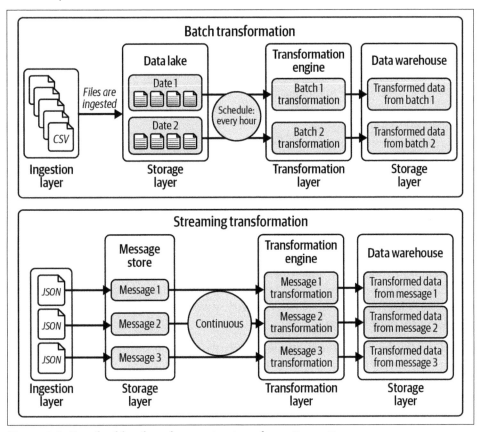

Figure 9-3. Standard batch and streaming transformation patterns

Memory-based versus disk-based transformations

A given data transformation, whether batch or streaming, can be processed either completely in memory or involving intermediary disk persistence steps. The best way to show the difference is with an illustrative example, as shown in Figure 9-4. A basic disk-based transformation is illustrated in the figure's upper part. In this setting, files are first ingested into a data lake. Subsequently, the transformation layer applies two transformation iterations on the files (e.g., cleaning + feature engineering) and saves the final results in a data warehouse. Note, however, that between the two iterations, the transformation layer had to store intermediary results back to the data lake and read it again for the second iteration. In the lower part of the figure, a memory-based transformation does the same thing, but instead of saving intermediary results to the data lake, it keeps it in memory and passes it as such to the next interaction.

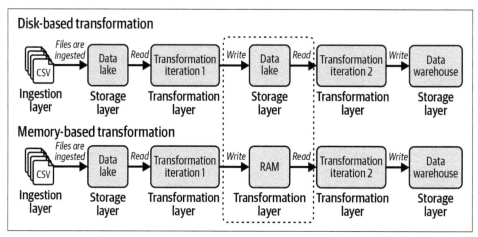

Figure 9-4. Disk-based versus memory-based data transformations

You might be wondering by now why this is necessary. The answer lies in the significant difference in data access speed between RAM and disk (random disk access, to be precise). This is the reason why in-memory software solutions for data storage and processing are quite popular.[12]

Many financial applications rely on memory-based data transformations, especially in time-critical scenarios like trading and fraud detection. For instance, in high-frequency and algorithmic trading, real-time data from feeds is processed directly in memory for immediate action. If data were to be stored on disk first, then the speed advantage would be lost.

---

12 For an insightful overview of financial markets, I recommend reading Nikita Ivanov, "In-Memory Computing Can Digitally Transform Financial Services and FinTech Applications for Capital Markets" (*https://oreil.ly/fyFqV*), *Forbes*, January 5, 2021.

Disk-based access modes don't all operate slowly. When compared to RAM access, random disk access—where data is retrieved at random locations on disk—is especially sluggish. Sequential disk access, on the other hand, is very quick since data records are retrieved in a predetermined order. Sequential disk access is leveraged by technologies like Apache Kafka (*https://oreil.ly/EnkF1*) in order to achieve high-performance data read/write operations.

Apache Spark: An In-Memory Computing Framework

When discussing data computing frameworks, it is difficult to avoid mentioning *Apache Spark,* a unified framework for large-scale data analytics. A bit of history is important to help understand the emergence of Spark. Early efforts at processing large data volumes led to the development of *Apache Hadoop*, a rich ecosystem of open source tools designed for managing multinode clusters and processing massive datasets. Hadoop's ecosystem incorporates two key components: the Hadoop Distributed File System (which we discussed in Chapter 8) for distributed storage with high-throughput access to data, and MapReduce for large-scale parallel data processing. Crucially, MapReduce's internal design processes data on disk, which was a major downside in terms of performance. In response, Apache Spark emerged as the next evolution in the Hadoop ecosystem. Compared to Hadoop MapReduce, Spark has demonstrated significant performance improvements (*https://oreil.ly/5tbsw*).

One of Spark's primary advantages is its native ability to perform computations in memory. While Spark can handle computations on disk when data exceeds memory capacity, data engineers typically configure sufficiently large Spark clusters to enable in-memory processing. Spark's core memory data abstraction is known as the *Resilient Distributed Dataset* (RDD), which is immutable and can be distributed across nodes within a Spark cluster.

Spark is a rich framework that combines Spark Core (execution engine), Spark SQL (for structured data querying and processing), Spark Streaming (for streaming processing), the Spark machine learning library, MLib (for building machine learning models), and GraphX (for graph data processing).

Furthermore, Spark seamlessly integrates with several programming languages such as Scala, Java, Python, and R, allowing developers to write Spark programs in any of these languages. Among data engineers, the Python API known as PySpark is particularly popular and widely used.

Spark can be deployed on premises and on the cloud (e.g., using a cluster of Amazon EC2 instances). Managed cloud solutions such as Amazon EMR allow users to configure a Spark cluster without the need to deal with cluster and node configurations. Additionally, some cloud-based AI and analytics frameworks are powered by Apache Spark, for example, Databricks and Azure Synapse Analytics.

Apache Spark has multiple applications in finance. For example, it can be used to perform fast data transformations that involve massive financial datasets, such as high-frequency trades and quotes. Fraud detection is another use. For an illustrative architecture design, consider starting with a Spark ML model, such as logistic regression, designed for fraud detection. Data begins by entering an event stream through a message broker like Kafka, continues to Spark Streaming for real-time processing, and finally undergoes fraud verification using the deployed Spark ML model.[13]

Another scenario that requires deciding between in-memory and disk-based transformations involves choosing whether to perform transformations dynamically in memory or precomputing and storing them in a database beforehand. This can be the case, for example, when performing feature engineering. Doing feature engineering dynamically in memory can be advantageous for large and changing datasets, enabling real-time processing without the overhead of storing and managing precomputed features. This approach allows flexibility in adapting to changing data requirements and quality, but it may require substantial computational resources (e.g., RAM) and execution time. On the other hand, precomputing and persisting features in a DSS can enhance performance by reducing computation time and memory consumption during model training and inference, which is optimal in scenarios involving expensive queries and complex feature engineering steps. Furthermore, this approach ensures consistency and reproducibility of features across different stages of model development and deployment. Therefore, the choice should be guided by balancing computational efficiency, reproducibility, traceability, data freshness, and scalability needs.

Full versus incremental data transformations

In a full data transformation pattern, the entire dataset (or its complete history) is transformed in one go, regardless of whether parts of it have been modified. This approach is typically used with small datasets that don't change frequently. Its main advantages are simplicity (no need for sophisticated logic to process parts of the data), consistency (the entire dataset is processed uniformly), and simpler error handling (if an error occurs during transformation, it's easy to detect since the entire operation will fail). This approach has drawbacks such as being resource intensive (especially with large datasets), limited scalability (if the dataset becomes large, processing it as a whole can become impractical or time-consuming), and potential latency issues (which may affect time-critical applications).

---

13 For more on this topic, I recommend reading A. Madhavi and T. Sivaramireddy's "Real-Time Credit Card Fraud Detection Using Spark Framework" (*https://oreil.ly/p6kJ7*), in *Machine Learning Technologies and Applications: Proceedings of ICACECS 2020* (Springer, 2021): 287–298.

Alternatively, incremental data transformation involves transforming only new or updated data, rather than the entire dataset. This approach is commonly used with large datasets or applications that continuously generate and update data. Its main advantages include resource efficiency, scalability, low latency, and reduced costs. Note, however, that incremental data transformation may introduce additional complexity, as it requires implementing a change detection mechanism (e.g., Change Data Capture), data ingestion logic to handle only new or updated records, and data processing logic capable of inserting or updating records without overwriting existing ones.

Change Data Capture

Change Data Capture (CDC) (*https://oreil.ly/CZowR*) is an essential concept in data engineering. It refers to the capability of a data infrastructure to detect changes—such as inserts, updates, or deletes—in an upstream data source and propagate them across downstream systems that consume the data. A common scenario is the propagation of changes from an operational database to an analytical system such as a warehouse or a data lake. CDC is extensively used to ensure data consistency and integrity across various systems, support up-to-date real-time analytics, and help organizations migrate from on-premises to the cloud.

A CDC mechanism can operate in either a push or pull manner. In a push-based CDC, the source data storage system sends data changes to downstream applications. In a pull-based CDC, downstream applications regularly poll the source data storage system to retrieve data changes.

Several methods exist for implementing CDC. A straightforward approach involves adding a timestamp column that records the time of the latest changes. Downstream systems can then capture updates by querying data with timestamps greater than the last extracted timestamp. The main disadvantage of this method is that it may not effectively capture deletes.

Another common method relies on database triggers. A trigger is a stored procedure in a database that executes a specific function when certain events, such as inserts, updates, or deletes, occur. Triggers can propagate changes immediately but may add additional load to the source database. Some data storage solutions, such as MongoDB (*https://oreil.ly/CFEIY*), implement a separate trigger layer that scales independently of the database server.

Finally, a highly reliable CDC approach involves using database logs. To ensure durability and consistency, many database systems log all changes into a transaction log before persisting them to the database. Logs are quite reliable as they capture all changes made to the data, along with metadata about who made the changes and when. The main challenge with this approach is the potential complexity of setting it up and maintaining it.

Computational Requirements

When designing the transformation layer, you must assess and plan your computational requirements. The main factors to consider are computing environments and performance.

Computational performance

Having a framework that outlines performance requirements and optimization strategies is essential for a reliable transformation layer. This framework should include features such as computational speed, throughput, efficiency, and scalability.

Computational speed.   Speed is a critical requirement for financial data transformations. It is typically measured by the time difference between the start and end time of a data transformation execution. A related and more specific concept is *latency*, which denotes the time it takes for a signal or message to travel over a network to its destination and receive a response back from it. Common latency metrics include the *average latency*, which is the mean time it takes for two systems to exchange messages, and *latency jitter*, which is the variation in latencies around the average value.

Throughout the rest of this section, I will use the term computational speed to describe the difference between the expected and the actual processing time of a given data transformation. This presupposes that you, as a financial engineer, should discuss and determine the ideal execution time for the many financial data transformations and keep an eye on your infrastructure to make sure it performs up to par. This can be linked to the data timeliness dimension that you learned about in Chapter 5.

In general, the higher the computational speed you aim for, the more technically challenging it becomes. It is simpler to reduce computation time from hours to minutes than from seconds to microseconds. For this reason, treat it as an economic problem by estimating the marginal gain from every unit of improvement in computational speed. Certain types of financial data transformations (e.g., monthly price extractions) may not require significant computational speed.

To guarantee fast data transformations, a common practice involves the definition of a Service-Level Agreement (SLA) that outlines the average duration of data transformations (e.g., five seconds) or the time by which a specific data transformation should have been finished (every Friday at 10 a.m.).

The Cost of Speed in Financial Markets

Speed in financial markets comes with its own set of risks. For instance, the drive toward instant payment and settlement processes increases exposure to fraud risks, as the system has limited time to analyze, detect, and prevent fraudulent activities and ensure compliance. Moreover, this can expose participants to liquidity, market, and credit risks. For example, during settlement, financial institutions must ensure they have sufficient liquidity to handle instant payments, particularly during peak times. Instant payments also expose market participants to credit risk if counterparties fail to settle transactions promptly.

High-frequency trading is another area where speed is key, with rapid data access and quick decision-making being critical elements. However, relying on real-time market data for fast trading might, in some cases, be risky because the data may contain errors or noise, leaving the trading system with limited time to properly assess the quality of the data.

Furthermore, fast trading systems like high-frequency and algorithmic trading can amplify market volatility, particularly during periods of stress. In addition, the pursuit of speed has contributed to events like flash crashes, where market prices drop sharply and recover within minutes. The reliance on sophisticated algorithms and high-speed trading infrastructure increases the risk of technical failures, such as software bugs, hardware malfunctions, or connectivity issues.

Fast order execution in trading poses challenges for regulatory compliance as well. For instance, rapid order cancellations or modifications by high-frequency traders can strain market surveillance systems responsible for upholding fair market practices and preventing market manipulation.

These examples highlight the distinctive characteristics of data engineering in finance compared to other industries. While speed may not pose major risks in certain sectors, in finance, rapid transactions and decisions can introduce substantial risks that must be carefully considered when designing financial data infrastructures.

Once an SLA is defined, the next step would be to compare the actual data transformation time against the SLA specification. Should the SLA be violated, you, as a financial data engineer, need to understand the main causes and propose potential solutions. Factors that might impact data transformation execution time include the following:

- Low-quality data that requires more steps to clean
- Poor querying patterns that take more time than necessary
- Dispersed data that requires multiple queries to collect
- A wrong data storage model (e.g., using a data lake instead of a data warehouse for structured data)
- Large batch jobs
- Limitations on the database side (e.g., max concurrent connections)
- Poor database design (e.g., missing or bad indexes)
- Too much complexity in the transformation logic
- Insufficient compute resources (e.g., low RAM or CPU)
- Shared resources that need to respond to requests coming from a variety of applications
- Bad queuing strategy (e.g., jobs are not ordered and executed in the right priority, big or time-consuming batch jobs run before small interactive requests, lack of asynchronous or parallel execution capabilities)
- Wrong transformation patterns (e.g., executing data transformations with synchronous blocking can slow down performance compared to asynchronous event-driven or streaming solutions; more on this in Chapter 11)
- Network issues
- Too many processing layers
- Inefficient data distribution among data centers (data is far from the processing engine)

Ideally, you should anticipate and test for such issues in advance. As discussed in Chapter 8, changing your data storage system is a costly operation that should be avoided. Similarly, once your data transformation layer is defined and implemented, you don't want to migrate or alter it.

Throughput. In data-intensive applications, an important performance measure is throughput. This refers to the amount of data that a system can process in a given time interval. Applications designed for high throughput emphasize the total amount of work that can be done in a given period of time. This is often measured using metrics such as bits per second (bit/s or bps), megabytes per second, or records per second.

In today's financial markets, especially trading systems, high throughput is essential due to the continuous influx of a massive number of orders that require immediate processing.[14] From an engineering perspective, it's crucial to define the desired level of throughput clearly. Simply aiming for "high throughput" is not specific enough. As such, it's essential to define a target throughput level through discussions with your business team and stakeholders.

The level of throughput may depend on a variety of factors, including the characteristics of the physical and networking infrastructure, the size and type of the data being processed in each request, and the type of operation being performed. For instance, when optimizing database read/write throughput, it is important to keep in mind that reading and writing have different internal mechanisms.[15]

Computational efficiency. The term computational efficiency is used to describe how well data transformations make use of available resources. An efficient data transformation minimizes resource consumption, which is increasingly important given the current emphasis on the environmental impact of data computations, such as carbon footprint.

The term *algorithmic efficiency* is often used in this context to measure the computational resources that an algorithm uses. Generally speaking, the more time and space an algorithm consumes, the less efficient it is. Interestingly, in 2020, a group of researchers from MIT's Computer Science and Artificial Intelligence Laboratory (CSAIL) presented evidence showing that data-intensive tasks benefit more from algorithmic efficiency than hardware improvement (*https://oreil.ly/xiNDo*).

---

14 For more context regarding this issue, I recommend the paper by John W. Lockwood, Adwait Gupte, Nishit Mehta, Michaela Blott, Tom English, and Kees Vissers, "A Low-Latency Library in FPGA Hardware for High-Frequency Trading (HFT)" (*https://oreil.ly/2UEtd*), in the *2012 IEEE 20th Annual Symposium on High-Performance Interconnects* (IEEE, 2012): 9–16.

15 For more on database throughput, see Felipe Cardeneti Mendes, Piotr Sarna, Pavel Emelyanov, and Cynthia Dunlop's *Database Performance at Scale: A Practical Guide* (Apress, 2023): 254.

High-Performance Computing in Finance

Finance has a lot of computationally expensive problems. Examples include risk valuation, derivative pricing, stress testing, scenario analysis, and Credit Value Adjustments (CVAs). Such problems are computationally expensive due to their nonlinear and high-dimensional nature, which results in a massive number of computations that need to be performed. I won't go into the details of these problems, but for those interested, I suggest reading the S&P Global blog entry "Accelerating CVA Calculations Using Quasi Monte Carlo Methods" (*https://oreil.ly/nTBF-*) on accelerating CVA calculations that illustrates the complexity of computing CVAs.

To address such computational challenges, the industry has responded with two streams of improvement: software-side and hardware-side improvements. Software-side improvements often entail the development of more efficient algorithms and computational models. On the hardware side, financial markets have expressed interest in what is called *High-Performance Computing* (HPC). HPC refers to the practice of aggregating and connecting multiple computing resources to solve complex computation problems efficiently. HPC isn't just one technology, but rather a model to build powerful computing environments (*https://oreil.ly/de-8e*).

Designing an HPC cluster leverages several concepts and technologies such as parallel computing, distributed computing, virtualization, Central Processing Units (CPUs), Graphics Processing Units (GPUs), in-memory computation, networking, and many more.

An HPC cluster can be implemented in a variety of ways. For example, an Apache Spark cluster can be considered an HPC. A cluster of connected EC2 instances is also an HPC environment. More complex forms of HPC clusters combine heterogeneous types of machines that serve different purposes (e.g., compute-optimized with high CPU count, memory-optimized, GPU-accelerated). Some organizations develop custom-built HPC supercomputers, highly optimized for superior speed and performance compared to standard computing systems. Supercomputers are often benchmarked using the *floating-point operations per second* (FLOPS) measure (*https://oreil.ly/EM8Jx*).

For more on HPC in finance, see Michael Alan Howarth Dempster, Juho Kanniainen, John Keane, and Erik Vynckier, eds., *High-Performance Computing in Finance: Problems, Methods, and Solutions* (CRC Press, 2018).

Scalability. Computational performance is very often dependent on the scalability features of the underlying infrastructure. When there is an increase in the number of data transformations or sudden peaks in workload, the computational capacity needs to scale proportionally to efficiently manage the increased load.

Taking a cloud context as a reference, scalability can be achieved by either adding more resources (e.g., additional EC2 instances or cloud functions) or by upgrading the capacity of existing resources (e.g., replacing smaller EC2 instances with larger ones). Scalability can be implemented following different strategies, such as the following:

Manual scaling
Where you manually scale existing resources to meet new demands

Dynamic scaling
Where you configure an autoscaling policy to automatically provision more resources in reaction to larger demands (e.g., if total CPU usage > 90% → provision X resources)

Scheduled scaling
When you configure an autoscaling policy to provision more resources on a given schedule (e.g., every Wednesday between 9 a.m. and 4 p.m., provision 200 more EC2 instances)

Predictive scaling
Where a machine learning model is used to predict and provision resources based on historical usage patterns

Scalability requires careful consideration. In particular, when planning the scaling requirements for the transformation layer, it's important to also assess the scalability features of the storage layer. For example, if you have a max concurrency limit on the data storage layer (e.g., 500 concurrent requests), it's essential to properly manage the number of concurrent requests arriving from the transformation layer to avoid overloading the storage layer. Ideally, the design of both the storage and transformation layers should be iterative, ensuring compatibility in scalability features to achieve optimal performance.

Computing environments

Once you have identified your computational requirements, the next step is choosing a computing environment that aligns with these specifications. Such an environment typically comprises three key components: software (e.g., operating system, programming language, libraries, frameworks), hardware (e.g., storage, RAM, CPU, GPU), and networking (e.g., TCP/IP, VPC, etc.).

There is a large variety of computing environments that can be configured to run the transformation layer tasks. Traditionally, many financial institutions, in particular banks, have relied on mainframe computing environments (*https://oreil.ly/HCSU2*) that run on languages such as Common Business Oriented Language (COBOL). However, modern financial applications are leveraging open source technologies and the cloud as a viable and simpler alternative.

If we choose to leverage cloud infrastructure, there are several approaches to consider when setting up the computing environment for the data transformation layer. The most flexible strategy is infrastructure-as-a-service (IaaS), where you provision and configure several computing machines to perform the data transformations. In this setting, you will be responsible for installing the required programming languages (e.g., Python, Java, Go, etc.), configuring security policies (e.g., ingress and egress rules), and installing all necessary packages (e.g., PySpark, Apache Airflow, etc.). The main advantage of IaaS is the extra control it offers over environment configuration. However, managing, configuring, and securing your instances under IaaS can potentially lead to a waste of time and effort.

As an alternative to IaaS, cloud providers offer several managed services that alleviate the need to configure and maintain the compute instances. In such settings, the user interacts with a declarative interface where they define the desired configuration of their environment. The cloud provider takes responsibility for provisioning, scaling, and managing the underlying infrastructure, offering greater convenience and often reducing administrative overhead for users compared to the IaaS model. For example, AWS offers *Managed Workflows for Apache Airflow* (MWAA), a managed service for running the data workflow management solution Apache Airflow (which we will discuss in "Extract-Transform-Load Workflows" on page 414).

Another popular choice for cloud-based computing environments is serverless cloud functions, which allow users to deploy and run code in a variety of languages without provisioning or managing servers. Cloud functions are ideal for short-time data transformation operations (several seconds or minutes). Examples include AWS Lambda and Google Cloud Functions (first and second generations). One of the main advantages of cloud functions is that they can be integrated with a wide range of other services and handle event-based workloads. For example, it is possible to configure a cloud function to run upon the arrival of a file in storage (e.g., Amazon S3), upon the arrival of a message in a queue (e.g., Amazon Kinesis), or with database updates (e.g., Amazon DynamoDB).

Case Study: FINRA's Transition to AWS Lambda for OATS Data Validation

The Financial Industry Regulatory Authority (FINRA) is a US nongovernmental organization responsible for protecting investors and ensuring market integrity by overseeing and regulating broker-dealers. To monitor the trading practices of member firms, FINRA has an integrated audit trail system of orders, quotes, and trade events for National Market System (NMS) stocks and over-the-counter (OTC) equities. To record such data, FINRA's audit trail relies on the Order Audit Trail System (OATS). Using OATS data, along with other sources of market and reference data, FINRA is able to reconstruct the lifecycle of a trade—from origination through completion or cancellation—and monitor the practices of its members.

Member firms submit daily OATS data to FINRA, totaling more than 50,000 files each day. Upon receipt, FINRA verifies the data's completeness and proper formatting against more than 200 rules, processing up to half a trillion validations daily. To handle the significant and variable processing demands, FINRA needed a scalable, cost-efficient, and secure solution (*https://oreil.ly/PfIlQ*).

Three options were explored—Apache Ignite on Amazon EC2, Apache Spark on Amazon EMR, and AWS Lambda. AWS Lambda emerged as the optimal choice due to its scalability, efficient data partitioning, robust monitoring, high performance, cost-effectiveness, and minimal maintenance needs. This choice supported FINRA's goal of transitioning to a real-time processing model.

Security was a critical factor, and AWS met FINRA's stringent data-protection requirements, including encryption of data in transit and at rest. The new system was developed in three months, with data ingested into Amazon S3 via FTP and validated using AWS Lambda functions. A controller, running on Amazon EC2, manages data feeds into AWS Lambda and outgoing notifications, as well as external data sources like stock symbol reference files.

To ensure continuous operation and reduce processing time, the new architecture leverages AWS Lambda's data-caching abilities and uses Amazon SQS for input/output notifications.

Data Delivery

Once data has been transformed, the next step is to deliver it to the final consumers to extract actionable insights. Financial data engineers must determine who the ultimate data consumers are and understand their specific needs, and then create the appropriate mechanisms to deliver the data. The following two sections will provide a brief overview of this process.

Data Consumers

Any user, application, business unit, team, or system that makes use of data generated by their company's data infrastructure is considered a data consumer. Human data consumers can engage in the data engineering lifecycle to varying extents. For example, compliance officers and marketing teams often specify their data needs and rely on data engineers to handle the rest. In contrast, analysts and machine learning specialists may be more involved in defining the data source, type, and necessary transformations.

Data consumers may also differ in terms of their data governance duties and responsibilities. For instance, senior individuals in control of the data in a certain domain are known as data owners. In a bank, for instance, the finance director may be the owner of client financial data. A related role is that of the *data steward*, who is responsible for maintaining and guaranteeing the quality and consistency of data as defined by the data owner. Data custodians are in charge of protecting the data by adhering to the rules outlined in the data governance framework.

Financial data engineers, being the data producers, must ensure that data consumers have clear and well-defined expectations and requirements to facilitate effective data delivery. A reliable way to formalize such an agreement between data consumers and producers is through data contracts, which were discussed in Chapter 5. A data contract can detail all consumer requirements such as the data type, fields, formats, constraints, conversions, SLA, and many more. Data contracts are often owned by the data owner or delegated to the data steward. With a data contract, one can be sure data producers know exactly what data consumers want, thus avoiding miscommunication issues around the data.

Delivery Mechanisms

Data can be delivered to its final consumers in a variety of ways. These include the following:

- Direct database access via a user interface (e.g., Snowflake UI, pgAdmin for PostgreSQL, Compass for MongoDB, etc.). This mechanism is often intended for people with basic SQL knowledge who want to conduct exploratory data analysis.
- Direct file access via a user interface (e.g., the S3 web interface). This is intended for easy interaction and sharing of the data.
- Programmatic access to databases and file repositories via APIs, JDBC (Java Database Connectivity), ODBC (Open Database Connectivity), and client libraries such as AWS Boto3. This delivery mechanism is widely used by applications, software engineers, and data engineers alike.
- Reports that contain essential summaries and aggregations of data used for supporting decision-making.
- Dashboard access that displays metric and summary data in a visual format, typically via a single web page. Dashboards are feature rich, and come with a variety of tools to visualize, explore, filter, compare, zoom, and query the data in a user-friendly way. They are quite useful for stakeholders who don't have much expertise or the time to perform raw data querying and analysis.
- Email delivery.

An important thing to keep in mind when designing a delivery mechanism is the need to provide users with the means to search and find the data they are looking for. As more data gets generated and stored in various locations, it becomes harder for data consumers to know where to find what they are looking for. Some good practices can be adopted in this regard. For example, the final location of the data needs to be specified in the data contract. Additionally, a data catalog can be created as a central search engine that allows users to search and find the data they are seeking.

Summary

This chapter discussed the third layer in the financial data engineering lifecycle: the transformation and delivery layer. Key topics covered include data querying patterns, query optimization, transformation operations and patterns, data consumers, and delivery mechanisms. Throughout the chapter, these concepts are applied within the context of financial markets, providing practical examples and case studies for better insights.

One thing to keep in mind is that financial data transformations, along with their associated patterns and optimizations, are fundamentally driven by business requirements. Custom transformations may need to be developed to specifically address unique business needs and challenges. This adaptive approach ensures that the financial data engineering lifecycle effectively supports and aligns with business objectives in the dynamic financial landscape.

As you learned toward the end of this chapter, once data has been transformed and prepared for its intended purposes, it is delivered to its final consumers, seemingly marking the end of its lifecycle. At this point, you might wonder if additional steps are still required. Crucially, ensuring optimal and flawless functioning across the ingestion, storage, transformation, and delivery layers is never completely assured. This underscores the critical importance of the final layer—monitoring—which will be the focus of the next chapter.

## CHAPTER 10

The Monitoring Layer

After designing and implementing the ingestion, storage, transformation, and delivery layers, the final layer to build is the *monitoring layer*. This layer is crucial for tracking and reporting on the financial data infrastructure's performance, reliability, and quality.

Data monitoring is a continuous task requiring close collaboration between financial data engineers and business teams. It enables financial institutions to operate securely, compliantly, and efficiently in a rapidly changing environment. More specifically, monitoring is needed for the following functions:

Operational continuity and efficiency
As financial data infrastructures grow in complexity, monitoring becomes vital to ensure operational continuity, system availability, efficiency, cost optimization, and optimal performance.

Compliance
Effective monitoring is crucial for financial institutions to meet regulatory requirements. It enables the detection and prevention of fraud and other suspicious activities, while also facilitating accurate and timely regulatory reporting.

Risk management
Financial institutions face a range of risks, including financial, credit, fraud, and operational risks, each with potentially significant costs. Monitoring plays a critical role in promptly and effectively detecting and mitigating these risks.

When designing this layer, the first question you should ask yourself is what components of your financial data infrastructure you need to monitor. This question is critical since monitoring can be a resource-intensive and costly commitment, so you must be clear on your monitoring plan from the start.

Monitoring every possible issue may not be feasible, which is an important consideration when designing the monitoring layer. There is always the potential for unexpected and unforeseen problems to arise.

There is no one-size-fits-all approach to monitoring, as financial data infrastructures may differ in terms of design patterns, data management maturity, software components, level of automation, and data governance policies. However, the following five categories are applicable to (almost) all monitoring approaches: (1) metrics, events, logs, and traces, (2) data quality monitoring, (3) performance monitoring, (4) cost monitoring, and (5) business and analytical monitoring. The following sections will examine each of these in more depth.

Metrics, Events, Logs, and Traces

The main building blocks of monitoring revolve around the generation and utilization of four fundamental types of data: metrics, events, logs, and traces. These elements provide essential inputs for financial data engineers to diagnose, understand, and resolve technical and nontechnical issues within the financial data infrastructure.

Metrics

Metrics are quantitative measurements that provide information about a particular aspect of a system, process, variable, or activity. Metric values are typically observed over a specific time interval or frequency, such as daily, hourly, or in real time. In addition, metric observations are often enriched with metadata represented as a set of key-value pairs, called tags. Tags are used to identify a given instance of a metric. A unique combination of a metric and its associated tags is called a *time series*. Table 10-1 illustrates this concept by displaying a time series view of the 30-day volatility metric across three distinct stocks traded on NASDAQ. Specifically, the table contains three separate time series: the initial two rows for AAPL-NASDAQ, the subsequent two rows for GOOGL-NASDAQ, and the final row for MSFT-NASDAQ.

Table 10-1. Metrics

Timestamp	Metric	Value	Tags
2023-07-09 09:00:00	Volatility (30-day)	0.025	Ticker: AAPL, Exchange: NASDAQ
2023-07-10 09:00:00	Volatility (30-day)	0.027	Ticker: AAPL, Exchange: NASDAQ
2023-08-11 09:00:00	Volatility (30-day)	0.020	Ticker: GOOGL, Exchange: NASDAQ
2023-08-12 09:00:00	Volatility (30-day)	0.022	Ticker: GOOGL, Exchange: NASDAQ
2023-03-11 09:00:00	Volatility (30-day)	0.014	Ticker: MSFT, Exchange: NASDAQ

Interestingly, this way of organizing metrics as time series is a key reason why many engineers prefer using time series databases for tracking and managing metrics. Common examples include Prometheus, Graphite, and InfluxDB. Advanced visualization tools like Grafana can be configured to retrieve data from the metric time series database, allowing users to explore and visualize metrics.

Data Monitoring with InfluxDB: Case Studies from Financial Markets

Financial institutions worldwide employ and continually invest in data monitoring technologies. One common choice involves using time series databases such as InfluxDB.

A good example is PayPal, a global leader in the international online payments sector, serving hundreds of millions of customers in over 200 markets around the world. When PayPal decided to become container-based to modernize its infrastructure, the IT team sought a scalable monitoring solution that could unify metric collection, storage, visualization, and smart alerting within the same platform. The final solution (*https://oreil.ly/ZVIvR*) involved using InfluxDB Enterprise (the enterprise version of InfluxDB) and InfluxData's open source plug-ins, such as Telegraf (*https://oreil.ly/qLL4r*).

Another example is Capital One, a US financial institution specializing in credit cards, car loans, and other products. Capital One generates a large amount of infrastructure, application, and business process metrics. This data plays a crucial role in maintaining high-performance systems and ensuring uninterrupted service. Capital One sought an advanced monitoring solution capable of ensuring high resilience and availability across multiple regions, while also integrating seamlessly with its machine learning systems to analyze data and generate predictive metrics. To this end, Capital One created a fault-tolerant system with disaster recovery features (*https://oreil.ly/9XaVz*) based on InfluxDB Enterprise, AWS, and the visualization tool Grafana (*https://oreil.ly/ORBrH*).

Another notable example is ProcessOut, a platform specializing in payment analytics and routing. ProcessOut provides two main products (*https://oreil.ly/QFdZU*): Telescope, which analyzes transaction data to aid clients in understanding payment failures, and Smart Router, which assists clients in selecting the optimal payment system provider for specific transactions. ProcessOut chose InfluxDB (*https://oreil.ly/xYx16*) to provide its consumers with the finest service while proactively monitoring and alerting them, depending on their payment actions. InfluxDB offers the functionality to collect, store, and manage critical payment information (logs, metrics, and events).

Examples like these, which you can check out online (*https://oreil.ly/xhPZj*), highlight the critical role of data monitoring in the financial sector. Financial institutions prioritize monitoring not just as a necessity, but as a means to create business value and drive innovation.

Events

Events are structured data emitted by an application during runtime. They are usually triggered by a specific type of activity and tend to belong to a predefined list of possible values. Examples include client HTTP requests such as POST and GET, response status (e.g., 404 NotFound), cloud resource operation (e.g., Amazon S3 object-level API activity such as GetObject, DeleteObject, and PutObject), and user permission changes (e.g., AmazonS3ReadOnlyAccess).

The structured nature of events makes them well-suited for storage and retrieval in tabular representations. That's why event data is commonly stored in SQL databases.

Logs

Logs are semi-structured data emitted by an application during runtime, providing greater flexibility in terms of content, structure, and triggering mechanisms compared to events. Logs are typically classified into five standard levels based on the severity of the issue. These levels, arranged from lowest to highest severity, are listed here:

Debug logs
Used for diagnosing system issues in testing and development environments.

Info logs
Information on normal system operations, which can be useful in case something doesn't look normal. For example, you may want to log detailed records about transactions, including timestamps, amounts, trade submissions, account details and updates, and status (success/failure). Such information can be critical for auditing, compliance reporting, and resolving disputes or discrepancies.

Warning logs
Information about potential issues that might lead to future problems if not addressed. These are used when something unexpected happens, but you want your application to continue running.

Error logs
Information about serious issues that affect the operation being executed but not the service or the application as a whole. They require a developer's intervention to fix. Examples include errors in processing a payment, a trade, or a loan application.

Critical logs
> Information about issues affecting the entire service or application and requiring immediate intervention, for example, if the primary database of a web application becomes completely inaccessible.

The extra flexibility of logs compared to events makes them essential for uncovering the root causes of issues. Logs can be general-purpose, such as errors related to software bugs or missing resources. They can also be software-specific, such as database-related errors like deadlocks, transaction conflicts, query timeouts, and the maximum connection limits reached.

A variety of tools can be used to store and query logs. Many companies use the ELK stack: Elasticsearch, Logstash, and Kibana. Cloud-based tools are also common, including Azure Monitor Logs, Google Cloud Logging, and Amazon CloudWatch.

Traces

Traces represent a more advanced form of system behavior records, capturing comprehensive details about each step taken by a process as it progresses through one or more systems. Examples include the following:

Business operation traces
> Store information describing the steps involved in completing a business operation. For instance, tracing a trade order lifecycle from submission until execution or failure; tracing a payment flow initiation, authorization, processing, validation, and settlement; and tracing a loan application from submission through credit scoring, approval, and final disbursement.

Application traces
> Store information about an application's behavior as it executes multiple components. This includes function calls, API requests, condition checks, input/output, resource usage, timeout, and execution time.

Security incident traces
> Store information on the events and activities associated with security incidents within a system.

Unique Transaction Identifiers: Cornerstones of Effective Transaction Tracing

To ensure effective tracing, a trace identifier, also referred to as a transaction ID or correlation ID, is essential for uniquely identifying and monitoring the path of a particular transaction or request across a complex system. Such identifiers ensure that all related activities can be linked together, providing a complete view of the transaction's lifecycle and ensuring transparency throughout the process.

In Chapter 3, you learned about transaction identifiers such as the Unique Transaction Identifier (UTI) defined in ISO 23897. The UTI was developed to offer a consistent reference that interlinks all related messages in an end-to-end financial transaction, allowing every party involved to refer to the transaction easily. This unique identifier remains unchanged throughout the various events of a transaction lifecycle, including amendments and version changes, thereby enhancing transparency and visibility across the settlement and reconciliation value chain.

Several frameworks, technologies, and tools come into play when designing a solution for storing and managing traces. OpenLineage is an open platform designed for collecting and analyzing data lineage. It tracks events related to data pipelines, including datasets, jobs, and executions. Apache Atlas is a metadata management and data governance tool that helps with data lineage, classification, and auditing. Apache NiFi enables the automated and efficient movement of data between systems, aiding in data lineage and flow management. For distributed tracing, Jaeger and Zipkin are widely used to monitor and troubleshoot errors and identify performance and latency bottlenecks in complex, microservices-based architectures.

Data Quality Monitoring

Data generated and used by financial institutions must consistently meet high quality standards. Chapter 5 focused on financial data governance and extensively addressed the topic of data quality, discussing dimensions such as errors, duplicates, relevance, biases, completeness, timeliness, and outliers.

The traditional approach to data quality monitoring starts with the definition and development of *Data Quality Metrics* (DQMs). These metrics are quantitative measures used to assess and summarize the quality of specific aspects or dimensions of data. Defining the right DQMs depends on several factors that relate to client expectations (e.g., a data quality clause in an SLA), business requirements (e.g., complete sales and customer data), and technical standards (e.g., formatting, decimals, etc.). For this reason, there isn't a fixed list of DQMs that fit all purposes. Instead, they are defined in an iterative and continuous process that involves financial data engineers, the business team, and data analysts/machine learning experts.

While there's no one-size-fits-all approach, there are several DQM techniques that are commonly utilized. The usage of *ratios* is one such approach. For example, the *error ratio* indicates the percentage of erroneous records in a dataset, the *duplicate ratio* computes the percentage of duplicated records compared to all records within a dataset, and a *missing values ratio* can be used to measure the rate of available data compared to a fully complete dataset. Temporal data quality metrics may also be used. For example, to ensure data timeliness, metrics can be constructed to measure the age of a data item in a dataset and compare it against a reference date (e.g., < 1 week ago). Another metric may check data arrival time against an expected arrival time (e.g., every day at 10 a.m.).

Once DQMs have been defined, a corresponding monitoring process must be implemented. A well-known approach in this regard is *data profiling*. This involves parsing and checking a given dataset to understand its content, formatting, structure, and the relationships between its records. By performing data profiling, potential data quality issues within the dataset can be identified. Profiling can be performed column-wise, where each column is examined separately, or row-wise, where all columns and their relationships are analyzed. At the end of a data profiling check, a short report can be generated to summarize the main features and issues of the input dataset and provide recommendations for addressing such issues. Figure 10-1 illustrates some of the elements a typical data profile report might contain.

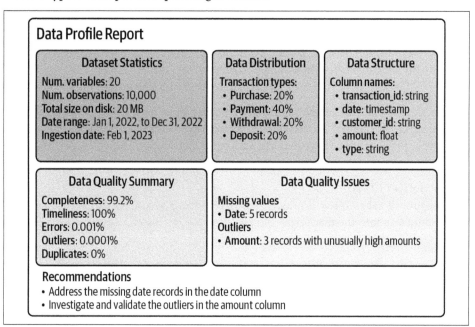

Figure 10-1. A simple example of a data profile report

Data profiling is a comprehensive procedure that scans the whole dataset to understand its data quality attributes. However, a complete data profile report may not always be required. Alternatively, a simpler approach could be to define and test data quality rules against one or more data records. A rule could state, for example, that the error ratio should not exceed 1%.

Once DQMs and the data quality monitoring process have been established, the next step is selecting a data quality tool or developing custom scripts to identify, validate, and flag any data quality issues. Commercial data quality tools include the Ataccama ONE Data Quality Suite, Informatica Data Quality, Precisely Trillium, SAS Data Quality, and Talend Data Fabric. There are also open source data quality tools such as the Python libraries Great Expectations, Soda Core, and DataCleaner.

It is essential to recognize that data quality monitoring is a continuous and evolving process. As the financial data landscape changes, with new data types, quality dimensions, and business requirements emerging, it is crucial to regularly revisit and refine your data quality monitoring process. This practice ensures the continued relevance and effectiveness of your data quality monitoring in safeguarding the quality of your data.

Performance Monitoring

Performance refers to the ability of the financial data infrastructure to meet key operational criteria such as speed, latency, throughput, availability, scalability, and resource utilization. These performance indicators directly impact business performance by influencing critical aspects such as the following:

Time to Insight (TTI)
> The time it takes to obtain actionable insights from data from the point it was generated. A shorter TTI enables fast delivery of financial data to end users, ensuring efficient decision-making, customer satisfaction, timely reporting, and revenue growth.

Time to Market (TTM)
> The time it takes for a product to progress from a conceptualized idea to its introduction into the market.

Innovation velocity
> The pace at which data-driven innovations are generated and implemented

Data cycle time
> The time required to complete an entire cycle of data analysis, starting from problem formalization to obtaining actionable insights.

Various metrics are frequently used to monitor data infrastructure performance. Some are software-agnostic and apply to any type of application:

RAM usage
    The amount of memory being used by the application

CPU usage
    The percentage of CPU being used by the application

Storage usage
    The amount of disk storage being used by the application

Execution time
    The time needed to execute a task or process a request

Requests per second (RPS)
    The number of requests made to an application every second

Ingress/egress bytes (bytes/sec)
    The amount of network traffic (in bytes) entering and leaving an application

Uptime/downtime
    The ratio of time a system is operational to the total time observed

API response time
    The time it takes for an API endpoint to process and respond to a request

Concurrent users
    The number of users accessing an application simultaneously

Additionally, performance metrics can be tailored to specific software systems. For example, database management systems may have metrics such as the following:

Read/write operations
    Count of read and write operations performed on the database within a specific temporal window

Active connections
    Number of currently open database connections

Connection pool usage
    Utilization of connections within a connection pool

Query count
    Total number of queries processed by the database during a specified interval

Transaction runtime
> Duration taken to execute a database transaction

Replication lag
> The delay between the time data is written to the primary database instance and the time it is synched with read replicas

You can even have more granular metrics defined for a specific software component. For example, database queries may be monitored via metrics such as the following:

Records read
> The number of data records read by the database.

Blocks read
> The number of data blocks read by the database.

Bytes scanned
> The total number of bytes fetched by a query.

Number of output rows
> The final number of rows returned by a query.

Scan time
> The time spent by the database scanning the data.

Sort time
> The time spent by the database sorting the data.

Aggregation time
> The time spent by the database aggregating the data.

Peak memory
> The maximum amount of memory used during query execution.

Query plans
> The execution steps that a data storage system follows to fetch data in response to a query. Monitoring query plans can help detect costly queries and unused DB objects such as indexes and provide insights into query performance.

Additionally, you can implement performance metrics specific to your business's technical needs. Examples from financial markets include the following:

Trade execution latency
> The time taken from when a trade order is placed until it is executed, which is critical for optimizing trading strategies and minimizing execution risks.

Trade execution error rate
> The frequency of failed transactions or trade orders, indicating operational inefficiencies.

Trade settlement time
> The duration from when a trade is executed to when it is settled, reflecting the efficiency of the settlement process.

Market data latency
> The time it takes for financial market data to be received from the exchange or data provider to the trading system, which impacts the speed of decision-making.

Algorithmic trading performance
> Includes metrics such as algorithm execution time and success rate, which can highlight the effectiveness and reliability of algorithmic trading strategies.

Risk exposure calculation time
> The time taken to compute and update risk exposure metrics, which is critical for managing and mitigating financial risks in real time.

Customer transaction processing time
> The duration from when a customer initiates a transaction (e.g., deposit, withdrawal) to its completion, which can impact customer satisfaction and operational efficiency.

Case Study: Monitoring Real-Time Financial Data Feeds

In today's fast-paced financial markets, real-time data feeds have become increasingly popular for providing the critical information necessary for making timely decisions. These feeds deliver up-to-the-second market data, including prices, volumes, and order book information, which are indispensable for traders, financial institutions, and automated trading systems. The reliance on accurate and timely data to capture market opportunities and manage risks effectively makes financial market feeds integral to the modern financial ecosystem. To ensure efficient and timely data delivery, providers of data feeds and related infrastructure need to thoroughly monitor the performance of their systems. Among the most important data feed performance metrics to monitor are the following.

Network Metrics

Packets per second (PPS)
> The number of data packets transmitted and received per second.

Packet size distribution
> The size of data packets being transmitted and received.

Round-trip time (RTT)
> The time for a signal to travel from sender to receiver and back.

One-way latency
> Tracks the time for a signal to travel from sender to receiver.

Bandwidth utilization
> Measures how much of the available network bandwidth is being used. Network bandwidth refers to the maximum rate at which data can be transmitted over a network connection in a given amount of time. Bandwidth utilization is about efficiency and capacity usage.

Data transfer rate (throughput)
> Measures the actual amount of data transmitted per second. It's about the speed of data movement.

System Metrics

CPU usage
> Percentage of CPU capacity used.

CPU time in I/O wait (iowait)
> Time CPU spends waiting for I/O operations to complete.

CPU interrupt time (irq)
> Time CPU spends handling software interrupts.

Memory utilization
> Percentage of memory being used.

Processing Metrics

Backpressure
> Tracks the system's ability to handle incoming data rates. Backpressure occurs if the system receives more message requests than it can handle.

Buffer/queue sizes
> Monitor data waiting to be processed.

A particular type of performance metrics are incident response and management metrics, which are used to evaluate the effectiveness of an organization at tackling and preventing system downtime/outage issues. Examples include the following:

Mean Time to Detect (MTTD)
> The expected time it takes to detect an issue or incident after it has occurred.

Mean Time Before Failure (MTBF)
> The expected time between two failures/downtime in a repairable system. The higher the MTBF, the more reliable and available the system is, and the more effective the data engineering team is at preventing future issues.

Mean Time to Recovery (MTTR)
> The expected time before a system recovers from a failure and becomes fully operational. A low MTTR indicates that the engineering team is quite effective at resolving the problem and that issue-fixing is efficient (e.g., through DevOps, DataOps, automated testing, etc.).

Mean Time to Failure (MTTF)
> The expected time until a nonrepairable failure occurs. A nonrepairable failure requires replacing the failed system with a new one.

Mean Time to Acknowledge (MTTA)
> The expected time from when an incident is reported to when someone starts working on the issue. A low MTTA indicates high team responsiveness and an effective alerting system.

Incident metrics are of primary importance in today's always-on financial market infrastructures. The costs associated with outages and downtime in financial markets can be substantial, potentially leading to significant repercussions, especially given the interconnected and high-frequency/high-volume nature of financial activities.

Turning to technological implementations, there are numerous tools and frameworks designed for performance monitoring. Some are integrated into data engineering tools; for example, Apache Spark includes a UI interface for monitoring cluster status and resource usage. Open source tools such as Prometheus (*https://oreil.ly/Y6EJ6*), designed primarily for metrics data, provide a rich set of monitoring and alerting features, including a multidimensional data model, flexible query language (PromQL), and multiple modes of dashboarding and visualizations. Another common approach involves using time series databases like InfluxDB, alongside advanced visualization tools such as Grafana.

Another popular and user-friendly option is cloud-based monitoring solutions. Using the cloud, it is possible to establish an alerting policy to get notified when performance-related issues occur. For example, Google Cloud provides a managed alerting service (*https://oreil.ly/2qrj6*) where you can create an *alerting policy* that defines the circumstances under which an incident is created and the notification channel through which you want to be notified.

Cost Monitoring

Cost monitoring is the process of keeping an eye on a financial data infrastructure's expenditures to ensure that they are within acceptable bounds and to spot patterns of excessive usage. The significance of cost monitoring has grown alongside the widespread adoption and migration to cloud services. While the cloud provides a plethora of accessible services with flexible on-demand pricing, managed scalability, and simplified configuration, there exists a potential risk of unforeseen, excessive, or misinterpreted cost structures.

To illustrate the issue, let's consider one of the most attractive cloud computing strategies: *serverless computing*. This term refers to a cloud-based application development model where the cloud provider takes full care of infrastructure configuration and management. This includes all features such as load balancing, auto-scaling, availability, security, operating system management, logging, monitoring, and storage management. Services such as AWS Lambda and Google BigQuery are among the most popular services that people often associate with serverless computing.

Crucially, the economics of serverless computing can be misunderstood, potentially resulting in unforeseen expenses. This is due to the variability in cost-effectiveness of the serverless model, which is dependent on factors like execution patterns and workload volume. Pennies can add up to thousands of dollars when running a massive number of jobs.

Furthermore, in services like AWS Lambda, pricing isn't solely determined by the frequency and duration of function invocations, as many might assume with *pay-as-you-go* models. You also indirectly pay based on the memory allocated to your function, which directly influences the cost of your function executions. Moreover, additional charges may be added if AWS Lambda reads data from AWS storage or transfers data between regions.

As of the time of writing this book, invoking an on-demand AWS Lambda function (*https://oreil.ly/znW-C*) costs \$0.0000000021 per millisecond for 128 MB of RAM and \$0.0000000167 per millisecond for 1,024 MB of RAM. This looks relatively cheap. However, costs can escalate significantly based on the nature of your workload. When assessing application scalability, a commonly used metric is transactions per second (TPS), also referred to as hits per second (HPS) or requests per second (RPS). Suppose our application processes a specific number of RPS over a total of 100,000 seconds in a month. Using this information, let's explore a few scenarios:

Scenario 1: 100 RPS with a duration of 10 seconds each
- *Cost per invocation*: \$0.0000000021 × 10,000 milliseconds (10 seconds) = \$0.000021
- *Monthly cost*: \$0.000021 × 100 RPS × 100,000 seconds = \$210

Scenario 2: Increasing execution time to 1 minute (60 seconds)
- *Cost per invocation*: \$0.0000000021 × 60,000 milliseconds (60 seconds) = \$0.000126
- *Monthly cost*: \$0.000126 × 100 RPS × 100,000 seconds = \$1,260

Scenario 3: Increasing allocated memory to 1,024 MB (1 GB)

- *Cost per invocation*: $\$0.0000000167 \times 60,000 = \$0.001002$

- *Monthly cost*: $\$0.001002 \times 100$ RPS $\times 100,000$ seconds $= \$10,020$

These calculations show how increasing execution time and memory allocation can significantly impact the monthly cost of running AWS Lambda functions. Adjustments in these parameters should be carefully considered based on performance requirements and budget constraints. Additionally, when assessing solutions like Lambda and other alternatives, it is important to consider your future scaling needs rather than just your current usage.[1]

Various practices and tools are available to manage cloud costs. For instance, cloud providers offer budgeting options (*https://oreil.ly/mkoVK*) that let users set target budgets and receive notifications if costs exceed predefined thresholds. Another promising approach is FinOps, a recent trend in cloud cost monitoring and management, which has been defined by the FinOps Foundation (*https://oreil.ly/gJSWy*) as:

> An operational framework and cultural practice which maximizes the business value of cloud, enables timely data-driven decision making, and creates financial accountability through collaboration between engineering, finance, and business teams.

A FinOps framework requires five pillars:

- Cross-functional collaboration among engineering, finance, and business teams to enable fast product delivery while ensuring financial and cost control.

- Each team takes ownership of its cloud usage and costs.

- A central team establishes and promotes FinOps best practices.

- Teams take advantage of the cloud's on-demand and variable cost model while optimizing the tradeoffs among speed, quality, and cost in their cloud-based applications.

- Decisions are driven by the cloud's business value, such as increased revenue, innovative product development, reduced fixed costs, and faster feature releases.

FinOps is an iterative and learning-driven process. Within organizations, the maturity of FinOps is commonly assessed using the FinOps Maturity Model (FMM) (*https://oreil.ly/E3VgV*), which consists of three stages: Crawl, Walk, and Run. As an organization progresses from Crawl to Run level, it moves from being reactive, where

---

1 To learn more about the economics of serverless computing, I highly recommend Adam Eivy and Joe Weinman's "Be Wary of the Economics of 'Serverless' Cloud Computing" (*https://oreil.ly/ASKET*), *IEEE Cloud Computing* 4, no. 2 (March–April 2017): 6–12.

issues are fixed as they occur, to being proactive, where teams are able to anticipate cloud usage patterns and expenses and incorporate such information into their cloud architecture design decisions.

Case Study: Financial Transaction Cost Monitoring with Abel Noser

Transaction cost monitoring and analysis is a common practice in financial markets. It entails monitoring and analyzing the expenses related to executing financial transactions, such as trades and investments. This process is vital for investment firms, asset managers, brokers, and other financial institutions to ensure that they are achieving optimal execution while minimizing costs.

Several companies specialize in transaction monitoring services for the financial sector. An industry leader in this market is Abel Noser (*https://oreil.ly/HAJej*), now part of Trading Technologies. Financial institutions submit their transaction data to Abel Noser, which conducts comprehensive cost analysis and returns insights to the clients. Over 350 global clients from the US, as well as other parts of the world, report their data to Abel Noser.

Abel Noser is also a data vendor, providing institutional investor datasets that contain transaction-related information such as the instrument traded, price, quantity, date, trade direction (buy or sell), commissions paid, and other market fields. Abel Noser's data is an essential source for scientific research on institutional trading.

Business and Analytical Monitoring

A more advanced form of data monitoring involves observing statistical, analytical, and business-related dimensions. This monitoring approach ensures that not only is the raw data monitored, but also the contextual and analytical insights that drive strategic decision-making.

For example, commercial banks must diligently and continuously monitor the status of their lending activities to ensure clients make timely payments and detect/predict defaulting clients. Moreover, to ensure resiliency and regulatory compliance, banks need to monitor their financial, credit, and operational risks as well as their exposures, risk concentration, capital adequacy, and leverage situation. Similarly, institutions such as investment firms need to continuously monitor their portfolio performance, asset allocation, diversification, and investment strategies.

Risk Monitoring in Financial Institutions: Data Engineering Challenges

Risk is an inherent aspect of financial institution operations, particularly in the banking sector. Consequently, most banking regulations emphasize principles and frameworks to ensure banks' resilience against the classes of risks they are exposed to.

The primary framework for international banking regulation (*https://oreil.ly/7XqUv*) consists of the three Basel Accords—Basel I, Basel II, and the more recent Basel III. The Basel framework groups bank risks into three broad categories:

Market risk
    The risk of financial loss deriving from movements in market prices.

Credit risk
    The risk of financial loss deriving from a borrower or counterparty not being able to meet the agreed-upon obligations.

Operational risk
    The risk of financial loss resulting from poorly designed or failed internal processes, people, and systems or from external events.

To be managed, these risks must be quantitatively measured. To do this, risk data is needed. Each risk category requires different sets of data fields. Market risk measurement requires data such as portfolio composition, historical prices, volatility, interest rates, and correlations. Credit risk measurement requires data such as credit ratings, credit scores, exposure data, collateral data, default data, probability of default data (likelihood of creditors defaulting on their obligations), and loss given default data (losses incurred in case of a default event). Finally, operational risk measurement requires detailed operational loss and risk event data as well as internal control data.

Importantly, effectively managing the diverse types of risk data poses significant data engineering challenges related to data collection, aggregation, integration, normalization, quality assurance, and timely delivery. In Chapter 5, we discussed the problem of data aggregation in financial institutions and illustrated how it mainly applies to risk data. As a reminder, Basel III introduced the *Principles for Effective Risk Data Aggregation and Risk Reporting* to ensure the adequacy of financial institutions' data infrastructure for managing and aggregating risk data efficiently.

To address operational risk, a common strategy involves establishing and maintaining an *operational event risk database*, which stores historical records stemming from operational incidents. This database may contain elements such as the event date, description (e.g., what happened), primary causes (e.g., human error), business line (e.g., risk management), and control point (e.g., trading desk). To learn more about this, consult the paper by Niclas Hageback, "The Operational Risk Framework Under a Retail Perspective" (*https://oreil.ly/mYnHH*).

Financial institutions relying on data analytics and machine learning must actively monitor the statistical, quality, and performance aspects of both their data and models. Within the machine learning community, concepts such as *concept drift* and *data drift* are frequently used in the monitoring and detection of changes in the underlying data distribution or model relationships.

Concept drift occurs when a machine learning model no longer accurately reflects the original problem it was trained to solve. For example, a well-performing fraud detection model trained on a specific financial dataset may become less effective over time if fraudsters adapt and modify their fraudulent tactics. As a result, the model's predictions may become less accurate because the underlying problem it was designed to address has evolved.

Data drift happens when the input data distribution to a machine learning model changes over time. Consider an ML model trained to forecast a company's stock price based on a given data sample. Suppose that throughout this sample, the stock price was relatively stable (low volatility). If the market becomes more volatile over time, the model might struggle to predict accurately because the statistical characteristics of the data have changed.

Interestingly, the ideas of concept and data drift are relatively familiar to finance. In financial markets, particularly among risk managers, the term *model risk* is used to describe the risk that financial models used in asset pricing, trading, forecasting, and hedging will generate inconsistent or misleading results.[2]

One prevalent area of business monitoring among financial institutions involves the monitoring of various fraudulent and illegal activities when conducting transactions. Examples include the following:

Money laundering
> The process of concealing the origins of illegally obtained money, typically by means of transfers involving foreign banks or offshore companies.

Terrorism financing
> Providing financial support to terrorist organizations or individuals to facilitate acts of terrorism.

Fraud
> Deceptive practices intended to secure unfair or unlawful financial gain, often involving misrepresentation or omission of information.

---

2 For more on model risk, see Jon Danielsson, Kevin R. James, Marcela Valenzuela, and Ilknur Zer's "Model Risk of Risk Models" (*https://oreil.ly/UfmCx*), *Journal of Financial Stability* 23 (April 2016): 79–91.

Corruption
Dishonest or fraudulent conduct by those in power, typically involving bribery, embezzlement, or abuse of authority for personal gain.

Another good example is market manipulation and securities fraud practices, which involve illegally influencing the supply or demand of financial instruments to gain advantage from market reactions. Examples include the following:

Pump and dump
This involves artificially inflating the price of a stock or other asset through false or misleading statements (pump). Once the price is high enough, the manipulator sells their holdings at a profit (dump), causing the price to collapse, and leaving other investors with losses.

Spoofing
This involves placing orders without the intention of executing them in order to create a false impression of demand or supply in the market. Once other traders react to these orders, the spoofer cancels or modifies their original orders.

Insider trading
Trading securities based on material nonpublic information, which can generate unfair advantages and distortions in market prices.

Front running
When a broker or trader executes orders on a security for their own account while taking advantage of inside knowledge of a future transaction that is expected to impact the security's price substantially.

Churning
Excessive trading of a client's brokerage account by a broker to generate commissions without regard for the client's investment goals.

Wash trading
Simultaneously buying and selling the same financial instruments to create artificial trading volume or a false impression of market activity without having exposure to market risk.

Lastly, an integral aspect of financial institution monitoring revolves around evaluating investment portfolio performance. This entails selecting, calculating, and monitoring key performance indicators like the Sharpe ratio, Sortino ratio, Treynor ratio, and information ratio. To illustrate one example, the Sharpe ratio is a measure of risk-adjusted return, indicating how well an investment performs relative to its risk level. These metrics allow institutions to assess the effectiveness of their investment strategies, enabling informed and timely decisions for optimizing portfolio composition and performance.

Data Observability

As the technological stacks supporting data infrastructures have grown in complexity and scale, the requirements for monitoring have evolved accordingly. This has led to the emergence of a more advanced and comprehensive monitoring approach known as *observability*.

Observability elevates monitoring to a new level, allowing software and data engineering teams to handle issues proactively and gain deep insights into the internal state and behavior of a given software application or infrastructure. Authors Charity Majors, Liz Fong-Jones, and George Miranda (*Observability Engineering*, O'Reilly, 2022) describe a software system as observable if you can do the following (the following list is a direct quote):

- Understand the inner workings of your application
- Understand any system state your application may have gotten itself into, even new ones you have never seen before and couldn't have predicted
- Understand the inner workings and system state solely by observing and interrogating with external tools
- Understand the internal state without shipping any new custom code to handle it (because that implies you needed prior knowledge to explain it)

Observability can be applied across various dimensions of IT systems, encompassing data, applications, infrastructure, networks, security, and business. *Data observability* is a vital area in this regard. Author Andy Petrella of *Fundamentals of Data Observability* (O'Reilly, 2023) defines data observability as:

> The capability of a system to generate information on how the data influences its behavior and, conversely, how the system affects the data.

With data observability, financial data engineers and other team members should easily be able to ask and answer questions such as: "Why is workflow A running slowly?", "Why is data not available yet for client X?", "What caused the data quality issue in dataset Y?", "Why is the data pipeline for report Z delayed?", or "Where is the bottleneck in a transformation or ingestion process?"

The main building blocks of data observability are metrics, events, logs, and traces.

In addition, data observability systems leverage concepts such as automated monitoring and logging, root cause analysis, data lineage, contextual observability, Service-Level Agreements (SLAs), telemetry/OpenTelemetry, instrumentation, tracking, tracing, and alert analysis and triaging.

OpenTelemetry: The Open Source Standard for Observability

OpenTelemetry (*https://oreil.ly/STFq-*) is an open source, vendor-neutral framework comprising a set of APIs, SDKs, libraries, agents, and tools to enable observability in software applications. It allows engineers to collect telemetry data, such as traces, metrics, and logs, from their applications and services to gain insights into their behavior, performance, and reliability. OpenTelemetry provides standardized instrumentation and integration capabilities for various programming languages, frameworks, and platforms, making it easier to instrument applications consistently across different environments. It allows exporter applications to send telemetry data to various backends and observability platforms for storage, analysis, visualization, and alerting.

A properly implemented data observability system can bring a lot of benefits for financial institutions, such as the following:

- Higher data quality (e.g., by observing data quality metrics)
- Operational efficiency (e.g., reduced TTD and TTR)
- Facilitated communication and trust between different team members (e.g., risk management and trading desk)
- Gains in client trust by being able to detect and understand the issues they might face
- Enabling complex data ingestion and transformation while maintaining reliability and visibility into the system
- Regulatory compliance (e.g., by keeping data privacy and security under control)

Financial data engineers play a vital role in embedding data observability capabilities within the financial data infrastructure. Observability is fundamentally a data engineering challenge. It entails instrumenting systems to generate vast amounts of heterogeneous data points, which must be efficiently indexed, stored, and queried in near-real time. This ensures comprehensive visibility into the behavior of various components of the financial data infrastructure, including data ingestion, storage, processing systems, workflows, quality, compliance, and governance.[3]

It's important to remember that implementing a data observability system requires a significant investment in both technology and people. For this reason, I highly recommend you evaluate your business needs, technical constraints, and growth

---

3 For a comprehensive discussion of observability data management systems, I highly recommend Suman Karumuri, Franco Solleza, Stan Zdonik, and Nesime Tatbul's "Towards Observability Data Management at Scale" (*https://oreil.ly/N9OXj*), *ACM Sigmod Record* 49, no. 4 (March 2021): 18–23.

perspectives before investing in a large-scale data observability system. In many cases, a simple monitoring strategy is all you need. As your organization grows and its technological stack becomes more complex, investing in data observability becomes increasingly beneficial and, eventually, essential.

Summary

This chapter discussed the final layer in the financial data engineering lifecycle: monitoring. Monitoring is critical for guaranteeing the reliability, performance, security, and compliance of financial data infrastructures.

This chapter explained and illustrated the significance of metric, event, log, and trace monitoring in tracking application activities and diagnosing and solving potential issues. Furthermore, it explored the key components of data quality, performance, and cost monitoring, outlining their techniques and giving practical advice and financial use cases.

In addition, it emphasized the importance of business and analytical monitoring in providing actionable insights and supporting informed decision-making within financial institutions. Finally, the chapter included a brief review of data observability, an emerging topic, highlighting its crucial role in providing deep insights into the internals and behavior of various data infrastructure components.

By this point of the book, you should have a solid grasp of the various layers comprising the financial data engineering lifecycle. To further simplify and enhance the modularity of financial data infrastructures, smaller data processing components, known as data workflows, are commonly developed. The next chapter will cover these data workflows in detail.

CHAPTER 11

Financial Data Workflows

Throughout this part of the book, you have explored the fundamental layers of the financial data engineering lifecycle: ingestion, storage, transformation and delivery, and monitoring. Adhering to this structured framework is crucial for building and maintaining efficient financial data infrastructures.

Importantly, as your company expands, the financial data infrastructure will become larger and more complex, generating many interdependencies and links between the different layers. To address this challenge, further refinement is required to build multiple independent and specialized data processing components. Data engineers call these components data pipelines or workflows.

This chapter will explore the foundational concepts of data workflows, introducing the ideas of workflow-oriented software architectures and workflow management systems. Then, it will cover the main types and characteristics of financial data workflows that can be implemented to handle financial data processing tasks.

Workflow-Oriented Software Architectures

Before explaining workflows, it's important to understand the business rationale behind their practicality. First, as a natural part of the growth journey of any digital company, the technological stack tends to increase in size and complexity, creating numerous interdependencies, logical flows, and interactions among various system components. For this reason, the software development community has identified the need for architectural designs and tools that organize software transactions into structured workflows that can be defined, coordinated, managed, monitored, and scaled following a specific business logic. In this book, I will use the term *workflow-oriented software architecture* (WOSA) to describe this design pattern.

The concept of WOSA is highly applicable to financial markets, where many financial operations are organized as a series of actions carried out in a specific sequence. A notable example is financial transactions, which generally follow a defined workflow consisting of multiple steps. Examples follow:

- The lifecycle of financial trades involves several steps such as trade initiation, order placement, trade execution, trade capture, enrichment, validation, verification, confirmation, clearing, and settlement.

- The lifecycle of credit card payments involves a chain of steps that may involve the customer, merchant, payment gateway, payment processor, acquiring bank, issuing bank, and card network. Along the way, the same payment goes through several steps that start with submission, authorization, balance and fraud checks, confirmation or rejection, clearing, and settlement.

In essence, WOSAs focus on organizing and executing complex processes through structured workflows, enhancing modularity, efficiency, and manageability in software systems. An important category within workflows is the data workflow, designed specifically for the processing and management of data. Let's examine some of its technical aspects and concepts in the following section.

What Is a Data Workflow?

A data workflow is a repeatable process that involves applying a structured sequence of data processing steps to an initial dataset, producing a desired output dataset.

Data workflows are fundamental to data engineering. As a financial data engineer, you will frequently build financial data workflows. To excel at this task, an important skill to learn is workflow abstraction. This involves defining a conceptual framework for your workflow that disregards technological implementation details to guarantee generalization. It is similar to how concepts of data storage models and data storage systems were used in Chapter 8 to abstract the specifics of storage technologies.

One of the most widely adopted data workflow abstractions is the *dataflow paradigm* (*https://oreil.ly/lyCsV*). Its core principle involves organizing an application into a directed computational graph. In this graph, nodes represent individual computation steps, while links express data dependencies or the flow of data between these computations. Typically, the computational graph underlying a workflow is designed without cycles. When structured in this manner, the graph is referred to as a Directed Acyclic Graph (DAG).

The most basic type of computational DAG is the linear DAG. It organizes tasks in a sequential order where each task N can have at most one preceding task (N–1) and one subsequent task (N+1). Figure 11-1 illustrates a three-task linear computational DAG.

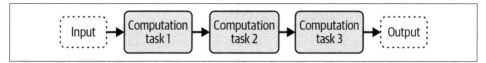

Figure 11-1. Linear DAG

Frequently, computational DAGs are more complex than the linear case. For example, a specific computing task may depend on multiple preceding tasks. Figure 11-2 illustrates such a scenario, where computation task 6 relies on tasks 3, 4, and 5.

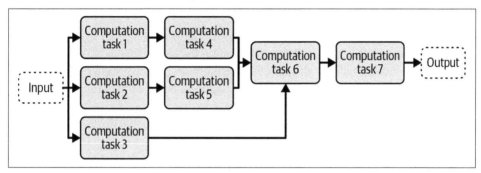

Figure 11-2. Complex DAG

When defining a computational DAG, a fundamental question arises: "What constitutes a task?" While there isn't a universal answer to this question, several best practices have been suggested. For example, a task needs to be an atomic unit of execution, meaning that it either succeeds or fails as a whole. Furthermore, it is considered a best practice to ensure that tasks are idempotent, meaning that running the same task multiple times will yield the same result as running it once, without causing any unexpected or undesirable side effects. This can be useful since it can allow you to add task checkpoint features to your DAG, allowing you to resume DAG execution from the failed step rather than execute it all over again.

Another consideration is the size of tasks within a computational DAG. They should strike a balance: they need to be small enough to facilitate debugging and traceability, but not so small that they introduce unnecessary overhead and degrade DAG performance. Conversely, overly large tasks simplify the DAG structure but can constrain debuggability and lead to costly retry operations.

Moreover, a good practice is to associate tasks with business logic. This can involve basic tasks such as data quality checks or more complex computations like modeling and analytics.

Workflow Management Systems

Once a workflow abstraction has been defined, the next step is to design a system that provides the infrastructure and tools necessary for building, orchestrating, and monitoring a WOSA. In this context, I'll use the term *workflow management system* (WMS) to refer to such systems. When developing a WMS, various properties must be considered. In the following subsections, I will briefly discuss the most common ones.

Flexibility

A flexible WMS is capable of managing a diverse range of tasks and workflows. For instance, it should support the creation of simple linear workflows as well as more complex ones. Additionally, it should offer flexibility in how workflows are initiated, allowing for scheduled executions as well as triggering based on specific events, such as the arrival of files or data in designated storage locations.

Configurability

A configurable WMS enables users to define workflow specifications according to their needs. For instance, many WMSs allow users to define workflows and tasks using infrastructure-as-code (IaC) methodologies. This can be achieved through programming languages like Python or Domain-Specific Languages (DSLs) such as JSON.

With IaC, users can programmatically define workflow and task specifications such as dependency structure, input/output parameters, error handling, timeout policy, retry logic, status update, workflow triggers, concurrent execution limit, logging, and many more. Figure 11-3 illustrates a typical approach to workflow and task definition, which contains all the information necessary to define the behavior of a workflow.

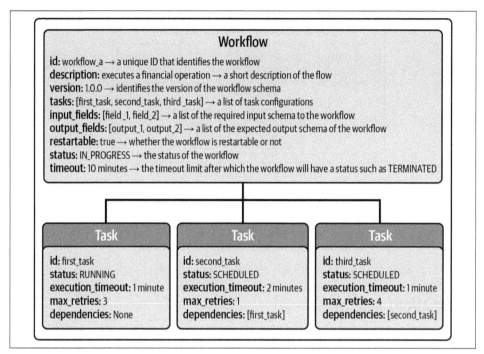

Figure 11-3. A workflow and task definition template

Dependency Management

WMSs vary in how they manage and configure dependencies between tasks and workflows. In simple WMSs, users are only able to define static and linear workflows. However, more advanced WMSs may allow for parallel workflow/task execution, dynamic and conditional task creation, and information passing between tasks. To illustrate, (a) in Figure 11-4 displays a workflow where tasks 3 and 4 are conditionally executed after task 2, depending on whether a specific condition is satisfied; if not, task 5 follows task 2. In contrast, (b) in Figure 11-4 illustrates a workflow that dynamically generates a variable number of tasks (N) at runtime, based on the input received from task 1.

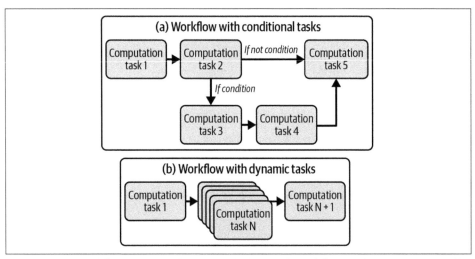

Figure 11-4. Workflow with conditional tasks (a), and workflow with dynamic tasks (b)

Coordination Patterns

In every WMS, components like workflows and tasks are designed to interact with each other. Various communication patterns have been developed to describe how these interactions occur. Two notable patterns are the *Synchronous Blocking Pattern* (SBP) and the *Asynchronous Non-Blocking Pattern* (ANBP).

The SBP involves one component calling another and waiting for a response, which is typical in systems using HTTP and RESTful APIs. In a WOSA relying on an SBP, each task within a workflow is executed sequentially within the same process, with each task waiting for the previous one to complete before proceeding.

Conversely, the Asynchronous Non-Blocking Pattern operates in a fire-and-forget mode, where a component sends a request or message to another component without waiting for a response or confirming its processing. In a WMS, this pattern can be implemented by running each workflow task independently on separate processes or machines and having a dedicated task queue that gathers incoming messages for execution. Figure 11-5 provides a visual representation of this concept.

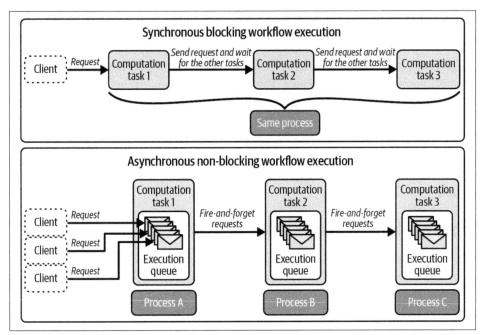

Figure 11-5. Synchronous Blocking Pattern versus Asynchronous Non-Blocking Pattern

Scalability

WMS scalability is typically assessed based on its capacity to handle concurrent executions of workflows and tasks. The scalability requirements vary depending on the nature of the WMS. Event-driven and high-volume WMSs, for instance, demand robust scalability capabilities to manage large volumes of tasks triggered by real-time events or continuous streams of data. In contrast, scheduled batch-oriented WMSs may have less stringent scalability needs as they operate on predefined schedules and process tasks in batches.

Integration

A highly desired feature of WMSs is their capability to seamlessly integrate with other tools and technologies, especially those that the WMS is designed to manage or coordinate. For example, when orchestrating applications in the cloud, it might be more convenient to rely on a cloud-based WMS as it will easily integrate with the cloud services running the applications.

Many WMSs incorporate operators, which are predefined tasks enabling seamless integration with a variety of technologies. These operators facilitate common and essential operations within workflows. For instance, a database operator allows users to establish connections and interact with specific types of databases like Postgres, Redshift, Snowflake, and BigQuery. This capability streamlines workflow execution by providing ready-made functionalities for interacting with diverse technological environments.

Now that you have established a foundational understanding of workflows, let's explore some of the most common types of data workflows, outlining their key characteristics, the technologies they employ, and their applications in the financial domain.

Types of Financial Data Workflows

This section explores four fundamental types of data workflows that are central to financial data engineering: *Extract-Transform-Load (ETL) workflows* streamline data movement and transformation; *microservices workflows* facilitate modular and scalable application architectures; *machine learning workflows* automate model training and deployment pipelines; and *streaming workflows* enable real-time data processing and analytics. Each type plays a critical role in enhancing efficiency and responsiveness across diverse data-driven applications and industries. Let's explore each of these workflow types in more detail.

Extract-Transform-Load Workflows

The predominant type of data workflow is Extract-Transform-Load (ETL), a three-phase workflow in which data is retrieved from one or more sources, transformed using predefined business logic, and saved in a target destination.

In a typical ETL workflow, raw data files are initially extracted and stored in a staging area within a data lake. Following this, various transformations are applied to each file. This can range from data quality checks and cleaning operations (e.g., drop duplicates, handle null values, remove erroneous records, standardize fields, etc.) to computation and data enrichment steps (e.g., scaling, normalization, feature engineering, etc.). Finally, transformed data is stored in the enterprise data warehouse, which serves as the central repository from which data consumers access and utilize the data they need.[1] Figure 11-6 illustrates this ETL use case.

---

1 For a comprehensive treatment of data warehouse-oriented ETL, I highly recommend the seminal work of Joe Caserta and Ralph Kimball, *The Data Warehouse ETL Toolkit: Practical Techniques for Extracting, Cleaning, Conforming, and Delivering Data* (Wiley, 2013).

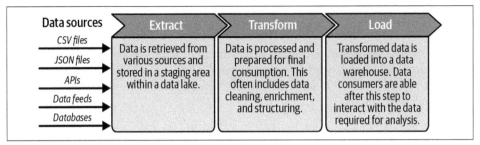

Figure 11-6. Illustration of the ETL workflow

ETL workflows may vary in terms of complexity and requirements. Traditional ETL workflows are often built as linear DAGs that process data in batches with a predefined schedule (e.g., daily or weekly). However, challenges can arise when new business problems create additional scalability and performance requirements. For example, you might need to implement parallel processing in your workflow to accommodate larger data volumes. This can involve, for example, splitting a large file into small chunks and transforming each into a separate dynamic task. Another major problem occurs when new types of data arrival processes must be handled. Nowadays, it is common to have data arriving in regular batches, as well as single data entries generated through event-based mechanisms.[2]

A large variety of ETL WMSs are available. These include commercial enterprise tools (e.g., IBM DataStage, Oracle Data Integrator, Talend, Informatica), open source tools (e.g., Apache Airflow, Prefect, Mage, Apache Spark), cloud-based tools (e.g., AWS Glue, Google Dataprep), and custom tools. These tools vary in terms of the features that we illustrated previously in "Workflow Management Systems" on page 410.

With so many ETL tools available, it can be overwhelming to choose the right one. I recommend starting by defining your workflows and identifying the features you need based on your business requirements. Subsequently, evaluate the various options in the context of your existing technological stack. For example, if you are running all of your stack on AWS, then you might benefit from using Amazon Managed Workflows for Apache Airflow or AWS Glue. Importantly, I highly recommend not using a complex tool to perform basic ETL operations. It might be that all you need is a simple job scheduler that runs a Python script on a provisioned server or managed services such as AWS Lambda or AWS Batch, or Python shell jobs in AWS Glue.

---

2 For more on ETL patterns, I recommend Vasileios Theodorou, Alberto Abelló, Maik Thiele, and Wolfgang Lehner's "Frequent Patterns in ETL Workflows: An Empirical Approach" (*https://oreil.ly/PW9GU*), *Data & Knowledge Engineering* 112 (November 2017): 1–16.

Apache Airflow: Why Is It So Popular?

Apache Airflow, developed and released by Airbnb in 2015, has become the leading open source tool for data workflow management. Airflow can be deployed as a containerized application and is also available as a managed service from cloud providers like Google and Amazon.

Airflow's high popularity is due to its extensive feature set and the frequent addition of new features and optimizations. It functions as an IaC tool, allowing workflows to be defined as DAGs written in Python. In addition, it offers a wide range of operators, triggers, customizable plug-ins, a flexible flow design (dynamic tasks, cross-DAG dependencies), SLA features, a security model, a rich UI, and operational control options.

Apache Airflow is fundamentally an orchestration engine with great versatility. It's designed to schedule, manage, and monitor different types of workflows, including data pipelines, machine learning pipelines, batch processing pipelines, reporting and monitoring pipelines, data migration, and data quality checks.

Like most tools, Airflow has several drawbacks to consider. First, while Airflow supports passing data between tasks using XCOM, it still does not offer a highly reliable and scalable method for cross-task data sharing. Second, Airflow is primarily designed for batch processing and does not natively support real-time or event-driven data streams. Third, being a workflow orchestrator rather than a dedicated data processing framework, Airflow lacks some performance and scalability features required for handling large volumes of data. In such cases, integrating specialized tools like Apache Spark for intensive data processing within an Airflow DAG can be a viable option.

ETL workflows are essential for financial institutions. They are extensively used to automate the extraction of subscription-based data from financial data vendors. Another common use case is data aggregation, where various types of data are periodically retrieved from multiple sources and consolidated into a single repository, such as a data warehouse. ETL workflows also automate the generation of risk and analytical reports for internal use, dashboarding systems, and compliance. Last but not least, they are used in financial research involving historical data analysis and processing, financial analysis, risk calculations, portfolio reconciliation, and performance tracking.

Stream Processing Workflows

A stream processing workflow consists of a sequence of data processing steps where data flows as a continuous stream of events and is processed in real time, enabling immediate reactions to new information. Figure 11-7 illustrates the concept visually.

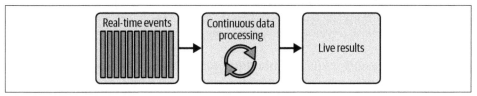

Figure 11-7. Illustration of a basic stream processing workflow

Stream workflow management solutions prioritize scalability for large data streams, fast transformations, in-memory computing, event-driven capabilities, and asynchronous non-blocking data processing.

A typical streaming architecture consists of four main components:

Ingestion layer
Handles the real-time reception of incoming data traffic from various sources. For example, a dedicated application can be deployed on AWS EC2 and load-balanced using AWS Elastic Load Balancing (ELB).

Message broker
Stores the event stream and acts as a high-performance intermediary between data producers and consumers. Examples include Apache Kafka and Google Pub/Sub.

Stream processing engine
Consumes data from a topic and applies transformations, analytics, or checks. Examples include Apache Storm, Apache Flink, Spark Streaming, and cloud functions such as AWS Lambda.

Data storage system
Persists the data for further consumption. Examples include Apache Cassandra, AWS DynamoDB, Google Bigtable, and Google Firestore.

Figure 11-8 illustrates this architecture.

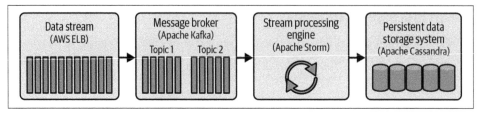

Figure 11-8. Example of a typical stream processing architecture

More complex stream workflow architectures can be built. One common pattern is the *lambda architecture*, which typically consists of three layers:

Speed layer
Handles real-time stream processing and creates real-time views for instant insights.

Batch layer
Consumes the same data stream to perform historical analysis, persisting a reliable view of the data (batch view).

Serving layer
Responds to queries made to both the speed and batch views.

The three layers can be implemented in various ways, but a basic illustration is shown in Figure 11-9. As depicted, data is first received by AWS ELB and then ingested into a Kafka topic. Once the new data enters Kafka, it is simultaneously consumed by the batch and speed layers' consumer groups. The speed layer generates real-time views for low-latency access to recent data, while the batch layer operates in a lower latency but higher throughput mode. This ensures that data is prepared, cleaned, preprocessed, aggregated, checked against existing historical data, and reliably persisted for later use.

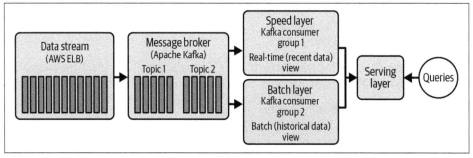

Figure 11-9. Illustration of a lambda architecture

Lambda architectures are often criticized for their complexity and the maintenance overhead they entail. A simpler alternative, known as the *kappa architecture*, integrates batch and real-time processing into a unified workflow that treats all data as a continuous stream. This approach leverages a single high-performance stream processing engine, simplifying both implementation and management.[3] Figure 11-10 provides an example. Initially, data is received by AWS ELB and then ingested into a Kafka topic. Once the data enters Kafka, it is consumed by the stream processing layer, which utilizes an Apache Flink engine to process these events in real time, performing various transformations. The processed data is subsequently stored in a Cassandra database, allowing for efficient querying and further analysis.

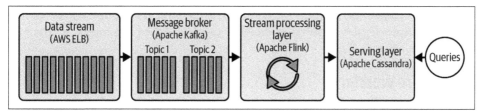

Figure 11-10. A kappa architecture

Stream processing finds numerous applications within the financial sector, with one prominent use case being real-time fraud detection and analytics. Financial institutions face significant threats from payment and credit card fraud, as highlighted by the 2023 Association for Financial Professionals Payments Fraud and Control Survey report (*https://oreil.ly/5HSVR*), underwritten by JPMorgan, which revealed that 65% of participants experienced payment fraud attacks or attempts in 2022. Effective fraud detection systems necessitate automation to reduce manual workload, high accuracy to minimize false positives and maintain customer satisfaction, scalability to handle large transaction volumes, and speed for real-time assessment and transaction execution.

Real-time stream processing architectures provide a robust solution to tackle these challenges. For instance, combining Apache Kafka as a messaging stream broker with Apache Spark ML for predictive modeling and Apache Spark Streaming for real-time stream processing can be highly effective. Similar architectures leveraging tools like Apache Flink and Apache Storm also offer robust alternatives.[4] Managed cloud streaming solutions cater specifically to these needs, such as Azure Stream Analytics, which includes built-in machine learning capabilities for anomaly detection (*https://*

---

3 To learn more about the Lambda and Kappa architectures, I highly recommend James Warren and Nathan Marz's *Big Data: Principles and Best Practices of Scalable Real-Time Data Systems* (Manning, 2015).

4 For a good discussion of this topic, I recommend "Fraud Detection with Apache Kafka, KSQL and Apache Flink" (*https://oreil.ly/ujJDz*), by Kai Waehner. To better understand how to assess the requirements of stream processing systems, I recommend the paper by Michael Stonebraker, Uğur Çetintemel, and Stan Zdonik, "The 8 Requirements of Real-Time Stream Processing" (*https://oreil.ly/TRN0z*), *ACM SIGMOID Record* 34, no. 4 (December 2005): 42–47.

oreil.ly/L20sT), Amazon Managed Services for Apache Flink, and Google Cloud Dataflow. In addition, AWS provides Elastic MapReduce (EMR), a versatile platform enabling users to build and manage big data environments encompassing Apache Spark and Apache Flink, among other tools.

Another application of stream processing in financial markets is for powering data feeds. Streaming architectures can be used to efficiently ingest, process, and analyze real-time market data sourced from stock exchanges, data providers, and trading platforms. Furthermore, financial institutions are progressively embracing streaming solutions to update their data infrastructure. This involves migrating diverse operational data from legacy mainframe systems to cloud-based platforms, a process known as *mainframe offload*.

Microservice Workflows

In Chapter 6, you were introduced to the concept of microservices. As a reminder, microservices are small, self-contained, and independently deployable applications that work together. There is a growing trend toward using microservice architectures to effectively implement and bring business ideas to life. Crucially, for microservices to collaborate effectively, coordination is essential. This typically involves defining and managing microservice workflows, which I will be discussing in this section.

Prior to designing a microservice workflow, it's crucial to assess several factors. First of all, determining what qualifies as a microservice requires careful consideration from both technical and business perspectives. From a technical standpoint, it's important to strike a balance between high cohesion and low coupling. This means minimizing dependencies between microservices while ensuring that related application logic remains cohesive within each microservice. Figure 11-11 illustrates the concept.

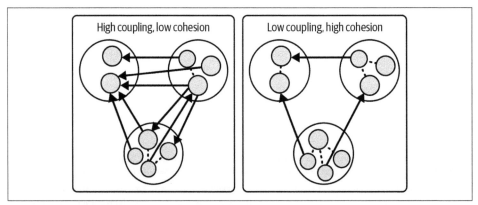

Figure 11-11. Coupling versus cohesion

From a business standpoint, a significant challenge involves deciding how to formalize and integrate business logic across multiple microservices. Various approaches exist for this purpose, including object-oriented principles such as the Single Responsibility Principle (SRP), procedural patterns like the transaction script pattern, and comprehensive frameworks such as Domain-Driven Design (DDD).

DDD is quite elegant and provides a reliable approach for designing business logic in a microservice architecture. In DDD, developers design the so-called *domain models* to capture and represent the business requirements and unique components of a domain, establishing a conceptual basis for building software applications. A business model includes the entities, relationships, rules, and logic that define a specific domain or problem space within an application.

DDD strives to establish a *ubiquitous language* that fosters shared understanding among domain experts and developers. Ubiquitous language helps bridge the communication gap between technical and nontechnical stakeholders, facilitating more effective collaboration and a clearer definition of requirements.

Another essential concept in DDD is *bounded context* (BC), which can be thought of as the setting that defines the meaning of a word. Just as "bond" can refer to different things depending on the context, a BC establishes clear and distinct definitions for terms and concepts within a specific domain area. This helps break down complex domains into manageable subdomains, ensuring clarity and alignment with business needs and allowing developers to focus on a specific area of the domain without being overwhelmed by the complexity of the entire domain.[5]

After you have defined and created your microservices, the next step is to organize them in a workflow. A microservice workflow coordinates multiple microservices to ensure they operate following a specific business logic, thereby achieving cohesive application functionality. To illustrate the idea, let's consider a simple example of an online store order processing system based on microservices, as depicted in Figure 11-12. As shown in the figure, when a customer submits a purchase order, six microservices collaborate to manage the various stages of the order lifecycle.

---

5 To learn more about how to use DDD in designing microservices, consult *Microservices Patterns: With Examples in Java* by Chris Richardson (Manning, 2018).

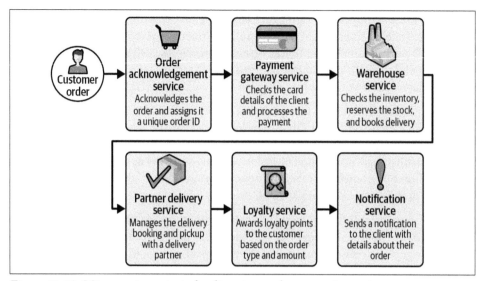

Figure 11-12. Microservice-oriented online store order processing system

In real-world scenarios, microservice workflows frequently exhibit greater complexity than the linear structure depicted in Figure 11-12. This happens when microservices are deployed in a distributed system. Here, establishing reliable communication mechanisms becomes critical for coordinating microservices and maintaining workflow consistency. Traditional application designs typically rely on ACID database transactions for this purpose. However, in distributed microservice systems, it is technically cumbersome to implement distributed ACID transactions.

As a reliable alternative, microservice engineers often rely on a popular design pattern known as the *saga pattern* (*https://oreil.ly/1LnOE*). A saga organizes a microservice workflow into a sequence of local transactions, where each transaction executes its logic and communicates with the next via update messages or events. Two primary approaches exist for coordinating a saga: choreography and orchestration.

In choreography-based sagas, microservices directly communicate and coordinate with each other to complete the workflow. Each microservice acts as both a participant and coordinator within the collaborative process. This means that each microservice needs to be aware of the business process, the services with whom to interact, the tasks to execute, and the messages to exchange.

On the other hand, orchestration-based sagas introduce a central orchestrator to manage the workflow execution. In this approach, participating microservices do not need to be aware that they are part of a larger orchestration process. Instead, they simply follow instructions provided by the orchestrator. Orchestration-based sagas commonly leverage a message broker to facilitate communication and ensure the orderly execution of tasks across distributed microservices.

Let's look at the two saga patterns. Part (a) in Figure 11-13 represents a choreography-based saga. In this instance, services interact directly with each other using specific topics. For example, Services A and B communicate with Service E via Topic E, while Services E and F use Topic B to interact with Service B, and Service C communicates with Service G through Topic G. In contrast, (b) in Figure 11-13 illustrates an orchestration-based saga, where all service communication is mediated by a central orchestrator. Each service receives instructions from the orchestrator via its designated topic and communicates back to the orchestrator through the same topic.

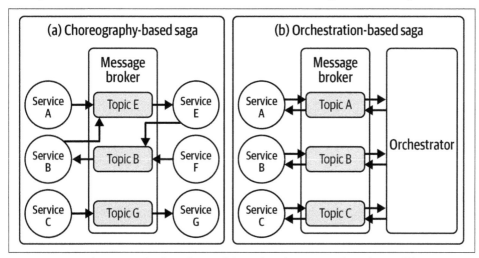

Figure 11-13. Choreography-based saga (a), and orchestration-based saga (b)

In terms of technological implementation, a microservice workflow management system can be designed in various ways. If we consider the more prevalent orchestration-based approach, a fundamental setup typically includes three components:

- A core orchestration engine responsible for managing workflows and facilitating communication among microservices. This engine could be a custom-built application using languages like Java or Python, an open source tool such as Orkes Conductor, or a cloud-managed solution such as AWS Step Functions or Google Workflows.

- A backend database to store details about workflow executions, ideally suited for OLTP systems such as PostgreSQL.

- A message broker for handling the queuing and exchange of messages between microservices. Options include Apache Kafka, Google Pub/Sub, or Redis, depending on specific requirements and preferences.

Keep in mind that the simpler your workflows are, the easier it will be to choose and design a workflow management solution. If you find yourself in a situation where existing solutions do not meet your microservice workflow requirements, it may be beneficial to carefully review and streamline the underlying structure and logic of your workflows before opting for more complex or custom solutions.

Microservices have been making a substantial impact across diverse industries, including the financial sector. A key driver behind this is the emergence of FinTech firms, leveraging cutting-edge technologies and design patterns to create disruptive financial solutions. By segmenting their applications into smaller microservices, FinTech firms gain the required agility to develop, update, and deploy individual functionalities independently.

Meanwhile, traditional financial institutions are embracing microservices as part of their digital transformation and reengineering endeavors aimed at fostering innovation while adapting to the evolving technological landscape. A prominent trend in this realm is the advent of platform and open banking (*https://oreil.ly/rEx4R*), wherein banks evolve into interconnected ecosystems of financial services. This often involves establishing strategic partnerships with FinTech firms to integrate and deploy their offerings seamlessly within the traditional banking infrastructure.

Through the utilization of microservices, banks can initiate new collaborations with FinTech firms by creating isolated microservices for each distinct application, facilitating streamlined integration and enabling rapid deployment of innovative financial solutions.[6]

Machine Learning Workflows

A machine learning project involves applying scientific techniques and algorithms to analyze and detect patterns from the data, build predictive models, or automate decision-making processes. These projects typically include stages such as data collection, preprocessing, model selection, training, testing, evaluation, and deployment. Given their structured and logical nature, ML projects are often organized as data

---

6 For an interesting case study from the financial sector, see how Danske Bank, the largest bank in Denmark, moved from a monolith codebase into a microservice-oriented architecture, as presented in Antonio Buc-chiarone, Nicola Dragoni, Schahram Dustdar, Stephan T. Larsen, and Manuel Mazzara's "From Monolithic to Microservices: An Experience Report from the Banking Domain" (*https://oreil.ly/KZm0h*), *IEEE Software* 35, no. 3 (May–June 2018): 50–55.

workflows to ensure their systematic and effective execution as well as optimal data and lifecycle management.[7]

In real-world scenarios, ML workflows can be designed in multiple ways, depending on the unique business needs, data characteristics, and technical requirements. To provide a basic perspective, I will divide the stages involved in an ML workflow into three categories: data related, modeling related, and deployment related. Let's explore each category in some detail.

Data-related steps:

Data extraction
> This very first step involves identifying and extracting all required data from various sources, such as databases, APIs, or files.

Quality checks
> Once the data is extracted, quality checks are performed to ensure multiple quality dimensions such as accuracy, validity, completeness, timeliness, and many more.

Preprocessing
> Once quality checks are completed, preprocessing steps are applied to get the data ready for model training. This includes tasks such as feature engineering, scaling, normalization, encoding, embedding, enrichment, imputation, and many more.

Modeling steps:

Model selection
> In this phase, you choose the appropriate machine learning algorithms, models, and optimization techniques based on the nature of your business problem and needs, data quality attributes, and performance requirements.

Training
> The selected model is trained on the preprocessed data to learn meaningful patterns from the data and achieve generalizability.

Evaluation
> Once trained, the model's performance is evaluated using various metrics and techniques to assess its ability to generalize to new, unseen data.

---

7 For a more detailed discussion of the value and the need for ML workflows, I suggest Hui Miao, Ang Li, Larry S. Davis, and Amol Deshpande's "Towards Unified Data and Lifecycle Management for Deep Learning" (*https://oreil.ly/IRNmt*), in the *2017 IEEE 33rd International Conference on Data Engineering (ICDE)* (IEEE, 2017): 571–582.

Model deployment steps:

Deployment
> After successful evaluation, the trained model is packaged and deployed into production or operational environments, where it can process requests for making predictions or classifications on new data.

Serving
> The deployed model is exposed to its final consumers via APIs or other interfaces to serve predictions in real-time or batch mode, depending on the business requirements at hand.

Model feedback
> Continuous monitoring and feedback mechanisms are put in place to assess the model's performance in production, collect feedback from users, and introduce improvements or updates as necessary.

For production ML workflows, additional features are often required. First, a *model registry* is often implemented to store and version persistent various ML workflow steps, including their code, parameters, and data output. This is useful as it enables a business to keep track of historical workflows, ensure point-in-time reproducibility, share ML models across teams, and ensure compliance and transparency.

Second, a highly desired feature of ML workflows is *checkpointing*. This involves periodically saving the workflow's state—including model parameters, data processing stages, and execution context—to persistent storage. In case of a failure, this allows the workflow to reload and resume from the last saved checkpoint.

Third, ML data modeling often requires a specialized, analytical approach. *Feature stores* represent a formal method for implementing this. A feature store is a centralized repository for storing, managing, and serving precomputed and curated machine learning features. Feature stores provide several benefits. First, they enable feature reuse by storing developed features for quick access and sharing across ML models and teams, thereby saving time and fostering efficiency in model development and cross-team cooperation. Second, they ensure feature consistency by centralizing feature definitions and development documentation, which helps maintain uniformity across large organizations. Last, they enhance security and data governance by tracking the data used for model training and deployment.

Fourth, an ML workflow often demands specific computing resources to ensure optimal performance. This can entail leveraging advanced technologies like GPUs for accelerated computation, distributed and parallel computing frameworks for handling large-scale data processing tasks efficiently, and specialized data storage systems such as vector databases, which store data as vector embeddings for fast retrieval and similarity search.

Finally, ensuring the stability, automation, and quality of an ML workflow's deployment and performance requires incorporating software engineering and MLOps best practices. MLOps, short for machine learning operations, encompasses methodologies and tools aimed at automating and optimizing the deployment and management of ML workflows.

Figure 11-14 illustrates the several stages involved in a typical machine learning pipeline as well as the undercurrents that underpin a reliable ML workflow management system.

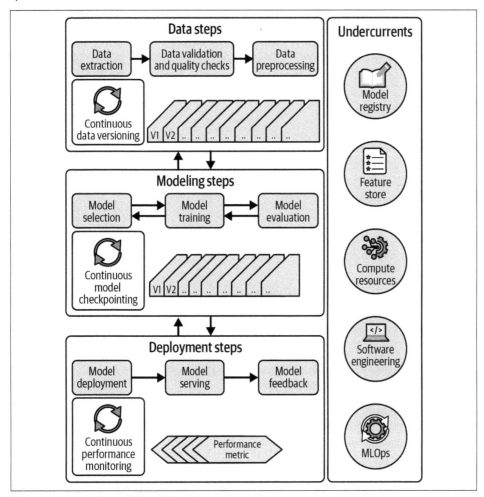

Figure 11-14. ML workflow lifecycle

Designers of ML workflows may need to integrate various domain-specific requirements. For instance, financial institutions must adhere to regulations and guidelines concerning fairness, transparency, and accountability in algorithmic decision-making. An example is the US Equal Credit Opportunity Act of 1974, which mandates creditors to provide applicants with specific reasons for credit denials or altered terms upon request. To comply, an ML workflow must include features to track, retrieve, and explain data, model mechanics, assumptions, and predictions.

Privacy-Preserving Machine Learning Workflows in Finance

In financial markets, the sensitive nature of financial data, coupled with growing public demand for privacy protection and the introduction of stringent privacy regulation worldwide, has imposed restrictions on how and what data can be analyzed, processed, and shared.

To address these issues, financial ML workflows must integrate privacy-preserving features to ensure that sensitive data used in machine learning tasks remains secure and confidential throughout the various phases of the workflow. Key techniques include the following:

Homomorphic encryption
    Enables computation on encrypted data without decrypting it, preserving data confidentiality during processing. This technique typically requires complex mathematical operations that can significantly slow down processing speed and increase computational overhead.

Differential privacy
    Introduces noise to query results to protect individual data privacy while maintaining statistical accuracy.

Secure multiparty computation
    Enables computations across multiple parties without revealing each party's private data to the others. This protocol ensures that each party can contribute their data securely to the computation process while maintaining confidentiality.

Federated learning
    Trains machine learning models on decentralized data sources without exchanging raw data, thereby preserving privacy.

Synthetic data generation
    Creates artificial data that retains statistical properties of the original dataset while protecting sensitive information.

Implementing these techniques ensures that financial machine learning workflows uphold privacy standards, fostering responsible data usage and enhancing security measures in the finance sector.

The challenges involved in building reliable and high-performance ML models largely revolve around effective data management and ensuring data quality. As a financial data engineer, your responsibility is crucial in establishing robust ML workflows. These workflows are indispensable in today's financial markets, where the integration of ML and AI technologies stands as the primary driver of transformation and innovation.[8]

Summary

This chapter provided a comprehensive examination of financial data workflows and their fundamental concepts. It started by emphasizing the value and need for workflows through the concept of workflow-oriented software architectures. The chapter then defined both data workflows and workflow management systems, highlighting their key features. Finally, it provided an in-depth examination of the main types of data workflows used within the financial sector, offering comprehensive insights into their fundamental concepts and applications. These are ETL, microservices, stream processing, and machine learning workflows.

Congratulations on reaching this point of the book. Your thorough understanding of the foundational concepts of financial data engineering has prepared you for the practical hands-on experience that awaits in the next and final chapter, where you will work on four engaging hands-on projects.

---

8 To learn more about the data-related challenges encountered in ML workflow design, I recommend Neoklis Polyzotis, Sudip Roy, Steven Euijong Whang, and Martin Zinkevich's "Data Lifecycle Challenges in Production Machine Learning: A Survey" (*https://oreil.ly/K4eIB*), *ACM SIGMOD Record* 47, no. 2 (December 2018): 17–28.

## CHAPTER 12

Hands-On Projects

Now that you've gained a fundamental grasp of financial data engineering, it's time to put it into practice. In this chapter, you will go through a series of practical projects designed to give you firsthand experience working with financial data.

Four projects will be discussed, each focusing on a different problem and employing a unique technological stack:

1. Constructing a bank account management system with PostgreSQL
2. Building a financial data ETL workflow with Mage
3. Developing a financial microservice workflow with Netflix Conductor
4. Implementing a reference data store with OpenFIGI, PermID, and GLEIF APIs

A few points should be mentioned about these projects. First, they are meant to provide hands-on experience with financial data engineering and may not necessarily represent complete solutions for real business problems. Additionally, they are intended to be executed locally on your machine and not deployed in a production environment. Finally, the employed technologies are not indicative of the author's personal preferences; instead, they reflect the author's prudent consideration of what would best clarify the problems and solutions for the reader.

Prerequisites

All projects in this chapter will be packaged and isolated with all their dependencies into Docker containers. Docker is the most popular open source software for operating system (OS) virtualization (aka containerization). It is available for Windows, macOS, and Linux through *Docker Desktop*. Therefore, to run the projects on your machine, you must install the Docker Desktop version that is compatible with your operating system. Please follow the instructions in the official Docker documentation (*https://oreil.ly/bWa1c*) to complete the installation. Furthermore, as you will be running more than one container in each project, you will be using a specific multicontainer orchestration tool called Docker Compose (*https://oreil.ly/KzSYO*), which is ideal for local testing and development.

The other prerequisite is to clone this book's GitHub repository onto your local machine. First, make sure you have Git (*https://oreil.ly/7Xnmv*) installed. Then, open a terminal in your computer, navigate to the location where you want to pull the project files, and finally, clone the repository (*https://oreil.ly/UeQyE*).

Project 1: Designing a Bank Account Management System Database with PostgreSQL

Account management is a core functionality for banks, allowing them to handle and oversee customer accounts, balances, and transactions. In this project, you will design and implement a relational database system for managing bank accounts. You will be using the conceptual/logical/physical data modeling approach discussed in Chapter 8.

Conceptual Model: Business Requirements

In the conceptual phase, the focus is on understanding business requirements and defining the high-level structure of the database system. Operational and business models vary from one banking institution to another, and not all banks offer the same products and services. As such, you will design a simple and generic bank account management system for this project.

We'll assume that stakeholders have defined their requirements and that these have been formalized them into entities, relationships, and constraints. Let's explore each in greater depth.

Entities

Our bank account management system needs to store data for seven types of entities: accounts, customers, loans, transactions, branches, employees, and cards.

Accounts are the most essential product that banks offer to their customers. For this reason, the account entity is needed to maintain detailed records of the various account types offered by the bank (e.g., savings, checking), along with account IDs, associated customers, balances, and more.

Loans are also a key banking product. Thus, the loan entity is needed to store information such as loan ID, terms (including amount, duration, interest rate, payment schedule, and start and end dates), type (such as mortgage or personal loan), and other relevant details.

In addition to accounts and loans, most banks provide a range of payment cards to their clients. As a result, the card entity is crucial for storing card-related information, including cardholder ID, associated accounts, card numbers, issuance and expiration dates, and other relevant details.

Customers represent the bank's client base, including both individuals and organizations. Therefore, the customer entity is essential for storing vital client information, such as IDs, names, addresses, statuses (e.g., active, inactive), and contact details (e.g., email addresses and phone numbers).

Employees are the individuals hired by the bank to deliver various services to customers. To manage employee information, the employee entity is required to store attributes such as employee IDs, names, job titles, and the branch where they are assigned.

Branches are the bank's physical locations where customers engage with employees to perform various transactions. The branch entity is essential for managing branch information, including branch IDs, names, addresses, and phone numbers.

Lastly, banks must track all transactions associated with customer accounts. Therefore, the transaction entity is vital for recording transaction details such as transaction IDs, associated account IDs, employee IDs (for transactions initiated by employees), timestamps, and amounts.

Relationships

The business team has requested that the following relationships be established between entities:

- Each account should be linked to a customer.
- Each loan should be linked to a customer.
- Each loan payment should be linked to a transaction and an account.
- Each employee should be affiliated with a branch.
- Each card should be associated with both a customer and an account.

These relationships ensure data integrity and facilitate efficient data retrieval and management.

Constraints

The business team has outlined the following constraints to be enforced within the database implementation:

- Account balances must never go below a customer-specific minimum amount.
- All entity records (e.g., accounts, loans, transactions) must be identified with a unique ID.
- Data redundancy should be minimized.
- Null values are not permitted for certain fields.
- Specific fields, such as email addresses, must be unique across records.

Constraints play a pivotal role in ensuring high data quality, consistency, integrity, and compliance, which in turn contributes to the reliability of the account management system.

Logical Model: Entity Relationship Diagram

Now that we have stakeholder agreement on the account management conceptual model, the next step is to build the logical model. This stage focuses on selecting the data storage model most suitable for our system (a concept discussed in Chapter 8).

After a thorough evaluation, the financial data engineering team has concluded that the relational model is the best fit. This model effectively organizes various entities into distinct tables and ensures data integrity through database constraints. Moreover, the relational model supports the implementation of a normalized data structure, which is essential for our system.

To implement this, we need to create the *Entity Relationship Diagram* (ERD) for our logical model. An ERD is a visual representation used to model the structure of a database. It illustrates the entities (such as tables or objects) within a system, their attributes (such as fields or properties), and the relationships among these entities. An ERD is constructed using information collected and summarized from the previous conceptual phase. Various tools are available for drawing ERDs, including Lucidchart, Creately, DBDiagram, ERDPlus, DrawSQL, QuickDBD, and EdrawMax. Figure 12-1 illustrates the ERD of our account management system.

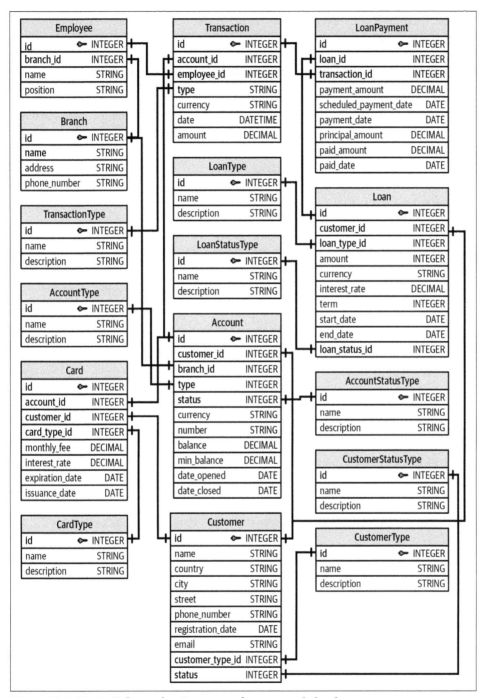

Figure 12-1. Entity Relationship Diagram of our example bank account management system

With the ERD design complete, let's move on to the next step: selecting the database technology and translating our ERD into database queries.

Physical Model: Data Definition and Manipulation Language

With our logical data model ready, it's time to choose a relational database technology and write the queries to create and populate our tables. Let's assume the financial data engineering team has selected PostgreSQL as the database management system due to its high reliability and strong adherence to SQL standards.

Now, let's shift gears and test things on your machine.

Project 1: Local Testing

To interact with PostgreSQL, you will need to run two Docker containers: one for the PostgreSQL database instance and another for pgAdmin, a user-friendly UI for interacting with PostgreSQL.

To launch the two containers, open a terminal and navigate to the following path:

```
# Bash
cd {path/to/book/repo}/FinancialDataEngineering/book/chapter_12/project_1
```

Then execute the following docker compose command (*https://oreil.ly/x3kBG*) to run our project containers:

```
# Bash
docker compose up -d
```

After that, open a browser and paste the URL *http://localhost:8080/* into a new tab. Wait until you see the pgAdmin UI and log in using the dummy credentials (PGADMIN_DEFAULT_EMAIL and PGADMIN_DEFAULT_PASSWORD) in the *.env* file (*https://oreil.ly/eRzH-*). Remember that this setting is for local testing purposes, and you should never share or store passwords publicly or explicitly in your project files.

Once logged in, click on Add New Server and insert the following values:

- In the General tab, give a name to the server (e.g., Bank Account).
- In the Connections tab, set:
  - Host name/address = *postgres*
  - Port = *5432*
  - Maintenance database = *bank_account*
  - Username = *admin*
  - Password = *password*

These are the values that you set in the project's environmental variables file *.env*. In the upcoming projects, we'll utilize pgAdmin, and you'll need to configure it by following similar steps. However, you'll need to use the credentials provided in the *.env* file specific to each project. Once completed, click on Save. Figure 12-2 illustrates these steps.

Figure 12-2. Creating a new server in pgAdmin

After that, from the left sidebar, follow these steps (as shown in Figure 12-3):

1. Navigate to Servers → Bank Account → Databases → bank_account → Schemas → public → Tables.

2. Right-click on Tables and select Query Tool.

Now, we are ready to create our tables. In SQL, using the term *Data Definition Language* (DDL) to denote statements that create or alter database objects is common. DDL statements include CREATE, ALTER, and DROP. The full list of table creation queries is available on this book's GitHub repo (*https://oreil.ly/ZltsM*). You will need to copy and paste all the queries into the Query Tool and click the Run arrow on the top, as illustrated in Figure 12-3. This will create all the tables for our bank account management system. To see the tables, right-click Tables from the left sidebar and hit Refresh. Then you will be able to see the 16 tables, as illustrated in Figure 12-4.

Figure 12-3. Opening the Query Tool editor

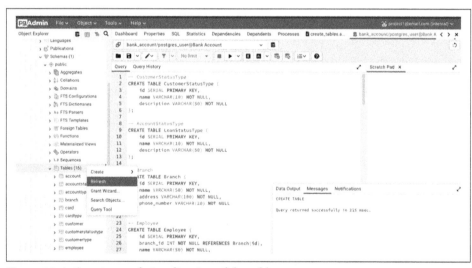

Figure 12-4. Creation and visualization of the tables

In this project, you'll manually copy and execute SQL commands directly within pgAdmin's query console. This approach was intentionally chosen to familiarize you with the SQL syntax. It's worth noting that databases can also be interacted with programmatically. For example, in the upcoming projects, we'll utilize Python's database driver, psycopg2, to interact with PostgreSQL.

As you will see, 16 tables were created. To have an idea about our DDL queries, let's take a closer look at the `CREATE TABLE` statement for the account table:

```
-- PostgreSQL
CREATE TABLE Account (
    id SERIAL PRIMARY KEY,
    customer_id INT NOT NULL REFERENCES Customer(id),
    branch_id INT NOT NULL REFERENCES Branch(id),
    type INT NOT NULL REFERENCES AccountType(id),
    currency VARCHAR NOT NULL,
    number VARCHAR NOT NULL UNIQUE,
    balance DECIMAL(10,2) NOT NULL,
    minimum_balance DECIMAL(10,2) NOT NULL DEFAULT 0,
    date_opened DATE NOT NULL,
    date_closed DATE,
    status INT NOT NULL REFERENCES AccountStatusType(id)
    CHECK (balance >= minimum_balance)
);
```

As you can see, the table has a serial ID as a primary key. This is used to automatically generate an increasing sequence of integers. Moreover, the table has four foreign keys referencing the IDs of four distinct tables: Customer, Branch, AccountType, and AccountStatusType. These keys are crucial for ensuring data integrity. Should, for example, a customer with ID 202 not exist in the customer table, the Customer ID foreign key will prevent the creation of an account associated with this customer. Lastly, a key feature of this table is the account balance, which specifies a minimum balance requirement for each customer. A check constraint is added to ensure the balance never falls below the customer-specific minimum. Any attempt to update the balance to a value lower than the specified minimum will result in an error.

Now, let's populate the tables with some data. In SQL, it is common to use the term DDL to indicate statements that add, update, and delete records in a database. For most tables in our system, the insert operations are quite simple. For example, to add a new customer, you would need to run the following:

```
-- PostgreSQL
INSERT INTO Customer (
  customer_type_id, name, country, city, street,
  phone_number, email, status
```

```
) VALUES (
  1, 'John Smith', 'US', 'New York',
  '123 Main St', '123-456-7890', 'john@example.com', 1
);
```

The full script of the insert queries is available in this GitHub file (*https://oreil.ly/ Hrgjp*). Copy all the insert queries, paste them into the Query Tool, and run the operation again. To see the data, right-click on a table name → View/Edit Data → All Rows. See Figure 12-5 for an illustration.

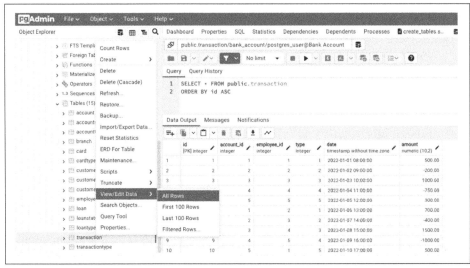

Figure 12-5. Visualization of table rows

Interestingly, some insert queries consist of multiple statements. For example, a payment transaction needs to be recorded in the transactions table and requires a concurrent update of the account balance in the account table. To this end, both statements need to be wrapped with an explicit SQL transaction. It is called explicit because PostgreSQL executes any statement by default within an implicit transaction. Here is an example where a transaction of 40 USD is recorded for the account with ID = 1:

```
-- PostgreSQL
BEGIN;
INSERT INTO transaction (account_id, type, currency, date, amount)
VALUES (1, 4, 'USD', '2022-01-01 08:00:00', -40.00);
UPDATE account
SET balance = balance - 40.00
WHERE id = 1;
COMMIT;
```

Last but not least, an even more complex operation is the loan payment. Here, we need to record the payment in the loan payment table, then store it as a transaction in the transaction table, and finally update the customer's balance in the account table. To illustrate, here is an example of a loan payment of 1,000 USD recorded for the account with ID = 1:

```
-- PostgreSQL
BEGIN;
DO $$
DECLARE
    payment_amount DECIMAL := 1000.00;
BEGIN
    WITH inserted_transaction AS (
        INSERT INTO Transaction (account_id, type, currency, amount)
        VALUES (1, 1, 'USD', -payment_amount)
        RETURNING id
    )
    INSERT INTO LoanPayment (
      loan_id, transaction_id, payment_amount, scheduled_payment_date,
      payment_date, principal_amount, interest_amount, paid_amount
    )
    SELECT
      1, id, payment_amount, '2022-04-01', '2022-04-01',
      900.00, 100.00, payment_amount
    FROM inserted_transaction;

    UPDATE account
    SET balance = balance - payment_amount
    WHERE id = 1;
END$$;
COMMIT;
```

To create more transactions, run the queries in this GitHub file (*https://oreil.ly/ nr_CS*). The query for creating a loan payment is available in this book's GitHub repo (*https://oreil.ly/9K_yn*).

Project 1: Clean Up

Once you are done with the project and you want to move to the next one, make sure you run the following command (*https://oreil.ly/iiFm2*) in the same root directory of Project 1:

```
# Bash
docker compose down
```

This command will stop and remove containers, networks, volumes, and images created by docker compose up.

Project 1: Summary

The goal for this project was to familiarize you with practical data modeling, database design, DDL and DML (Data Manipulation Language), and multistatement transactions. While this project provided a foundational understanding, it's important to note that a real-world bank account management system demands more extensive development. For example, implementing database security features like user roles and permissions, authentication, and data encryption will be necessary. Moreover, you will need a database optimization strategy that involves indexing, clustering, and typing. Finally, you will need to establish a reliable integration between the database and your application. This involves using database connectors, clients, connection pooling, object-relational mappers (e.g., SQLAlchemy), and more. Tackling all of these features is beyond the scope of this book and would require a lot more detailed explanation.

Project 2: Designing a Financial Data ETL Workflow with Mage and Python

In this project, you will design and implement a financial data ETL workflow. This involves retrieving historical stock price data from a financial API, applying various transformations, and ultimately storing the processed data in a database.

More specifically, we will be fetching the intraday open, close, high, and low prices, alongside trading volume, for four prominent stocks: Google, Amazon, IBM, and Apple. The source of our data will be the free version of the Alpha Vantage Stock Market API (*https://oreil.ly/f_GVm*). Subsequently, we'll aggregate the intraday values to derive daily averages. Both the raw data and the transformed daily data will be stored in a PostgreSQL database. Let's assume that the workflow must be run once at the start of each month to retrieve data for the previous month.

Project 2: Workflow Definition

This project's workflow will have a linear structure consisting of the following steps:

1. Data retrieval
   - Fetch adjusted intraday time series history for the past month using the TIME_SERIES_INTRADAY endpoint (*https://oreil.ly/jWueo*). As the free API version allows for 25 requests per day, we'll query data for 4 stocks: Amazon, IBM, Apple, and Google. The API request specifies the following parameters:
     — A one-minute time interval between consecutive data points.
     — adjusted=true to retrieve a time series adjusted by historical split and dividend distributions.

— The month parameter is set to the past month for monthly data retrieval.

— `outputsize=full` to obtain the full intraday history of the specified month.

— `datatype=csv` to receive the time series as a CSV file.

2. Raw data storage

- Store the raw data in the database, recording the ingestion timestamp.

3. Data aggregation

- Select the required columns for the primary transformation task, which will involve aggregating intraday values to compute daily averages.

- Compute daily aggregates by averaging the open, close, high, low, and volume columns, grouped by date and ticker symbol.

4. Deduplication

- Select columns for deduplication to address the aggregation step's behavior of computing aggregates without row grouping, where each row receives the corresponding aggregate of its group.

- Deduplicate the data, retaining the aggregated columns

5. Data export

- Export the daily averages to the database for further analysis.

We will execute each one of these steps in a linear sequence.

Project 2: Database Design

In our database, we will need two tables: one to store the raw intraday data retrieved from the API and another to store the transformed daily data produced at the end of our workflow. Figure 12-6 illustrates the ERD of these tables.

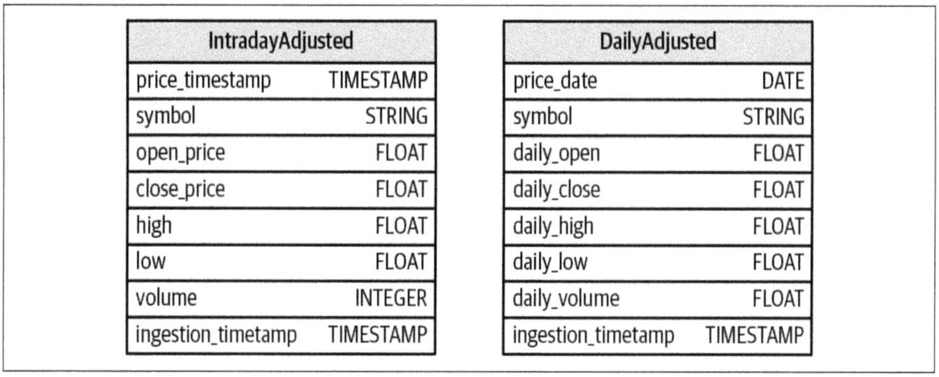

IntradayAdjusted	
price_timestamp	TIMESTAMP
symbol	STRING
open_price	FLOAT
close_price	FLOAT
high	FLOAT
low	FLOAT
volume	INTEGER
ingestion_timetamp	TIMESTAMP

DailyAdjusted	
price_date	DATE
symbol	STRING
daily_open	FLOAT
daily_close	FLOAT
daily_high	FLOAT
daily_low	FLOAT
daily_volume	FLOAT
ingestion_timetamp	TIMESTAMP

Figure 12-6. ERD of the API stock data

Let's move ahead to test our workflow in action.

Project 2: Local Testing

To begin testing, the initial step is to claim your Alpha Vantage API key on the Alpha Vantage website (*https://oreil.ly/N-SW2*). Follow the instructions you find on the page, and you will receive an API key that you need to keep as a secret and never share it with anyone else.

Once you have the API key, you will need to navigate to the project's main directory. As before, this can be done by typing in the following command in your terminal:

```Bash
# Bash
cd {path/to/book/repo}/FinancialDataEngineering/book/chapter_12/project_2
```

Once you are in the main project directory, you will find an *.env* file with a variable called ALPHAVANTAGE_API_KEY. Without using quotes, you must assign this variable the API key you get from Alpha Vantage (i.e., ALPHAVANTAGE _API _KEY=YOUR_API_KEY).

After that, run the project containers with the following command:

```
docker compose up -d
```

Once completed, you will have three running containers:

- Mage (*https://oreil.ly/-s1mz*) running on *http://localhost:6789/*. Mage is an open source data pipeline tool renowned for its user-friendly UI, ease of use, and extensive feature set, making it an ideal option for ETL workflows.
- A PostgreSQL instance where we will store the data.
- The pgAdmin client running on *http://localhost:8080/*. As before, you will use pgAdmin to create the project tables and explore the outcome of your workflow data outputs.

To begin, let's create our tables. Open a tab in your browser and navigate to *http://localhost:8080/*. Log in with the PGADMIN_DEFAULT_EMAIL and PGADMIN_DEFAULT_PASS WORD that you have in your project's *.env* file. Follow the same steps as you did in the first project to create a server, and from the left sidebar, open the database called *stock_data*, then navigate to the schema called *public*. From there, you should be able to open a query tool and execute the queries you find in the *create_tables.sql* file (*https://oreil.ly/YQ5Z7*) to create the tables.

Once the tables are created, it's time to move on to build our ETL workflow. Open another browser tab and navigate to *http://localhost:6789/*. You should be able to see Mage's overview page, as illustrated in Figure 12-7. From the top left, click on "+ New

---

pipeline" and select "Standard (batch)." You will be asked to give your pipeline a name; let's call it *Adjusted Stock Data*. Once done, click on Create.

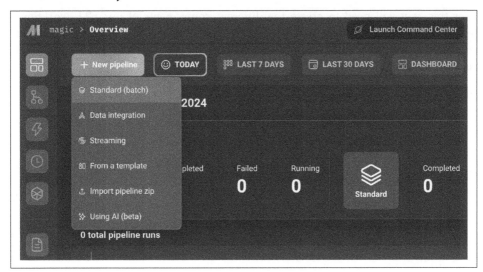

Figure 12-7. Mage overview page

After creating your pipeline, you will be redirected to the pipeline edit page, as shown in Figure 12-8.

Figure 12-8. Pipeline edit page

From the left sidebar, open the file called *io_config.yaml*, delete all its content, and add the content of the *io_config.yaml* file (*https://oreil.ly/6O8RI*) to it. Once done, from the top menu, click File → "Save file" and then close the file editor. The *io_config* file (*https://oreil.ly/7gBzq*) is used by Mage to store and access credentials required to connect to databases and various storage systems.

After this, you will need to create the different components of our ETL workflow. From the same pipeline edit page (Figure 12-8), you can see different buttons that can be used to create an operator, such as data loader, exporter, and transformer. Let's create what we need as follows:

1. Create the API data loader:

   a. Click on +Data loader → Python → API.

   b. Name it *Load Data from Alpha Vantage* and then click "Save and add."

   c. In the code editor that appears, delete all code and replace it with the code in *fetch_intraday_data.py* (*https://oreil.ly/W_AE-*).

   d. From the top menu, click File → Save pipeline.

   e. Use the small up arrow (^) on the top right of the data loader block to close it so you can better see the structure of your pipeline.

   f. In the subsequent phases, repeat steps d and e.

2. Create the raw data exporter:

   a. Click on +Data exporter → Python → PostgreSQL and call it *Export Raw Data*.

   b. Delete the content of the editor that appears and replace it with the code in *export_intraday_data.py* (*https://oreil.ly/bhB6W*).

3. Create the aggregation column selection transformer:

   a. Click on +Transformer → Python → Column removal → Keep columns and name it *Select Aggregation Columns*.

   b. Paste the code from *select_columns_for_aggregation.py* (*https://oreil.ly/fJHCE*) into the editor.

4. Perform the aggregation:

   a. Click on +Transformer → Python → Aggregate → Aggregate by average value and name it *Compute Averages*.

   b. Paste the code from *compute_daily_aggregates.py* (*https://oreil.ly/jAy8K*) into the editor.

5. Create the deduplication column selection transformer:

   a. Click on +Transformer → Python → Column removal → Keep columns and name it *Select Deduplication Columns*.

   b. Paste the code from *select_columns_for_deduplication.py* (*https://oreil.ly/awAQa*) into the editor.

6. Drop the columns that contain duplicates:

    a. Click on +Transformer → Python → Rows actions → Drop duplicates and name it *Drop Duplicates.*

    b. Paste the code from *drop_duplicates.py* (*https://oreil.ly/6eW39*) into the editor.

7. Export the daily average data to the database:

    a. Click on +Data exporter → Python → PostgreSQL and call it *Export Daily Data.*

    b. Paste the code from *export_daily_data.py* (*https://oreil.ly/DFsyG*) into the editor.

Once these steps are done, your workflow is complete and ready to be executed. It should look like Figure 12-9.

Figure 12-9. Overview of the full financial data pipeline

To perform a workflow execution test, navigate to the Pipelines section using Mage's left sidebar. Locate your pipeline named adjusted_stock_data. Click on the pipeline name, then select Run@once from the top menu, and confirm by clicking "Run now." A new execution line with a random name will appear in the table. Click on the name displayed, then patiently observe the execution progress as it advances through the seven steps.

Once completed with success, navigate to the pgAdmin tab in your browser and check the data in the database. You should see that both tables are populated with the data produced by your pipeline.

Project 2: Clean Up

Run the following command in the same root directory of Project 2:

```bash
# Bash
docker compose down
```

Project 2: Summary

Throughout this project, you've gained hands-on experience building a financial ETL workflow with Alpha Vantage API, Mage, Python, and PostgreSQL. In real-world scenarios, you'll probably design and build similar pipelines. Yet, you will very likely need to incorporate more complex transformers and data quality validations. Additionally, you'll need to deal with challenges in pipeline management, such as scheduling, variable and secret management, triggers, scaling, concurrency, and data integration, among others. I strongly advise consulting the official Mage documentation (*https://oreil.ly/-s1mz*) to learn about these subjects and beyond.

Project 3: Designing a Microservice Workflow with Netflix Conductor, PostgreSQL, and Python

In this project, you will implement a microservice-based order management system (OMS) to process orders for an online store. Any online company that wants to streamline the entire order fulfillment process must have an OMS.

It's important to note that microservice workflows often entail more complexity than other types of workflows. Additionally, because microservices tend to be distributed in nature and deployed across diverse environments, accurately replicating microservice architectures locally can be quite challenging. Nonetheless, this project will offer a minimal example to provide insight into the structure and characteristics of microservices.

Project 3: Workflow Definition

The first step in designing a microservice workflow is to define its structure. To this end, let's start by outlining the microservices that will constitute our OMS system. Here are the five microservices we'll need:

Order acknowledgement service
> Handles the acknowledgment of customer orders. It receives a client order, persists it in the database, and returns an acknowledgment message to the customer.

Payment processing service
> Processes customer payment transactions and returns a message informing the customer about the status of their payment operation.

Stock and inventory service

Manages the inventory and stock levels of products available for sale. It tracks and checks the quantity of each product in stock, books and updates inventory based on incoming orders, and returns a message to the customer about the stock booking.

Shipping service

Manages the shipment of orders. This service coordinates with shipping carriers to book a delivery, generate a tracking number, and update the delivery status of orders. It returns a message informing the client about their upcoming delivery.

Notification service

Sends notifications to customers at various stages of the order fulfillment process.

As a next step, we need to define the dependency structure among our services. To keep things simple, we will design a linear workflow that executes one service after another. Once an order is submitted, it first gets acknowledged, then the payment gets processed, then the stock gets booked, and finally, a delivery is scheduled. Figure 12-10 illustrates the workflow.

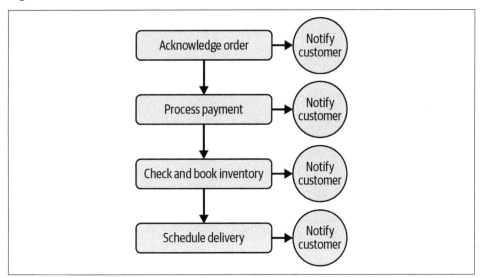

Figure 12-10. OMS workflow structure

Project 3: Database Design

A reliable database system is required to store and manage order-related data. In line with the other projects in this chapter, PostgreSQL stands out as our database solution of choice. Different database design patterns exist for microservices. While some advocate for a dedicated database per service, others favor a unified database shared across all microservices. To simplify our microservice structure, let's proceed with the latter approach—the single shared database pattern.

In our database, we will have five tables:

- The orders table stores orders along with their unique identifiers.
- The payments table stores transactional data related to order payments.
- The inventory table stores product inventory details.
- The stock bookings table stores the allocation of order items within the inventory.
- The delivery schedule table stores tracking delivery and shipment details.
- The notifications table stores customer notifications.

Figure 12-11 illustrates the ERD of our OMS database.

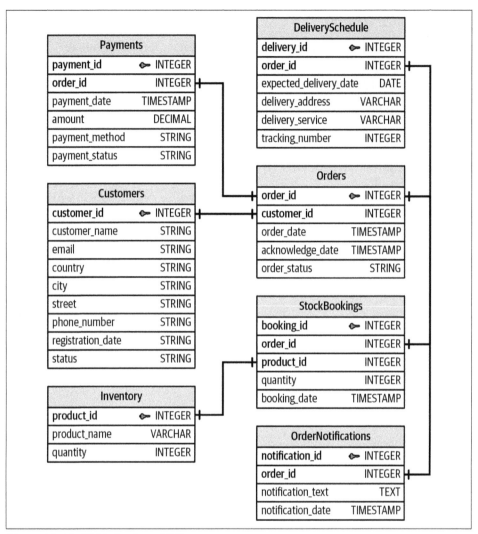

Figure 12-11. OMS database ERD

Next, let's move on to see our microservice system in action.

Project 3: Local Testing

As usual, you will need to navigate to the project directory in your terminal:

```
# Bash
cd {path/to/book/repo}/FinancialDataEngineering/book/chapter_12/project_3
```

Then, run our containers with the following command:

```
# Bash
docker compose up -d
```

Once completed, you will have three services running that we will be interacting with:

- JupyterLab to program and execute our workflow in Python. It will be running on *http://localhost:8888/*.

- Conductor orchestrator to explore and monitor workflows and executions via a user-friendly UI. It will be running on *http://localhost:5000/*.

- PgAdmin client UI to explore the data generated by executions. It will be running on *http://localhost:8081/*.

Open three browser tabs and paste the three localhost URLs into each. We will be interacting mostly with JupyterLab, so navigate first to the tab for *http://localhost: 8888/*. Once it's ready, open a terminal from the Launcher tab. Consult Figure 12-12 for an illustration.

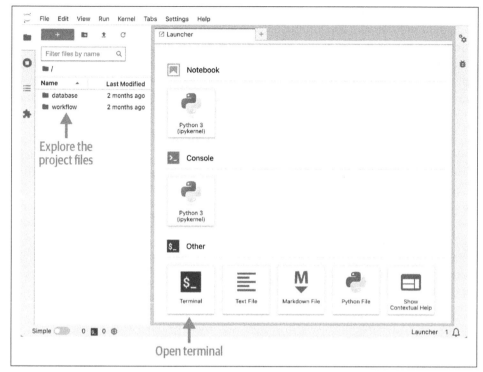

Figure 12-12. JupyterLab main overview page

In the terminal, type the following command and hit Enter:

```Bash
# Bash
python3 database/create_tables.py
```

You should see a few logs that say "SQL executed successfully." This means that the tables we want for our OMS have been created in Postgres.

Next, we want to insert some data into the customers and inventory tables. This is needed because, later on, we will be executing our workflow with orders that already contain the customer and product information. Again, in the terminal, type the following command, then press Enter to execute it:

```Bash
# Bash
python3 database/populate_tables.py
```

The customer and product tables are now populated with data. If you wish to view the content of these files that you have just executed, you can navigate to the database folder using the right sidebar, as shown in Figure 12-12. If, in addition, you want to see the populated tables in the database, switch to the tab with *http://localhost:8081/* and log in with the PGADMIN_DEFAULT_EMAIL and PGADMIN_DEFAULT_PASSWORD values, which you can find in the *.env* file of the project. Once logged in, proceed with the same steps you learned in the first project to create a server and explore your tables.

The next step is to create and register our microservice workflow. First, we need to implement each mircoservice individually. This has been done for you, with each microservice residing within its respective folder within the *workflow* directory. You can use the left sidebar in JupyterLab to navigate to the *workflow* directory. You'll find five folders in there, each corresponding to one of the previously defined microservices. Within each microservice folder, you'll discover two scripts: one named *service.py*, which contains the microservice's code, and the other named *worker.py*, containing the Conductor worker program (*https://oreil.ly/sJlB_*) for the respective microservice. Each worker is tasked with executing a specific task, where the task corresponds to a microservice in our context.

To keep things simple, the logic defined in each *service.py* contains a database insert/update operation. In real business problems, you will obviously need to include more functionality and business logic in your microservices. This may involve computations, transformations, API calls, database calls, and various other operations.

Moving to our workflow, to see how it is defined using Conductor, open the *order_workflow.py* file in the *workflow* directory from the sidebar. You will see how each task is defined by passing a reference name and the values for its parameters. The first task (acknowledge order) receives its input from the workflow input, while the other tasks take their input from the output of their previous tasks. More on passing input to tasks in Conductor is available in the Conductor documentation (*https://oreil.ly/MOuaK*). Using Conductor, it is possible to create a linear flow using the >> operator. You can see how this is done at the bottom of the *order_workflow.py* file.

Now that our workflow is ready to be created, the next thing you can do is register the workflow in the Conductor database. To do so, go back to the Terminal screen in JupyterLab and paste the following command:

```
# Bash
python3 workflow/register_order_workflow.py
```

You should see a log message saying that the workflow has been successfully registered. To review your newly created workflow, go to the tab running *http://localhost:5000/*. There, you'll find the Conductor UI, which lets you check and monitor your workflow and task definitions and executions. Once there, use the top toolbar and navigate to the Definitions tab. You will find a table containing your workflows in your local instance. Click on the Order Workflow button to see the full details of the OMS workflow you created. Figure 12-13 illustrates what this page looks like.

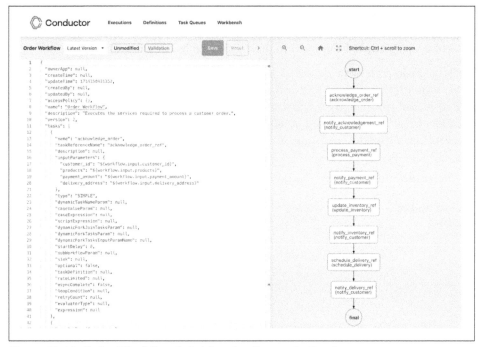

Figure 12-13. Order Workflow definition details page in Conductor

On the left side of Figure 12-13, you will see a lot of workflow definition parameters, many of which can be configured. To avoid extra complexity, we won't be setting any custom variables in this project. On the right side, you will see a visual representation of our OMS workflow. As you can see, it's a linear flow where tasks run in a sequence.

Now that we have our workflow registered, let's execute it. To do so, we need to run the file called *execute_order_workflow.py,* which you can find in the *workflow* folder. If you open this file, you will see that I already prepared a dummy workflow input with customer_id, products, payment amount, and delivery address. You can change these input values if you wish, but you need to make sure that the customer and products you add to the order exist in the database.

To execute our workflow, navigate to the Terminal tab in your JupyterLab and paste the following command:

```Bash
# Bash
python3 workflow/execute_order_workflow.py
```

You should see a few log messages being printed that inform you about the successful outcome of the different microservices.

Now that you have executed the workflow, you can check the results in the database using pgAdmin. You'll find a record of your order in the orders table, payment details linked to your order in the payments table, updates in the inventory and stock bookings tables, and a booked shipment in the delivery table.

Finally, you can review the details of your workflow execution via the Conductor UI. Simply visit *http://localhost:5000/* and click on Executions from the top toolbar. In the table displayed on that page, you'll find a record corresponding to your workflow execution. Click on the ID listed under the workflowid column to access the details of this particular workflow execution. You should see a page similar to Figure 12-14.

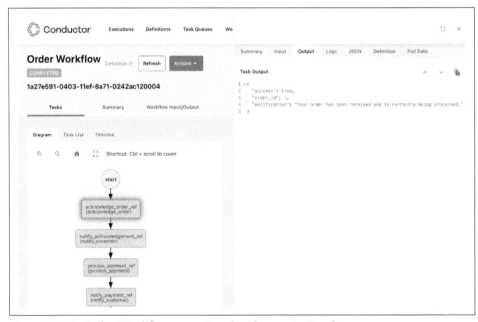

Figure 12-14. Order Workflow execution details page in Conductor

As shown in Figure 12-14, our workflow execution has completed successfully. By clicking on a specific task in the diagram on the left side, you can view its execution details, including the input it received, the output it produced, its logs, and its task definition details.

Project 3: Clean Up

Run the following command in the root directory of Project 3:

```Bash
# Bash
docker compose down
```

Project 3: Summary

This project aimed to familiarize you with the process of building and executing microservice workflows. In real-world situations, you'll likely tackle similar projects but with more complex requirements. For example, you are likely to deploy each of the services we defined into a separate environment, such as Cloud Functions or container-based deployment services, and configure security and access policies to allow them to communicate. Moreover, you will need to have a way to handle concurrency and dependencies in distributed transactions that span multiple services. Additionally, you might need to configure the workflow and task definitions to handle issues such as failure, retries, timeouts, etc.

Project 4: Designing a Financial Reference Data Store with OpenFIGI, PermID, and GLEIF APIs

In this project, you will develop a basic reference data store that holds information for identifying financial instruments and various entities, including the following:

- The full list of ISO 3166 Country Codes.
- The FIGIs, ISINs, Thomson Reuters Open Perm IDs, and RICs for the S&P 100 stocks (*https://oreil.ly/RYylN*). The S&P 100 is a primary stock index comprising 100 of the largest and most established companies listed on US stock exchanges.
- ISO 17442 Legal Entity Identifiers.
- ISO 10383 Market Identifier Codes.
- LEI-to-ISIN mappings.
- LEI-to-BIC mappings.

Throughout this project, you will be using three open APIs:

- OpenFIGI for retrieving FIGI data (*https://oreil.ly/VPX6F*)
- Open PermID for retrieving PermIDs and RICs (*https://oreil.ly/Zvx15*)
- GLEIF API for retrieving LEI and country code identifiers (*https://oreil.ly/jCttr*)

If you are not familiar with financial identifiers, I strongly recommend reading Chapter 3 before beginning this project.

Project 4: Prerequisites

The only prerequisite for this project is to obtain a PermID API token. To do so, follow these steps:

1. Go to *https://permid.org*.

2. From the top right, click on REGISTER and follow the steps to complete your sign-up.

3. Once completed, go back again to *https://permid.org* and sign in with your login credentials.

4. Once signed in, from the top menu, click on APIs → Display my API Token (see Figure 12-15 for an illustration).

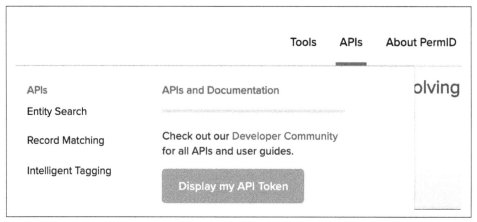

Figure 12-15. Finding your API token on PermID.org

In the following section, you'll use this token to communicate with the PermID API.

Project 4: Local Testing

To start, navigate to the project directory in your terminal:

```
# Bash
cd {path/to/book/repo}/FinancialDataEngineering/book/chapter_12/project_4
```

Once you are in the main project directory, you will find an *.env* file with a variable called PERMID_API_KEY. Without using quotes, you must assign this variable the API access token you got from PermID (i.e., PERMID_API_KEY=YOUR_API_TOKEN).

Run our containers with the following command:

```
# Bash
docker compose up -d
```

Throughout this project, you will be mainly interacting with JupyterLab notebooks. To begin, open your preferred browser and visit *http://localhost:8888/* to access JupyterLab.

The first thing we want to do is to create our tables in the database. These tables will store the various types of reference data that we will be loading. From the main JupyterLab overview page, open a Terminal and execute the following command:

```
# Bash
python3 scripts/create_tables.py
```

To view the tables, log in to pgAdmin on *http://localhost:8081/* using the PGAD MIN_DEFAULT_EMAIL and PGADMIN_DEFAULT_PASSWORD credentials you find in the *.env* file of the project. Once logged in, create a server with the POSTGRES_DB, POST GRES_USER, POSTGRES_PASSWORD credentials following similar steps as in Project 1. When done, you can check the tables using the left sidebar (Databases → reference_data → Schemas → public → Tables).

Now that you've created the tables, it's time to populate them. To accomplish this, you'll need to run multiple notebooks that have already been prepared for you. In JupyterLab, navigate to the *scripts* folder using the left navigation sidebar. Inside the scripts folder, you'll find several directories. Open the first one named *country*. Inside, locate a file named *country.ipynb*. Double-click to open it. Then, from the top menu, select Run → Run All Cells. This action will execute all the code cells in your notebook, fetching and uploading the ISO 3166 Country Codes from the GLEIF API.

Follow the same steps with these files:

- *scripts/figi/figi.ipynb*
- *scripts/lei/lei.ipynb*
- *scripts/lei_bic/lei_bic.ipynb*
- *scripts/lei_isin/lei_isin.ipynb*
- *scripts/mic/mic.ipynb*
- *scripts/permid/permid.ipynb*

After running all these scripts, our reference data store should be ready. Switch to the pgAdmin tab and examine the contents of the tables to observe the data in action.

Project 4: Clean Up

Run the following command in the same root directory as Project 3:

```
# Bash
docker compose down
```

Project 4: Summary

This project was designed to offer you an introduction to the world of financial reference data. Constructing and managing reference data stores are essential and common tasks in the financial industry. Although the reference data used in this project was simple and limited, handling reference data often presents much more complex challenges. For more information on this topic, refer to the section "Reference Data" on page 77.

Conclusion

Congratulations on finishing the final chapter of the book! This is a significant milestone, and I want to thank you for your dedication and commitment to completing this journey.

Throughout the first 11 chapters of this book, you've gained knowledge about a range of foundational and finance domain-specific subjects essential for your journey as a financial data engineer. In this final chapter, you worked on hands-on projects crafted to solidify your understanding from earlier sections and refine your abilities through practical implementation.

Although this chapter concludes our journey through this book, your exploration of financial data engineering is just beginning. This field is continuously evolving with new trends that will shape the future of financial markets. In "The Path Forward: Trends Shaping Financial Markets", I'll briefly highlight these emerging trends, providing you with a glimpse of what lies ahead.

Follow Updates on These Projects

If the projects featured in this chapter undergo any updates or changes, I'll document them on the GitHub page (*https://oreil.ly/c7TJt*). Feel free to refer to it if you encounter any issues.

Report Issues or Ask Questions

Should you encounter any challenges while setting up or executing any step in the projects outlined in this chapter, please don't hesitate to create an issue on the project's GitHub repository (*https://oreil.ly/XCV4f*). I will make sure to reply to you in a very short time.

The Path Forward: Trends Shaping Financial Markets

As we look toward the future, the financial industry is expected to undergo significant transformations, driven by technological advances, regulatory changes, evolving consumer demands, and shifting market dynamics. Financial data engineering will be central to these changes, playing a key role in guiding and shaping the financial landscape. The skills and knowledge you have gained through this book will equip you to tackle these future challenges head-on. Let's take a quick look at these major trends on the horizon.

Financial Integration

The global financial system is becoming more interconnected, breaking down barriers among different markets, regions, and institutions. This trend toward financial integration is driven by the need for seamless cross-border transactions and investments.

Digitalization of Financial Markets and Cloud Adoption

The shift to digital financial markets is accelerating, with cloud technologies emerging as the key driver of innovation. This digital transformation enhances scalability, reduces costs, and improves access to financial services.

Financial Regulation

Regulations in the financial industry are becoming more stringent and complex, with increased demands for privacy protection, transparency, accountability, and risk management. Ensuring compliance through accurate data collection, storage, security, protection, and reporting will be essential.

Financial Data Sharing and Marketplaces

Data sharing is reshaping financial markets by boosting collaboration, innovation, transparency, and efficiency. Financial data marketplaces are emerging as key platforms for sharing and exchanging data, providing easy access to financial data for those who need it.

Financial Standardization

Standardization is key to achieving interoperability and reducing complexity in financial data management. The financial services industry has fallen behind other sectors in collaborating to create and adopt comprehensive interoperable standards for storing and exchanging information. However, this is beginning to change, with initiatives such as the adoption of the Legal Entity Identifier (LEI) and ISO 20022 marking significant progress in this direction.

Artificial Intelligence and Language Models

Artificial intelligence is revolutionizing financial markets by addressing a wide range of applications such as trading, risk management, fraud detection, customer service, and financial advising. Generative AI and LLMs are set to redefine the future of financial services, revolutionizing everything from front-office customer interactions and trading strategies to back-office operations such as risk management and compliance.

Regulations such as the EU AI Act are being established to ensure that AI systems are safe, transparent, and ethically sound. Additionally, standards for AI are being developed, with ISO creating the ISO/IEC JTC 1/SC 42 committee to oversee AI standardization. The committee introduced ISO/IEC 42001 (*https://oreil.ly/9WXAX*), the first global standard for AI management systems, providing guidelines for managing AI technologies effectively and ethically.

Architectures for Specific Business Domains

In financial institutions, distinct business units—such as trading, risk management, compliance, and retail banking—have specific data needs and regulatory requirements. Adopting a domain-oriented approach allows for scalable and efficient data management by customizing the architecture to meet the particular needs of each unit.

Data Collection

The scope of data collection in financial markets is expanding rapidly, encompassing everything from market transactions and customer interactions to alternative data sources like social media and IoT devices. This broader data collection offers financial institutions and regulators deeper insights, enabling more detailed analysis of market trends and risks.

Speed and Efficiency

Speed and efficiency are in high demand within financial markets, reflected in the ongoing push for rapid, real-time transactions, fast access to market data, and the ability to quickly respond to market changes and opportunities. Efficient financial processes enhance customer satisfaction, enable the development of optimal trading strategies, allow for prompt and accurate fraud detection, and ensure the stability and efficiency of the financial system.

Tokenization, Blockchain, and Digital Currencies

The future of financial markets will be profoundly influenced by tokenization, blockchain technology, and digital currencies, which promise to revolutionize transaction security, enable decentralized finance (DeFi) innovations, and enhance transparency across the financial ecosystem. These advancements will facilitate more efficient asset management, streamline cross-border transactions, and create new avenues for investment and financial inclusion.

Regulations are being introduced to provide legal certainty and consumer protection for crypto-assets and their service providers. The best example is the EU's *Markets in Crypto-Assets* (MiCA) regulation, which aims to establish a uniform set of rules for the issuance, trading, and custody of crypto-assets across EU member states.

What Can You Do Next?

Now that you have acquired the skills and knowledge outlined in this book, it's your turn to explore the diverse and dynamic world of financial data engineering. The trends and challenges discussed here present numerous opportunities to make a meaningful impact. Dive into the various data problems faced by financial markets, identify the areas that excite you the most, and think about how you can contribute to solving these issues.

Whether it's developing innovative solutions for financial integration, leveraging cloud technologies, ensuring regulatory compliance, facilitating data sharing, or harnessing the power of AI, the possibilities are endless. As a financial data engineer, you have the power to shape the future of finance. Embrace the challenge, push the boundaries of what's possible, and become a key player in the next chapter of financial innovation.

The future is in your hands—go out there and make a difference!

Afterword

As you reach the conclusion of *Financial Data Engineering*, I trust your answer to the question, "Are you ready to navigate today's complex financial data landscape?" is a resounding "yes." Like Tamer Khraisha and myself, you've likely realized by now that the journey of a financial data engineer is one without a clear endpoint. There is no final "pot of gold" waiting at the end of this path. Instead, the true reward lies in the continuous development of creativity, skills, and insights. Each step you take in mastering the intricacies of financial data is a reward in itself, contributing not only to your own growth but also to the ongoing evolution of the financial industry.

At the intersection of finance, digital data diversity, and data engineering lies an exciting and dynamic frontier. The opportunities for innovation are limitless, and each new challenge brings with it fresh insights. In an industry driven by data, transformation is constant, and we are all part of this exhilarating change.

Tamer Khraisha's contributions to this field are a testament to the importance of embracing this journey. From his mastery of network science, analysis of lending practices, and numerous financial and technical analyses, to his pivotal work, "A Holistic Approach to Financial Data Science: Data, Technology, and Analytics," published in *The Journal of Financial Data Science*, Spring 2020, Tamer has provided a critical foundation for understanding the relationship between data, technology, and finance. His motivation to develop this book reflects a desire to share knowledge, offer guidance, and inspire future financial data engineers.

As we continue to wrestle with the transition from traditional representations of value—such as coins and bills—to a purely data-driven financial ecosystem, it becomes clear that finance is now an information industry at its core. Data is no longer just a reflection of value; it is value. In this book, Tamer provides a comprehensive guide that combines finance domain expertise with software engineering, data science, and analytical techniques. These tools are crucial for extracting insights from financial systems and evaluating data-driven hypotheses.

The industry itself is a marvel. Despite countless complexities, idiosyncrasies, and convoluted relationships between financial entities, it operates smoothly on the backbone of data. This is where the power of financial data engineering shines, and Tamer's book draws from personal experience, as well as the shared experiences of many professionals in this field, to help us navigate these complexities.

Part one of the book lays the essential foundations: an understanding of finance, the key concepts of financial data engineering, and the interrelationships between financial entities. Tamer brings order to the chaotic, diverse nature of financial data, identifying patterns and structures within the financial ecosystem. It is within this "primordial soup" of data that infinite creativity, innovation, and financial ingenuity thrive.

In part two, the book shifts to the technical frameworks and technologies needed to manage financial data. Tamer outlines critical decisions regarding the shape, size, and velocity of data and provides practical examples for applying data engineering techniques. These hands-on exercises are invaluable for deepening your understanding of real-world financial data solutions.

Finally, Tamer guides us into the future of the financial industry, where ongoing digital transformation demands ever greater mastery of data engineering. Financial system integration, product innovation, and technological advancements will continue to drive the need for financial data engineers who can navigate this new world with confidence and expertise.

You now possess a deeper understanding of the financial data landscape and the analytical frameworks needed to unlock its potential. The tools and skills you've gained from this book have empowered you to analyze complex data and derive actionable insights that will contribute to the financial industry's future.

Your journey, like Tamer's and mine, will be one of continuous learning, adaptation, and exploration. The world of financial data is vast, and the challenges it presents are complex—but the rewards for those who embrace these challenges are profound. This book is just the beginning of what promises to be an exciting and fruitful career as a financial data engineer. Take with you the inspiration, creativity, and innovation that define this field, and know that every discovery you make brings you closer to designing the art and mastering the science of financial data engineering.

— Brian Buzzelli
Director, Head of Data Practice at Meradia
Author of Data Quality Engineering in Financial
Services *(O'Reilly, 2022)*

Index

VPNs (Virtual Private Networks), 248

W

warehouse model, DSMs and, 335-341
warning logs, 388
Weather Source, 84
web access mode, 277
Wells Fargo
  Cards 2.0, 318
  multi-cloud strategy, 239
Wharton Research Data Services (WRDS), 51
Wikification, NER and, 146-148
winsorization, outliers and, 178
WMS (workflow management system), 410-414
workflow-oriented software architecture
  (WOSA), 407-408
workflows

abstraction, 408-409
Apache Airflow, 416
ETL (extract, transform, load), 414-416
microservices, 420-424
ML (machine learning), 424-429
stream processing, 417-420
WOSA (workflow-oriented software architecture), 407-408
World Bank Open Data, 46
WOSA (workflow-oriented software architecture), 407-408
WRDS (Wharton Research Data Services), 51

X

XBRL (eXtensible Business Reporting Language), 20, 261

About the Author

Tamer Khraisha is a senior software and data developer, as well as a scientific author, with over a decade of experience in both industry and research. Tamer's experience combines a solid background in financial markets with substantial expertise in software engineering. He did his undergraduate studies in finance and economics and earned a PhD in network science. Tamer's research interests are focused on financial markets, data, and technology. During his professional career, Tamer has worked with various FinTech startups, where he designed and built data-driven cloud platforms for financial research, artificial intelligence, and asset management, as well as international payment systems.

Colophon

The animal on the cover of *Financial Data Engineering* is a pearl oyster.

All species in the *Pinctada* genus of saltwater oysters produce pearls, as do various other oysters and some non-oyster mollusks. Pearls are created when the oyster coats a foreign particle with nacre, or calcium carbonate (of which its shell is also composed), as a protection against the irritant.

In the wild, only one in around 10,000 oysters will produce a pearl, and a small percentage of those pearls form in a desirable shape and color. As such, most of the pearls obtained for the commercial jewelry market are farm raised.

Many of the animals on O'Reilly covers are endangered; all of them are important to the world.

The cover illustration is by Jose Marzan, based on an antique line engraving from *Natural History of Ceylon*. The series design is by Edie Freedman, Ellie Volckhausen, and Karen Montgomery. The cover fonts are Gilroy Semibold and Guardian Sans. The text font is Adobe Minion Pro; the heading font is Adobe Myriad Condensed; and the code font is Dalton Maag's Ubuntu Mono.

9 781098 159993